CAPITAL INTENTIONS

THE LUTHER H. HODGES JR. AND LUTHER H. HODGES SR.

Series on Business, Society, & the State

William H. Becker, *editor*

EDITH SPARKS

CAPITAL INTENTIONS

FEMALE PROPRIETORS IN SAN FRANCISCO,

1850–1920

THE UNIVERSITY OF NORTH CAROLINA PRESS

Chapel Hill

© 2006 THE UNIVERSITY OF NORTH CAROLINA PRESS
All rights reserved
Manufactured in the United States of America
Designed by Amy Ruth Buchanan
Set in Janson by Tseng Information Systems, Inc.

The paper in this book meets the guidelines for
permanence and durability of the Committee on
Production Guidelines for Book Longevity of the
Council on Library Resources.

Library of Congress Cataloging-in-Publication Data
Sparks, Edith.
Capital intentions : female proprietors in San Francisco,
1850–1920 / Edith Sparks.
p. cm. — (Business, society, and the state)
Includes bibliographical references and index.
ISBN-13: 978-0-8078-3061-1 (cloth : alk. paper)
ISBN-10: 0-8078-3061-5 (cloth : alk. paper)
ISBN-13: 978-0-8078-5775-5 (pbk. : alk. paper)
ISBN-10: 0-8078-5775-0 (pbk. : alk. paper)
1. Businesswomen—California—San Francisco—History.
2. Women-owned business enterprises—California—
San Francisco—History.   I. Title.   II. Series:
Business, society & the state.
HD6096.C3S63 2006
338.7082′0979461—dc22   2006014320

cloth   10 09 08 07 06   5 4 3 2 1
paper   10 09 08 07 06   5 4 3 2 1

FOR LUCY,

who inspires me,

and

FOR RICK,

who sustains me

CONTENTS

————————— ❖❖❖ —————————

ILLUSTRATIONS AND MAP

———————————— ❀❀❀ ————————————

ACKNOWLEDGMENTS

———————————— ❖✿❖ ————————————

It is with great pleasure that I acknowledge the help and support of the many people who have contributed to this book and its completion. First and foremost among them is Gary Nash. When I asked him to direct the committee for my dissertation, he replied that he thought it would be fun! It was that intellectual curiosity and enthusiastic support that drew me to him as an adviser in the first place and which informed his mentorship throughout my graduate education. Through him I sought to master the tools of social history that enabled me to uncover the stories of San Francisco's nineteenth- and early twentieth-century female proprietors. He has taught me more than how to practice social history, however, also providing a model as a teacher, scholar, leader, and lover of life. I am grateful for his enduring friendship, and that of his wife Cindy Shelton, for his contributions to the words and ideas in these pages, and for the many ways that he has helped me to forge my own intellectual freedom.

I have also benefited from the guidance of several other teacher-scholars at the University of California. It was in a graduate research seminar at UCLA with Ellen DuBois that I stumbled upon this topic; she made several important contributions to my conceptualization of the project and helped steer me through the dissertation. Carole Shammas, at the time a professor at UC Riverside, generously agreed to help me master the field of women's economic history during meetings at her home. Eric Sundquist helped me to think about the ways in which literary depictions of women in business could contribute to my project. When he left UCLA, Karen Rowe graciously stepped in to replace him and read the manuscript with great care, providing several helpful suggestions. Joan Waugh also helped me develop the project in a guided study of nineteenth-century economic history, asking decisive questions and piquing my interest in the field with her own enthusiasm for the topic. Mary Yeager generously shared an early list of the articles that would eventually become her edited collection, *Women in Business*. I would also like to acknowledge the mentorship of three undergraduate advisers in the English Department at UC Berkeley, where I completed my Bachelor of Arts degree: Dorothy Hale, Susan Schweik, and the late Jenny Franchot. Each of them contributed in important ways to my development as a critical thinker, careful reader, and enthusiastic writer.

Crafting this project into the book it has become was only possible because of the critical feedback and support of several individuals. In addition to providing an example of excellence in her own scholarship on women in business, Wendy Gamber has been generous with her time, helping me develop as a scholar and professional historian more generally. She read an early draft and provided several key suggestions—among them incorporating more comparisons between male and female proprietors of small businesses —that have made the book substantially better. Angel Kwolek-Folland and Lynn Hudson, both of whom reviewed the manuscript, provided an enormously helpful set of recommendations for how to complete the manuscript's transformation into a book. I cannot thank them enough for the care with which they both read the manuscript and for their many insights about how to make it better. Both pushed me in ways I at first resisted but can finally acknowledge now to have been wise. It wasn't until I set out to implement their suggestions that I had the pleasure of seeing this project's full potential and not until then that I "got" what it meant to write a book. I owe both reviewers a debt of gratitude for helping me to write the book that *Capital Intentions* finally became and am delighted to be able to thank them by name.

I have been fortunate to work with many talented professionals at the University of North Carolina Press. Chuck Grench, my editor at the press, provided a helpful critique that inspired substantial rewriting of Chapter 1 and has provided helpful feedback throughout the publishing process. He and his assistants, Amanda Macmillan and Katy O'Brien, as well as assistant managing editor Paula Wald, adroitly steered the book through the publication process. Copyeditor Liz Gray improved the book in countless ways. I thank them all as well as the many other individuals there who contributed to this book's publication.

Several colleagues have read the manuscript or earlier renditions of it and provided helpful critical feedback. The members of EATS, the Early American [History] Thesis Seminar at UCLA, shared their insights, support, and good food during my first conceptualization of the project. Anastasia Simmons, Jen Koslow, and Lisa Materson read early renditions of my research while we were all graduate students at UCLA, contributing ideas and moral support at a crucial time. Later on, members of the Urban History Dissertation Group at the Newberry Library in Chicago provided a much needed intellectual forum during the two years I lived in the Midwest. Since my good fortune to be hired as a faculty member at the University of Pacific, in Stockton, California, I have found myself surrounded by colleagues who have supported me and the project in numerous ways. Gesine Gerhard, Cynthia Dobbs, and Amy Smith briefly formed a writing group that got me started with the arduous process of turning the project into a book. Ken Albala shared his advice and experience as an author during numerous conversations. And Caroline Cox, a model colleague in every way, has been enormously generous with her time, reading multiple drafts of the introduction and fortifying me throughout the book-writing process with helpful feedback and encouragement. I have been happy to rekindle a friendship with Lisa Materson since her arrival at UC Davis; her insightful reading of the introduction has improved it substantially. Finally, my writing group partners, Jessica Weiss and Samantha François, have kept me on my toes with hard questions, delicate prodding, great ideas, decisive criticism, and deadlines. The entire manuscript has been touched in innumerable ways by their careful readings and came to completion in part because of their support and friendship.

I am glad to acknowledge the help of several students. George Yagi, Sharlene Messer, and Daniel Ender all provided valuable research assistance, while Jennifer Powers graciously shared her own research findings and materials on African American women in San Francisco.

I would also like to acknowledge the archivists and librarians at numerous institutions who helped make this book possible. Staff at Harvard University's Baker Library, the Huntington Library, the California Historical Society, the Bank of America Archives, and the San Francisco History Center at the San Francisco Public Library facilitated the research behind this project and helped make the countless hours I spent in historical archives happy periods of discovery. I would also like to thank Dunn & Bradstreet for permission to quote from the R. G. Dun & Co. Collection credit reports and Bank of America for permission to quote from the Bank of Italy collection.

The crew at the highly understaffed and underfunded National Archives and Records Administration (NARA) facility in San Bruno, California, deserve to be singled out for their warm reception and cheerful assistance during my research there using the bankruptcy court records. Claude Hopkins, now happily retired, deserves particular recognition for his willingness to retrieve box after box of records since I worked without the benefit of an index and thus had to literally search through all the court records for each year I examined in order to locate the women whose cases I used for the project. In spite of this, he always seemed happy to see me. It is my hope that historians' public recognition of the value of the federal records contained in NARA facilities such as this one will one day lead to an increase in the resources that our government allocates toward their management.

Of course, the ability to devote hours of study in historical archives such as these has only been possible because of generous financial support from a variety of institutions. I benefited from the Barbara Kelly Memorial Fellowship and a Dissertation Year Fellowship while a graduate student at UCLA. An Alfred Chandler Jr. Traveling Fellowship facilitated my first trip to the Baker Library at Harvard University, while a W. H. Keck Foundation Fellowship allowed me to spend four blissful weeks as a researcher at the Huntington Library. A faculty research grant from the University of the Pacific enabled me to return to Harvard's Baker Library for a second time.

Finally, it is my great privilege to acknowledge in print the friends and family who have made it possible for me to write this book. First, I would like to thank my uncles, Tom Lutzy and Jim Laprade, who generously hosted me in their two-bedroom, one-bathroom flat in Cambridge for several weeks during my first trip to the Baker Library and who again shared their home with me during the second trip. Wendy Sheanin, too, graciously agreed to take me on as a roommate in her San Francisco apartment for six weeks while I embarked on the first intensive period of research. She and Lara Schultz could always be counted on for support and cheerleading; I am deeply grateful for their friendship. I would also like to thank my mother- and father-in-law, Gloria and Emilio Mendez, for their unconditional support during this long process and for providing a present-day example of immigrant enterprise. My father, Frank Sparks, deserves acknowledgment for teaching me to recognize "capital intentions" among ordinary and extraordinary people. Thanks to my sister, Elizabeth Brownlow, for always remembering to ask how the book was coming and for innumerable examples of support. My parents, mother and stepfather Patty and Robert Murar, have provided constant encouragement, always believing in me and inspiring me with their own life-long intellectual curiosity.

Anyone who has written a book of this nature while parenting a young child knows that the undertaking presents unique challenges and is only possible because of the help of other people. Lucy showed an appreciation of my quandary as a working mom early on by coming almost two weeks after her due date so that I could finish the first version of the manuscript. Since then she has filled my life with new joys even as she keeps me running, sometimes literally, from one thing to the next. I have been able to focus on writing this book only because of Lucy's many "second moms" at HGG whose loving expertise has provided me with the peace of mind necessary to take this intellectual journey. Thank you to all of them. Last, but certainly not least, my husband Rick Mendez deserves to be singled out for all of the ways he has lovingly shouldered the responsibilities of our family and household so that I could lock myself in the office to write. Additionally, this book has benefited from his critical feedback, intellectual creativity, business knowledge, and enthusiastic support. In celebration of his true partnership, I share this accomplishment with him.

CAPITAL INTENTIONS

INTRODUCTION

———————— ❖ ❀ ❖ ————————

For most Americans today, the word "businesswoman" brings to mind women who have enjoyed spectacular success in big business corporations. Of course, it is only recently that such female success stories have emerged from what remains a male-dominated business world. Yet female corporate executives are minorities not only in the world in which they circulate, but also in the overall population of businesswomen today. Unlike the female executives we read about in today's business newspapers, most businesswomen operate small-scale enterprises that promise only modest success, if any at all. Limiting our definition of businesswomen to corporate icons, therefore, obscures the many thousand small-scale retailers and service providers whose neighborhood establishments provide "stuff" and sustenance to countless Americans on a regular basis. In spite of their often-tenuous hold in the marketplace, these ordinary women who own businesses arguably have a much greater impact in the world of commerce than any female executive simply because of how ubiquitous they are in our everyday lives.

San Franciscans encounter small-scale female proprietors in nearly every section of the city today. Such businesswomen can even be found in the busy financial district along California and Montgomery Streets that houses many of the city's corporate giants. But instead of fourteenth-floor offices with views of the Bay, these retailers and service providers inhabit closet-sized flower stands and mobile espresso carts in the glass-and-marble lobbies that welcome executives to work each day. Still others operate small establishments in the districts beyond downtown: gift shops in Noe Valley, restaurants in the Sunset, T-shirt stands along Fisherman's Wharf, laundries in the Mission, and card stores near Union Square. San Francisco residents patronize these businesses on a daily basis, perhaps not even knowing that their money is helping to support one of the myriad female business owners that populate the city. This pattern is replicated in cities around the country, where scores of female proprietors compete for the business of local consumers in small-scale establishments peppering the urban landscape.

Yet when such women are newsworthy it is not as business success stories but as human-interest stories. Neither national magazines such as *Businessweek* nor the business section of city newspapers such as the *San Francisco Chronicle* typically covers such establishments because they rarely offer models for management and often are short lived and marginally successful at best. Instead, the city's female business owners might appear in the "lifestyle" section of a newspaper, in an article highlighting a local grocer's struggle to support a family, a dress shop owner's recovery from theft, or a manicurist's loss of patronage during a period of street construction. These women are interesting, such news stories imply, not because they are business owners but because they are people just like the rest of us trying to make ends meet, to raise their children, to eke out a living doing something they know how to do. What we learn from such human-interest stories is not the role that these entrepreneurs have played in the world of business, but the role that their businesses have played in their lives.

Small businesses serve not only the needs of consumers but also those of the business owners and their families. A neighborhood clothing store owner, for example, can reasonably open for business at ten o'clock in the morning, allowing enough time to prepare breakfast for her children and get them off to school with lunch bags in tow. When school is not in session, during holidays, weekends, and afternoons, the children might join their mother in the store, where they can be safely supervised with no additional cost to the family. For the owner of a dry cleaning business, the labor-intensive enterprise might provide work for several family members whose free or below-market-value labor in turn helps the business persist. A small ethnic restaurant might enable a non-English-speaking immigrant to build status for herself as the proprietor of a social institution central to the community of immigrants who share her language and country of origin. In each case, the small business is the owner's solution to a particular problem—how to accommodate or employ family, for example, or build status and companionship for one's self within a particular community. The business thus grows out of both the demands of the marketplace and the demands of the owner's personal and familial needs.

Even small businesses enmeshed in webs of personal relationships such as these, however, ultimately hold their owners accountable to the public: as providers of goods and services, as taxpayers, as debtors. This fact underscores that proprietorship is, of course, a commercial activity, one that exposes owners to the scrutiny of strangers and thrusts them into the difficulties of business management. The high rate of business failure among small-scale proprietors, male and female, highlights the difficulty of this aspect of proprietorship.[1] Yet year after year, female small-business owners are one of the fastest growing categories of participants in the commercial economy, turning to independent enterprise over and over again in spite of its challenges and the uncertainty of success because it accommodates both their family and their income needs.[2] Thus for women, small-scale proprietorship must be understood in terms of both public and private—commercial and domestic—rewards and responsibilities.

Female business owners in San Francisco at the end of the nineteenth and beginning of the twentieth centuries, almost all of them owners of small, indeed "tiny," businesses, are interesting for similar reasons.[3] Their stories reveal the ways in which ordinary women navigated the exigencies of everyday life by engaging in the commercial marketplace as proprietors. Their businesses played a crucial role in their own lives, bridging the gap between family and paid labor, pushing them into the public eye and engaging them in challenging commercial decision making on a regular basis. Like the female small-business owners who appear in human-interest stories in our urban newspapers today, most businesswomen one hundred years ago did not pioneer original marketing strategies, develop new products or market niches, or demonstrate exceptional managerial insight.[4] Instead, their most remarkable achievements consisted of paying their debts, drawing customers consistently, and having enough cash to purchase new inventory without credit. At a time when small-business proprietorship was more or less a revolving door for men and women, both of whom failed at significant rates, simply staying afloat *was* an achievement. This was all the more true for women who faced a variety of gender-specific legal and social limitations complicating and constricting their commercial activity.

San Francisco's women business owners are worthy of our attention both because they were representative of larger national patterns in female proprietorship at the end of the nineteenth and beginning of the twentieth centuries and because they faced several unusual circumstances particular to the business climate in their city. Like female business owners elsewhere, the women who operated small businesses in San Francisco crowded into a small number of domestic service–oriented industries and struggled to compete with more-experienced male proprietors who enjoyed greater access to capital, credit, and free family labor. Yet while women competed with men, they also relied on them as customers, creditors, employees, and occasionally even as partners. Thus this study reveals that as a group, women business owners operated in a heterosocial commercial world even if certain segments, such as the much studied apparel and beauty industries, comprised a "female economy."[5] Declining fortunes due to expensive technological advances, adoption of brand-name goods, competition from large-scale retailers, and increased opportunities in other, more-remunerative job sectors eventually would help to bring an end to the heyday of female proprietorship across the nation, just as it did in San Francisco.

Yet as a case study, female proprietorship in San Francisco also offers several interesting and important exceptions to the norm. First, the city experienced phenomenal demographic and economic growth during the late nineteenth and early twentieth centuries punctuated by periods of dramatic market contraction (over and above the two depressions that plagued the nation). In addition, several natural and human disasters during the period (in the form of fires, earthquakes, and an outbreak of bubonic plague) threw thousands of proprietors out of business. Keeping the doors of a small-scale retail or service establishment open in the face of such challenges set San Francisco proprietors (male and female) apart from those in other cities. Women, in particular, also exhibited San Francisco–specific patterns of proprietorship in two ways: they were uniquely active in the accommodations industry because of the city's gender imbalance and remarkably absent from the laundry industry because of competition from Chinese immigrant men driven to laundering clothes by sinophobic laws and neighbors. Thus, while the experiences of San Francisco's businesswomen reflect many of those of women elsewhere in the country, the city's female proprietors also rose to several unique challenges.

This is revealing of San Francisco as a place but also of women's commercial actions in response to setbacks and opportunities regardless of location. San Francisco's dynamic marketplace elicited from female proprietors decisive action, innovative strategies, modest success, and spectacular failure— sometimes all by one business owner. Thus, for the study of late nineteenth- and early twentieth-century female proprietorship, San Francisco's case is both mirror and microscope, reflecting national trends even as it complicates and deepens our understanding of them.

As is often the case in histories of "ordinary" people, San Francisco's

female proprietors left an incomplete record of their past, one that highlights "failure" more than it does "success."[6] This is both because going out
of business was a commonplace experience, as already mentioned, and because women who failed in business left behind the most extensive record of
their day-to-day operations in the form of bankruptcy court records. Thus
the stories told here are not the celebratory biographies Americans often
associate with the world of business. Neither does the book trace the lives
of individual entrepreneurs over time, partly because of the length of their
business careers—which were almost uniformly short-lived—and because of
the nature of the sources documenting their business lives. Late nineteenth-
and early twentieth-century female proprietors appear in a number of public sources, including court records, credit reports, city directories, and advertisements, but do so for only fleeting moments. Because not all women
declared bankruptcy, bought enough on credit to merit an investigation by
outside evaluators, were captured by the spotty demographic accounting in
city directories, or could afford advertising, no one woman appears in all
four sources, and few even in two. Thus the study of female small-business
proprietors is a study in ephemera. Such women maintained their businesses
for short periods and appeared in the historical record only briefly. Making
historical sense of their lives requires generalizing across the momentary experiences of multiple women and reading into the meaning of the records
they left to uncover what they do not tell us about intentions and inclina-
tions. Thus, while you will not get to know the women you meet in these
pages in depth, the glimpses of their lives permitted by the extant historical
record are revealing of the ways in which the city's female proprietors delib-
erately engaged in the business of everyday life in late nineteenth- and early
twentieth-century San Francisco.

Mrs. Stites Miller is a good example. Her simple business card, printed
from a wood etching dating from the 1870s, at first appears to reveal little.
Those San Franciscans among whom it circulated at the end of the nineteenth century learned only where her boardinghouse was located and the
name of the house's proprietor.[7] Yet beyond these factual details, the card reveals a great deal about Miller's perception of herself as a businesswoman.
Most importantly, it illustrates her engagement in the commerce of domesticity. This was not a woman who simply opened her home to occasional
paying guests, as was common among urban residents at the end of the nineteenth and beginning of the twentieth centuries. Miller's home was a business, one to which she hoped to draw a steady stream of paying customers.
That, of course, was the point of the business card. Fanciful scrolling etched
around the name and address of the business highlighted the information she

Mrs. Stites Miller's trade card, clearly designed to draw customers to her boardinghouse, exemplifies the "capital intentions" with which San Francisco's female proprietors engaged in business. (California Historical Society, North Baker Research Library)

most wanted people to remember. The cozy portrayal of the boardinghouse, on the other hand, was meant to have the greatest emotional impact. Complete with curtains in the window and smoke curling out of the chimney, the image would have tugged at the heartstrings of any homesick and homeless city resident. Printed in a deep green color to set the whole design off, the scene may have evoked pleasant memories for those who traveled to California from the East, reminding them of the family homes and verdant gardens they left behind. These details of design were meant to lure customers to the boardinghouse and clearly indicate the degree to which Miller engaged in the *business* of boarding. This was a woman who crafted her own economic opportunity by appealing directly to potential customers, who knew how to market her establishment to the best effect, and who recognized that the best way to draw boarders to a boardinghouse was to make it feel like home.[8] She clearly operated as a business owner whose goal was to increase the profitability of her enterprise.

This intentionality—implicit in distributing a business card—makes Mrs. Stites Miller and her boardinghouse a valuable example of late nineteenth-century San Francisco businesswomen and their commercial behavior. For in the very act of soliciting patronage, a woman demonstrated an impulse for business and a desire for profit. This was not a skill honed through the formal training or experience that some businessmen received. Rather, most women had to follow their instincts and rely on the various pieces of business know-how they managed to pick up wherever they could. Yet the informality of women's business impulses did not detract from their intentionality. For by crafting and distributing a business card, Miller, in essence, declared herself a businesswoman—a woman engaged in the selling, marketing, and managing of goods and/or services for her own gain, with all the risks and liabilities the venture entailed. Such women were unlikely to refer to themselves as businesswomen, however, since by the end of the nineteenth century that term typically connoted a woman engaged in clerical work. Women like Miller were even less likely to use the term "entrepreneur," since that word evoked images of tycoon capitalists such as Charles Crocker, Colis Huntington, Leland Stanford, and Mark Hopkins, the "Big Four" of the Central Pacific Railroad. For some, especially those in the accommodations industry, the term "proprietoress" may have seemed an apt description. Yet in spite of the hesitations late nineteenth- and early twentieth-century women had using these terms, all of them—"businesswoman," "entrepreneur," and "proprietoress"—accurately describe female business owners because they capture the engagement in commercial decision making that characterized the daily lives of women who operated small-business enterprises.[9]

Indeed, it is in women's day-to-day struggle to start and maintain a business that their commercial conduct emerges most clearly and their lives become most interesting to historians. For in operating even the smallest of businesses, female proprietors were engaged in the management of economic risk, forced to confront the vagaries of the market, the caprice of customers, the ruthlessness of creditors, and the inflexibility of bankruptcy courts. Women business owners regularly made conscious, indeed conscientious, decisions that indicate they had a keen awareness of their economic environment, an instinct for how to maneuver in the marketplace, and a penchant for commercial capitalism. In the course of such transactions they had to employ an understanding of supply and demand, customer needs and preferences, suppliers' costs and conditions, creditors' terms and allowances, inventory management and protection, and competitive pricing and strategies. All this was in addition to demonstrating the particular skills their endeavors required and understanding the attributes that distinguished them from competing proprietors. Even a businesswoman such as Mrs. Stites Miller who marketed skills long associated with women's work—homemaking, cooking, sewing, and laundering—relied on commercial know-how and economic savvy, not just home-spun proficiency, in the daily operation of her boardinghouse.

Like women business owners in other cities in the country at the end of the nineteenth century, and not unlike women business owners today, San Francisco's female proprietors between 1850 and 1920 operated small-scale enterprises concentrated in the accommodations, apparel, beauty, laundry, and retail industries. With some exceptions, they filled economic niches performing what might accurately be described as commercial domesticity—jobs historically related to women's culturally prescribed role as stewards of house and home.

However, neither the argument that women had a "natural" proclivity for such work nor the assertion that such jobs were perceived as "women's work" satisfactorily explain the sex segregation of the marketplace. Women were agents in their own commercial destinies to a far greater degree than either of these two explanations would have us think. In dressmaking and millinery, for example, women did not simply transfer their domestic skills to the marketplace but achieved proprietorship only after years of apprenticeship as expert sewers in another woman's shop.[10] Thus dressmaking and millinery businesses were learned, planned, and pursued, and not occupations into which women fell because they had no other choice. To miss this intentionality in women's business pursuits is to miss the nature of their economic engagement.

This study eschews superficial explanations of women's marketplace activities, insisting on a deeper investigation of women's commercial behavior. I argue that women did not simply *end up* operating businesses in the domestic service industry but that they pursued them as viable opportunities within market niches where their skills and resources could be leveraged to meet an economic need. Entering the accommodations, apparel, laundry, beauty, and retail trades, in other words, was a commercial decision for San Francisco women, one that reflected "capital intentions"—a determination for profit and marketability.

This is not to say that women freely chose the kinds of businesses they pursued or that their concentration in the domestic services industry was purely a function of preference and profitability. Even today female small-business proprietors flock to those businesses with the lowest barriers to entry and the highest compatibility with their skills and responsibilities. This channels most into the service industry in a few specific niches such as retail and food service. For women at the end of the 1800s and beginning of the 1900s, the factors shaping their business decisions were even more numerous and more trenchant. In fact, "choice" was a misleading notion for women at the end of the nineteenth century, especially when it came to the economy. Many scholars have detailed the ways in which ideology, law, and discrimination constrained women as workers.[11] This was especially true for married women and formerly married women (widows and divorced women), who comprised the majority of San Francisco's female proprietors. These women "chose" proprietorship because there were not many other options. They were penned in by laws that restricted married women's access to capital and enforced women's responsibility for the care of home and children, and by a job market that offered few accommodations for women with children and formally barred married women from some of the most lucrative employment opportunities. Race, ethnicity, and class further hampered women's employment options, forcing some to choose between taking degrading personal service jobs in private homes or striking out on their own as independent enterprisers, often utilizing the same domestic skills. Ethnically specific cultural values, too, prescribed that, once married, women find ways of increasing a family's income without having to engage in wage labor outside the home. Irish immigrant women—who comprised a significant proportion of San Francisco's female proprietors—may have been particularly constrained by such cultural expectations. Late nineteenth- and early twentieth-century female proprietorship, therefore, was more often than not the result of creative problem solving rather than the enlightened inspiration with which Americans have typically associated entrepreneurs through history. Reacting to a host of legal and economic restrictions as well as the cultural expectation that, even as income earners, they retain responsibility for child care and housekeeping, women resolved to launch their own businesses, capitalizing on their ability to respond simultaneously to family and marketplace demands for their domestic services.

Domestic concerns shaped women's commercial activities so dramatically because, regardless of race or ethnicity, most female proprietors in San Francisco retained charge of their children and their homes. In the late nineteenth and early twentieth centuries, this was as much a duty imposed on women (economically, socially, and culturally) as it was one inspired by a desire to protect and care for their families. Recent scholarship on small business emphasizes that for many male small-business owners too, perhaps especially those in the retail trade, the long-term goal of providing for their families and not "short-term profit maximization" took precedence in day-to-day business decisions and was a foundational motivation for entering proprietorship in the first place. Thus male and female proprietors alike pursued small-business ownership as a strategy for "family survival and advancement."[12] Yet female proprietors labored under a set of gendered restrictions and expectations that meant family was both instigator and obstacle to their economic enterprise. In other words, men and women both may have been motivated by the care of their families, but only women faced a set of limitations on *how* they cared for their families. Men were not tied to the home and thus chose small business as one among many options, a choice women with families did not share. In addition, if family served as motivation other than as a set of mouths to feed for male family heads, it was because family could be used to best advantage in small business as unpaid laborers. Male small-business owners, scholars have noted, regularly relied on the help of their wives in the day-to-day operations of their stores, groceries, and hotels. Women did not share this same ready access to free family workers since very few could rely on the help of husbands, and sons and daughters figure only rarely in the historical record as laborers in their mothers' enterprises.[13] Thus, for women, family shaped their proprietorship in both positive (motivating) and negative (challenging) ways.

The phrase "capital intentions," therefore, captures the dual goals of female proprietors: to generate a source of income and to fulfill their principal obligation to their families. It also underscores the fact that women were *intentional* about the ways in which they engaged in marketplace activities. The types of businesses, start-up strategies, and management approaches they pursued reflect, in part, clear deliberation about what actions were most prudent and profitable.

This book also highlights the informal, impulsive, and sometimes insufficient skill women applied in their daily business operations. Female proprietors may have *intended* to raise capital, in other words, but they did not always or even often achieve this goal. As later chapters will detail, engaging in commercial enterprise and demonstrating an aptitude for it were not necessarily the same thing; some women (and men) engaged in business recklessly and foolishly. In fact, few displayed consistently excellent judgment as business owners. For women, this weakness grew from their lack of formal training and education. Whatever skill women displayed as the managers of their own establishments was more likely the result of instinct or a knack for business, since women did not have access to the same learning opportunities that some men had at the end of the nineteenth and beginning of the twentieth centuries. This book argues, therefore, that intuition, guts, and guesswork governed women's activity in the marketplace as much as anything else. In truth, this probably described *all* small-business owners, male and female, at the beginning of the last century, since contemporaries and scholars alike have depicted male small-business owners in the early 1900s as driven to irrational decisions by a burning desire for independence and a lack of proper preparation.[14]

In spite of these similarities, however, men and women came to proprietorship unequally equipped to capitalize on their skills and services. Scholars have emphasized that the enduring advantage enjoyed by small businesses historically, if there was one, was their low labor costs. Businessmen worked "harder, longer and/or more cheaply than paid employees would require" for the "non-economic reward of personal independence" and "depended on . . . the help of unpaid family members."[15] Women no doubt worked equally long or longer hours as the managers of their own businesses. But they did so less out of a desire for independence (an elusive pursuit for many women, particularly, of course, married women) than out of compulsion, combining as they did the management of their businesses with the management of their homes and families. Additionally, as noted above, few San Francisco women utilized the help of husbands and children in the operation of their businesses. More importantly, proportionally the number of female small-business owners who did rely on free family labor pales in significance when compared to the percentage of men who relied on the unpaid labor of their wives in the running of their small businesses. What this meant for female proprietors is that they did not have the same nearly universal access to unpaid labor that men enjoyed.[16] Because women generally had a harder time obtaining credit and capital and had less experience than men often did as first-time business owners and because the consequences of failure were grave, especially for female heads of households with children, women adopted comparatively conservative financial strategies when starting their businesses. As we shall discuss later in the book, chief among the start-up methods they employed was buying out an already established business, a strategy almost universally rejected by male proprietors.[17] These and other differences suggest that while the commercial know-how women displayed (or did not display) was not unlike men's, there were significant ways in which the day-to-day experience of proprietorship diverged for men and women. This examination, therefore, adds to the scholarship investigating how the practice of business was gendered and shows that we must learn more about the day-to-day customs of both businessmen and -women, since each sheds light on the other.[18]

Of course the history of San Francisco female proprietors illuminates not just the experiences of women and men but also the experience of place. For women who operated businesses in California's biggest and most important city at the end of the nineteenth and beginning of the twentieth centuries did not just interact with the marketplace at large but with a particular marketplace, one with its own unique features.[19] One of the city's most distinctive features was a significantly higher proportion of men than women. This gender imbalance started with the gold rush in 1849 and lasted until 1920, inflating the market for domestic services. As already mentioned, this had an impact on the accommodations industry (hotels, boardinghouses, restaurants), where it created unusually high opportunity for women proprietors compared to other cities. On the other hand, large numbers of Chinese male immigrants in the city, handicapped by race- and class-based violence, discrimination, and exclusion laws, were pushed into the laundry industry, consequently shrinking the number of female laundry operators compared to their earlier numbers and relative to other U.S. cities during the same period of time.[20] Both factors made San Francisco unique as a marketplace in which women operated businesses.

This does not mean that the city's female proprietors enjoyed singular opportunities that women in other large American cities such as New York, Cincinnati, or Buffalo did not. Businesswomen probably resided in all cities in the United States between 1850 and 1920, operating enterprises in the same industries as those in San Francisco. My comparison between female proprietorship in San Francisco and six other U.S. cities, in fact, demonstrates remarkable continuity, suggesting that this study sheds light on the experience of women business owners generally and not just in one particular city.[21]

There was one period in the city's history, however, during which female San Franciscans enjoyed exceptional opportunities compared to women elsewhere, and that was the gold rush that dominated the city's economy from 1849 through the 1850s. During these years female "forty-niners" in northern California enjoyed unique and expanded marketability in every occupation from prostitute to restaurateur, wife to hotel operator. During this one period, women in San Francisco and the greater northern California region enjoyed unparalleled business opportunities as well as access to credit and capital to a degree unusual for women in other parts of the country. But by at least the end of the 1860s, when the completion of the transcontinental railroad tied together the nation's two coasts, the inflated economy of San Francisco's rough-and-tumble gold rush years evolved into a complex, national market akin to urban centers throughout the country. At that point, with the exception of the accommodations and laundry industries, which, as already mentioned, offered unusually high or low opportunity, respectively, the business opportunities afforded women in San Francisco were remarkably similar to those in other cities around the nation.[22]

Thus, over time, the business climate in which San Francisco women operated became more typical of that of cities further east. Certainly, in the midst of the 1850s, San Francisco was a small, sandy outpost (with a population of 35,000 people in 1852), pitched with the tents of sojourners on their way to the gold fields; it would have been a foreign environment to anyone traveling from other American cities expecting to find a familiar urban marketplace.[23] But by the 1870s contemporary observers likened San Francisco to Paris for its urbane sophistication and abundant hotels, cafes, and stores. Many visitors would have found it overwhelmingly large, since by 1880 it had a total population of 233,959 and was ranked the ninth largest city in the country.[24] By 1900 San Franciscans enjoyed access to both national markets and brand-name products, and small-business proprietors found themselves competing with local department stores such as the Emporium and I. Magnin and purchasing cash registers and telephones to keep up with the technological changes sweeping the nation. By the 1920s what one historian has called the "incorporation of America" was complete. In San Francisco, as in other big cities across the country, the consequent demand for clerical workers drew women away from proprietorship and into office jobs in the skyscrapers that now hummed with the sounds of typewriters and telephones.[25] Thus the city endured several dramatic transformations in the seventy-year period between 1850 and 1920 that brought San Francisco closer and closer to the commercial profile of other U.S. cities.

The changes that occurred in San Francisco at the end of the nineteenth and beginning of the twentieth centuries made it a dynamic environment in which to operate as a businesswoman. The growth that the city experienced in a few decades took cities such as Boston and New York centuries to complete. That rapid expansion, combined with the host of catastrophic events that plagued the city—everything from frequent fires to epidemic illnesses and, of course, earthquakes—made it an unusually provocative setting for entrepreneurship. Over the course of seventy years San Francisco businesswomen witnessed a constant influx of new residents from the United States and abroad, extreme inflation during the city's isolationist period and then deflation after the sudden introduction of national competition following the completion of the transcontinental railroad, military buildup during the Spanish-American and Filipino-American Wars, the development of an international port, and the rise (1849), fall (1906), and rise again (1915) of their city. These San Francisco–specific developments occurred alongside major national changes already mentioned, such as the evolution of national markets and brand-name products, the growth of department stores and other commercial giants, the introduction of new technologies, and the expansion of the clerical sector.

Over time these developments changed the nature of women's economic and commercial choices, on the one hand making it more and more difficult to compete as a small-business owner and, on the other hand, opening new, remunerative avenues for employment. San Francisco women followed the new opportunities and left proprietorship in large numbers. The decline began after 1880, the apex of female business ownership in the city, and sped up after 1920, when married women and women with children finally began to transcend the discriminatory hiring practices barring them from new jobs in the clerical sector. Even as these developments drove and drew women out of proprietorship, they consistently made the city an exciting and challenging place for those who remained business owners. No wonder, then, that so many San Franciscans penned their reflections about the ever-changing marketplace. The number of personal recollections in letters, diaries, and memoirs that discuss female economic enterprise in San Francisco are numerous. Such insight into the economic details of daily life is probably unique compared to the records available for other regions. It exists because San Franciscans saw themselves as participants in an especially historic series of events—the gold rush and 1906 earthquake and fire, first and foremost—and, as a result, wrote about their experiences, their financial experiences in particular, in voluminous detail.

San Franciscans' recollections about their economic circumstances at the end of the nineteenth and beginning of the twentieth centuries contribute much depth to this volume's focus on the details of everyday life for the city's businesswomen and the choices they faced as independent proprietors. Such documents are valuable partly because they record women's own voices and perspectives about the city's business climate and their own economic exploits. But to answer the questions this book seeks to address—questions about who these female proprietors were and what drove them to go into business, about the kinds of businesses they operated, about the successes and failures they met with in their ventures—I have found another source even more indispensable. Bankruptcy court records, heretofore unused by historians of women in business and certainly underutilized as a source generally, provide an invaluable window into the day-to-day operations of San Francisco female proprietors at the end of the nineteenth and beginning of the twentieth centuries. Particularly because R. G. Dun & Company credit reports—the records upon which historians of women business owners have tended to rely—only exist for the 1870s for San Francisco, it was the bankruptcy court records that provided much of the material I used to examine how women managed their businesses. These records, in combination with newspaper advertisements, city directories, printed census reports, credit reports, and the aforementioned personal recollections, enabled me to peer over the shoulders of the city's businesswomen as they undertook daily tasks such as paying bills, borrowing money, and purchasing supplies. Examining such ordinary details is important because it highlights women's commercial behavior and the intentionality with which they engaged in daily economic decision making.

We have much to learn about the day-to-day operations of small-scale owners because business historians have been much more interested in the impact proprietors have had on business than on the impact business has had on proprietors. Training their lens on the entrepreneurial stories that have something to teach present-day business leaders, many of these scholars have traditionally overlooked small-scale proprietors in favor of big business managers and the strategies they employed that led variably to success or failure in the marketplace.[26] More recently, a growing number of scholars have examined small-business owners, focusing on their marketplace innovations and accommodations.[27] But in fending off the world of big business and its scholarly champions, these historians of small business have themselves remained focused on the contributions small-business proprietors and entrepreneurs have made to the economy.[28]

This emphasis on "contribution" history has caused business historians to overlook several aspects of small business proprietorship. First, such scholars have generally ignored female business owners since women generally operated tiny enterprises and rarely pioneered innovations or strategies that shaped the larger marketplace.[29] The men whose corner groceries, cigar stands, and tailor shops dotted cityscapes from the nineteenth century to the present day also escape notice for similar reasons. Both omissions are due in part to the sources and methodology business historians have traditionally relied on—company records and case studies. Most operators of the smallest business establishments did not even keep daily account books, let alone the kinds of company records business historians have typically used, those that document the internal and external operations of larger firms and corporations, spanning decades.[30] Neither have such individual proprietors persisted long enough nor left behind enough documentation of their existence to merit a case study. Thus the smallest businesses at the end of the nineteenth and beginning of the twentieth centuries are beyond the purview of business historians who focus on the contributions of businessmen and -women and their enterprises.

On the other hand, business historians have introduced several concepts that are applicable to and useful for the study of female proprietors. Scholars have refocused our attention on the importance of individual initiative and insight to the life-course of any small business. They have zeroed in on the way that small businesses persisted in spite of encroachment by large, nationwide chains by "embedding themselves in their local communities." And they have emphasized the importance of experience in enabling small-scale proprietors to identify a market niche that protected them from competition with larger firms.[31] Underscoring all of these studies is the business historians' insistence that "regardless of gender, race, ethnicity, or class, business is still business and only survives in the long run if it generates some income above its costs." Thus, incorporating the scholarship of business historians into an examination of female proprietors provides specific clues for interpretation as well as a general filter through which to view these women's actions, highlighting the degree to which they were commercial or "market-oriented" behaviors.[32]

While small-scale female proprietors have eluded most business historians, they have intrigued women's historians. Ironically, it was the focus on contribution history that initially caused female business owners to capture the attention of scholars in women's history. The first such studies typically celebrated the achievements of successful businesswomen, keeping the focus on what they contributed to the masculine world of business.[33] In this sense women's historians were following the pattern of business historians who continue to examine proprietorship through the lens of innovation and contribution.

But other women's historians were critical of this approach. Mindful of the importance of studying women on their own terms, they argued that scholars needed to move beyond contribution history and stop simply inserting women into the existing masculine paradigm.[34] Initially, women's historians took this to an extreme, identifying a separate sphere within the business world that set female proprietors apart from men both economically and culturally.[35] More recently, scholars have straddled these two positions, demonstrating both that women made important contributions to the business world and that their experiences in that world were shaped significantly by gender. These studies situate female business ownership at the intersection of women's, business, labor, and urban history.[36] For example, businesswomen are examined as participants in the "female economy" of the late nineteenth- and early twentieth-century custom-crafted women's apparel trade, a world characterized by complicated and often-exploitive relationships between women proprietors, employees, and customers.[37] Scholars assert that such women created "semipublic" spaces in stores and shops located on the margins of the business world where they struggled to redraw the lines of gender and class proscribing an exclusively domestic life for them.[38] Ultimately, women's historians have demonstrated that the business world was an arena in which women participated broadly as family members, professionals, laborers, and entrepreneurs; thus, as one scholar tells us, "Women have always been in business in America."[39] In these latest studies, female proprietors are at the center of economic development, helping to shape the geographic, commercial, and moral economy of their communities. As a consequence, the scholarship of women's business historians provides an important foundation for the research presented here.

But none of the books published on women in business is a detailed, micro-level study of women's specific practices as female proprietors, and thus many questions remain unanswered. From whom did businesswomen borrow money? What strategies did they adopt to protect themselves from failure? How did they respond to larger market forces, such as the impact of the department store on merchandising? These are among the everyday details of female proprietorship that this study aims to address by focusing on women business owners across all fields and in one particular location.

This study takes a city in the western United States as its setting, a region entirely neglected in women's historians' accounts of female proprietorship but one with economic and demographic circumstances that had a significant impact on women's commercial activities. As a result, this study will add to the cast of characters we generally associate with women's business ownership. Female proprietors in San Francisco were overwhelmingly married or formerly married (widowed and divorced) and foreign born, a majority hailing from Ireland. This finding conforms with one recent study of female "micro-entrepreneurs" in Albany, New York, at the end of the nineteenth century, suggesting that patterns of female proprietorship probably have many common threads across space and time.[40] But since most published studies have overlooked Irish immigrant women, emphasizing the predominance of native-born white women (both those whose parents were native-born and those whose parents were foreign-born), Jewish immigrant women, and African American women—and have focused on single women—this book helps to fill a hole in our understanding of female small-business owners at the end of the nineteenth and beginning of the twentieth centuries. To be sure, all of these categories of women could be found among San Francisco's female proprietors, but the preponderance of Irish immigrant wives and widows among the city's businesswomen makes them a population that must be better understood, as this study aims to accomplish.

One of the reasons that Irish female proprietors have been overlooked is that market niches drew different types of women. Women in the apparel trades, the "female aristocracy of labor," were more likely to be unmarried, native-born women, or the daughters of (often Irish) immigrants.[41] Women in retail tended to be Jewish immigrant women who drew on a long tradition of active participation in family businesses and household finances, and an even longer tradition of commercial experimentation and enterprise dating

back to life in the shtetl.[42] Jewish women found opportunities in the burgeoning beauty industry as well, along with African American women, who
also operated confectionery, catering, restaurant, hotel, and laundry businesses.[43] The importance of Irish women to the history of female proprictor-
ship has been largely overlooked because current historiography has focused
on women in particular kinds of businesses and particular regions of the
country. The apparel, retail, and beauty industries have received the attention of several talented scholars, but the accommodations and laundry fields,
where most Irish women in San Francisco concentrated their businesses, have
been largely ignored as sites for female economic enterprise.[44] Irish immigrant women in business have figured prominently in general studies of Irish
immigrants but not in the histories of women in business.[45] Of course ethnic
and racial variations among businesswomen in different cities also reflect regional demographics.[46] Studies of women in business, including this one,
have been regionally focused, and thus some of their conclusions—especially
those related to ethnicity and race—can not be applied broadly.[47] Until we
know about female proprietors in many regions of the country, however, we
will not be able to generalize persuasively about their circumstances or their
history.[48] Thus, in addition to shedding light on female proprietorship generally, this study adds a western perspective to our understanding of the history of women small-business owners.

This book's multi-industry focus also leads to a new interpretation of
the nature of women's business relationships. Because of this approach, the
study demonstrates the extent to which women were participants in the larger
urban marketplace. The most widely studied proprietors—those in the apparel trade—were important in San Francisco but never dominated the world
of female proprietorship there. This is significant because unlike the millinery, dressmaking, and beauty industries, every other field in which women
operated businesses involved men as well as women. Thus the majority of
women business owners transacted business not in a "female economy" but in
a heterosocial world in which they employed male as well as female laborers
and drew customers of both genders. As this book will argue, these businesswomen were participants in the hustle and bustle of everyday commercial life
and played an extremely public role in the urban economy—one that is key
to understanding their experience and image as business owners.

Thus where other histories have repopulated the nineteenth-century public domain with politically active women, this study returns economically
active women to the streets and squares of urban America at the end of the
1800s.[49] Women small-business owners inserted themselves into the city's
business and residential districts as tenants and property owners, into the

city's newspapers as advertisers and bankrupts, into its wholesale houses and courthouses as debtors and borrowers, and into the pocketbooks and routines of residents as the providers of goods and services. They were an integral part of the fabric of economic life, with threads connecting them to more corners of the city than their numbers—10 percent of women in the paid labor force—might suggest. Thus, this study positions female proprietors squarely at the center of the late nineteenth- and early twentieth-century urban marketplace by viewing them as intentional participants in city commerce.

Because this book focuses on female proprietors in San Francisco, it also makes a contribution to western history. This is not to say that scholars in the field have ignored gender or its impact on economic opportunity in the West. In fact, many have taken to heart the suggestion that gender is a "useful category of analysis" and have begun to rewrite the region's history, forcing us to rethink events such as the California gold rush that have previously been portrayed as gender neutral.[50] The subject of San Francisco history, too, has benefited from gender analysis, recently receiving the attention of scholars who have inserted women into the political, social, and economic contests that dominated headlines during the second half of the nineteenth century.[51] But there exists no previous study of San Francisco that treats female business owners comprehensively or as integral to the city's development.[52] With a few exceptions, those accounts that have taken up the subject of western businesswomen have treated them as an impressive yet anomalous and transient group.[53] Small midwestern towns have received some attention by scholars as dynamic economic environments in which women played influential roles in such a wide variety of market and nonmarket activities that they seemed to "do everything."[54] Even these studies, however, have not explicated the details of women's commercial engagements, focusing instead on the interconnections between private and public spaces as well as on women's contributions to their communities. Yet to situate female proprietors at the center of western, urban development, where they rightfully belong, requires an examination of their day-to-day interactions with big-city market forces.[55] That is precisely what this study aims to do.

Change over time is an important part of this story. The economics of female proprietorship in San Francisco between 1850 and 1920 were linked to larger changes taking place in both the female labor market and the world of business. Female proprietorship declined during this seventy-year period as other income-producing opportunities for women increased. At the same time, and linked to this trend, operating a business became more and more complicated by the turn of the century, requiring female business owners to invest in start-up strategies that would mitigate competition and cost.

Chronological developments such as these, while fundamental to this book, do not guide its organization, however. In order to maintain the emphasis on women's commercial behavior and daily business operations, the book is organized thematically rather than chronologically. Each chapter traces change over time between 1850 and 1920 in relation to its own theme.

The chapters roughly follow the stages in a businesswoman's commercial life: identification of opportunity, development of an idea, strategizing for start-up, and managing success and failure. Chapter 1 lays out who the city's businesswomen were and what types of enterprises they operated. It examines San Francisco's unique business opportunities compared to six other cities during the same period and argues that women's focus on the high-demand accommodations market highlights their commercial intentionality as proprietors. Chapter 2 discusses the economic, legal, and personal circumstances behind women's entrance into the world of proprietorship, placing particular emphasis on the lack of alternative income opportunities for married, widowed, and divorced women. It highlights the personal stories of several proprietors to demonstrate the circumstances that drove women to start their own businesses. Chapter 3 argues that women took a cautious approach to starting their own businesses, analyzing their use or rejection of several strategies in comparison to men and the reasons why some strategies were better than others. Chapter 4 looks at the increasingly demanding patrons that female proprietors had to contend with and the ways in which this, in combination with competition, especially from department stores and national brands, made operating a successful business more and more expensive and difficult over time. Chapter 5 dissects the importance of financial management and argues that in comparison to men, women were especially poorly prepared for this aspect of their role as business owners. Finally, Chapter 6 explores the longevity, or lack thereof, of women's businesses as well as the many catastrophes that drove San Francisco women out of business. It also highlights how careful planning and persistence enabled some women to recover from such setbacks.

Ultimately, each chapter examines women as intentional economic actors who relied on impulse and intuition to guide their commercial behavior in the city's challenging and competitive marketplace. Who pursued proprietorship and what kinds of businesses they chose reveal the degree to which women responded to their own economic circumstances as well as market conditions by entering the world of commerce. Why women started businesses, on the other hand, tells us a great deal about their motivations for caring for their families by combining economic and domestic responsibilities, a commercial response to the gendered restrictions and requirements imposed on women with families. How San Francisco women chose to start their businesses shows that their impulses for business were often cautious, as befitted a group with so much at stake. Keeping picky customers coming in the door, by comparison, required a sense for customer service, one that many women exercised in order to keep up with the increasingly sophisticated marketplace in which they found themselves operating. When it came to finance, on the other hand, women's commercial impulses were of less use because it was training and experience that made a skilled money manager —precisely the qualities that most San Francisco female proprietors lacked. Finally, women with a yen for proprietorship and a commitment to the opportunities it provided showed a remarkable ability to bounce back from failure, even in the face of disaster, if they were careful about planning for such challenges. Thus, the story of San Francisco's female proprietors between 1850 and 1920 is a story about women as economic actors, family managers, marketplace innovators, resource protectors, financial blunderers, and failure survivors—all roles that elicited deliberate commercial behavior, or *capital intentions*.

CHAPTER 1

FEMALE PROPRIETORS AND THE

BUSINESSES THEY STARTED

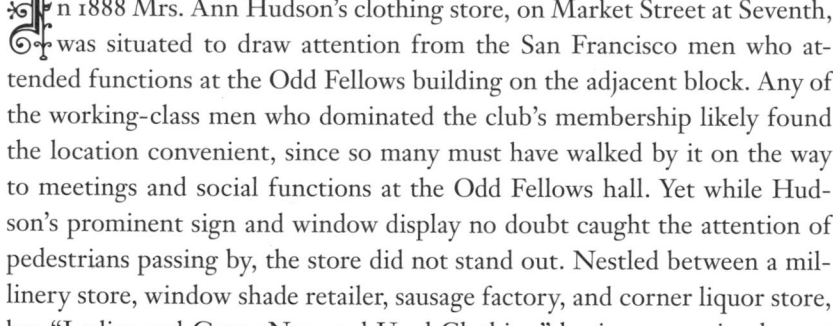

In 1888 Mrs. Ann Hudson's clothing store, on Market Street at Seventh, was situated to draw attention from the San Francisco men who attended functions at the Odd Fellows building on the adjacent block. Any of the working-class men who dominated the club's membership likely found the location convenient, since so many must have walked by it on the way to meetings and social functions at the Odd Fellows hall. Yet while Hudson's prominent sign and window display no doubt caught the attention of pedestrians passing by, the store did not stand out. Nestled between a millinery store, window shade retailer, sausage factory, and corner liquor store, her "Ladies and Gents New and Used Clothing" business was simply part of the commercial landscape, a customary sight to San Franciscans who encountered women-owned businesses on a daily basis.[1]

This was especially true during the 1870s and 1880s, when female proprietorship in the city reached its peak. Thereafter storefronts such as Hudson's were on the wane, as mechanization transformed the production of clothing and department store competition made it increasingly difficult to succeed as a small-scale independent business owner. For each of the five main types of businesses women operated—apparel, laundry, accommodations, beauty, and retail—this trend, in which industry-specific changes altered the opportunities women pursued, was repeated. Growing employment in clerical occupations, a new and burgeoning field for women, further reduced female proprietorship. By 1920, in fact, San Franciscans had witnessed dramatic changes in the commercial contours of their city and would have been hard pressed to locate the kinds of women-owned businesses that had been a dime a dozen just four decades earlier.

Apparel stores such as Hudson's were among the most common types of establishments operated by businesswomen throughout the country, but in San Francisco female proprietors demonstrated a preference for accommodations businesses. Women-owned hotels, boardinghouses, lodging houses, saloons, and restaurants catered to laborers from working-class neighborhoods, uptown gentlemen, and traveling families. This preponderance of female-operated businesses was not coincidental but a calculated response to the unusually high commercial opportunities in San Francisco's accommodations industry. That women responded to such market incentives underscores that capital intentions, not domestic proclivities or happenstance, guided their business decisions.

On the other hand, female proprietors' responses to the city's commercial conditions were constrained by their own economic and cultural circumstances. Most women-owned businesses were modest establishments operated by immigrant women. Whether or not she was an immigrant, Hudson herself was typical in that her commercial and residential addresses were the same. Most likely she lived in a room or small apartment located above or behind her store. Such an arrangement facilitated women's need to find a source of income that did not require them to leave their homes. This seemed especially important to Irish immigrant women, who traditionally did not work outside their homes after marriage and who comprised the largest individual group of businesswomen in the city. The fact that native-born white women, the largest group of women in the paid labor force, constituted much smaller proportions of the population of female business owners suggests the degree to which proprietorship was a humble pursuit, one not expected to bring women glory or riches.

Examining who San Francisco's female proprietors were, the types of businesses they operated, and when they operated them, therefore, illustrates important proprietary patterns. It highlights the rise and fall of female proprietorship in the city, the similarities and differences between women's business ownership in San Francisco and that in other cities, and the kinds of women most likely to pursue proprietorship. All are important foundations for understanding female proprietorship in San Francisco and the capital intentions that guided women's commercial endeavors there. Before we can make sense of Mrs. Hudson, we must understand the patterns she represented.

When the Women's Banking Department at the Bank of Italy opened in the 1920s, it drew a steady stream of female proprietors who were concentrated in four main industries: accommodations, apparel, retail, and beauty. Among the accommodations proprietors were Miss de Gomez, who operated Courtyard Tea Rooms, and Mrs. Washington, owner of the Kentucky Tavern. Apparel proprietors included Mrs. Berry and Miss Ready, proprietors, respectively, of the Berry Corset Company and the Panchon Hat Shop. Mrs. Powell and Miss Cook were among the retailers who utilized the bank's services for their stores: the Children's Book Shop and Candle Glow. And beauty business owners included Miss Rolin, owner of the Flo Rie Beauty Shop, and Miss Berio of Tiny's Beauty Studio.[2]

Women such as these were typical of female proprietors during the late 1800s and early 1900s, who tended to operate establishments in these main lines of business. Accommodations proprietors operated hotels, boardinghouses, lodging houses, saloons, and restaurants. The owners of businesses in the apparel industry included milliners (hat makers), dressmakers, and corset makers who designed, constructed, and sold custom-made women's apparel. Female retailers operated stores that sold everything from toys to used furniture, groceries to sheet music. And proprietors in the beauty industry operated hair and manicure salons and sometimes sold human hair (for wigs and hair pieces) and hair jewelry. Laundry industry proprietors, whose businesses were among the most marginal, were also plentiful, but because of their modest enterprises they were less likely to utilize the bank's services. They operated small-scale wash houses that cleaned and pressed residents' clothing, sometimes specializing in the "French" laundry method and the care of fine linens to distinguish themselves from less-expensive and, they would argue, less-careful washerwomen.

By the 1870s, in fact, San Francisco residents had come to rely on the female purveyors of all of these goods and services. Indeed, the city's commercial district was well populated with woman-owned businesses. A person could hardly walk through the center of the city without encountering one. An imaginary stroll east on Market Street and then north on Montgomery in 1870 illustrates how ubiquitous women's businesses were and how entrenched their commercial presence was in the heart of the city.[3] Walking east on Market Street, for example, a pedestrian would have passed Mrs. G. W. M. Croles's millinery establishment, with an attractive sign hanging in front and perhaps an elegant window display calling ladies inside.[4] A few blocks east, at the intersection of Market and Montgomery, another millinery store was for sale. It was being sold at half the stock's cost on account of the sickness of the proprietor—in all likelihood a woman since female proprietors dominated the hat-making industry.[5]

Nearby but somewhat less obvious would have been Mrs. F. McAuliff's modest business on Market Street. It was a confectionery counter and small restaurant that may have catered to mechanics like her husband, many of whom lived in boardinghouses just south of Market Street.[6] Demand for services such as these was boosted by the city's dramatic gender imbalance—one of the factors discussed later in greater detail that made female proprietorship in San Francisco unique compared to other cities. Unmarried men and men who had traveled to the city without their families relied on boardinghouses, lodging houses, and small hotels as well as on modest establishments such as McAuliff's restaurant for their room and board needs.

At the junction of Market, Montgomery, Kearny, Second, and Third Streets, a traveler would find herself standing at the center of the city's commercial district and the locus of women's small businesses. Two blocks to the right, where New Montgomery Street (in between Second and Third) intersected Mission just south of Market, ladies would find Mrs. S. A. Dewey's hairdressing establishment. There they could have their hair "dressed in the very latest styles" or buy Dewey's own brand of hair tonic "for preventing the hair from falling out."[7] Competing for the business of black beauty customers was Miss C. T. White, a ladies' hairdresser located around the corner at 303 Third Street and one of several businesswomen the city directory identified as "colored."[8] Nearby, at 639 Mission, was the custom shirt business of Mrs. Hagan, who was venturing into the world of proprietorship for the first time after working with the Co-operative Union, most likely as a seamstress.[9]

Above Market Street, north on Montgomery and Kearny, lay the most refined shops and lodging establishments, many of them operated by women. Turning left and strolling past 28 Montgomery Street, for example, anyone might have seen Mrs. M. A. Butler, who had recently moved her millinery store from under the Occidental Hotel to this new location on Montgomery.[10] There was considerable competition at this spot. On Kearny Street, one block to the west, lodgers could also find "large, sunny rooms, handsomely furnished" at the Arlington House, offered at moderate prices with "first-class board" by the hotel's proprietor Mrs. E. M. Gillan.[11] In order to keep her rooms filled, Gillan may have had to draw customers away from the nearby Nucleus House, a popular city hotel that was operated by David Stern in 1870 but would eventually become the domain of Mrs. E. R. Worth.[12]

Walking beyond the successful female-operated businesses of this cen-

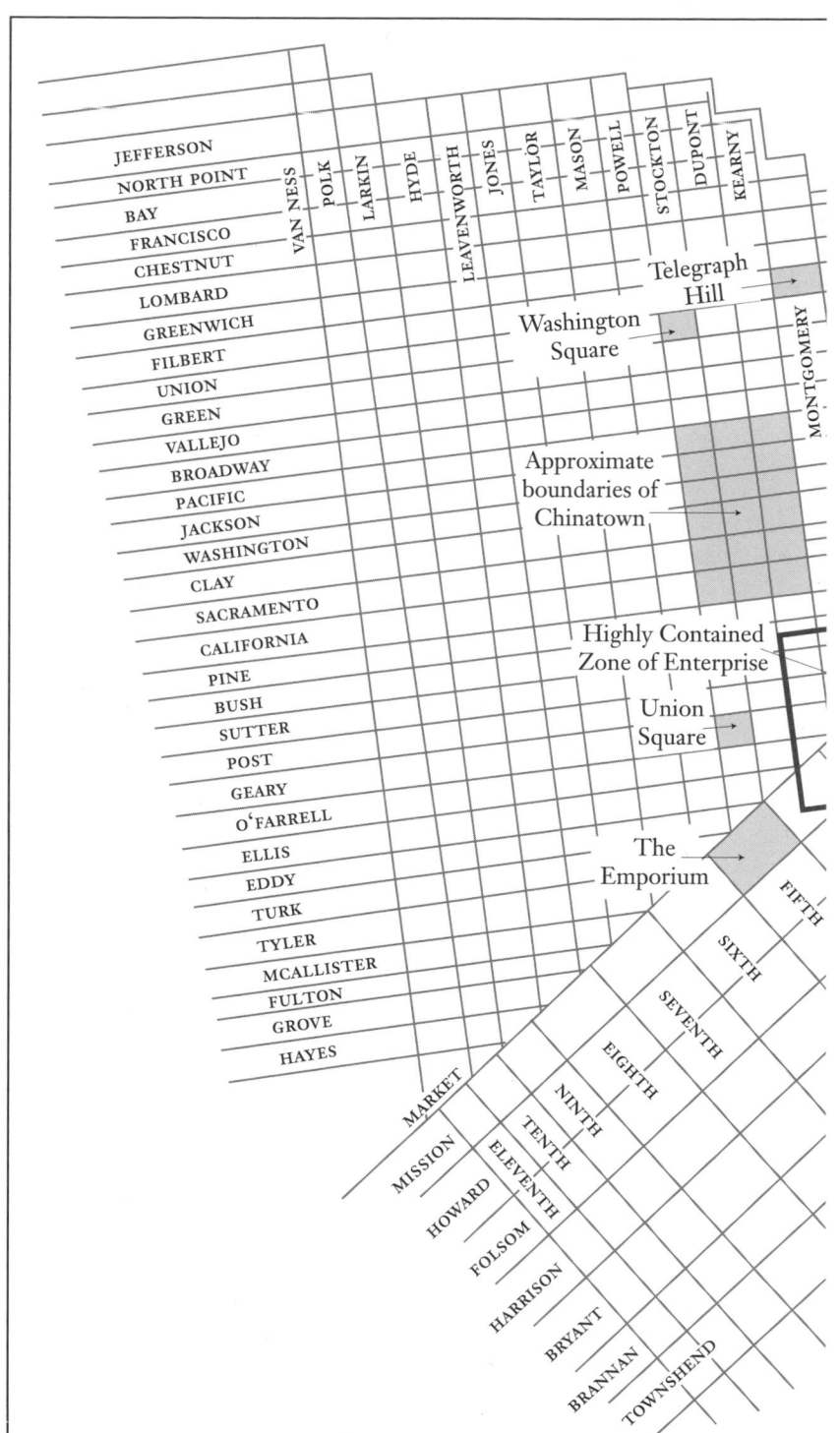

Downtown San Francisco, ca. 1876

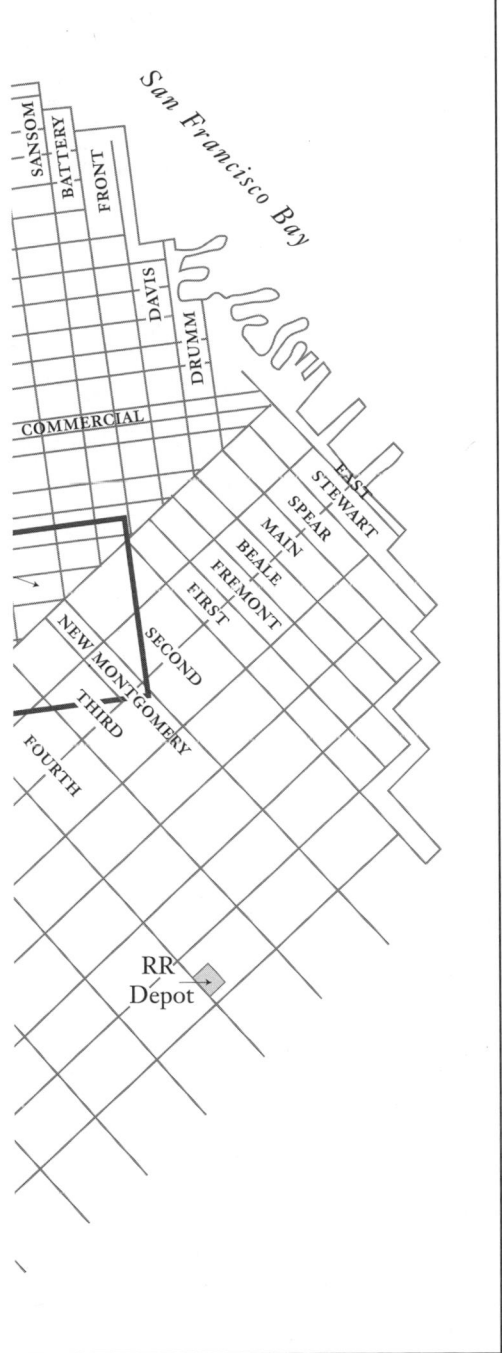

San Francisco Bay

SANSOM

BATTERY

FRONT

DAVIS

DRUMM

COMMERCIAL

EAST

STEWART

SPEAR

MAIN

BEALE

FREMONT

FIRST

SECOND

NEW MONTGOMERY

THIRD

FOURTH

RR
Depot

This ramshackle lunch counter on Mission Street exemplifies the restaurants catering to male laborers concentrated south of Market Street. (California Historical Society, FN-23813)

tral commercial district, passers-by would have seen other establishments that were obviously struggling to stay afloat. Five city blocks above Market, Montgomery crossed Commercial Street, where Sue Long's tobacco store teetered on the brink of commercial failure. On July 16, 1870, credit reporters had succinctly declared that Long was "not safe for credit."[13] Far beyond, near where Montgomery ran to Telegraph Hill, Mrs. Stopplekamp, a fifty-five-year-old widowed grocer, "barely eeked out a living" to support herself and one child. Her grocery, located on the corner of Stockton and Union across from Washington Square, had been started by her husband in 1857

The Nucleus House, which occupied an entire city block, is shown here in 1880 when it was under the management of Mrs. E. R. Worth. (California Historical Society, FN-32514)

and remained her family's primary source of support for over twenty years.[14] Nearby, small numbers of Chinese immigrant women supplemented their laboring husbands' incomes by taking in boarders in their Chinatown homes. Most would have purchased necessary supplies at one of the ethnic groceries in Chinatown, however, and would have had little to no contact with vendors such as Stopplekamp or the rest of the non-Chinese world.[15]

Once at Washington Square, North Beach cafés beckoned weary walkers with coffee and a newspaper in which published advertisements brought even more businesswomen into view. Mrs. C. Cook, for example, ran a prominent advertisement in the paper offering a $1,000 reward to anyone who could return three cases of hair jewelry stolen from the front of her store at 519 Montgomery Street.[16] Less obvious was a much smaller notice, toward the bottom of the page, announcing that Julia A. Forbes, wife of David Forbes, intended to "carry on in her own name and on her own account the business of general dealer and vendor of drugs and medicines."[17]

While female-owned businesses such as these were widespread in the 1870s, fifty years later significant changes in the commercial face of the city overwhelmed what was then a smaller number of female proprietors. San Francisco businesswomen's public presence had declined noticeably. By 1920, in fact, residents walking through the city center were far more likely to come in contact with one of the new "business" women employed in office jobs than with an actual female business owner. Those proprietors whose businesses *were* located along the city's main commercial arteries were dwarfed by gigantic department stores, movie theaters, and large-scale hotels all jostling to be the destination of choice for downtown visitors.

Tracing the same route along Market Street in 1920 that was followed in 1870, a pedestrian would have encountered one of three millinery stores owned by Mrs. Elizabeth Lynch. This one, located at 826 Market, must have catered to a niche crowd, since it would have been hard to compete with the Emporium, one of the city's best-known department stores, which was located just across the street. There men's, women's, and children's apparel and household furnishings were sold in elegant surroundings by knowledgeable and courteous saleswomen—some of them probably defectors from female proprietorship themselves—who were at the ready to promote the latest fashion or provide an encouraging compliment. The Emporium's service, variety, and glamour literally overshadowed Mrs. Lynch's, and she would have had to work hard to give customers a reason to patronize her store.

Mrs. Annie Brownlee's millinery establishment, just a few blocks further east, would have faced similar challenges, as would the businesses of three dressmakers located nearby. By 1920 factory-made and mass-marketed hats and dresses, all displayed seductively in professionally decorated department store windows, made operating a small-scale apparel business a particularly difficult task compared to the halcyon days of the late nineteenth century. While female millinery and apparel store proprietors permeated the city's commercial center during the 1870s, by the early 1900s few could afford to compete with department store opulence and increasing male competition in a craft tradition newly wrenched from female dominance. Not one of the city's female vendors of ladies' furnishing goods, in fact, could afford to locate her establishment on the city's fashionable thoroughfares in 1920, while nearly one-fifth of comparable male vendors did.[18]

Keeping an accommodation business open along Market Street in the central district of the city was also difficult by 1920. Only five lodging houses operated by women were listed with addresses on or near Market Street. Now that the city's gender imbalance had evened out, lodging in San Francisco was

The Emporium overwhelmed small business proprietors with its size and the grandiosity of its claims. (California Historical Society, FN-32511)

no longer in such high demand, and the female owners of hotels, boarding-houses, and lodging houses joined other proprietors in their decline, constituting just 2 percent of all working women counted in the census that year.[19]

The conspicuous absence of female-owned lodging businesses along Market Street, however, may have had a more-particular explanation too. First, several blocks had been inundated with motion picture theaters by 1920. In the 700, 800, 900, and 1000 blocks of Market, ten theaters were listed in the directory, with two additional ones nearby on Kearny and Third. Movie palaces such as the Imperial Theater, the Majestic, and the Odeon, which might attract as many as one hundred paying customers at a time, likely drove up the cost of real estate along the city's central arteries, pricing small-scale accommodations proprietors out of business. Second, San Franciscans had grown increasingly interested in modern improvements and, when given the choice, may have been less likely to spend their money at a simple lodging house than at an establishment such as the Cecil Hotel, operated by Mrs. O. E. Morris on nearby Post Street. Every room she rented had a private bathroom, and reservations for either the "American or European [meal] plan" could be procured by telephone.[20] Like so many proprietors of the late nineteenth and early twentieth centuries, Morris had invested in all the latest conveniences because that was what it took to command a share of public patronage — especially in the city's most central locations. Since most large-scale, highly capitalized hotels were owned and operated by men, however, establishments such as Morris's were unusual, more the exception than the rule in the city's commercial layout.

Finally, what would have been most noticeable to a San Franciscan perusing the city center in 1920 would not have been the ubiquity of female-owned businesses, as in 1870, but public dependence on the clerical skills of women who were employed in offices located along Market, Kearny, and Montgomery Streets. What had been the commercial center of the city was quickly becoming a hub for the expanding financial, accounting, and book-keeping service sectors, and women were an important part of the change. Mrs. Marie Stanyan (240 Montgomery) and Margaret Hart (703 Market) dispensed insurance policies, while Ivy Borden (417 Montgomery) and Mrs. Morrell (681 Market) processed loans. Still more noticeable to a pedestrian would be the twelve women who offered their services as notary publics and the eleven women who hired themselves out as stenographers, all located along Montgomery and Market Streets.[21] Harder to detect as a passerby but still more important to the administrative revolution reconfiguring San Francisco's downtown were the thousands of female clerical workers and secretaries who spent the work day in offices, providing the record keeping and paper processing necessary to keep modern, twentieth-century corporations humming smoothly.[22]

As our walking tour of San Francisco makes clear, the heyday of female economic enterprise was short-lived in San Francisco. Starting in 1870, female proprietors comprised 7 percent of all gainfully occupied women listed in the census (see table A1). Ten years later, at the peak of women's small-business ownership in the city, that figure had risen to 10 percent. Thereafter the proportion of gainfully employed women who operated small businesses decreased significantly, until by 1920 only 4 percent of women in the paid labor force were proprietors.[23] Thus, the rate of women's business ownership rose until 1880 and then declined steadily through 1920.

This decline in female proprietorship in San Francisco was not gender specific and represented larger economic changes sweeping the nation. Like female small-business owners, small businessmen in the city declined from roughly 13 percent of those in the paid labor force in 1890 to 7 percent in 1920.[24] In addition, printed census figures confirm a similar decline in female small-business proprietorship in six other sample cities: Buffalo, Cincinnati,

New Orleans, New York, Boston, and Chicago. As in San Francisco, the proportion of women in the paid labor force employed as proprietors peaked at an average of 10 percent in most of these cities in 1880.[25] Thereafter female proprietors in the paid labor force in all six cities declined steadily until 1920, when only 5 percent of gainfully occupied women worked as proprietors. These figures mirror almost exactly the statistics for San Francisco female proprietorship during the same period.[26] The parallel declines in female and male small-business proprietorship in San Francisco and in female proprietorship in other cities indicate that larger changes were occurring in the nature of work and business. Closer examination of individual industries confirms this.

In the apparel industry, for example, the rise of ready-to-wear women's clothing and the industrialization of clothing manufacturing precipitated the decline of female proprietorship. But it was a process that was not complete until the early twentieth century. Until then, demand for complicated dresses with tailored bodices and long, full, structured skirts as well as elaborate hats provided employment to a large population of dressmakers and milliners.[27] These workers commanded significantly higher wages than women in most other occupations. And a determined minority found they could turn their years of experience and careful savings into careers as proprietors. In 1870s San Francisco, some 19 percent of apparel workers did just that, operating as independent owners of small-scale businesses.[28] In other cities around the country, the trend in the industry was similar.[29] But by the beginning of the twentieth century, proprietorship had become significantly harder to obtain in the apparel industry. The reason, one scholar explains, was that "beginning in the 1890s ready-made dresses and mass-produced hats threatened the fortunes of custom clothiers[, and] sumptuously furnished department stores forecast a grim future for tiny, female-operated concerns."[30] The changes affected both laborers and proprietors. But it was business owners who experienced the more-precipitous decline. By 1900, dressmaking and millinery proprietors comprised just 9 percent of their trade in San Francisco, half of the share they had enjoyed thirty years earlier.[31] Again, the trend was repeated in other cities throughout the country.[32] This was a classic case of deskilling and proletarianization, in which independent artisans were drawn away from control over the production process and increasingly put in the position of selling their labor rather than their products.[33]

Women in the laundry industry faced a similar downward trajectory nationwide as mechanization and competition transformed the nature of their work. Individual washerwomen who operated small-scale laundry businesses, usually out of their homes, persisted into the twentieth century in the United

States but became rare icons of an earlier era. More common by the end of the nineteenth century were "laundrymen" who employed several laborers to operate the new steam-powered washers and mangles that made the work of laundering clothes and linens more efficient and cost-effective.[34] Eventually "a number of innovative ironing and starching machines were introduced," as well, "mechanizing what had been previously considered the most skilled jobs in laundries."[35] In these new steam-laundry factories, foreign-born white men generally filled the more-prestigious and higher-paid washing and distributing jobs. The women who were hired as shirt finishers, ironers, starchers, manglers, and folders worked for substantially lower wages and enjoyed none of the independence that characterized the work of female laundresses and laundry owners decades earlier.[36] In San Francisco the displacing of women from the laundry field was preceded and augmented by substantial competition from Chinese men, who dominated the industry in the city by 1880.[37] By then Chinese immigrants already had experienced a long history of ethnic antagonism in California, where it was made clear from their arrival that they were not welcome by Anglo Californians. After being driven out of jobs in San Francisco's shoe and tobacco industries, Chinese men turned to operating laundries.[38] It was one of the few opportunities they had for independent income generation, and they fought hard to maintain their rights within the industry, using the courts to protect themselves against anti-Chinese laws that targeted laundry owners.[39] But the persistence of Chinese men in the industry doomed the enterprises of the city's laundresses. The economic relationship between Asian male success and female failure seemed so clear, in fact, that San Franciscans organized the "Anti-Coolie Co-Operative Laundry Association" to try to stamp out Chinese competition and appealed to consumers to "give labor to the whitewoman of our city in preference to the coolies."[40] Similar tactics were used decades later when Anglo San Franciscans formed the "Anti-Jap Laundry League" to target Japanese launderers who "inherited much of the resentment and prejudice that had been directed against the Chinese."[41] In combination with mechanization, this perceived incursion of Asian men in San Francisco's laundry industry resulted in substantially depressed opportunities for women. This was not a broader phenomenon in the West or even in the rest of the state, but one confined to northern California cities such as San Francisco and Oakland that contained high concentrations of Asian immigrants.[42]

In contrast to the apparel and laundry industries, women in San Francisco's beauty industry enjoyed expanding opportunity. Nationwide, women began establishing a presence in the industry as proprietors by the 1870s. Though early on only the ladies' hairstyles popular for special occasions—

upswept hairdos ornamented by flowers and feathers—demanded the employ of a hairdresser, by the 1870s casual styles became elaborate enough to create a significant market for business owners in the beauty industry.[43] But only a small number of these proprietors were female. By the end of the decade, women comprised 10 percent of the 245 hairdressers listed in San Francisco. Mrs. E. A. Jordan, Mrs. C. Marchard, and Miss Nora Scully, for example, all located on Washington Street, competed with four other hairdressing establishments on the same street that were operated by men.[44] Women such as these trying to carve out a niche for themselves in the male-dominated beauty industry represented less than 1 percent of all gainfully occupied women by the end of the decade and under 2 percent of the city's businesswomen.[45] Female proprietors in the beauty industry in comparable cities around the nation comprised similarly small populations, both as a proportion of all businesswomen and as a proportion of all gainfully employed women.[46] But as the number of businesswomen in the apparel and laundry industries declined, the number of beauty proprietors grew as a proportion of all businesswomen. Opportunity in the industry grew at the same time. This was true because of the development of a new "beauty culture" between the 1890s and 1920s, "formulated and organized . . . to a remarkable extent" by women. Working-class, immigrant, and African American women in particular capitalized on the growing demand for beauty services engendered by this new cultural emphasis on shaping women's appearance. Female proprietors offered women's hair care, cosmetics, and manicuring services at genteel beauty parlors or salons popularized throughout urban America at the beginning of the last century.[47] Such businesses became fixtures in the business directories of cities, including San Francisco, and constituted an increasing share of all female-owned enterprises.

Like businesswomen in the beauty industry, female retailers in San Francisco comprised a small but increasingly significant population that resembled that of female proprietors in the industry elsewhere. In San Francisco retailing was important early on because of the demand for equipment and supplies by gold rush miners. For some men who entered the trade to provision the miners, retail proved enormously profitable. Men such as Levi Strauss, for example, built an empire supplying comfortable yet durable canvas work pants.[48] But women retailers in the city tended toward more-modest enterprises ranging from tobacco to jewelry sales. Though retail dealing was an attractive occupation in San Francisco, women traders comprised only a small proportion of businesswomen in the city. By the 1870s, for example, women identified as "traders and dealers" or "hucksters and peddlers" constituted just 6 percent of all female proprietors in the city and less than 1 percent of all gainfully occupied women. The population was comparably small in other major U.S. cities, where female retailers hovered within a percentage point of San Francisco's population as a percentage of all gainfully occupied women.[49] Among the many kinds of stores that existed in the city, the five areas that drew the largest numbers of women retailers by 1920 were groceries (190); dry goods, fancy goods, and notions (85); candy and confectionery (70); clothing and personal furnishings (53); and drugs and medicines (47). In these five retail occupations and all others, San Francisco women faced stiff competition from men and comprised just 7.5 percent of the city's total number of retailers.[50] In spite of the competition and women's small numbers in the industry, retail was an occupation that grew increasingly important over time for women interested in operating their own businesses. From 1870, when they constituted just over 2 percent of all businesswomen in San Francisco, retailers grew to approximately 12 percent of all female proprietors by 1920. This was a consistent trend in other cities and resembled the change that occurred in the beauty industry.[51] As proprietors in the apparel and laundry industries decreased, businesswomen in those industries that offered consistent opportunity—retail and beauty—comprised an increasingly significant proportion of the city's female entrepreneurs.

Along with these industry-specific changes we must lay two additional factors in the decline of female proprietorship in San Francisco. The first was the expanding opportunities in clerical work that drew women out of proprietorship. The second was the increasing costs and complications of starting and maintaining a business. Both subjects will be taken up in detail in the following chapters: Chapter 2 on why women started businesses, Chapter 3 on how women started businesses, and Chapters 4 and 5 on what it took to manage a business. What is important here is simply to identify the ebb and flow of female proprietorship in the city.

CAPITAL INTENTIONS AND MARKET INCENTIVES

Businesswomen in San Francisco, as in cities across the nation, found the most plentiful opportunities for proprietorship in trades correlated to the sorts of domestic tasks women performed in their own households without pay.[52] Dressmakers, milliners, and laundresses made, repaired, and cleaned clothes, tasks in which countless wives and mothers engaged as unpaid, reproductive laborers. Boardinghouse, lodging house, and hotelkeepers provided "homes away from home" for unattached men and unsettled families. Female restaurant, saloon, and café owners nourished the empty stomachs of many with the kind of meals married women usually provided for their families at private tables. And a variety of store owners stocked shelves with products that women had previously produced by hand for their households.

Women did not choose such jobs to satisfy some abstract social ethic regarding their role as nurturers but because they knew how to do the work, because they knew there was a demand for these services, and because these jobs fit with their family and household responsibilities. In pursuing proprietorship in industries such as retail and apparel, women demonstrated "capital intentions" — that is, they assessed their own skills and abilities and matched them with the opportunities they saw in the marketplace in order to make the most profitable and prudent business decisions. Because most women entered business ownership with no previous experience or training as proprietors, it was instinct and intuition that guided many of their economic choices, including the decision to concentrate their efforts as entrepreneurs in commercializing domesticity. In simplest terms, they went where the opportunities were.

It was for this very reason that so many women pursued opportunities in San Francisco's accommodations industry, since it offered unusually high opportunities for proprietors compared to other cities. In fact, San Francisco female proprietors operated businesses in the hospitality industry in dramatically higher proportions than women in the rest of the country. Compared to Boston and New York, for example, where hospitality proprietors made up 2.2 and 1 percent, respectively, of all gainfully occupied women in 1900, San Francisco proprietors in the industry comprised 4.5 percent — more than twice the proportion (see figure A1).[53]

The concentration of San Francisco's female proprietors in the accommodations industry was a trend that started early and lasted into the beginning of the twentieth century. In 1877, for example, over 500 female proprietors were listed in the city directory as owners of accommodations businesses.[54] By comparison, 142 were listed in Boston, a substantially bigger city.[55] These female hotel, boardinghouse, lodging house, restaurant, and saloon owners found that in San Francisco, "home-making" was a uniquely profitable enterprise, and they entered this niche in the economy in large numbers throughout the period between 1850 and 1920 (see figure A2). In fact, businesswomen in the accommodations industry consistently outstripped female proprietors in laundry, retail, beauty, and apparel, making up 35–36 percent of the total number of San Francisco's female business owners over time.[56] What these women found is that in San Francisco unique economic and demographic factors conspired to generate an unusually high demand for accommodations services from the gold rush through the beginning of the twentieth century.

Finding housing had been a problem from the start in San Francisco. After

1849 men began arriving in such large numbers in such a short time that the only housing available for many was canvas shacks. "[A] large portion of the fixed inhabitants live in tents and places which cannot be described with any accuracy," wrote Charles P. Kimball, the first San Franciscan to try to record the city's population.[57] Even the earliest "hotels" in northern California were rough-hewn. In Nevada City, north of Sacramento, for example, Luzena Stanley Wilson started with just a table; walls and a roof grew up around it as money allowed.[58] The first hotels in San Francisco must have been similarly primitive, relying on the scarcity of local comforts to bring customers to their doors.

The demand for lodgings was, in fact, tremendous, and it was met by an unusually large number of accommodations service providers. Already by 1850 the temporary housing business employed hundreds in the city. As one historian found, "the number of people running boardinghouses or hotels to house transients [in San Francisco] far exceeded the national figure. In 1850, for every thousand Californians gainfully employed, over nine were in the hotel or boardinghouse trade, more than double the figure for the country as a whole."[59]

One of the main prohibitions to real estate development in early San Francisco was a lack of lumber. For while the surrounding mountains were certainly full of trees that could have been felled and put to good use in building construction, northern California's new residents had come to mine gold, and few had any intentions of setting up semipermanent, capital-intensive businesses such as lumbering. In addition, the city's labor shortage made hiring construction workers prohibitively expensive.[60] Those who did put up new buildings, therefore, seemed more ready to ship prefabricated structures around the Isthmus then build their own from scratch. A San Francisco agent for prefabricator Joseph G. Bearly & Co. reported that "had the Boarding house been here 8 weeks sooner I could have sold it for 4000 dollars instead of 2000 dollars." Nonetheless, along with his report, he enclosed a "draft on New York for 2500 dollars . . . full payment for the Boarding House and the balance for the small Houses and the hardware" that he had also sold on behalf of the company.[61]

For those who had such capital, a boardinghouse or sturdy home may have seemed like an especially good investment in a city where housing was scarce. The owner of either could have made a pretty penny selling room and board. But while prefabricated buildings were better protection against the elements than tents, they could not withstand the firestorms that swept through San Francisco regularly. A total of eight fires during the 1850s caused property damage totaling $25 million.[62] Scarcity and the risk of fire made San Francisco one of the most expensive cities in the country when it came to real estate. Mary Jane Megquier, an early resident of San Francisco, reported: "If I could only get a house to live in I should make money but one boarding house rents for eighty thousand dollars a year."[63]

Even after the challenge of securing building materials, the risk of fire, and the prohibitively high real estate prices had been reduced, San Francisco remained a city predominated by temporary living arrangements. In addition to functioning as the outfitter of the mining hinterlands, the city was also accommodation headquarters for a seasonal influx of miners and agricultural workers who wintered there each year. By the 1880s they were joined by a sizable population of sailors who spent their time enjoying the city's many entertainments when on leave. Together these sojourners "filled every available shelter to overflowing" and lined the pockets of those male and female proprietors who provided beds and meals for a reasonable price.[64] Even permanent residents of some means tended to choose hotel or boardinghouse accommodations. Between 1849 and 1860, for example, most of the city's merchants lived with "a friend, relative, or business associate in a multi-room dwelling, boarding house, or hotel and paid exorbitant prices at the myriad of local restaurants."[65] Contemporary Benjamin E. Lloyd was just one of many to comment on the city's reliance on hotels and boardinghouses. He observed: "The hotel is the San Franciscan's home. A man of domestic habits is a rarity . . . so attached are San Franciscans to hotel life, that 'let come what may come,' they will not forego its attractions."[66]

Absence of family was one of the most important factors in this trend. Most of the early settlers viewed their residence in the state as temporary and the journey as treacherous. Therefore, they saw no reason to uproot their families from their permanent homes elsewhere.[67] But even as the tide of migration changed with the end of the gold rush and a more-stable lifestyle took hold in San Francisco, the city continued to be dominated by men. In fact, the gender imbalance did not begin to approximate parity until 1920, when there were 117 male residents for every 100 women (see table A2).[68] Even then, there would have been a significant proportion of men who had to rely on restaurants and lodging establishments for the services that family men received at home.

Perhaps most remarkable about life in San Francisco was the preponderance of families who also shunned housekeeping in favor of boarding out. In his 1876 account of San Francisco Benjamin E. Lloyd wrote that "women ha[d] come to regard family cares and duties as a sort of drudgery without their province" and happily embraced the practice of eating family meals at restaurants and taking private rooms in hotels and lodging houses. The "drudgery" of keeping house may have been particularly acute for women of some privilege who were accustomed to the help of several servants but whose family budgets could not afford the notoriously high wages servants commanded in San Francisco. In his comments in *Hotels and Hotel Life at San Francisco California in 1876*, William Laird MacGregor seconded this observation: "Owing to the difficulty of obtaining good servants, to the wandering habits of many of the population, to their love of society, amusement and pleasure . . . many of the Americans seem to prefer life at a hotel to domestic life at home." Some, he reported, resided in hotels for years at a time.[69] Of course, low demand for private family homes could also be explained as a function of cost. While the exceptional inflationary prices characteristic of the gold rush did not persist beyond the 1850s, geographical isolation kept the cost of almost everything high until the completion of the transcontinental railroad in 1869. By then the hotel and restaurant tradition was sufficiently entrenched that the arrival of cheaper lumber, household furnishings, or servants may not have been able to reverse the trend. As contemporary observer Benjamin E. Lloyd commented, by the 1870s San Franciscans had been "wean[ed] from home."[70]

The majority of opportunity for proprietors in the hospitality industry, however, was concentrated not among the fashionable thoroughfares of the city populated by middle-class families but in the working-class environs. South of Market Street lay the "half city, half camp" region known as Happy Valley in 1849 and thereafter as home to the exclusive Rincon Hill and South Park neighborhoods—province of the city's earliest elite. But by 1860 the region had "become highly industrial, with the houses and shelters of its laborers growing up around it." Capitalists and laborers coexisted there uneasily for a decade, each claiming particular avenues for their commercial exchanges. Second Street showcased the shops of upscale milliners, jewelers, and modistes, while a block away, "First Street ran to sailors' boarding houses, German groceries, Irish saloons, gas works and boiler shops."[71] But when Rincon Hill was "sheared in two" in 1869 to extend Second Street further south, property values there plummeted, and the wealthy residents left the area for good. Thereafter "South of Market" was "known as a working-class quarter" and quickly became home to the majority of San Francisco's hospitality proprietors.[72] Depressed housing prices must partly explain the trend. Affordable real estate permitted working-class families to procure a business location (either separate from their residence or not) for the purpose of operating an accommodations enterprise. The city directory's "Progress of the City" report for 1879–80 stated that South of Market was home to nearly one-third of San Francisco's boardinghouses, a quarter of its hotels, half of its lodging houses, and one-third of its restaurants.[73]

The South of Market Street district of the city always housed a large share of the city's single men, but before 1906 it was also home to many families. Typically the family heads worked in unskilled or semiskilled occupations and rented rather than owned their homes. To make ends meet, their children often worked as well, bringing money into the household through unskilled labor. Also key to many family's budgets was taking in boarders. One survey of a street in the district found that eleven out of twenty-four households had boarders: "Seven families had a boarder not related by kinship or marriage, three families had two boarders, and one had six."[74] Since most of the families consisted of both husband and wife and all the men labored outside the home, the work of keeping boarders fell to the women in the household. As economic historians of women's labor have pointed out, such work was usually undercounted, either by census takers or by the women themselves, who may not have considered keeping boarders an "occupation" in the late nineteenth- or early twentieth-century sense of the word.[75] It is not surprising, therefore, that only one woman was listed as a "landlady." Such informal boarding businesses supplemented the more-obvious lodging houses (14) and restaurants (7) that also appeared on the street.[76]

While single women were occasional renters and boarders in the South of Market region—three washerwomen lived in the same building on Tehama Street where Timothy Gill and his wife Bridget kept six boarders—unattached men were the primary customers.[77] All types of local unskilled and semiskilled laborers and migratory casual workers sought shelter in the area while residing in San Francisco during the late nineteenth and early twentieth centuries. But most numerous among the group by far were the men employed as sailors. At the end of the nineteenth century, San Francisco had more mariners than any other American city, including New York. The population was so large that it overwhelmed the other occupations men pursued. "In 1890, one working man in forty found employment as a seafarer, and by 1910 the proportion of sailors and deck-hands among working males had increased to one in thirty-two." Most lived along the waterfront, where almost 70 percent of the residents in 1900 and nearly 90 percent in 1910 were men. The waterfront district bristled with boardinghouses, restaurants, saloons, brothels, and gambling houses, all of which catered to young, single men.[78]

Female proprietors as well as male took advantage of the city's composition by operating businesses in the hospitality industry. As early as 1850 the city directory recorded 22 female proprietors of boardinghouses, hotels, and restaurants.[79] "Many females came here to establish boarding houses," wrote one contemporary observer in a letter home.[80] That figure grew more than 400 percent to 114 in 1860 and more than quadrupled again in 1877–78, when it reached 586 (see table A3).[81] The 1870s increase in accommodations proprietors certainly was linked with the national depression of that decade that forced thousands into bankruptcy and still more out of work.[82] Historians of small business have noted the relationship between economic downturns and independent enterprise. As one scholar argues, "more [small businesses] were started during the trough of the business cycle than during any other of its stages." This trend suggests that "many Americans go into small businesses when they find other employment options cut off."[83] Housing lodgers and boarders certainly followed this pattern. For women with families, taking in boarders might be a minimally disruptive income generator when economic tragedy struck. One study found that 15 to 20 percent of urban households relied on this strategy to supplement the ebb and flow of a male household head's income into the early twentieth century.[84]

Between 1890 and 1910, opportunities in the accommodations industry surged along with the city's fortunes in conjunction with military build up for the Spanish-American and Filipino-American Wars. The city was strategically positioned to benefit from the conflicts. Nine federal military bases founded between 1851 and 1900 and ten munitions and explosives plants in the San Francisco Bay Area stood to gain from the militarization. The United Iron Works, for example, which had enriched its owners through the production of hydraulic mining machinery starting in the 1860s, redirected its attention to shipbuilding once the company secured a government contract for the *Charleston*, an armored cruiser, in 1886. Thereafter it remained one of the biggest employers in the city, joining other firms in capitalizing on the creation of America's great Pacific fleet and drawing millions of dollars into the region for the production of warships, bolstering the local economy through the 1890s depression. By the outbreak of violent conflict with Spain and then the Philippines, San Francisco power brokers understood clearly the positive commercial impact that war would have on the city; they promoted American engagement in both conflicts unabashedly, in spite of the moral contradictions that writers such as Mark Twain identified in the racist American agenda in the Pacific. "War meant business for San Francisco's leading merchants and manufacturers and unlimited trade opportunities for the future," as well as federal subsidies for the region's military installments.[85] For decades thereafter city leaders worked hard to ensure that it would be their city and not some other West Coast urban center that benefited from the nation's imperialistic ambitions in the Pacific.[86]

The economic benefits of war and imperialism did not just make the rich richer, however, but trickled down as well to small-scale service providers in San Francisco and the surrounding region. "Troops stationed at [the region's military] bases, or passing through [on their way to the front], did wonders for the local economy."[87] A total of some 126,500 American troops served in the Filipino-American War, for example, and most of them departed through San Francisco; the 122,266 who returned from the war again came through the city's golden gates.[88] While in San Francisco, these men needed food and shelter, stimulating the city's service economy. Women were among those who benefited. Following their capital intentions and going where they saw the opportunity, the number of women working as the proprietors of restaurants, hotels, lodging houses, and boardinghouses increased dramatically between 1890 and 1900 to meet the increased demand for domestic services by American soldiers and sailors.[89]

By 1910 the number of businesswomen in the city employed in hospitality began to decline, but not dramatically, because a new population of single and unattached men who needed temporary housing kept them in the industry. Thousands of carpenters, masons, and general laborers descended on San Francisco after the devastating 1906 earthquake and fire to help rebuild the city. Before the fires were entirely extinguished, the *San Francisco Chronicle* was already publishing a call to arms; its headline proclaimed, "San Francisco Will Rise From The Ashes A Greater And More Beautiful City Than Ever."[90] Under pressure from the Downtown Businessmen's Association, city leaders decided to forgo plans for a new "city beautiful" and instead rebuild the city as it had been as quickly as possible. "Within three and a half years downtown San Francisco was rebuilt along pre-earthquake lines. Within five years, recovery was total."[91] To accomplish this amazing feat, thousands of additional workers made their home in San Francisco. For shelter and warm meals, they turned to one of the city's boardinghouses or inexpensive hotel apartments, hundreds of which were run by female proprietors. Their presence kept women who might otherwise have pursued one of the new jobs in sales or bookkeeping in the hospitality business and probably attracted others who would have occupied themselves with wage labor.[92] Operating a business in the hospitality industry never made a woman rich, but it was a lucrative pursuit during the flush and crowded times between 1906 and 1910.

That businesswomen catered to the stereotypically churlish sailing and laboring crowds may seem doubtful. After all, might an unmarried woman's moral decency come into question if she spent her days and nights among single men?[93] This was apparently not the case with Mrs. Mary Frances

Male workers such as these flocked to San Francisco after the 1906 earthquake and fire to help rebuild the city, creating ample opportunity for female accommodations proprietors. (California Historical Society, FN-32504)

Tighe, who had been operating just such an establishment for eleven years when she came to the attention of the *San Francisco Chronicle* in 1918. Tighe operated the St. Dunstan Hotel Apartments with the help of her unmarried daughter, Lucile. Together they provided a haven for "homeless" San Franciscans, "[a] large number of [them] Army and Navy people," who liked the place for its "home-like atmosphere . . . the comfort afforded being especially attractive to them." Far from questioning the propriety of Tighe's working in a business that catered to single men, the newspaper declared her "one of California's leading women." She and her daughter were described as "standard-bearers of their sex in America," their achievements as "shining criterion by which the women of this country gauge their hopes and ideals."[94]

That the Tighe women were participating in a trend unique to San Francisco—the unusually high number of female proprietors in the accommodations industry—may have been the real reason they seemed so remarkable. Because women hotel, boardinghouse, lodging house, saloon, and restaurant owners constituted a larger percentage of all gainfully occupied females in San Francisco than in other cities in the country, they may have stood out to city residents and visitors. This difference in women's proprietary patterns underscores the degree to which specific market conditions, rather than predictable domestic habits, motivated the commercial decisions of female business owners.

GENDER, CLASS, RACE, AND NATIVITY:
THE DEMOGRAPHICS OF PROPRIETORSHIP

As participants in San Francisco's unusual trend in women-owned accommodations businesses, the Tighes were actually no more remarkable than any other female proprietor in the city. In fact, what truly makes them stand out is that the *Chronicle* mentioned them at all. For as a group, San Francisco's businesswomen were typically immigrants who operated modest commercial establishments and were unlikely to draw the attention of newspaper writers or readers.

If they did get mentioned in the press, it was less likely for laudatory reasons than for their status as lower-class members of society. It was in this way that female proprietors seemed to occupy the popular imagination. A sketch taken from "The Misadventures of Charley," a cartoon series that appeared in *Harper's Magazine* beginning in 1857, illustrates the point.[95] In it, Charley, the son of a prosperous city family, brings home the son of a woman who runs the local candy store—much to the horror of his class-conscious mother. This sketch was meant to entertain middle-class readers by "playing upon the perplexities and anxieties of real householders and parents."[96] A middle-class mother's anxiety is raised by the prospect of her child befriending a lower-class child—the son of a female retail dealer. As a minor character, significant only for the class status she represented, such a businesswoman had to have been familiar, even ordinary, to *Harper's* readers. Her appearance here reveals how ubiquitous such figures were in the nineteenth-century urban landscape. The cartoonist chose a female candy store owner for the part both because she could stand in as a class signifier, and because she would not stand out.

The use of the female candy store owner to represent the taint of class underscores that while businesswomen may have been common, they were often perceived as commoners as well. Of course, the *Harper's* cartoon played on well-worn stereotypes, so it is not a particularly reliable gauge of the actual class status of female proprietors. And as later chapters will reveal, the class backgrounds of businesswomen in San Francisco were in reality varied.[97] Privileged female property holders and working-class renters, fortunate estate inheritors and desperately impoverished widows, middle-class wives of handsomely paid government employees and abandoned mothers of several children were all among the city's female business owners. For some, proprietorship was a proud accomplishment of independence, for others a necessary income generator, and for still others an embarrassment they would rather not reveal. Middle-class, American-born women, for example, commonly resorted to business operation when they suffered financial reverses; yet because middle-class prescriptions defined female paid labor as a loss of status, such women often operated their enterprises informally, and thus invisibly, to census enumerators and others.[98] On the other hand, an unmarried milliner who labored doggedly for years under the tutelage of a master hat maker likely experienced independent proprietorship with pride, advertising to all she knew that she was now in business for herself (a sign of good marketing instincts as much as hubris). Finally, some women were encouraged to operate small businesses as a matter of course. "Urban Jewish women," for example, "were among the most active entrepreneurial women in the United States at the turn of the century . . . [because] Eastern European Jewish culture afforded women . . . importance as economic actors within the family."[99] Similarly, while female immigrants from Ireland labored under cultural expectations that they remain in the home after marriage, married women controlled the purse strings in Irish homes and were granted wide latitude when it came to supplementing their husbands' income, especially through remunerative household labor.[100] Many business enterprises fit these expectations, and thus Irish women were also among the most populous group of female business owners in urban America.[101] But if women came to proprietorship from different class backgrounds and with different attitudes, their outcomes as business owners were much more uniform. Female proprietorship did not provide a ladder for the upwardly mobile to a higher class level. There were a handful of exceptions, of course, but not many. Indeed, as subsequent chapters will show, few if any businesswomen accomplished enduring economic security, let alone wealth.[102] Here was the grain of truth in the *Harper's* stereotype: female proprietorship was rarely in and of itself a badge of class attainment, and it could be a symbol of class slippage.

The 1880 peak in female proprietorship underscores this point. That census was taken just a year after the nation's first depression came to a close. Women's income became even more important during such hard times. Those dislocated from wage work during the economic slump turned to business ownership as a source of replacement income. Others may have taken on business proprietorship as an addition to wage work during hard times. And still others, as discussed above, were forced to enter the paid labor force for the first time because of financial tragedy. The increase in the portion of employed women who were engaged as independent proprietors in 1880, therefore, indicates that economic necessity, or as one scholar puts it, "self-preservation," was a driving force behind small-business ownership.[103]

Indeed, what the rates of proprietorship for women *and men* underscore is that small-business ownership was a humble economic achievement, one that often afforded a "respectable" income but accorded proprietors little status in the eyes of class-conscious women like Charley's mother. Those most likely to share her cultural values, native-born white children of immigrants and native-born white children with native-born parents, were least likely to become business owners in San Francisco. Immigrants and nonwhites, however, operated according to a different set of ideals.[104] As one early twentieth-century study found, "recent immigrants in particular 'look[ed] upon a job as a workman as lower in the social scale' than any sort of independent proprietorship."[105] Thus, long after native-born white Americans had begun to reject small-scale enterprise, immigrants "clung to the independent status of the small proprietor."[106] This was true for both men and women. Thus foreign-born whites were most likely to enter the world of small-business proprietorship (tables A5–A11).[107]

Computations from the 1890 printed census illustrate these trends. Among women, 57 percent of business proprietors were "white" immigrants, compared to a slightly smaller 47 percent for male proprietors. Foreign-born white women were overrepresented in proprietorship relative to their presence in the labor market, then, as they comprised only 41 percent of gainfully employed women in the city.[108] Women who hailed from Ireland were the largest group of immigrants, comprising 39 percent of foreign-born female proprietors and 23 percent of all businesswomen. They dominated all fields of business except apparel. German (16 percent), British (8 percent), and Scandinavian (6 percent) immigrants comprised the second-, third-, and fourth-largest groups of immigrants.[109]

Irish women's predominance among San Francisco's female proprietors fits with larger trends. First, hawking and peddling wares in Ireland was the province of women in the late nineteenth and early twentieth centuries, so Irish immigrant women arrived with experience and/or a proclivity for small-business enterprise. Second, because Irish women eschewed work outside the home once married, proprietorship was an attractive option for them. Housing laborers, providing sewing and laundry services, or operating small retail stores—all of which could be done from the home and combined with unpaid family labor—was a means of income to which Irish women frequently turned.[110] Studies of Irish immigrant women around the country during the period confirm this trend and underscore that their predominance in San Francisco's world of female proprietorship should be no surprise, given the city's significant Irish population.[111]

Irish credit networks could also help explain the trend. Scholars have argued that the ability to draw "on family and kin networks as well as voluntary associations and mutual aid groups" has facilitated immigrant business ownership by reducing the need for capitalization.[112] Most point to well-documented cases of such lending and borrowing in the Jewish community as examples.[113] But the Irish community also had a history of microlending to draw on and may have employed such capitalization techniques in urban America as well, easing the entrance of Irish immigrant women into small-scale proprietorship.[114]

Of course Irish women's predominance in San Francisco's workforce also contributed to their tendency toward proprietorship.[115] Before marriage Irish women worked as teachers (comprising 30 percent of the city's total), laborers (40 percent of total), and servants (37 percent of total). After marriage they continued working in jobs compatible with their family responsibilities, dominating the population of laundresses (37 percent of total) and merchants (33 percent of total), among other proprietary occupations.[116] Their exclusion from expanding opportunities in the clerical sector, which was generally closed to foreign-born white women, was further reason for Irish women to hold on to their opportunities as female proprietors.[117]

To some degree, Irish women's persistence in the laundry industry was their own doing, a result of the privileged position they had carved for themselves in the marketplace as white women under attack by Chinese men. While appeals to consumers were not entirely successful, as the Chinese continued their stronghold on the industry, some must have been moved by the racially and sexually charged peril of white women losing jobs to Chinese male workers. The "degradation" of white women that consumers allegedly participated in by patronizing Chinese (and eventually Japanese) laundries certainly must have stirred some to boycott such businesses, just as organizations such as the Anti-Coolie Co-Operative Laundry Association had intended.[118] Thus while market forces such as price and convenience, both areas in which Chinese laundry providers triumphed, were pushing out Irish laundresses, racialized morality helped preserve a space for them.[119] In other words, the activities of anti-Chinese groups most likely helped keep Irish women in business.

Irish immigrant men did not enjoy the same dominance in small-business proprietorship that their female counterparts did. For among San Francisco's businessmen, Irish and German immigrants traded places, with Germans comprising 40 percent of all immigrant proprietors.[120] This predominance in male small-business ownership in the city is mirrored in and substantiated by the R. G. Dun & Company credit reports, in which Germans are the most common ethnic group captured.[121] These German men dominated the hospitality and retail industries.[122] Irish men's comparative rebuff of small-business ownership (they constituted only 15 percent of all foreign-born white proprietors) can be interpreted two ways. On the one hand, it reminds us that, historically, Irish immigrant men occupied the lowest rungs of the economic ladder in this country, higher only than nonwhite men. Their high rates of involvement in industrial accidents added to their economic dislocation and point to their concentration in the most dangerous and lowest-paid positions in the labor force.[123] On the other hand, the San Francisco Irish enjoyed a greater degree of success than their brethren elsewhere, finding opportunity in a variety of jobs. Irish settlement patterns in the city, for example, show a concentration of poor Irish residents clustered in the largely working-class Seventh Ward (south of Market Street) and wealthier descendants from Ireland spread throughout the city's other wards. One study found, in fact, that in the Second Ward, 23.2 percent of Irish men had white-collar occupations in 1880.[124] Such opportunities may have kept Irish men out of less predictable occupations as proprietors.

High numbers of Irish men in San Francisco's laundry industry (second only to "colored" men) could be interpreted as a reflection of economic achievement as well.[125] This census category mingled laborers and proprietors, so it is impossible to determine whether this is a reflection of business ownership or not. But even if the numbers simply capture a concentration of Irish male laborers, it occurred at precisely the moment when mechanization, standardization, and professionalization made the laundry industry a more-profitable and thus desirable field for men. Scholars of the industry tell us that white men dominated the managerial and high-skill roles in the newly mechanized power laundries by the end of the nineteenth century, leaving only the least skilled and lowest-paid jobs to women. Chinese men and, later, Japanese men certainly dominated the field, but they competed as owner-operators of low-tech businesses, able to offer competitive prices because of their reliance on large numbers of free or low-paid Asian immigrant workers.[126] Typically the predominance of nonwhite men and women in an industry depresses its appeal for white men. But in the case of laundry, the sweeping changes transforming the business of cleaning clothes and linens may have engendered a new niche, one that promised economic and social gains because it enabled Irish immigrant men to distinguish themselves from the industry's nonwhite and female employees. Thus, ironically, while Irish women fought to maintain a foothold in the laundry industry as independent proprietors, their brothers, fathers, and husbands found burgeoning opportunity there.

Since the foreign-born so dominated women's business ownership in San Francisco (57 percent), the remaining groups of women, of course, comprised significantly smaller proportions of the city's female proprietors. For example, the second-largest group of businesswomen, white women who were born in the United States but whose parents were immigrants (native white/foreign parentage), comprised 25 percent of all businesswomen in 1890. Women born in the United States whose parents were also native-born (native white/native parentage) were the third-largest group, comprising 16 percent of all female business owners. Combined these two groups of native-born, white San Franciscans comprised 41 percent of all female proprietors, a figure far lower than their overall proportion of gainfully occupied women in the city (56 percent).[127] Finally, African American, Chinese, Japanese, and "Indian" women, grouped together under the title "colored," comprised a tiny 2 percent of all San Francisco businesswomen. Since 9 percent of all non-white women who were gainfully occupied worked as businesswomen, however, they clearly turned to proprietorship at a significant rate.[128]

While the printed census figures discussed here provide a broad overview of the racial backgrounds of San Francisco's female proprietors, in fact, it is very difficult to talk about race in the story of San Francisco's late nineteenth- and early twentieth-century female small-business owners. Extant historical records either do not provide or do not readily yield enough information to be feasible for use in this study. Spanish surnames, for example, are scattered throughout extant records; but because of their disparate and infrequent appearances, women of Mexican or Latin American descent are difficult to examine in any systematic way. There are similar challenges when studying black and Asian women business owners. Black newspapers are not as reliable as one might think because non-African Americans advertised in them as well. Chinese newspapers are inaccessible to me because of language barriers. Not even the city directory can provide reliable data about the race of San Francisco's women business owners because, in addition to containing a spotty record of existing residential and commercial addresses, it also ceased noting the race of those listed in 1875. The sample of bankruptcy court records used for this study is silent on the matter of race, as are the R. G. Dun & Company credit reports, which occasionally identify a woman as Jewish, but never as black or Asian.[129] The manuscript census, of course, mentions race, but since its use was not feasible for this project, printed census records had to suffice.

Because San Francisco's populations of nonwhite women were particularly small, however, the shortcomings of the sources used for this project are not as detrimental as they might be. African Americans (male and female) never comprised more than 1 percent of the city's population before the 1940s. "Although the Chinese community was eight times larger than the black population in 1900," Chinese women were distinct minorities, too.[130] They "never exceed[ed] the 5,000 mark, or 7 percent of the total Chinese population . . . through the nineteenth century."[131] Though once large, the Californio population in the state was declining during this time due to the devastating Land Act of 1851; but these native sons and daughters of Mexican California had been rancheros and thus never concentrated in urban San Francisco.[132] Mexican immigrants, by contrast, did settle in San Francisco, but only in very small numbers.

Secondary scholarship on black women in San Francisco can alleviate the problem to a degree, and what it tells us is that they found the greatest opportunity in the accommodations industry.[133] For African American women, this was a long-standing and nationwide trend. Research on free black women in the antebellum South, for example, shows that the hotel and boarding-house business was "one of the most remunerative occupations," attracting 5 percent of all free black women in business.[134] Self-employment in the service sector, including the operation of boardinghouses, continued to attract a sizable proportion of African American women in 1910, when the census showed that black female entrepreneurs outstripped white female entrepreneurs throughout the nation.[135] Scholars studying black San Francisco have made similar determinations, commenting on the degree to which African American women made inroads as small business proprietors in the accommodations industry. One study, for example, found that by 1930, "28 percent of Afro-American San Franciscans had households with boarders."[136] Yet because of the small size of the city's black population, San Francisco could not support the kind of thriving black business community that large populations of African American consumers stimulated elsewhere.[137] Perhaps more then in other locales, therefore, black entrepreneurs were forced to rely on the business of nonblack city dwellers. There was considerable precedent for this, since antebellum free black women in the South had specifically catered to whites, including aristocratic white slaveowners accustomed to being waited on by black women.[138] African American women in San Francisco clearly carried on in the same tradition, as the history of Mary Ellen Pleasant indicates. Probably the city's leading boardinghouse keeper, Pleasant catered to powerful white men, leading figures in politics and finance. Taking a lesson from the Old South, her clientele fondly referred to her as "Mammy Pleasant." Yet Pleasant cleverly capitalized on both this servile title and the heightened accommodations market.[139] According to one contemporary, "she handled more money during pioneer days in California than any other colored person."[140] Evidence shows, however, that black women in the city capitalized on more-ordinary boarding arrangements as well. Diana Plumber is an example. A widowed, fifty-year-old black woman, she housed two white male boarders in addition to taking in washing.[141] Widows in particular conducted boarding businesses, one study has found, because they could often make more money that way than by engaging in wage labor.[142] This was probably especially true for black women, hindered in the job market by restricted choices and low wages.

It was this type of common boarding arrangement that most likely typified the boarding businesses operated by Chinese women as well. While less has been written about them, we know that Chinese women also took in boarders to supplement the earnings of their laboring husbands. It was in this way that Chinese women's income was most valued by their families. "A Chinese wife's earnings from sewing, washing, or taking in boarders could mean the difference between having pork or just bean paste with rice for dinner, or between life and death for starving relatives back in China." Thus, in addition to maintaining their households, Chinese wives "played an important role in the family economy."[143] Chinese and black women alike probably turned to the accommodations business because it was especially profitable in San Francisco and because it enabled them to combine their household responsibilities with income generation.

According to the printed census, however, nonwhite women in San Francisco were almost equally likely to operate enterprises in laundry, retail, or apparel as in accommodations.[144] While these figures may in fact obscure a concentration in the boarding business that the scholarly literature on African Americans suggests, they most likely also indicate that such women were even less "free" then white women to "choose" their occupation. Perhaps for nonwhite women, any opportunity to work as a business proprietor was a good one, especially given their paucity of job choices and the depressed wages of their husbands. What black and Chinese businesswomen's industry distribution illustrates, therefore, is not a democratic market, but one shackled by longstanding prejudices that confined and controlled the choices of nonwhite women.

By comparison, there were dramatic divergences in white women's industry preferences, indicating that cultural expectations, social status, and economic imperatives all played an important role in determining the type of business a woman operated. Foreign-born white women, for example, were almost equally likely to concentrate their businesses in the laundry (32 percent) and hospitality (38 percent) industries. Of all the choices, these two types of small-scale businesses were most easily conducted from home, suggesting that for immigrant women work outside the home was less tolerable culturally and that accommodating domestic responsibilities was of utmost importance.[145] The fact that 20 percent of the native-born daughters of immigrants also conducted laundry businesses underscores that such traditional expectations could even carry over to the next generation, upheld by conservative immigrant parents. Yet the clear majority of native-born white women proprietors with foreign-born parents (47 percent) entered the apparel trades, a business that more often than not took a woman outside the home. That preference was most likely influenced by the availability of apprenticeships in which talented young women might learn the craft of dressmaking or millinery before striking out on their own. In addition, a successful apparel proprietor dressed the part and often interacted intimately with the most sophisticated ladies in urban society. To the daughter of immigrants, these aspects of the business may have seemed like the trappings of success, a way to distinguish herself from her immigrant heritage and to establish herself as an American.[146] Native-born white women with native parents were also drawn into the apparel trades in significant numbers (27 percent), but they were most likely to operate accommodations businesses, which drew 48 percent of them. This preference may, as with foreign-born women, reflect a desire to contain paid labor to the home, where a woman might conduct a lucrative trade as a boardinghouse owner or hotelier. But since millinery and dressmaking was their second choice, this conclusion is not so clear as it is for foreign-born women. An alternative explanation is that since there was more opportunity in the accommodations industry than in any other in San Francisco, native-born white women with native parents simply went where there was the most commercial opportunity.[147]

Not surprisingly, in contrast to female proprietors, male proprietors in San Francisco showed a preference for traditional "male" businesses and generally eschewed those occupations seen as feminine. The notable exception was the hospitality industry, which was dominated by foreign-born white men who no doubt relied on the help of their wives, since 70 percent were married. Retail businesses were the most common pursuit among all male proprietors (59 percent), and men concentrated in the sale of "masculine" provisions such as meat, groceries (a traditionally male-dominated area in the late nineteenth and early twentieth centuries), drugs, and men's furnishings. A full 73 percent of native-born white male proprietors operated retail establishments, while 63 percent of foreign-born white men were retail store owners. A much smaller 41 percent of black, Chinese, and Japanese male proprietors were in retail, underscoring the perceived status (and thus racial exclusivity) of this type of business. Those nonwhites unable to enter the more-desirable types of business ownership found that the laundry industry, perceived as a female profession and thus rejected by most white men, offered them opportunity. Forty-nine percent of black, Chinese, and Japanese proprietors operated such businesses.[148] This phenomenon alone largely accounts for the much higher proportion of nonwhite men (in contrast to nonwhite women) in the business world. As with the women, foreign-born whites comprised the largest proportion of all male business owners, at 47 percent. But unlike businesswomen, "colored" proprietors were the second-largest group, comprising 29 percent of the city's business owners.[149] This difference, of course, also reflected the large population of nonwhite men in the city, especially Chinese immigrants, whose numbers were not matched by similar numbers of women. Thus, business proprietorship in San Francisco at the end of the nineteenth century was clearly gendered. Men and women both made decisions about what kinds of businesses to operate based on cultural, social, and economic needs, ever mindful of the "proper" role for men and women in American society, when they had a choice.

What the demographics of female proprietorship illustrate, therefore, is that businesswomen sought out ways to earn an income that could feasibly be combined with their responsibilities at home, they went where they found the best opportunities, and they were most likely to be immigrant women for whom business ownership was a familiar female recourse. Thus the women on whom San Franciscans had come to rely for the purchase of their meals, clothes, laundry services, haircuts, and groceries were likely to transact business with a foreign accent over a counter located but a few steps away from where they managed their own family affairs. At the height of female proprietorship, such businesswomen were a regular part of city life, widely patronized for the goods and services they made available throughout San Francisco.

By the 1920s, Ann Hudson and the other female business owners who had enjoyed the peak of proprietorship in the 1870s and 1880s, would have found San Francisco a foreign place. Accustomed to walking down Market Street and encountering fellow store owners, boardinghouse keepers, milliners, manicurists, and laundresses all eagerly competing for the dollar of pedestrians, they would not have recognized the commercial landscape before them. The diminished numbers of businesswomen had virtually disappeared into the hustle and bustle of the modern city. The sense of communion and economic significance they may have enjoyed as members of the city's much larger late nineteenth-century population of female proprietors would have vanished, replaced by a humbling sense that they were becoming extinct.

Yet while they enjoyed their heyday during the end of the 1800s, San Francisco female business owners such as Hudson displayed patterns that reveal the ways in which opportunity, culture, and economics shaped their proprietary ambitions. First and foremost, these proprietors followed opportunity, flooding into the unusually large and lucrative openings in the city's accommodations industry in especially large numbers to serve the uniquely male-dominated city population. In four additional industries—apparel, retail, beauty, and laundry—they also carved out niches for themselves where, like other small-scale businesswomen around the country, they competed for a share of public patronage, often amidst overwhelming competition from men. Second, proprietorship was pursued overwhelmingly and disproportionately not by native-born, white San Franciscans but by the foreign-born women of the city. Such immigrant women found that owning a small business could earn them a modest and respectable income in a marketplace that afforded them fewer choices than native-born white women. In addition, owning a business—especially in the accommodations and laundry industries—afforded these women the opportunity to combine household responsibilities with paid labor, a cultural value that seemed to influence both immigrant women and their native-born daughters.

These proprietary patterns were eclipsed in the twentieth century by the dramatic decline in the number of women who pursued independent enterprise. Economic change, specifically the decline in opportunities for business ownership and the development of new jobs in the clerical sector, caused San Francisco's female proprietors to reject business ownership in increasing numbers by the early twentieth century. Understanding this transformation of the marketplace more fully and how it changed why women started businesses is the subject we turn to in the next chapter.

CHAPTER 2

WHY SAN FRANCISCO WOMEN

STARTED BUSINESSES

The stereotypical entrepreneur was motivated by a desire for riches and independence. But for businesswomen in San Francisco between 1850 and 1920, such dreams provided only brief inducement. Gold, the dust that inspired a worldwide migration to northern California, pulled women into proprietorship during the first decade of statehood. Yet gold's lure was short-lived and, after 1860, women in search of a stable income sought it in more-predictable realms.

For those single women pursuing economic independence, proprietorship continued to be an attractive option, but one that required calculated risk and no promise of a steady income. Comparatively few single women were willing to take those odds, and they pursued proprietorship in only very small numbers relative to their presence in the paid labor force.

But married and formerly married (divorced and widowed) women accepted the risks of proprietorship because they had few other income opportunities. Economic and family circumstances restricted their employment options so severely that proprietorship was perhaps their only choice—an enterprise they could pursue while maintaining their responsibilities to home and family. At the same time, however, changes in small business ownership such as increased difficulty securing capital, competition from mass marketers and large-scale retailers, and the rationalization of the commercial marketplace made proprietorship a decreasingly attractive option. In short, turning to small business ownership was a decision made within increasingly restrictive parameters. Thus, once alternative employment options became available to women with families at the beginning of the twentieth century, they fled business ownership in large numbers. The utility of proprietorship, it seems, had expired.

Why San Francisco women started businesses, therefore, has much more to do with the factors pushing women into proprietorship than it does with the popularized, romantic pull of entrepreneurship. The city's business-women were problem solvers who turned to economic enterprise to support themselves and their families because it allowed them to combine their do-mestic responsibilities with economic opportunity. The lure of profits drew only the earliest adopters to gold rush California. Thereafter, proprietorship was less about wealth than about subsistence for most small-scale business-women.

AN "APRON FULL OF GOLD":

THE EARLY LURE OF PROPRIETORSHIP

As soon as the earliest reports of "Gold!" reached communities around the world in 1848, San Francisco quickly became a city populated by hoards of hungry and homeless men expecting to strike it rich. At first, men were forced to provide themselves and each other with "domestic" services such as cook-ing and laundering that women had always provided for their sons, husbands, brothers, and fathers. But as soon as married and single women arrived, many men were willing to pay them a high price for the same services, and women began to believe they too would "strike gold" in California.

It did not take much for women to turn a profit selling their skills as cooks, homemakers, and laundresses to this first wave of migrants. For miners who had been away from their families and on their own for months, even years, a woman's cooking was especially valuable. One female settler appears to have been turned into an entrepreneur on the spot by the appeals of a hun-gry miner: "Attracted by the unusual sight of a woman . . . a hungry miner . . . said to me 'I'll give you five dollars, ma'am, for them biscuit.' It sounded like a fortune to me, and I looked at him to see if he meant it. And as I hesi-tated as such . . . he repeated his offer to purchase, and said he would give me ten dollars for bread made by a woman . . . In my dreams that night I saw crowds of bearded miners striking gold from the earth with every blow of the pick, each one seeming to leave a share for me."[1] Luzena Stanley Wilson was not surprised that a miner wanted to buy her biscuit—such transactions were commonplace in cities throughout the United States where women sold boarding services to single male workers. What she had a hard time believing was that her cooking could be worth so much to anyone.

In letters home to family and friends, women commented on the unusually profitable enterprises they could conduct in the city during the early 1850s. One woman wrote to a friend in Boston that "[a] smart woman can do very well in this country. . . . If I was in Boston now and know what I now know of California I would come out here if I had to hire the money to bring me out. It is the only country that I ever was in where a woman rece[ive]d anything like a just compensation for work."[2] Mary Jane Megquier agreed to accompany her doctor husband from Maine to San Francisco for similar reasons, explaining to a friend, "as the ladies are very scarce I expect to make money in the way of odd jobs such as cooking and attending the sick."[3] After several months she reported that by operating a medical practice, drug store, and boardinghouse she and her husband had struck gold; she wrote: "We have made more money since we have been here than we should make in Winthrop in twenty years."[4] In subsequent letters home, Megquier bragged that she intended to stay and work in San Francisco until she could "get [her] pile" and return home with an "apron full [of gold]."[5]

The remarkable profits that women generated providing domestic services in early California were due primarily to what Megquier called the "scarcity" of women. Late nineteenth-century American men were accustomed to living in a world where women took care of their domestic needs. Mothers, daughters, and wives prepared food, maintained clean and tidy homes, and laundered clothes for male family members as a matter of course. Such work was gendered female—thought of as within women's "sphere" of labor—and men generally performed it only when they had no choice. Whenever possible men preferred to secure the services of a woman, whether in the form of a wife or a boardinghouse keeper, to perform such labor.

Thus the significant population of "unattached" men in gold rush California, either single men or married men who traveled to the state without their families, constituted an important customer base for cooking, laundering, and boarding. The 5 percent of "forty-niners"[6] who were female were rewarded highly for such services because most men believed them to be "women's work," thought women to be superior homemakers, and coveted the company of a woman—even one standing behind a counter. The gender imbalance that fueled this service economy was more balanced in the city of San Francisco, where the lure of jobs (including prostitution) attracted a higher proportion of women than in the mining towns—but only slightly. By 1853, 16 percent of the city's 50,000 residents were women—three times the proportion statewide yet small enough that women such as Luzena Stanley Wilson could name their price when selling domestic services to men.[7]

Even for some African American women, historically confined to the lowliest of jobs, this translated into extraordinary opportunity. The success of Mary Ellen Pleasant attests to this. Beginning in 1858, Pleasant engaged in everything from real estate investment to accounting, from operating a laundry chain to running a boardinghouse. Eventually she amassed $30,000 worth of property, "the equivalent of at least a million dollars today," making her the second-richest black resident in the city and an influential woman among even the wealthiest San Franciscans.[8]

Her nickname, "Mammy Pleasant," reveals that a woman made rich selling domestic services was problematic in the minds of many San Franciscans, however, especially if the woman was black. That the domestic services of any woman had a market value inherently challenged the original legal and cultural framework from which the definition of "women's work" had emerged. The coverture laws that had originally helped Americans to articulate the status of women in marriage and the expectation that they minister to the domestic (and sexual) needs of their husbands, for example, were intended to inscribe economic dependency—and certainly not opportunity—for women in American society.[9] So the fact that any woman would become wealthy by capitalizing on men's domestic dependence inverted the intended social and economic roles for men and women. But San Franciscans seemed to chafe particularly at the thought of a black woman gaining such elevated status in the second half of the nineteenth century. White city residents tried to recast Mary Ellen Pleasant in a subservient role in which, like the mammies of the slaveholding Old South, her job was to attend to the needs of whites. Yet according to her most recent biographer, "the ways in which Pleasant exploited gendered and racialized codes of behavior constituted one of her most profitable strategies"; she herself used the term "mammy" to insinuate herself into economic, legal, and social positions in which she might not otherwise have appeared.[10] Thus, under the guise of a servant, Pleasant worked her way into a fortune. She was not the only woman to exhibit cunning in her marketplace maneuvers in mid-nineteenth-century San Francisco.

Female economic activity in gold rush California often reflected calculation and ingenuity. Profit-oriented women developed a multitude of ways to make money. A Mrs. Smith, for instance, traveling by ship around Cape Horn in 1850, heard of the California vegetable shortage and determined to capitalize on it during a stop on a Pacific island. When her husband would give her no money for speculation, she sold her jewelry for $20 and invested the money in onions, which she reportedly sold in California shortly thereafter for $1,800.[11] Another woman turned a half-barrel of salted pickles into a money-making venture by soaking them and selling them in fourteen quart bottles, each priced at six dollars more than the original price of the whole lot.[12] And legend had it that Mrs. Peter Wimmer, wife of a Sutter employee at Coloma and the owner of a few pear trees, "sold her pears when they were still blossoms, tagging each flower with the name of the purchaser."[13] These unusual commercial schemes underscore how clever women could be as gold rush enterprisers and how eager they were to capitalize on the opportunities of the market. For them, as for most mid-nineteenth-century northern Californians, profitability was the motivator, and it encouraged innovation.

Thus women did not simply extend the domestic activities they performed for family members to the large number of "unattached" men in the region because it was expected of them, nor did they provide such services to their new communities because of their social value. Instead, they "read" the economic signs around them and seized the most promising business ideas. In short, gold rush women exhibited capital intentions: they started commercial ventures because they saw opportunity in them.

The abundance of such economic opportunities made the decision to start a business both simple and popular in 1850s San Francisco. Women wanted to "make their pile," and proprietorship seemed to provide a golden opportunity to do so. Female San Franciscans responded to this chance, streaming into business ownership in remarkably high numbers. Of the 47 women listed in the 1850 city directory, for example, 85 percent can be identified as businesswomen.[14] By 1860, women appeared in a much larger variety of occupations ranging from doctress to domestic servant, and 40 percent were listed with no occupation at all. But still 406, or 40 percent, of the women in the directory (and 66 percent of all those listed with an occupation) can be identified as proprietors. In comparison, an 1876 directory for Boston—a city four times the size of San Francisco in 1860—listed 650 female proprietors.[15]

The profit potential that drew gold rush women into proprietorship was equally seductive to men. Indeed, California boasted more merchants per capita in the 1850s than any other state in the country save Louisiana. Most were concentrated in San Francisco, the state's commercial center, since it was the distribution depot for the mining hinterlands. So extensive was San Francisco's maritime trade, in fact, that by 1852 only New York exceeded the total tonnage entering the city's port. Those who oversaw the disbursement of trade goods, whether at the wharves and warehouses or retail counters and concession stands, reaped the benefits. For as trade fueled the growth of San Francisco, it also enriched the fortunes of its merchants. Most of those who made considerable amounts of money in trade during the gold rush were commission merchants that bought and sold goods for large wholesale houses. But the largest number of merchants in the city were petty proprietors who provided miners and other city residents with everything from beans, picks, and housing to oysters, champagne, and gambling. Their upward mobility—over one-half were upwardly mobile during the span of their careers in San Francisco—set them apart from retailers in other cities (only one-quarter were upwardly mobile in Boston and Poughkeepsie, New York). This fact underscored that capitalizing on the needs of gold rush San Franciscans was not gender-specific: men and women seized the opportunity.[16]

One commercial possibility was unique to women in gold rush San Francisco, however, and that was prostitution.[17] Not all San Francisco prostitutes became wealthy. Indeed the majority of them were Chinese women who lived a life of both sexual slavery and abject poverty, forced to turn their profits over to their masters.[18] But some women, especially those "madams" who operated their own brothels, did report considerable earnings. One estimate based on the 1860 census found that over 1,000 reported financial assets totaling $3,000.[19] In a city dominated by men throughout the second half of the nineteenth century, prostitutes were numerous and often powerful. According to one study, the most successful ran "large-scale and widely ramified" enterprises which helped keep the city's police, politicians, doctors, liquor salesmen, and theater managers in business. Until the 1870s when they were segregated within the notorious Barbary Coast region of the city, the madams who operated the city's most successful establishments could be seen in any of the city's leading public venues, "parading their finery on the most popular avenues."[20]

Often this wealth poured into the coffers of one of San Francisco's many dressmakers or milliners, for many of the most successful prostitutes kept open accounts with city apparel shops to stay abreast of the latest fashions. So distinguished looking were such women that one contemporary observed that while "in Eastern cities the prostitutes tried to imitate in manner and dress the fashionable respectable ladies . . . in San Francisco the rule was reversed—the latter copying after the former."[21] Thus prostitution, a largely female business opportunity, fueled yet another economic sphere that was also dominated by women—the apparel industry.[22]

Word of San Francisco's unique economic opportunities in the 1850s drew women from around the globe. Whether prostitutes, milliners, restaurateurs, or hotelkeepers, all hoped to find their fortune in what they believed to be the deep pockets of the city's residents. More than one left her hometown with an earnest belief in the promise of the gold rush and the "expectation that," in San Francisco, "one's destiny could be transformed by one's energy."[23] When Jane Hale closed up her fancy goods store in Princeton, Illinois, in January 1861, for example, she did not simply warn her customers that they must settle outstanding bills with her before she left, she advertised that she was "leav[ing] th[e] county for California the first day of January next," proudly brandishing her destination a full year in advance as though it were a ticket to the promised land.[24] Like so many other women who had traveled to California in the first few years after the gold rush, Hale expected the move to change her economic fortunes.

Jane Hale was most likely disappointed, however. For with a handful of exceptions such as Mary Ellen Pleasant, after the early years of the gold rush came to an end neither cooking biscuit, keeping boarders, nor selling fancy goods made even the most enterprising and hard-working woman wealthy. When the flush days of the early 1850s came to an end, business proprietorship rarely yielded the kinds of returns that gold rush entrepreneurs such as Luzena Stanley Wilson and Mary Jane Megquier had earned. Gold production peaked early (1852) and died hard, sending both income and expectations spiraling downward.[25] Trade goods flooded the market, sending prices tumbling. Activity in the once-bustling port came to a halt. Between 1854 and 1858, business failures doubled, led by the folding of the city's biggest and most important bank, Page, Bacon, & Co. "Fortunes made in good times were destroyed as quickly as they had been accumulated. The early optimism of 1849 gave way by 1860 to caution, and in many cases, despair." For some the answer was flight—almost one-half of the first generation of merchants had departed by the end of the 1850s.[26] Those men and women who stayed were forced to rely on more-conventional and less-profitable means of support. San Franciscans pursued the same kinds of jobs that employed men and women in other cities around the country and set their sights on earning a subsistence rather than a fortune.[27] By 1860, for example, 15 percent of all female residents were employed in teaching, nursing, or domestic service, whereas no women had been listed with such common occupations ten years earlier.[28] Those women who remained in business had to adjust their goals. The arrival of economic normalcy meant that female proprietors could rarely get rich and sometimes could barely make a profit operating a business establishment in San Francisco. Women who started businesses after 1860, therefore, entered the world of commerce for reasons other than the pursuit of wealth.

Some women continued to be pulled into small-business ownership by the emotional rewards it promised. Independence, the chance to express creativity, and the opportunity to do what one loved and did well on a daily basis could set proprietorship apart from more-mundane wage work. In such instances, the personal profits to be reaped transcended the financial uncertainty that had come to characterize business ownership. This was true generally for small businessmen for whom, one historian argues, "a desire for freedom more than a quest for large profits provided their motivation."[29] But for female business owners, the intangible rewards of small-business proprietorship drew only certain kinds of women—those never-married women not legally bound to the care of home, husband, or children. Thus marital status was a significant factor in why women started businesses in post–gold rush San Francisco.[30]

Single (Never-Married) Women

The story of Miss Eliza McGearny, a young single woman, illustrates the degree to which a yearning for independence and personal fulfillment, or "nonpecuniary" and "psychic" rewards as one scholar calls them, might motivate a woman to pursue proprietorship.[31] At the age of twenty-seven McGearny commenced a millinery business of her own. Over the course of several years in the 1870s, she had mastered the craft of women's hat construction while employed in another proprietor's shop. If she was good, she may have built a loyal customer base willing to follow her to her own millinery parlor.[32] She may also have saved up her earnings, for she had enough money to pay cash for her first batch of stock.[33] But even if she was lucky enough to have entered the ranks of proprietor with cash and customers, McGearny was gambling a lot by betting on her own ability to succeed as a milliner. By leaving behind her job as a millinery worker she gave up the certainty of a wage, one that was—in contrast to the money women earned in other jobs—especially good.[34] Doing so took courage, confidence, and the willingness to take a risk.

The motivation driving single women such as McGearny in the face of such vulnerability was independence. For "proprietorship had the *potential* (albeit one that was not always realized) to free women from economic dependence on men."[35] Those who succeeded as business owners had the opportunity to direct their own destinies in a way that was foreign to most nineteenth-century women. No financial, domestic, sexual, or personal concessions would have to be made for marriage if a woman could succeed as a proprietor of her own enterprise. At the same time, a woman like McGearny gained independence from her former employer through proprietorship as well. No more would her boss control her earnings, oversee her work, or manage her performance. She would be putting her skills in the service of her own success rather than the success of her employer. Though independence was a more culturally appropriate goal for American men, women who pursued small-business ownership were likely as enthralled by the promise it held to transform their lives as those male entrepreneurs who had been dreaming of "control[ling] an independent business of their own . . . [since] their childhood."[36]

But the seduction of independence, while powerful, was not enough for most women; the uncertainty of business success drove the vast majority of single women in San Francisco into another line of work altogether during the second half of the nineteenth century. In fact, only 6 percent of all single women in the city's labor force in 1890 were listed as business proprietors in the census.[37] Since nearly three-quarters of all gainfully employed women in 1890 were single, this figure is remarkably low. It underscores that while never-married women were the largest individual group of San Francisco's female proprietors that year (42 percent), they were grossly underrepresented in the field given their dominance of the female paid labor force. Over the course of the next forty years, single women represented a smaller and smaller proportion of all female proprietors. By 1930, only 20 percent of all businesswomen were single. These female business owners constituted a tiny 2 percent of all unmarried women in the paid labor force.[38]

Unmarried women such as McGearny chose proprietorship in such small numbers after 1860 because they had other more-reliable and often more-lucrative ways to earn money. For those willing to forgo the independence and personal fulfillment that might come with proprietorship, domestic service, teaching, and clerical work were all promising employment options. Though categorized as "women's work" generally, these jobs were in actuality open to single (never-married) women almost exclusively. And in contrast to business ownership, they afforded a comforting degree of predictability and provided a level of income that far surpassed what the lowliest proprietors made.

Domestic service was particularly lucrative in San Francisco because the city's marked gender imbalance resulted in a "shortage" of female servants. Between 1849 and 1853, city residents unwilling to hire a Chinese man-servant[39] competed for female servants by offering $50 to $70 per month, more than ten times the amount earned by servants in New York.[40] While such inflated wages did not persist through the nineteenth century, working as a servant remained a dependable option to which many women continued to turn. In 1870, for example, 42 percent of San Francisco women employed in all occupations worked as domestic servants.[41] And among the Irish, whose female population dominated the job up to the turn of the century, 71.3 percent worked as domestic servants.[42] Because servants were usually required to "live-in" with their employers, such jobs were generally filled by unmarried and childless women and attracted only the most economically disenfranchised married women and mothers. In San Francisco, that group was comprised of African American women and, later, Japanese immigrant women; both groups found that labor discrimination and economic vulnerability combined often made domestic service the only work available to them, whether they were married or single.[43]

Teaching was another financially rewarding occupation "reserved" for unmarried women. As a teacher, a young, single woman could often earn a higher income than that enjoyed by female proprietors. Clara Rix, for example, earned $100 per month teaching at the San Francisco Mission in 1854, while her sister Tina earned only $30 a month taking in boarders, sewing, and laundry.[44] Unlike in domestic service, however, the dearth of married women in the teaching profession was not a matter of preference but was formally imposed. School boards throughout the country barred married women from employment as teachers, effectively keeping them out of the profession for decades in the name of upholding the sanctity of marriage and women's unpaid work in the home. According to one study, such practices began in the late 1800s and increased after the turn of the century. In fact, "[e]xtensive surveys of local school districts beginning with 1928 indicate that 61 percent of all school systems would not hire a married woman teacher and 52 percent would not retain any who married while on contract."[45] These policies helped create another profitable employment niche for single women. For even though female teachers were segregated into the lowest-paid primary school positions in San Francisco, their income was markedly higher and more consistent than that earned by women selling goods and services in the marketplace.[46]

While domestic service began to wane after 1870 and teaching opportunities in the city failed to grow, by the last quarter of the nineteenth century single women had abundant new employment options in the exploding clerical sector.[47] Nonwhite women were typically excluded from these new jobs, as were foreign-born whites, but the native-born daughters of those immigrants for whom domestic service had been a primary option could find well-paid and respectable positions as stenographers, typists, clerks, and bookkeepers.[48]

The expansion of office jobs for women was a national trend that re-flected important changes in the organization of the economy. "As large busi-ness organizations of the late nineteenth century stitched regional networks together to create a national market," correspondence and record keeping became essential tools for effective management.[49] Face-to-face business transactions could not be conducted with distant customers, clients, and creditors, and so with the increase in the "amount and geographic range of a firm's activities," clerks, bookkeepers, accountants, typists, and stenogra-phers played crucial roles in the day-to-day operations of American compa-nies.[50]

While men initially performed clerical work, office jobs increasingly were reserved for young, educated white women. One important reason for this change was the ready supply of female job candidates. By the end of the nine-teenth century, there were more and more women graduating from American high schools and colleges. Since education was a prerequisite for clerical posi-tions, there were thousands of female candidates for such jobs in any given year.[51] A second reason for the feminization of clerical work, however, had to do with the changing nature of the job. As business processes came under the purview of scientific management and were organized into discrete, rational units of work, the work became more tedious and repetitive and less chal-lenging. The result was that clerical workers were seen as support staff and the work they did as "women's work." This combined with the ready supply of trained office workers pushed wages down and drove away any new male employees who would otherwise have pursued such jobs. Those men who had an education as well as previous clerical experience were happy to leave the lowly clerical work to women because they found increased opportunities in management.[52]

For women, for whom there were few if any employment opportunities in management or other professions, office positions were the best jobs avail-able. They paid relatively well. And they promised a respectable, even genteel job environment, something attractive both to middle-class women hop-ing to maintain their status when they entered the paid labor force and to working-class women in pursuit of upward mobility.[53] Finally, it was easy to gain the training necessary for office work. Classes in typing, dictation, and bookkeeping that qualified women for clerical positions might be taken at night, making it affordable for women who could not forgo wage work en-tirely to prepare for a new job.[54]

The growth in office jobs for women had a dramatic impact in San Fran-cisco. After 1870, clerical workers comprised an increasingly important sec-tor of the city's female labor force. Heald's Business College, established in the 1870s, made acquiring the necessary technical skills easy. The demand for such training was so great that in 1876, the college "enlarged to double its former size," opening at a new location on Post Street.[55] Fifteen years later, Pacific Business College also began advertising in city newspapers.[56] By 1890 clerical workers grew to 5 percent of all gainfully occupied women in the city, up from less than one-half of 1 percent in 1870. By 1910, that figure had grown to a remarkable 19 percent.[57] With the stimulus of World War I, the demand for female office workers grew exponentially, and between 1910 and 1920 the total number of women working as office clerks in the city rose 277 percent; the number of female stenographers, typists, bookkeepers, accountants, and cashiers rose an average of 87 percent.[58]

Evidence of this new army of female laborers turning the wheels of industry was not always readily available to contemporary San Franciscans. Most office workers spent their days stashed behind tall building walls methodically executing their new jobs. But some San Francisco women trained in the clerical sciences advertised their services as independent contractors. By 1920 passersby might catch a glimpse of a sign, posted in a second-story window, announcing stenography services available to the public.[59] Such notices were a visual reminder that economic opportunity in the city had shifted away from the volatile, independent enterprise characteristic of gold rush days and toward the staid, bureaucratic administration of a mature city at the beginning of the twentieth century. And single women were following the change, abandoning proprietorship almost entirely.

The increasing costs and complications of conducting small business certainly pushed unmarried women out of proprietorship as well. While this topic will receive more in-depth treatment in later chapters, especially Chapter 4, it should be noted here that small-scale economic enterprise changed in substantial ways over the course of the late nineteenth and early twentieth centuries. "From the 1880s onward," one scholar writes, "big businesses arose in America . . . and small businesses, although continuing to increase in absolute numbers, declined in their relative importance to the American economy."[60] Even in the retail sector, where small city and country stores dominated, mass marketing of brand-name goods and the rise of chain and department stores altered the commercial landscape. Proprietors responded to these changes by adopting new sales and marketing strategies, embracing technological innovations, and engaging in new financial management techniques. Even niche production, a widespread strategy adopted by small businesses faced with competition from big business, could not permanently ward off the successful incursion of national, brand-name products and mass retailers into local markets. All this made persistence as a small business owner significantly more challenging and more costly. National figures for small-business ownership tell the story: in both 1900 and 1910, almost as many small firms discontinued operation as started.[61] So why would women presented with alternative and remunerative employment options have taken the risk of proprietorship if it was becoming so difficult? The answer, of course, is that most did not.

Married and Formerly Married (Widowed or Divorced) Women
If alternative opportunities explain why never-married (single) women shunned proprietorship after 1860, then they also provide the key to explaining why married and formerly married (widowed or divorced) women did not. For while single women could secure more-reliable jobs in domestic service, teaching, and office work, women with families typically did not have such options. The small numbers of married and widowed/divorced women in these professions illustrates the point. In 1890, for example, only 14 percent of domestic servants and 8 percent of teachers were married or formerly married women. The figures were equally dramatic for women office workers. Only 10 percent of clerks and copyists and 8 percent of stenographers and typists in San Francisco were married or formerly married women. Overall, of the new occupations available to women at the end of the 1800s — saleswoman, clerk, stenographer, typist, and telephone/telegraph operator — 89 percent were filled by single, never-married women.[62]

The very jobs that single women found more profitable and reliable than business ownership were largely off limits to married women in the late nineteenth and early twentieth centuries. Clerical work provides a striking example. A comprehensive survey of 178 companies conducted by the Women's Bureau in 1931 uncovered the prevalence of discretionary rules and company policies that kept married women out of office work. In studying these surveys, one economist found that "more than 50 percent of all firms in the sample would not hire married women as a condition of policy and discretion." In addition, "about 35 percent of all female [clerical] employees were working in firms that would not retain them if they married."[63] As discussed earlier in the chapter, such exclusionary policies were typical of school districts as well as office environments through the beginning of the twentieth century and were designed primarily to uphold the expectation that married women devote their labor to their homes rather than paid employment.

Such employment restrictions effectively *pushed* married and formerly married women into proprietorship in significantly larger numbers than single women because their job choices were so much more limited between 1860 and 1920. Statistics reflect this dynamic. One-fifth of married and divorced women and one-fourth of widowed women gainfully employed in San Francisco in 1890 operated their own businesses. These female proprietors were overrepresented in the field of business given their low rates of participation in the female labor force overall. For example, married women represented only 11 percent of all gainfully occupied women and yet comprised 20 percent of all businesswomen. Similarly, widows constituted only 14 percent of all women in gainful occupations but accounted for 26 percent of all businesswomen in 1890.[64] For these married, widowed, and divorced women proprietorship was not one in many employment options, as it was for single women, but one of the *only* options.

Even when companies did not specifically prohibit their employment, women with families were excluded from clerical jobs by the time commitment such positions demanded. This was as true for widows with dependent children—53 percent in one study—as it was for married women.[65] The care of children, then, was a primary motivator for those women drawn into proprietorship. For before the 1930s, the work week for wage laborers exceeded fifty hours and generally included five and a half to six days. Part-time work was, for the most part, unheard of until the 1950s.[66] Few if any women with children could manage a full-time schedule, therefore, given late nineteenth- and early twentieth-century expectations of women's family and household responsibilities.

Herein lay the pull of proprietorship for married and formerly married women after 1860. Business ownership could potentially provide a woman with an income while allowing her to continue to care for her children, her home, and, if she was married, her husband. A hotel, boardinghouse, restaurant, saloon, grocery, or store might be run in a woman's own home or in an adjacent commercial space and could be operated according to her own schedule, making it easier to juggle paid and unpaid labor. For the gendered division of labor gave women exclusive responsibility for child care and domestic work regardless of their additional pursuits. Underscoring this point are the findings of one regional study that 50 percent of all female proprietors in 1880 had school-age children, and 20 percent had children under the age of five.[67] Thus businesswomen with families had the dual responsibilities of managing their own households at the same time they managed their businesses.

For widowed and divorced women domestic responsibilities persisted in spite of their legal status as "feme soles," or unmarried women. The legal and economic independence that this status afforded widows and divorcées—the right to own property, make wills and contracts, and retain their earnings— was circumscribed by the ongoing responsibilities of children and household. In fact, most formerly married women who exercised these rights upon separation from their husbands did so out of a desperate need to provide for the children dependent on them. In the words of one historian, "divorced women, like widows and women whose husbands merely deserted them, struggled to make a living." Similar to "unskilled, undereducated, or racially marginalized women," such women found that the only income opportunities open to them traditionally were working as boardinghouse keepers, laundresses, and hawkers of prepared food. Historically, such women had "few other options."[68] Thus, starting a business selling traditional domestic services was often the first and last strategy for providing physically and economically for their families.

Julia Lyons, for example, raised her children in the boardinghouse she operated after her separation from her husband. In 1861 her husband James informed her that she was no longer his wife and that "he would contribute nothing further toward her support" but that she was "at liberty to take her children, then minors, and make her own living in whatever way she could." This forced Julia to find some way to support herself and her family. Starting a business was a reasonable solution provided her husband would not interfere in its operation, since they were not legally divorced yet. Once she received his assurance "that he would never interfere with her in her business; that he would never claim any interest in her business, or any portion of her earnings or accumulations, or those of her children," Julia pressed forward with the plan. Soon after she opened a large boardinghouse "in her own name" and "called herself a widow" in her business transactions with diverse tradesmen and creditors. The upstairs portion of 17 Fourth Street at the corner of Market, which Julia rented for use as a lodging house, was her children's home for seven years between 1865 and 1872. In that time she managed to turn a $125 per month flat into a successful business worth $1,500. By the time her landlord filed a bankruptcy petition against her for $1,100 in back rent, Julia had sold her business, "turned all the balance of her property and effects into cash," and "abandoned said premises and business," disappearing with some unknown but significant amount of gold coin.[69] For her, the boarding business had been a means to an end—an avenue that led, albeit surreptitiously and illegally, to a financial independence that few divorced women with dependent children obtained. But more importantly, the business had sustained her and her family during financial hard times.

Like Julia Lyons, most divorced women were usually left entirely to their own devices when their marriages ended. California instituted alimony laws as early as the 1870s, but payments could be suspended when the wife had separate property. Even absent such additional assets, alimony payments were not always forthcoming, as the lawsuits filed by unpaid spouses attest.[70] A divorced woman, therefore, could expect to shoulder responsibility for the care of her children and herself for the rest of her life, or until she remarried. In cases where women contemplated filing for divorce themselves, more than half of all cases in the state, they had to figure out how to provide a new home and a new vocation for themselves before making any moves toward separation.[71] Operating a business was one solution to this predicament—an especially good one for women with children.

For widows, unlike divorced women, business ownership often grew naturally from enterprises left behind by their husbands. According to one scholar, in fact, "widowhood, inheritance, and the need to support families" remained the key reasons why women engaged in business.[72] For many widows who had been active in their husbands' businesses, the move into proprietorship was seamless. Some women, such as Mrs. Alvin Finke, who succeeded her husband at the helm of their retail champagne business when he died in San Francisco during the 1870s, were determined by credit reporters to be the "real manager[s] of the bus[iness]" long before they acceded to the title.[73] Female involvement in family-run businesses was common, in fact, as were widowed business owners. Indeed widows had been inheriting the management of their husbands' businesses for decades by the end of the nineteenth century. One historian of colonial America found that 9.5 percent of the merchants who advertised in the *Boston Evening Post* during the first half of 1773 were women.[74] For women in colonial America, their tenure as proprietors was generally temporary, a short-term solution to a family's predicament until a grown son could take over management of the business. During the late nineteenth and early twentieth centuries, this was most likely to be true when a widow was pressed into business in a sector of the economy usually "reserved" for men, as in the case of Mrs. Rosanna Short, who took over her husband's Japanning (shellacking) business temporarily in 1876.[75] Women who inherited businesses from their husbands were among the more fortunate; widows swelled the ranks of charity cases, often forced to rely on odd jobs in nursing, sewing, and domestic service provided by benevolent societies.[76] But occasionally business ownership was itself a burden to widowed women. When Michael C. Murphy died in 1870, for example, he left his wife a small store that one and a half years later was still mortgaged for all of its worth. His widow kept a small stock of liquors for sale but evidently could not get ahead. The business became a liability rather than an asset. Unable to find a tenant to rent the store and take the responsibilities of operating a business out of her hands, Mrs. Murphy was forced to consider alternatives. At the time that R. G. Dun & Company credit reporters evaluated her, she was planning to open either a bakery or a small grocery in the hapless space. For Murphy, business proprietorship was an unhappy consequence of widowhood and did not provide a reliable means of support for herself and her family. Difficult circumstances such as Murphy's caused one historian to conclude that "perhaps more than any other group, widowed proprietors resembled the stereotypical victims of Victorian melodramas."[77]

For women thrown on their own resources by the death of husbands who left nothing behind, commencing a business enterprise may have seemed like the least disruptive option. The right arrangement could allow them to keep on living the way they had always lived by simply taking on customers who would pay them for the skills they utilized in their homes every day. The following advertisement captures just such a scenario: "A LADY, WHO HAS HERETOFORE occupied a social position and been suddenly thrown upon her own resources, is desirous of meeting with a few families, or gentlemen, who will be responsible for the rent of a first-class furnished house, as an equivalent for the best of board and a refined and agreeable home."[78] This woman, who had previously been able to avoid work altogether, had suddenly lost her "social position," most likely because she had been widowed and was forced to think up her own money-making plan. Since she already occupied a "first-class furnished house," taking in boarders who would pay for her rent must have been an obvious choice. Counting on her skills and experience as the keeper of a "refined and agreeable home," this resourceful woman sought to turn her domestic space into a commercial one. Relying on the only assets she had, her property and her domestic skills, she transformed herself from "lady" to ladylike, from socialite to superintendent.

The advertiser's case was common enough to be imagined and immortalized in one California writer's story. In Frances Fuller Victor's 1877 novella, *The New Penelope*, a recently widowed young mother, Mrs. Anna Greyfield, agrees to use her housekeeping talents to earn money taking in boarders. "Though I was wholly inexperienced in any business," she says, "I thought it better to venture the experiment than to keep on as I was doing."[79] Having lost her husband on the overland journey to Oregon, Greyfield arrives in Portland nearly penniless and with a young son to support. She is desperate for a way to earn more than the paltry sum she makes taking in sewing but unable to work for wages outside the home because she has no one to care for her infant son. Household management, it seems, is the one asset she can cash in on.

In creating the fictional Anna Greyfield, Victor struck at the heart of why widows started businesses after 1860. Not all were as inexperienced in business as Greyfield, nor did they all rely on homemaking skills to operate businesses. Mrs. L. H. Lichtenstein, for example, used the money left to her by her husband to open a small brokerage shop—an enterprise that required business proficiency rather than domestic knowledge.[80] But Greyfield's determined and desperate search for a source of income to support herself and her son typified the inspiration behind San Francisco widows' decisions to start their own businesses. Suddenly responsible for providing for the economic well-being of themselves and their families, widows found themselves boxed in by the demands of their domestic responsibilities and the paucity of job opportunities that would accommodate those demands.

These circumstances, combined with the fact that many widows inherited their husbands' enterprises, explain why proprietorship remained such an attractive option to San Francisco's widowed women into the twentieth century. Compared to single and married women, in fact, widows constituted the largest proportion of gainfully occupied women employed in proprietorship between 1890 and 1930.[81] These figures conform to the findings of other scholars that widows throughout the country were among those women most inclined toward proprietorship.[82]

When one considers that the increasing complications and costs of small business ownership, which likely pushed single (never-married) women out of proprietorship, made it a riskier and riskier income option, the true desperation of such women is revealed. Married, divorced, and widowed women, in other words, continued to pursue proprietorship in spite of its increasing challenges. Sometimes they did so because the opportunity presented itself, as in the case of widows who inherited businesses from their husbands. But as the data indicate, women also entered business because the market afforded them few other job opportunities, especially in the case of women who retained responsibility for the care of husbands and/or children.

THE TRICKY ISSUE OF ECONOMIC CHOICE: WOMEN AND PROPRIETORSHIP AFTER 1920

For those who "chose" proprietorship, particularly married and formerly married women with few other possibilities, operating a business was a conscious choice not to capitulate to the limitations of the labor force, their responsibilities at home, or, in some cases, their financial troubles. That is, proprietorship was a solution to a problem. But economic choice was a tricky issue for late nineteenth- and early twentieth-century women. For even if "abstract market goals indicate that people *choose* jobs," women made such choices within a complex system of social, legal, and familial expectations.[83] Women were bound by the "family claim," which "defined women primarily as family members." As encoded in the law and customs of the country, this status determined that women would have only limited access to economic opportunity.[84] These economic, social, and legal restrictions severely restricted women's array of income options during the nineteenth and early twentieth centuries, particularly for married and formerly married women, effectively driving them into proprietorship.

But after the 1920s, when job opportunities expanded dramatically for women, especially in desirable fields such as clerical work, fewer and fewer women turned to business ownership as a source of income. Single women had, of course, been flocking to these jobs for several decades. But after the World War I boom in white-collar jobs, demand for office workers outstripped the populations of workers that had typically filled such positions. Businesses previously committed to barring married women and women with children from their office spaces, therefore, for the first time invited these women to enjoy the spoils of what one historian has aptly called the "incorporation of America."[85] Married and formerly married women wasted no time taking advantage of these newfound employment options. By 1930, for example, married women comprised 22 percent of all clerks, stenographers, typists, and telephone/telegraph operators, and widowed and divorced women comprised 15 percent of this total. Just forty years earlier, in 1890, these two groups of women comprised just 5 percent and 4 percent, respectively, of the same categories of workers. San Francisco schools also opened their doors to married, widowed, and divorced women, who together comprised 25 percent of all teachers by 1930, up from just 12 percent in 1890.[86]

The dramatic increase in the numbers of married and formerly married women entering nonbusiness occupations after 1920 suggests that when alternative employment opportunities existed, women with families seized them, shunning business proprietorship. Census data recording the portion of gainfully occupied women who chose proprietorship in 1930 substantiates a mass exodus of women from business ownership. This was true for all women. Between 1890 and 1930, the portion of married female proprietors dropped from 20 percent of those gainfully employed to 7 percent, and widowed and divorced businesswomen dropped from 26 percent to 8 percent of all such women in the labor force. Similarly, the portion of single women in the labor force who chose proprietorship dropped from an already low 6 percent to just 2 percent.[87] In each case, the percentage of gainfully employed women who took up business ownership dropped by two-thirds. The point that these figures drive home is that, regardless of marital status, class, or race, all women who entered the job market after 1890 chose business proprietorship at a lower rate and flocked into new job opportunities as soon as they became available.

The women who left proprietorship may not have done so entirely by their own choice. As discussed earlier, changes in the marketplace made small business ownership increasingly challenging over the course of the early twentieth century. What once may have seemed a likely solution to the problem of earning an income while supporting family over time may have come to be seen as impossible. This must have been truer then ever after 1920, when Americans "witnessed a marked decline in the importance of small firms relative to larger companies." "As America's national economy matured," one historian argues, "small businesses in many fields found their roles shrinking relative to big businesses."[88] In combination with the devastating boom-and-bust cycles that punctuated the decades after 1920, the predominance of big business, with all its ramifications for capitalization and competition, created daunting circumstances for small businesses across the country. For women who had the privilege of weighing their options, proprietorship must have looked less and less attractive at the same time that employment in clerical and other positions looked more and more enticing and, for women with families, more and more of a possibility.

In spite of a general broadening of employment opportunity for American women, married women continued to face severely limited choices. Census figures indicate, for example, that married women, who comprised the largest percentage (42 percent) of San Francisco's businesswomen by 1930, were least likely to be able to take advantage of the new employment opportunities that were drawing other women out of proprietorship.[89] This is not to say that married women's circumstances had not changed substantially. On the one hand, the average number of children for women who came of age around 1930 was approximately 2.5 for both white and nonwhite women, a lower birthrate than at any time previously in U.S. history.[90] With smaller families, these women were freed from child rearing and some household duties earlier in life, theoretically enabling them to take advantage of the many new job opportunities available. Yet married women continued to be tied to their families and their homes by the same set of expectations and obligations that had been keeping them out of the paid labor force and pushing them into business proprietorship since the middle of the nineteenth century. Indeed, the restraints that marriage, motherhood, and household management placed on this category of women far surpassed the restrictions faced by either widowed or divorced women. The key ingredient, of course, in this distinction was the added responsibility that husbands brought into the lives of their wives.

Late nineteenth-century California divorce cases highlight the degree to which marital expectations bound women to their households. For the most common complaint lodged against women by their husbands was desertion, or "dereliction of domestic duty." Louis Franklyn, for example, alleged that he had only left his wife because she "refuse[d] to assist him in the conduct and management of his home." Similarly, Robert Lucas, an unemployed laborer, countered his wife's charges of nonsupport with the accusation that "her management of the household became so improvident and slothful that he became entirely discouraged"; after supporting her for one and a half years he had simply stopped working because of it. The state courts upheld men's expectations that their wives act first and foremost as homemakers, finding women guilty of desertion more often than men. A wife's duty to provide a refuge for her husband, therefore, was paramount, and unless she could find a way to combine wealth production with household production, she would have to forgo participation in the paid labor force.[91]

That men were much more likely to be granted divorce on the grounds of neglect than women also reflects the degree to which married women's hands were tied if they found their husbands to be "improvident and slothful." If her husband did his job poorly or not at all, took unreasonable financial risks, or continued to invest in failed business ventures, a woman did not have the same opportunity for divorce on the grounds that her husband was neglecting his duty to provide for his family. A house in disarray, the state suggested, was unacceptable, but financial disorder was simply unlucky. As a result, not only were married women burdened with the task of combining paid labor with unpaid household management, but they were also burdened with the task of finding a way to make ends meet themselves if their husbands failed at the task.

The story of Mrs. Joseph Newmark exemplifies this. When she married her husband in Sacramento sometime in the 1860s or 1870s, she did so knowing that "his means were not more than $2,000." She was "modest in [her] demands," though, and trusted that he would be able to provide for her. But once Joseph's retail tobacco store failed and he was asked to leave his brother-in-law's business to make room for another family member, Mrs. Newmark's faith in her husband's ability to support the family faltered, and she decided to take things into her own hands. In 1882, Mrs. Newmark hatched her own plan for supporting the family and convinced her husband to participate. As she later recalled in a brief autobiography: "I suggested to my husband that we go to San Francisco and open a business there, of children's ware, etc. I would participate and we could, I hoped, support ourselves. This plan was adopted. We moved to the corner of Bush and Kearny and rented the whole house for $100 and established the business here. . . . Our business was very good; a child from babyhood up to twelve years could find clothes here."[92] Starting their children's clothing business was, for Mrs. Newmark, an economic imperative. It was driven both by a need to satisfy the domestic expectations of her and by Mr. Newmark's failure to support his family.

This was only the first of several occasions when economic hard times visited the Newmarks; Joe, as he was affectionately called by his wife, seemed to have a peculiar ability to bring such troubles upon himself and his family. Indeed, compensating for or suffering through her husband's business failures and financial blunders became a persistent occurrence in Mrs. Newmark's life. Learning to balance this with her responsibilities as a wife and mother was a challenge she faced over and over. When her daughter Millie, born after the couple started their business in San Francisco, became seriously ill, Mrs. Newmark was forced to take a vacation from the store. Worn down herself, with a bad cough that did not seem to get better, she and Millie were sent to San Rafael, known for its dry and sunny climate, to recuperate.[93] When both she and her daughter had recovered and returned to the city five months later, Mrs. Newmark learned that Joe had "given up" their children's clothing business and planned to go to White Pine "to make his fortune there." He and a friend planned to take a stock of clothes with them to sell at great profit. While away Joe punctually sent checks to San Francisco to cover his wife's room, board, and other expenses, but he never found the wealth he had expected. A year later he was back, and Mrs. Newmark summed up the whole endeavor glibly: "As he did not make his fortune, it was better that he returned."[94]

Although the loss of her business frustrated her, Mrs. Newmark understood her position well. She could do little to counter the decisions her husband made without potentially causing enormous domestic strife. Mrs. Newmark's disadvantages were widely felt by married women throughout the country in the nineteenth century, but the situation may have been worse for women in California. While the state was an early adopter of married women's property laws (largely the heritage of Mexican laws regarding community property), California ultimately was highly conservative in the rights it extended to women.[95] By 1880, it was among a minority of states (37 percent) that had not yet enacted laws protecting married women's wages from their husbands.[96] This fact underscored married women's dependence and vulnerability. Even as co-owner of a business in the state, Mrs. Newmark was virtually powerless unless she had her husband's consent or filed a petition to "conduct business in her own name."[97] The fact that Joe could and did decide to sell the business without consulting her proved how uneven their control over the joint enterprise was. If Mrs. Newmark's autobiographical account is any indication of how she responded upon discovering that the business was gone, then she must have said little. Prudence was required even in the way she remembered the event: "How I felt I will not state here. It was [a] very unpleasant surprise for me, but what could I do?" In the end, the dejected Mrs. Newmark could do nothing but watch for another chance to bend her husband's ear and his will to her way.

She did not have to wait long. Shortly after the family's return to Sacramento, where Joe accepted yet another job, Mrs. Newmark had one final opportunity to pull the family through "hard times." Their landlord, one Mr. Garrison, from whom the Newmarks rented a house for $30 per month, was "constantly dinning in Joe's ear what an advantage it would be to him to buy the house and that it could be paid off with the rent." Although undoubtedly advised by his wife to the contrary, Joe decided to buy the house and found himself instantly burdened with repair bills, taxes, street repair assessments, and the cost of a gardener. As Mrs. Newmark remembered it: "My Joe bought the house but if one does not have the means one should not buy houses. This was my experience." Determined to overcome the "constant worries . . . tied up with the house," Mrs. Newmark came up with yet another business plan. Tipped off by a gentleman who came to her wanting to rent rooms, she decided to run a lodging house. Because of the home's proximity to the State Capitol, she could fill every available furnished room throughout the duration of the legislative session. In her own words: "I rented rooms on the upper floors and so I paid off the house."[98] Once again Mr. Newmark's poor financial decision put the family's fortunes at risk, while Mrs. Newmark's business initiative saved them.

As the Newmark story suggests, business proprietorship could be a feasible way for married women to protect their families' financial welfare when their husbands failed to do so. Because it provided women with the opportunity to earn an income while still fulfilling their domestic obligations, economic enterprise may have been one of the only ways that a woman could improve the family's finances without jeopardizing her role in the home. Consequently, business ownership was a strategy to which many married women turned when they found their family fortunes sinking under the management of their husbands.

The R. G. Dun & Company credit reports reflect this. Roughly one-quarter of all married female proprietors in the credit reports (and 12 percent of all women in the reports) were married to men who had failed in business and seemed unable to support their families. In these situations, women took things into their own hands and either assumed their husband's failing businesses or started their own enterprises. Mr. C. H. Mercer, for example, was "dissipated," "drank, sometimes excessively," and neglected his confectionery business, so his wife took out sole trader papers and took over its management herself. Mrs. Ward's experience was similar. After failing in the drug business, her husband decided to study to be a physician while his wife supported him by opening her own drug store. Not all stories were so dramatic. Another 20 percent of all married female proprietors in the credit reports were motivated not by their husbands' failure but by the men's menial jobs and accompanying poor pay.[99] Business proprietorship was also, therefore, a feasible way for women to supplement the income their husbands earned as mechanics, journeymen, retail grocers, or other occupations in which the financial rewards were especially low and/or unpredictable. Research by other scholars confirms that this was a national trend among female proprietors, not a local one.[100]

In California, the 1852 law[101] authorizing married women "to transact business in their own name" was in fact designed to give them an opportunity to provide for themselves and their children in the event that their husbands could not.[102] This motivation for the law was specifically laid out in an 1862 revision requiring petitioners to take an oath swearing that their purpose in availing themselves of the law was to enable them to support themselves and their children. Beginning that year petitioners were also required to state the reasons for their application. A husband's inability to support his family was an acceptable reason for the petition.[103]

While the law technically released married businesswomen from their legally imposed economic dependence on their husbands, the restrictions it imposed were a reminder that married women's commercial and domestic responsibilities were intertwined. First, women who exercised their right to operate a business under the law were automatically put in charge of the financial maintenance of their children. The expectation, evidently, was that if women became business owners they would have to accept added responsibilities with their expanded rights. In essence, they became heads of household and were held accountable for their dependents. Taking over financial liability for their children, however, did not release married women from responsibility for their children's physical care. Thus, ironically, starting a business simply multiplied married women's ties to their households. Second, the law restricted the amount of money married women could invest in their businesses. The original law capped the investment at $5,000 un-

IN THE DISTRICT COURT OF THE Fourth Judicial District of the State of California in and for the City and County of San Francisco—In the matter of the application of SARAH McDONALD for an order of said Court permitting her to carry on business as a Sole Trader,—Notice is hereby given by the undersigned, Sarah McDonald, wife of Charles McDonald, and residing in the city and county of San Francisco, State of California, that it is her intention to make application to the District Court of the Fourth Judicial District of the State of California, in and for the city and county of San Francisco, on SATURDAY, the 10th day of April, 1869, at 10 o'clock A. M. of that day, at the Court-room of said Court, in the City Hall, in said city and county, for an order of said Court permitting her to carry on business in her own name and on her own account. The nature of the business to be carried on by her is keeping a lodging-house in said city and county. Dated March 12, 1869.

mh12-td*   SARAH McDONALD.

A married woman who intended to conduct business in her own name in San Francisco was required by law to run a notice such as this one, from an 1869 newspaper. (National Archives, Pacific Region, San Bruno, California)

---

less a married woman could demonstrate that any additional moneys came neither from her husband nor from their joint property. By 1862, the law restricted the amount to $500. While this aspect of the law was designed to regulate married men's behavior, preventing them from "hiding" their assets in their wives' names, in practice it restricted married women's behavior, severely limiting their business investment and thus their chances for getting a business off the ground.[104] Concerns over allowing married women to independently control significant amounts of money in their own businesses were most likely at work here, too, ultimately underscoring the state's belief in married women's dependent economic status. Thus, a married businesswoman's commercial stakes were intertwined with her husband: at the same time the law recognized her husband's economic foibles it reiterated that it was he who was the proper manager of the family's finances.

The extraordinary burdens placed on married women who exercised their rights under California law to operate businesses in their own names were likely replicated elsewhere. In Massachusetts, for example, "a comprehensive statute passed in 1855 granted married women the right to engage in business independently of their husbands and guaranteed them control over their earnings." Such laws initially appear progressive but, as one scholar observes, "often worked to men's advantages."[105] Other studies have also emphasized the degree to which changes in nineteenth-century laws for women were often not what they seemed and ultimately may have hindered more than helped women's economic advancement and gains in status.[106] Existing scholarship does not, however, explicitly discuss the details of laws granting married women the right to operate business in their own names.[107] Since the laws governing married women's businesses reveal the degree to which female proprietorship sometimes challenged traditional expectations of women's role in their families—and thus needed to be controlled—further research in this area will be fruitful. Regional comparisons would, of course, be revealing. Tracing married women's business laws over time offers equal promise for providing insight into the ways female proprietorship has remained a touchstone issue for women's economic status in American society. The California law, for example, changed in significant ways over time and was not repealed until *1980*, at which time the law still required married women to justify their application and explain the source of the capital being invested.[108] Clearly the law existed to protect creditors from fraud, and yet, in doing so, it placed the rights of capitalists above the rights of women—and suggested the two parties were at odds. There could be no clearer message from the California legislature: married women's economic activities must not interfere with their responsibilities for their children. It was a message designed originally for women such as Mrs. Newmark that reverberated throughout the state for over one hundred years.

While a small proportion of San Francisco's female proprietors were single, never-married women drawn by the promise of economic independence and personal fulfillment, the majority were women with families who turned to business ownership for more-practical reasons. With the exception of the unusually profitable gold rush era, proprietorship in San Francisco provided these women with the opportunity to earn a modest income that accommodated their personal and legal obligations to husbands and/or children. Employment options that fit these criteria were limited both because married and formerly married women were barred from many of the more-lucrative jobs that never-married women took advantage of, and because their domestic responsibilities limited the types of employment they could realistically pursue.

Economic choices for San Francisco women, therefore, were limited by formal and informal restrictions yet changed over time. By 1920, the barriers that previously pushed women with families into proprietorship began to fall, and married, widowed, and divorced women started to move into expanding opportunities in clerical and teaching work, rejecting business ownership to an increasing degree because it did not offer the same reliability or remuneration. Small-business ownership changed too, likely pushing many women out of proprietorship as it became increasingly complicated and costly. Historical circumstance, therefore, influenced why women started businesses, for the economic and personal circumstances that defined their choices were transformed by the demographic and marketplace changes sweeping the nation at the beginning of the twentieth century.

Yet in spite of these changes, one thing remained the same: proprietorship was the province of those women least free in the job market. Hampered by socially and legally enforced responsibilities for homes, husbands, and/or children, married, divorced, and widowed women turned to small-business ownership as a solution to overcoming the restraints they faced as economic actors. Often a blending of domesticity and commerce, reproductive and productive labor, female proprietorship enabled such women to meet economic and familial imperatives simultaneously. But they did so only by pursuing carefully considered start-up strategies, the subject to which we turn in the next chapter.

CHAPTER 3

HOW WOMEN STARTED

BUSINESSES

Once San Francisco women seized on proprietorship as a way to over-come the economic, legal, and personal restrictions that limited their employment choices, they faced the daunting task of getting their businesses started. This too was a test of a woman's capital intentions. For what start-up strategy she adopted might determine whether or not her enterprise took off at all. Such a decision involved careful consideration of the risks and require-ments of each approach. Because female proprietors had few other income options to turn to, prudence was necessary every step of the way.

Easy access to credit during the flush and male-dominated years of the gold rush made starting a business during the early 1850s simple. This was particularly true for white women, who were idealized in nineteenth-century American culture as nurturers and homemakers. Demand for their domestic skills and services, fueled by a dramatic gender imbalance, meant female pro-prietors were unusually safe risks in the eyes of most creditors, and women enjoyed generous terms for financing new enterprises as a result. A woman with an "honest face"—typically the face of a married white woman—found she needed little else to access almost unlimited credit. Yet such beneficial commercial conditions were short-lived. Indeed, the gold rush era was the only period when their gender seemed to be an advantage for some women.[1]

Thereafter women found access to credit—that is, the ability to purchase necessary inventory and fixtures with extended payment plans—particularly difficult. By at least the 1870s, credit dispensation became an impersonal, rationalized process in which "an honest face" counted for very little. Instead, creditors relied on evaluations of a proprietor's capital assets and experience. This put all women at a distinct disadvantage both because most came into proprietorship with no previous business experience and because the economic and legal restrictions on women's ability to earn and control money made saving cash out of reach for most would-be female proprietors.

These financial disadvantages, in combination with women's lack of alternative employment options, made San Francisco women cautious when it came to how they started their businesses. First and foremost among their concerns were practicality and cost. Women sought ways to limit the capital they needed to get started as well as to contain their liability. Their start-up strategies reflect this. Instead of expensive loans from institutional lenders, the city's female proprietors sought out loans with more-lenient and forgiving terms from informal lending networks comprised of female and male acquaintances. Partnership, a second strategy, contained both the amount of money and the responsibility a businesswoman took on for her new business. But because a partnership also made a woman liable for someone else's blunders, it increased the risks of business start-up, and therefore relatively few women employed this strategy. The most popular means of start-up by far was taking over or buying out an already established business. As this chapter will show, San Francisco female proprietors utilized this strategy to a much larger degree than men, who may have viewed it as a compromise to their independence. But for women it was the safest way to start because it enabled a first-time proprietor to build her own business on the successful foundation that another had already established. Instead of risking the complete unknown, any businesswoman who utilized this strategy got started with a solid track record already in place and did not have to build her enterprise from the ground up. Lenient payment terms made getting started this way widely available. Thus buying out or taking over another person's business contained both cost and risk, making it the best approach for the city's new businesswomen.

These start-up strategies tell us that when it came to how women commenced business, penny-pinching practicality characterized San Francisco's female proprietors throughout the post–gold rush years. The costs were too high, the alternatives too few, and the risks too great to adopt any other approach.

Luzena Stanley Wilson had no money in 1851, so getting herself, her children, and her stove from Sacramento to Nevada City, where she intended to start the El Dorado Hotel, seemed hopeless. But then Wilson met "a man with an idle team" who said he would take the party and offered to extend her credit for the $700 trip. "I must have carried my honesty in my face," she recalled years later, "for he looked at me a minute and said 'I'll take you Ma'am if you will go security for the money.'" Wilson promised the man he would be paid if "she lived and made money." In the end, he accepted her pledge and took her to Nevada City.[2]

Taking her promise as collateral was indeed profitable for the kind man. Within six weeks Wilson used her earnings at the El Dorado to pay him his $700. For trusting a woman's honest face, he had made $14 per mile on the fifty-mile trip from Sacramento to Nevada City—more than five times what a man made in one month for working in a California store.[3] Wilson, on the other hand, had gained even more. From the extension of credit, she had gained the opportunity to gross from $1,875 to $5,000 a week operating the El Dorado. This was six times the average *annual* income of male workers in the trades in 1850 New York, and more than 500 times the weekly pay of female operatives in Massachusetts textile mills.[4] Of course, the high inflation in gold rush California would have cut these profits down to size. But even Wilson's net income must have surpassed what a woman could earn anywhere else in the country. Such profits were enjoyed by white and nonwhite women alike who, in dance houses, gambling halls, and crude hotels throughout Northern California mining towns, capitalized on men's willingness to pay for women's domestic and sexual services, and even for what one scholar has described as "quite simply, proximity to a woman."[5]

Such dramatic earning potential during the gold rush made many women good credit risks, and thus during this unique and brief period of time, they found credit easy to come by. This was a gender-specific privilege enjoyed exclusively by would-be businesswomen. The cost of this privilege, however, was women's confinement to domestic labor—that is, commerce historically rooted in "women's work" in their own homes. The hotel and restaurant start-ups made possible by women's access to credit kept women precisely where men wanted them during the gold rush: serving men's needs, albeit this time for pay.[6] The fact that women operated businesses that provided men with domestic services made their ventures both socially acceptable and profitable. Combined, these factors loosened creditors' purse strings. Stories of spectacular profits such as Wilson's assured a would-be creditor that a woman who asked him for credit would be able to make good on the loan.[7]

But at issue was not only whether women *could* repay their debts but also whether they *would*—a question of character that was as responsible for a good credit rating as any financial indicator in the nineteenth century. Here too the gold rush period was unique because it was characterized by a fantasy, held especially about Anglo-American women, that those few women in the state who were not prostitutes were gatekeepers of morality and civic responsibility and thus especially worthy of trust. This was particularly true once the wives and daughters of white merchants and professionals arrived in the mining camps, bringing with them white middle-class conceptions about their own role in the community. In stark contrast stood those women who profited unabashedly from men's extravagant spending on liquor and games of chance. French women, for example, earned opprobrium rather than praise from male contemporaries for their "profligate, shameless, avaricious and vain" ability to take men's money.[8] Clearly these were not the sort of qualities that attracted creditors. But women who sold domestic services and could conceal their profit motivation in the guise of womanly care benefited from the belief in women's character and their inherent virtue and trustworthiness.[9] This belief served the commercial interests of Anglo-American women especially well.

Mothers were viewed as particularly safe credit risks in gold rush California because they epitomized virtue. "There was no credit in '49 for men," recalled Luzena Stanley Wilson, "but I was a woman with two children and might have bought out the town with no security other than my word."[10] A hardworking white mother such as Wilson, it seems, appeared automatically trustworthy compared to the gold diggers, gamblers, and sex workers who populated western towns. Thus motherhood, a job market handicap that was one of the key factors driving women into proprietorship in the first place (see Chapter 2), was for a brief period in northern California, a financial advantage in the eyes of creditors.[11]

Scarcity of women in the region underpinned such preconceived notions about female trustworthiness. Whether or not she could or would repay a debt voluntarily, a woman living in a city of men could easily be found by her creditors to arrange repayment. Gender imbalance, therefore, also made women good credit risks because they were unlikely to abscond. This factor gave women in the nineteenth-century West, a region characterized by a significant gender imbalance in the nonnative population, access to credit to a degree not found in other regions of the country.[12] San Francisco women were not alone in this regard. In nearby Denver, Colorado Territory, women were found to have an "edge over men" in the dispensation of credit between 1858 and 1876. One study argued that "women without collateral could usually get recommendations for credit where men could not, even when everything was equal except their sex."[13] This regional gender advantage temporarily evened out the playing field for many female proprietors.

Easy credit made launching a new business simple for such women. It allowed first-time business owners to get started without having to produce any capital up front. Like Luzena Stanley Wilson, female proprietors could pay for the start-up costs out of the business's monthly profits, thus requiring no out-of-pocket expenses from the new entrepreneur. Monthly installments, and a wholesaler willing to accept them, enabled a potential business owner to obtain the merchandise and other supplies she needed to start a modest enterprise with very little effort or cost.

But this unusual window of opportunity for female proprietors was specifically tied to the unique conditions of 1850s and 1860s Northern California. It was a period when the gender imbalance and sex role stereotypes characteristic of the gold rush created social and commercial capital for the city's women, particularly for morally upright, white, married mothers such as Luzena Stanley Wilson. The advantages of the period were fleeting, however, for by the 1870s, obtaining credit became much more difficult for women and stayed that way for the next fifty years.

The R. G. Dun & Company credit reports (which exist only for the 1870s for San Francisco) provide the best insight into women's experience as credit-seekers, and what they indicate is that by the last quarter of the nineteenth century, gender had in fact become a *disadvantage* for women who sought credit to start their businesses. Indeed, by the time the company began sending credit reporters around the country to evaluate men and women as credit risks, obtaining credit became an increasingly distant possibility for San Francisco women. This was a change mirrored in the rest of the nation. As one scholar argues, "the shift to corporate capitalization beginning in the 1860s made it more difficult for women to access capital since financial markets became more formal, restrictive, and driven by the need for long-term creditworthiness."[14] By then, the dispensation of credit was an impersonal and rationalized process, one in which credit reports rather than "hunches" were the oil that lubricated the deals. An "honest face" such as had won Wilson the $700 credit she needed to start her hotel in 1851 counted for little, since applicants for credit were scrutinized for their ability—and not their commitment—to repay their creditors. Capital assets, experience, and connections were the name of the game now, one that many small-scale businesswomen would not even qualify to play. Thus, by the 1870s, San Francisco women came to resemble female business owners elsewhere in the country for whom obtaining credit had always been a problem.[15]

The chief determinant of a high credit rating was a person's capital, and this put women at a disadvantage. As one historian found, "there was a high correlation between property holdings and a favorable R. G. Dun evaluation."[16] This meant small-business owners in general, and women in particular, were distinctly handicapped. Low start-up costs were partly what drew women into the field of small business in the first place. So few if any had the real or personal property to make them safe risks for anything beyond very small amounts of credit. Those with successful husbands or fathers willing to cosign for their indebtedness were fortunate, and widows left with the property of their deceased husbands even more so, but most female proprietors drew on scant resources to start their businesses.

Women's comparative lack of business experience also hindered their ability to procure credit. Only 6 percent of the San Francisco women evaluated by R. G. Dun & Company during the 1870s had previous experience operating a business in another location or field. By contrast, 30 percent of male small-business owners in the reports had previously conducted business in a different locale or line of work.[17] Men's business experience often opened up lines of credit for them when they started new enterprises. William Searby, for example, a thirty-five-year-old Englishman, failed in business in Victoria, Canada, before coming to San Francisco to start over again with a new drug store. Although he "had no means when he commenced" business in San Francisco, Searby's two or three years experience earned him a line of credit from a "prominent wholesale house." Thus, in spite of his previous failure, he "managed to build up a nice little trade."[18] Because women did not typically have previous business experience when starting up a new enterprise, they did not have the same generous (and forgiving) offers of credit extended to them. In fact, widespread lack of experience among businesswomen encouraged negative generalizations about female creditworthiness. Consider the opinions stated in the *Milliner*, a trade journal published for retail milliners: "It is appalling the presumption of some women in the matter of credits. They think that the wholesaler will provide them with all the merchandise they need and that with them having little or practically no experience."[19] Thus, in combination with lack of capital, women's lack of experience meant that most San Francisco businesswomen had little hope of procuring a line of credit to start their businesses.

For a very few women, personal connections could mitigate these strikes against them when it came to qualifying for credit. Occasionally male creditors took pity on female proprietors they knew. Imagining themselves as benevolent fathers saving ladies in distress, these wholesale merchants felt the women needed protecting. Yet even in instances such as these, creditors were more interested in the bottom dollar than anything else and did not allow their benevolence to get in the way of their profit margins.[20] On other occasions, ethnic ties could be profitable for women. Mrs. H. Jacobs, for example, a thirty-five-year old widow who traveled to San Francisco from the Sacramento area in 1872, relied on family and community connections to get started. She arrived in the city bearing letters of recommendation from Alexander & Hyman, a Yolo County firm in which she had family members. These and her connections to the city's Jewish community earned her lines of credit from Michael Friedlander & Co. and Rosenbaum & Friedman, dry goods wholesalers who provided her with the stock necessary to launch her fancy goods store. In the opinion of R. G. Dun & Company credit reporters, Jacobs was "credited by Jewish houses full as much on account of being a widow with a family depending upon her as upon any means that she is thought to possess."[21] In fact, several scholars have noted the degree to which Jewish businessmen and -women helped each other with capital.[22] This was a long-standing tradition in the community, in fact, one that gave birth to active mutual aid societies for Jews as well as to generous extensions of credit.[23] Yet truly forgiving terms were extended to female credit applicants only in rare cases. Moreover, family and community connections could also be liabilities when they linked a would-be businesswoman to a particularly disdained racial or ethnic group.

Jews, African Americans, Irish immigrants and others who did not fit Anglo-Saxon, middle-class norms were far more likely to find their ethnicity or race an obstacle than an advantage in obtaining credit. As others have noted, the R. G. Dun & Company credit reporters consistently documented non-Anglo backgrounds and more often than not used such information to generalize about a man or woman's "personal character" and declare him or her unsafe for credit.[24] African Americans' racial background appears to have escaped comment by Dun reporters some of the time. No female proprietors were identified as black or "colored" in my sample for San Francisco, and, according to one study of black business in American history, this was a trend repeated in the reports for other cities. Yet on other occasions, credit agency reporters recorded the derogatory racial epithet "nigger," betraying the same racism that was rampant throughout the rest of society.[25] If credit reporters did not always mention race, they did identify ethnicity, usually because they considered it a negative attribute. Jewish men and women, for example, were consistently depicted as untrustworthy, while Irish residents were likely to be described as dissipated, even drunk.[26] Such racial/ethnic stereotypes had far-reaching effects on access to credit. This was particularly true for small-business owners in San Francisco who were, as explained in Chapter 1, over-whelmingly immigrants. Thus for the preponderance of Irish and German-Jewish immigrant women among the ranks of the city's female proprietors, unless they had personal connections in the business world, obtaining credit to cover start-up costs was very likely impossible. Such women, along with the many others turned down for credit due to insufficient financial resources and lack of business experience, had to look to strategies other than obtaining credit to cover their start-up costs after the 1870s.

RAISING CAPITAL: SAVING AND BORROWING MONEY

Using savings to finance a new business was, in general, a popular strategy among small-scale proprietors.[27] This was no different in San Francisco than in other parts of the country. Thus when thirty-three-year-old Louis Beyers-dorf bought a half interest in a saloon business in San Francisco in 1873, he furnished $2,500 of the $5,700 purchase price from his own savings, accu-mulated from his earnings as a barkeeper.[28] Similarly, N. J. Wyman was able to save some $10,000 from his wages working as a clerk for Joseph Bros. be-fore opening his jewelry and fancy goods business in the city in 1874.[29] Both men were among the 4 percent of male proprietors in my sample from the credit reports who utilized savings as a start-up strategy. They were, in this regard, typical of small businessmen around the country. "Personal savings," one scholar argues, "provided most of the initial capital" for the owners of small-scale businesses around the country, though many supplemented this with funds from family, friends, and loans.[30] In contrast, utilizing personal savings was a strategy few women could use. No female proprietors in the credit reports for San Francisco, in fact, were described to have launched their businesses with savings.

The disparity between men's and women's ability to save highlights the degree to which would-be businesswomen were hampered by economic and legal restrictions on their ability to accumulate financial assets. In fact, in comparison to women, men had numerous benefits when it came to their ability to save money. First, 11 percent of all small businessmen in the credit reports worked previously as clerks (keeping a business's account books, pro-cessing paper work, placing orders, etc.).[31] Such jobs were highly desirable white-collar jobs that early in the nineteenth century launched thousands of young men into the middle class. By the end of the 1890s, clerking jobs were no longer a training ground for men interested in "making it to the top . . . [in] business leadership."[32] But in the 1870s male clerks still had the opportunity to gain valuable business experience and, if careful, to save money—both of which they might then channel into starting their own businesses.[33] For women, saving enough money from their own wages to start a business was extremely difficult. Some milliners and dressmakers, among the highest paid female laborers in the job market, did so, but as one study found, it took them thirteen to twenty years of careful penny pinching to save enough.[34] Thus men's higher income levels (men made several times the amount women made in typical industrial jobs and had access to higher-paying jobs off limits to women) were a distinct advantage.[35] The ability to maintain control of their own earnings was also a benefit men enjoyed that many would-be business-women did not, since this was a privilege not granted to married women in California until the twentieth century.[36] In combination, these advantages meant men were far more likely than women to be able to save money to cover the start-up costs for a small business.

The few San Francisco women who were able to invest cash in new businesses without borrowing money almost always did so with the assistance of a male family member. Mrs. Jane Thomas, for example, a divorced woman who supplied $1,500 cash to start up her own millinery business, reportedly relied on aid from her father.[37] Miss E. Van Winkle, a twenty-year-old milliner, may also have been assisted financially by her father, the proprietor of a distillery. Her mother, a former milliner, was already assisting her daughter in the day-to-day operations of the business.[38] The widowed Mrs. L. H. Lichtenstein, who inherited some $5,000 from her husband, was in particularly good shape; two years after his death she used a portion of the money to open her own small brokerage shop—the same type of business her husband had operated.[39] Other scholars have noted as well that the dependence on family for capital was a widespread strategy for women business owners.[40] In fact, male proprietors of small businesses typically also relied on family for help with capital, underscoring that at least some of the time, it was the modest size of women's commercial establishments, rather than the gender of their owners, that determined their start-up strategies.[41]

Married women whose husbands enjoyed a secure middling income probably had the greatest access to capital. For example, Mrs. S. Fiala, a Hungarian immigrant to San Francisco, must have had little problem pulling together the money to start her business. Her husband was a draughtsman in the U.S. surveyor general's office, bringing home a good, steady wage. The substantial amount of money she invested to start her dry goods and fancy goods store in 1875 could probably have been saved from the couple's household income with little difficulty.[42] And unlike the single, divorced, and widowed women discussed above, Fiala may have continued to access the family's capital for her business needs. For women such as Fiala, married to men with steady and substantial incomes, the benefits of a husband's wages were evidenced in their own success. One historian argues that "married women had access to far greater resources than their single counterparts and their businesses, on average, lasted twice as long."[43] Of course Mrs. Fiala's class status was atypical. As discussed in Chapters 1 and 2, San Francisco's businesswomen were largely immigrants whose husbands often had difficulty locating steady, well-paying jobs (this was particularly true for Irish immigrants) and who therefore pursued proprietorship as a source of income compatible with their household responsibilities.[44] Thus women whose husbands were capable of providing the start-up costs for their wives' businesses were most likely unusual among the population of female proprietors in San Francisco.

But while these examples of men's financial assistance to their daughters, widows, and wives underscore women's dependence on men, it was the intervention of the state that truly illustrated the gender inequality inherent in access to capital savings for business start-ups. For by the 1860s, California put restrictions on the money invested in a married woman's business. Any married woman who did *not* declare herself a sole trader, that is, an independent entity in the eyes of the law, was not restricted in the amount of capital she could invest in a business. This was because a married woman who did not officially file her intention "to conduct business in her own name and on her own account" (as a sole trader) according to her rights under the 1852 Married Women's Business Act, did not own her own business in the eyes of the law. Instead, like a married woman's wages, the business belonged to her husband; thus *he* was free to invest as much money in it as he wanted.[45] But for any married woman who assumed all the risks and benefits of operating a business herself by publicly declaring the business her own and claiming sole trader status, the 1862 revision of the law restricted her investment to no more than $500 if the money did not come from her separate account. This constrained a married woman's access to both a couple's community property and her husband's separate property.[46] Since only the wealthiest women brought valuable real and personal property into marriage, California's law disadvantaged most married women when it came to start-up capital.[47] In effect, because it so severely restricted married women's access to capital, the law encouraged them not to operate their businesses independently, as sole traders, and reinforced their economic dependence on their husbands.[48]

Those married women who insisted on economic independence as proprietors were reduced to pawning their personal belongings to generate cash. A woman's "personal effects" were considered her separate property even if she was married, and so could be sold or traded for cash or credit in the event she wanted to start her own business.[49] An 1894 advertisement for a pawn-broker, for example, reminds female readers, "Always Money If You Need It On Your Jewelry."[50] Business owner Johanna Pulfer acted on this suggestion when in 1921 she secured a $2,500 loan from the Remedial Loan Association after pledging one solitaire diamond ring, one lady's platinum, diamond-set watch, and one diamond-set bar pin.[51] Because such transactions only became public when bankruptcy proceedings were initiated, however, we will never know just how many married women were moved out of desperation, frustration, or ambition to trade in a family heirloom for the start-up capital to launch their own businesses.

While investing savings was a start-up strategy unavailable to most women by restrictions on their ability to make and control money, borrowing—also used far less frequently by women (1 percent) than by men (6 percent)—was more likely a strategy that women rejected of their own accord.[52] Here the point is really a matter of degree. That is, though scholars have shown that small-business owners generally were unlikely to rely on bank borrowing, women clearly rejected (and probably were rejected by) banks as lenders to a greater degree than men.[53] Like other creditors, banks probably turned women away because of lack of capital assets. Yet women's own financial caution most likely prevented them from borrowing start-up money from lending institutions as well. Because such loans were typically expensive and dispensed with less than favorable terms, women, so often cautious when it came to money management, shied away from such help.

The few examples in the bankruptcy records of women who took advantage of commercial loans illustrate this point. Mrs. Nancy C. Noyes, for instance, borrowed $3,000 from Hibernia Bank in 1877, secured by a mortgage on a lot of land she owned that was valued at $4,000. In one year's time, she had accrued $500 interest on the loan, which computes to a high annual interest rate of 17 percent.[54] Others such as Teresa Holden borrowed from "capitalists" who advertised "money to loan" in the city newspapers.[55] Such individuals probably charged lower interest rates, but like banks and other institutions, they loaned money to make money. Charles Heisen, for example, loaned $300 to Diana O. Anderson on September 1, 1872, at 3 percent interest. The loan was to be paid back in ninety days, and interest was payable monthly or would be added to the principal (capitalized). While the terms of the agreement between Heisen and Anderson were far more reasonable than those offered Noyes by the Hibernia Bank, they were still designed to make Heisen money and were enforced in court three years later. After defaulting on the loan for thirty-eight months, Anderson was found to owe Heisen

$342.35 in interest on top of $299 in principal (since she had managed to pay back $1 the day after borrowing the money). A $300 loan ended up costing her $641.35.[56] As Anderson learned, borrowing money from professional lenders was costly. And few women could afford to engage in high-cost business start-up strategies; only 12 percent of the loans taken out by women in the bankruptcy records sample were contracted with institutions or professional money lenders.[57]

Even when lending institutions such as the Bank of Italy (later called Bank of America) specifically targeted female proprietors as customers, they failed to draw borrowers. When the Bank of Italy opened its Women's Banking Department in 1921, offering banking services to San Francisco women of all professional and economic backgrounds, it officially stated that applications for loans would be accepted. Because so many of its customers were small-scale businesswomen, the department may have expected this service to be popular. But while many women kept checking and savings accounts in the department and probably consulted its knowledgeable (and all-female) staff for money-management advice, there is no evidence that such women applied for the commercial loans it offered. In interviews conducted by the company's head office with several department customers, no female proprietors mentioned using the bank's services for loans.[58]

The unpopularity of bank loans among female proprietors signaled a conscious rejection of high costs and not just a rebuff of institutional help, for when San Francisco women were presented with the possibility of *low-cost* financial aid from formal channels they took advantage of it. When, for example, San Francisco businesswomen had the rare opportunity to apply for business rehabilitation funds from the city after the 1906 earthquake and fire, they did so in droves because the money was available to them for free. Female proprietors, in fact, comprised a disproportionately large share of the total pool of grant applicants and recipients. Of the 894 grants for which demographic information is available, 394 were made to married couples (44 percent), 286 were made to widowed, divorced, or separated women (32 percent), and 93 were made to single women (10 percent). These business funds were granted to proprietors "so crippled by the fire . . . they [could] not now provide themselves with the necessary equipment or stocks in trade, and [had] no other way of supporting themselves or their families." The grants, ranging from $50 to $500, were designed to help them get back on their feet commercially. They were allocated mainly to proprietors of accommodations (32 percent), apparel (13 percent), beauty (3 percent), and retail businesses (11 percent)—the kinds of enterprises in which San Francisco businesswomen were concentrated. Two years after the devastation of the city, 57 percent of the grant recipients were in business as planned, and 15 percent were in a different line of business than formerly proposed but still in business. All in all, nearly three-quarters of the grantees had their enterprises up and running again. They had used the money provided to invest in new locations, fixtures, and stock and were once again running successful businesses. These female proprietors had made good use of free institutional funding, indicating that when the terms were right, they did not shy away from formal channels for financial aid.[59]

As already mentioned, the small number of institutional loans utilized by San Francisco businesswomen was in fact typical of the behavior of male and female business proprietors around the country during the late nineteenth and early twentieth centuries. According to business historians, the capital needed for starting a small enterprise came "very seldom from banks or finance companies."[60] When they did borrow money, proprietors most commonly relied on family, friends, and business associates.[61] In this respect too, the city's female proprietors resembled small-scale business owners elsewhere in the United States.

Bankruptcy court records show that women borrowed almost equally from male and female acquaintances, enlisting the help of an array of characters from their day-to-day lives. Customers, suppliers, laborers, colleagues, and even competitors could all be found among the lenders in women's informal borrowing networks. They turned to such associates for financial aid because they typically provided female proprietors with free capital and the most lenient repayment terms. Not all of these lenders provided interest-free loans or forgave a failure to pay.[62] But the vast majority did and thus provided an essential boost to the economic fortunes of the city's female small-business owners. Miner Andrew Curtain's 1878 loan to Nancy Noyes, his landlady, and Ella Fisher's 1915 loan to fellow dressmaker Bertha Root served the same purpose: they got the businesswomen through a significant financial hurdle by providing much-needed capital at no cost. The only thing that seems to have changed over time is that businesswomen's personal contacts were stretched over larger distances by the early 1900s. Whereas Noyes's loan had come from a friendly customer living in San Francisco, Root's loan forty years later came from an acquaintance in New York City.[63] But no wonder such advantageous financial relationships crisscrossed the nation by the turn of the twentieth century: they fit squarely with female proprietors' practical, penny-pinching approach to financing.

It would be incorrect, however, to suggest that friendliness and forgiveness characterized *all* of women's financial transactions. For there is also scattered evidence of women taking advantage of other women. Martha Bal-

Credit statement for a grocery owner who secured a loan from a female acquaintance with a chattel mortgage on her store furniture in 1916. (National Archives, Pacific Region, San Bruno, California)

---

linger is one such woman. In 1907 she allegedly borrowed money from her housekeeper, Clara Evarts, and then instead of paying it back offered to invest the money (inherited by the young woman from her grandfather) to earn her a better return on her investment. Ballinger never provided any documentation of the "investment," instead giving Evarts a note declaring her the intended beneficiary of Ballinger's life insurance policy. When Ballinger declared bankruptcy two years later, however, Evarts found she could not recoup her money. The note, the only security she had, yielded nothing, since policies with premiums of less than $500 per year were exempt from creditors under California law. Ballinger had swindled her trusting young housekeeper.[64]

Even when their motives were not strictly dishonest, women who loaned money to businesswomen sometimes did so to make a profit rather than support a friend in need. Mrs. Vioget, for example, used a broker to loan out $350 for interest. Though the broker seemed to keep women's money in women's hands (loaning it exclusively to other women), his clients never interacted with each other. Unlike the "friendly" loans discussed earlier, these transactions were impersonal and designed to achieve financial gain.[65] Multiple examples from the bankruptcy court records, in fact, highlight that women at the beginning of the last century were not strangers to financial investment. Indeed more female than male lenders in the sample charged interest to the women business owners who borrowed from them, and female lenders were more likely than male lenders to file lawsuits against female borrowers who failed to comply with the terms of their loans.[66] This finding conforms with recent scholarship emphasizing that nineteenth-century women "used the financial markets" and grew their assets through a variety of investments.[67] Those women who loaned out money to businesswomen as an investment rather than charity fit this pattern.

The fact that women lenders could not always be counted on to provide interest-free loans helps explain why businesswomen borrowed money from men as frequently as from women. In deference to their need to keep operating expenses low, the city's female proprietors turned to whoever was willing to offer them the best deal. This is especially interesting given the long history of women relying on other women for capital assistance in their day-to-day lives. European women's history of informal lending, for example, goes back as far as the seventeenth century.[68] In a more-recent example, nineteenth-century women played important roles as borrowers, depositors, and managers of Irish "loan funds," "an important microcredit institution which operated in Ireland for over 200 years."[69] Similarly, Jewish immigrant women in the United States frequently took advantage of loan networks in which more-fortunate Jewish women pooled resources in order to make small loans to poorer community members, typically for basic household expenses.[70] One of the leading historians of women in business in the United States also stresses this point, arguing that "female entrepreneurs often helped other women to get a start in business."[71] Yet for female business owners in San Francisco at the end of the nineteenth and beginning of the twentieth centuries, there appears to have been no gender division in who borrowed money from whom. If male acquaintances, whether lodgers or provisioners, competitors or colleagues, had the best terms, female proprietors jumped at the opportunity. This underscores the fact that the commercial world in which San Francisco's women small-business owners operated was a heterosocial one, characterized not by an all-female cast of characters, as others have asserted, but by female *and* male customers, employees, and lenders.[72]

In spite of this reality, early twentieth-century institutions such as the Bank of Italy persisted in the belief that women were more comfortable interacting with women when it came to money management. Following in the footsteps of other banks around the country, San Francisco's Bank of Italy created a Women's Banking Department in 1921, conceived, managed, staffed, and patronized entirely by women.[73] The department successfully drew thousands of female depositors but, as discussed earlier, apparently no female borrowers. Offering the friendliest of service provided by female staff trained to address the special needs of women customers, the department still could not convince female business owners that borrowing from the bank was a practical solution to their monetary problems. No matter the story the Women's Banking Department sold them, San Francisco's businesswomen rejected their terms in favor of the more-friendly ones offered by acquaintances, male and female.

Thus while credit dispensation in the city became more impersonal and objective between 1850 and 1920, borrowing continued to occur according to highly subjective and personal standards. While this likely characterized borrowing relationships for small-business owners, male and female, throughout the country, what makes it particularly significant for San Francisco is that others have characterized the late nineteenth century there as a period of rapid "vertical segregation." By at least 1880, one scholar argues, "the city's social and physical topography were one and the same."[74] Yet private loans from attorneys to their widowed, boardinghouse-keeper neighbors, from unmarried women to their millinery colleagues or suppliers, from Berkeley farmers to Oakland hotelkeepers, and from painter's wives to female tire store owners indicate commercial borrowing crossed geographic and class boundaries into the twentieth century.[75] This does not, of course, contradict previous suggestions that San Franciscans recreated the stratified societies they left behind in the eastern United States. But it does suggest that at least between middle-class professionals, petty entrepreneurs, and laborers, personal connections could trump class distinctions when it came to who loaned money to whom and on what terms. Such fluid lending networks superimposed on the city's otherwise segregated landscape opened channels to capital that facilitated at least short-term commercial persistence (though not necessarily success or occupational mobility) for the city's small-scale female proprietors. The same pattern was likely true for small-scale businessmen in San Francisco as well.

BUSINESS PARTNERSHIPS

Women's use of business partnerships to start up their businesses was likely motivated by the same penny-pinching practicality that caused them to avoid institutional lending in favor of informal, personal loans. For such alliances inherently reduced an individual's financial and legal obligations in the business since partners shared ownership and responsibility. Would-be female proprietors came together to combine their capital, to share the labor of running a business, and to double the palate of skills from which they drew. Doing so made opening a business possible for those women unable to raise the necessary start-up capital on their own and was, therefore, probably the strategy employed by San Francisco's least likely businesswomen. In addition, because it offered the opportunity to share business liability, information, and skill, partnership buffered against failure and made success more probable both for experienced proprietors expanding their enterprises and inexperienced businesswomen entering the commercial world for the first time.

Women's partnership relationships ranged from mother-daughter, mother-son, and wife-husband pairings to partnerships between two parties with no apparent familial connection. Occasionally business alliances were formed between men and women, but most often they joined two women with compatible talents and interests. In fact, by far the most common business partnerships for San Francisco women recorded in credit reports, bankruptcy records, and advertisements were with other women.[76] This finding conforms to other studies of female proprietors that also assert that partnerships between women were most common.[77] Women's business alliances sometimes involved female relatives, such as sisters or mothers and daughters (33 percent of all businesswomen's partnerships)[78], but more often brought together two unrelated women with a common goal.[79]

The partnership between Mesdames Gillam and Touchard, for example, may have been key in the success of their two businesses, a ladies' and children's apparel store and a boardinghouse, perhaps operated in the same building. Their 1851 notice advertised "a general assortment of ladies' and children's wearing apparel . . . of the latest Parisian fashions" and, almost as an afterthought, "a comfortably and well situated" boardinghouse. The syntax of the ad suggests that the two businesses were started simultaneously, so the Gillam-Touchard partnership was likely not formed to combine two separately established enterprises, nor was it the result of one business's expansion.[80] Instead, the women must have joined forces in order to start the two businesses at the same time. But why would they want to take the risk of trying to start two enterprises simultaneously?

The answer may lie in the addendum—the secondary, supportive role the boarding announcement seemed to play in the ad. "Mesdames G. & T. have also established a private boarding establishment," it read, tacked onto their apparel shop ad as an indented "N.B.," or side note. Perhaps, because the clothes business was so new and the competition so great, it was not possible (or prudent) to rely on the profits of the store alone. Selling room and board could, in effect, be a night job that would provide supplementary income until the apparel shop was well established. Considering how common it was for women to supplement their family's income by taking in boarders, such a line of reasoning must have come easily to a woman starting a business in San Francisco, especially since the housing demand in that city was so high.[81] The problem, however, lay in the execution of the plan: how could one woman operate both a store and a boarding house?

The combination of the two certainly would have been overwhelming if not impossible for a single woman to do by herself, so taking on a female partner was a reasonable solution. The profits would, presumably, be shared, but so would the work. While Gillam stayed at the store helping customers until closing, Touchard might return home early to prepare supper for their boarders. Her partner must have joined her as soon as business hours had ended, most likely with a pile of sewing. Such a division of labor would have facilitated greater profits, ensured minimum staffing for the two businesses, and, not least of all, provided companionship. Finally, as the old adage goes, "Two heads are better than one"; surely the two women relied on each other's strengths and compensated for each other's weaknesses by making business decisions together. The announcement, after all, was for a partnership, and gives no indication that either woman played a dominant or subordinate role; this suggests that they worked like a team.

Six years later, however, Touchard alone had climbed to the top of the lodging industry and appeared in the paper as the sole proprietor of the Union Hotel. As a result of her initial partnership with Gillam, she had enjoyed a great deal of success and now offered "the most fashionable and comfortable [accommodations] of any in the city."[82] To reach this standard of service, she must have relied on her experience in the lodgings industry, a steady stream of faithful customers, and a healthy income for reinvestment, all of which might be tied to her strong start. Her "side job" as boarding-house keeper had certainly taken center stage over her foray into the apparel industry. This should not be surprising given the high demand for accommodations in the city, as discussed in Chapter 1. Even more important to this discussion, though, is that her stint as a business partner had laid the foundation for independent success. While Touchard's solo rise might be a sign that partnerships between women did not always work, it also underscores the degree to which partnering with another woman could provide the initial momentum that eventually allowed women like Touchard to move out on their own.[83]

The business relationship between Mrs. M. A. Fowler and Miss Lawlor provides another example of how working in pairs must have helped women to succeed. Their 1855 ad for the Female Employment Office included a lengthy description of the services they provided to both employers and employees and then, like Gillam and Touchard's ad in 1851, ended with the brief announcement of an additional business. In the penultimate line of the ad they wrote: "Also, dressmaking and plain sewing." Once again, here was an attempt to make some additional money on the side (by sewing), perhaps only until the new employment office was up and running. Fowler and Lawlor's ad appeared on the same day that Mrs. Butler announced that she had taken over the Alta Female Employment Office. Later that same year Mrs. E. V. Homer announced that she was opening her Intelligence Office for Ladies. All this a mere five years after Mr. Butler had first identified the demand for job placement services and opened Clarke & Co.'s Pioneer Employment Office in 1850.[84] Clearly this was an industry in which there was competition. In fact, considering the small size of the city's female population and the even smaller number of women in that population seeking paid labor outside of prostitution, four female employment agencies may have been as many as the city could sustain. With this in mind, Fowler and Lawlor must have planned to rely on sewing and dressmaking to supplement low initial profits or, if necessary, replace their new business venture altogether if it failed.

The fact that they intended to fall back on dressmaking and not some other skill reveals the care with which Fowler and Lawlor had laid out their business plans together. Their ad stated confidently that "private families, boarding houses, hotels, milliners, dressmakers, and others wanting help of any kind, may rest assured of being supplied, free of charge."[85] In essence they were in business to collect "finder's fees" from young women seeking employment in San Francisco; they offered these referrals to employers without charge. This strategy placed the burden of success on their ability to attract unemployed women willing to pay a fee for job placement. At the same time, Fowler and Lawlor could not have been successful without a strong and far-reaching network of employers to work with. Dress and millinery shop owners were likely among these contacts, since San Francisco's apparel industry was already a large employer by the 1850s. Surely it was by no coincidence, then, that these two businesswomen also sold their own sewing skills. They had created (or reserved) for themselves the opportunity to offer clients their own services as dressmakers when they were in need of extra money.

As the business transactions that San Francisco women participated in became more and more complex after the early 1850s with the increase in transcontinental commerce (a subject to which we will turn in the following chapters), increasing numbers of businesswomen turned to the legal protection provided by formation of a partnership contract. Like the informal alliances created between business partners such as Gillam and Touchard or Fowler and Lawlor, legally enforced partnership agreements also multiplied the labor, capital, and skill available to women's enterprises. But partners bound by legal contract had the added benefit of shared legal and financial liability since they were accountable "severally and jointly" for all firm blunders. The law did not consider a partnership a single person, as in the case of the corporation, so forming a partnership contract did not provide the same financial and legal freedoms that incorporation provided. But since each partner was accountable for a firm's debts and legal contracts, entering into a partnership agreement assured that partners would share the burden of liability incurred during business.[86]

This could be an advantage or a disadvantage for businesswomen. For Miss May Thompson, a partnership with Mrs. Amalie Dannenberg had launched her career in 1873. After working several years as a saleswoman with S. Rosenblatt, she knew the Ladies Cloak business well and had many regular customers but no start-up capital to venture out on her own. The opportunity to enter into a partnership with Amalie Dannenberg, whose Ladies and Children's Clothing store drew the "cream of society," gave her the chance to publicize her skills in association with an already well-known name. Since the partnership was an expansion for Dannenberg, she demanded no financial investment on Thompson's part, relying instead on an interest in the profits that she expected the new line of cloaks would bring to the store. When Dannenberg withdrew from the firm two years later on account of ill health, Thompson continued the business under her own name and was still in business four years later, when she was listed in the 1879 directory. Dannenberg fared less well. Upon withdrawing from her partnership with Thompson, she "received oo for her interest," and creditors "refused to grant [her] a release from the liabilities" of the firm.[87]

But Amalie Dannenberg fared better than others. For Mrs. H. E. Booker, a retail fancy goods dealer in the early 1870s, partnership was ruinous. Her business failed after only two years, "owing to [the] bad management of a partner she then had." When credit reporters spoke to her four years later, she had recovered and was "doing [a] fair business," "manag[ing it] carefully," and upholding a "good reputation." But this time she was in business alone.[88] Booker's story underscores how important it was for businesswomen (and -men) to choose reliable, competent, and trustworthy partners, especially if they intended to entangle their fortunes through a partnership agreement. In San Francisco, where out-migration was especially high during the first thirty years after the gold rush, population turnover must have made it particularly difficult to determine whom one could trust as a business partner.[89]

By the early twentieth century, female partnerships were well represented among the northern California women who filed bankruptcy cases in the District Court. For example, four of the twenty-four cases filed by women in 1915, or one-sixth, involved business partnerships between two women. This does not necessarily mean that partnership agreements contributed to business failure, but it suggests that formalized business partnerships had become more and more common. This was very likely due to the fact that operating a small business had become too costly and complicated for many would-be proprietors to try alone, a subject that will be explored further in the next chapter.

Several of the cases also highlight how complex it was to extricate oneself from a partnership contract and how costly it was to defend one. Ethel Watson and Eva Applefield, for example, co-owners of the Oakland Song Shop, owed $60 to attorney J. Lawrence Jr. for dissolution of their partnership agreement. Bessie Newman and Doris Morley owed $165.28 for defending themselves and their partnership against litigation filed by the Retailers Credit Association of San Francisco.[90]

The expense and complication associated with partnerships help explain why, in spite of this start-up strategy's advantages, joining forces with another was not a worthwhile risk for most businesswomen. On the whole, San Francisco female proprietors were too cautious to enter into such alliances. In fact only 10 percent of those who appeared in the credit reports took on partners in order to launch their businesses. By contrast, this strategy was utilized far more often by small businessmen, 48 percent of whom created commercial partnerships.[91] For men who took on partners there may have been several advantages. First, as one scholar has demonstrated, partnership was often necessary to procure the assistance of a clerk, many of whom were sensitive about the "blot" of dependence associated with being an employee and thus agreed to take on the role only under the guise of becoming a partner in the business.[92] Greater access to credit was also a big attraction for men who took on partners.[93] For as one historian found, "merchant partnerships . . . were more likely to obtain a higher credit rating than were single proprietors."[94] But San Francisco's businessmen may also have been drawn to partnership to a larger degree than businesswomen because they were more comfortable with the idea of risk. Certainly turn-of-the-century definitions of American manhood celebrated the idea of fearlessness, encouraging men to take risks, including those financial risks associated with taking on a partner.[95] In contrast, one study has argued that late nineteenth- and early twentieth-century ideology "crippled [female] capitalists" by hounding and intimidating them into submission so as to "preserve" the financial markets for men.[96] This may have contributed to women's rejection of partnership. But practical economic factors alone explain this phenomenon. Male proprietors had so many economic advantages over women that they were in a better position to rebound from a partnership gone bad when necessary. For women, however, the risks of entering into a disadvantageous partnership and the potential legal battles over partnership dissolution added financial uncertainty and unpredictability to proprietorship, already an inherently insecure proposition. That was enough of a reason for most women to avoid partnerships altogether.

Thus while sharing the liabilities, costs, and responsibilities of business ownership with a partner lightened the load of starting up a new enterprise, when such alliances went sour they could send an otherwise successful proprietor into ruin. Because most businesswomen had few alternative options to fall back on, that was a risk they were unwilling to take. Once again, caution and practicality won out in the start-up strategies San Francisco women chose to embrace.

BUYING OUT OR TAKING OVER AN ESTABLISHED BUSINESS

This same risk aversion was precisely why women overwhelmingly tended toward buying out an established business as a start-up strategy. Unlike forming a partnership, taking over someone else's already successful enterprise gave a proprietor the advantage of a foundation on which to build. Careful examination of the previous owner's business performance might even enable a businesswoman to project costs and returns, mitigating some of the many risks first-time proprietors faced.

These advantages made buying out or taking over an already established business the most highly utilized start-up strategy for San Francisco businesswomen. Among those women business owners evaluated for credit during the 1870s by R. G. Dun & Company, some 16 percent "bought-out" a business, and another 18 percent "took one over." Thus one-third of San Francisco's female proprietors eschewed building a business from scratch, opting instead to "piggyback" their business careers on someone else's success.[97]

It was probably this inherent dependence on the previous owner that discouraged men from buying out or taking over an established business to the same degree as women. For while 34 percent of women chose this start-up strategy, a comparable sample of small businessmen in the R. G. Dun &

Company credit reports for the 1870s reveals that only 10 percent bought out or took over preowned businesses.[98] Given the American obsession with masculinity and independence at the end of the nineteenth and beginning of the twentieth centuries, perhaps this should not be surprising. For, as one historian argues, American middle-class men's "deepest concern was independence—to determine their own fate, achieve their own status, choose their own governors, exercise their own economic options."[99] Certainly building a business atop someone else's foundation of success might be interpreted as compromising a man's ability to "achieve his own status." Perhaps the added security that came with such a strategy was not worth the independence that a would-be owner was forced to give up.

Yet it was precisely this certainty that women—perpetually encouraged to be *dependent*—found attractive about buying out or taking over an already established business. In fact, this strategy was one of the easiest ways for a woman to enter into business for herself. Unlike women who put together their own enterprises piece by piece, those who took over someone else's could usually open for business right away. Those who "refitted" already established boardinghouses or stores stalled that process but nonetheless enjoyed several advantages over those who started from scratch. For when a woman took over someone else's enterprise, she acquired the business's physical location and its stock and fixtures as well as the previous proprietor's clientele, reputation, and recognition. For those who had no business experience or reputation of their own to rely on, it may have been an especially good tactic. One lump sum bought place, product, and patrons—assuring a first-time businesswoman a solid start.

Since San Francisco was in such flux during the 1850s and early 1860s, buying out an already established business was a particularly effective strategy in those early years. Because of its constantly changing structure and layout, the city lacked a numerical address system. Residents were obliged to describe their locations using street intersections and well-known neighbors. As late as 1866, for example, Miss Woods advertised the location of her dress and cloak-making business at the "corner of Clay and Kearny Streets, over Hinckley's Drug Store."[100] References to previous owners also helped businesswomen bring in customers. Here was the special advantage of taking over a preowned establishment. If a new owner kept the name and mentioned the previous owner, it helped her both to retain regular customers and to draw new customers to her business. Several examples make this point. Mrs. Bosley ran an ad in the paper on November 1, 1851, stating that she had just leased the Crescent House and was prepared to take in boarders. Madame Rosalie advertised on January 11, 1852, that she had "newly fitted up the Union

Restaurant." And Mrs. Eliza Beach announced on February 3, 1855, that she now managed the hotel "formerly occupied by Mrs. Haley." [101] Each of these three women made a point of advertising her business using the establishment's original name and/or owner. What all of them knew is that starting with a name that city residents recognized could make the difference between failure and success.

By the late 1860s, the process of buying and selling businesses became a business itself. Prior to this period, owners advertised their businesses themselves, and transactions occurred directly between buyers and sellers. When Mrs. Schaffer's Saloon was advertised for sale in the *Daily Alta California* in 1853, for example, interested parties were instructed to "apply on the premises." [102] But, like all other aspects of the business world, the process started to become an impersonal, rationalized, and managed business operation during the second half of the nineteenth century. [103] Agents took the place of business owners as the advertisers and became the go-betweens who executed the sale or lease. San Francisco newspapers aided them in this endeavor by creating a column entitled "Business Opportunities" for anyone advertising the sale of an established business.

By the 1870s, on any given day one might see some thirty to forty notices advertising small businesses for sale, with nearly all of them offered by business agents. Lines such as "For Sale At A Bargain—A News Depot, stationery, and fancy goods store," "Must Be Sold—A Candy and Fruit Store . . . for cheap," and "Restaurant For Sale . . . doing a business that cannot be beat," may have not only convinced already interested parties that entering into business for oneself was feasible, but might actually have planted the idea of proprietorship in the minds of some unsuspecting readers too. [104] For as little as $400 in 1870 one could purchase a cigar store "splendidly located and doing a fine trade," while $1,100 would buy "an old established millinery business situated on a prominent corner south of Market street [which] clear[ed] $150" (presumably per month). [105] Like franchise sellers in the nineteenth and twentieth centuries, these agents, whether appointed by court order or by the owner him- or herself, sold "the opportunity for business ownership," helping to democratize the field of small-business proprietorship. [106]

In some notices for business opportunities, agents appealed specifically to prospective female proprietors. For just $350, one ad offered "a chance for either a lady or gentleman to engage in a business paying large profits." As further inducement to female readers, who knew that the millinery industry was dominated by women proprietors and customers, the notice suggested that the business "would be splendid in connection with a millinery store." [107] Another ad claimed that "a man or woman with the above amount [$600] can buy a retail business that will realize them $100 each month, clear of expenses."[108] A third ad in 1869 read: "$3,000 — To Ladies Looking for Millinery Business — For sale, one of the handsomest millinery establishments in the city, beautifully fitted up; location cannot be surpassed: with splendid stock and a most extensive business of 12 years standing."[109] Clearly aimed at an elite audience, this ad targeted current or prospective female proprietors with significant money to invest and the credentials and experience required for operating such an exclusive establishment. In conjunction with the other ads discussed, it underscores the range of opportunities being presented to would-be businesswomen.

But how did a woman afford such an established business? As these ads indicate, by the 1870s it generally took anywhere from $300 to $3,000 to buy out a business.[110] Some of the women who took advantage of this strategy may have been from elite backgrounds with large savings or access to generous loans. Others who got started this way may have had help from friends and family. Mrs. Jane Thomas, for example, the purchaser of Mrs. Jeanie Evans's millinery business, was thought to have received assistance with the $1,500 purchase price of her business from her father.[111] But given the popularity of this start-up strategy, it is doubtful that only well-to-do women took advantage of it.

In fact, there is ample evidence that women arranged favorable terms that made buying out or taking over an established business more affordable than it might seem. One strategy evident as early as the 1850s and popular for decades after was the possibility of renting or leasing a business. Mrs. Clark's Boarding House, for example, was advertised for rent in February of 1854. Even the furnishings could be leased with the house if they went "to a good tenant."[112] Sixteen years later, Mrs. E. M. Gillan advertised herself as the "lessee" of Arlington House.[113] But renting or leasing was just one of several strategies that made starting with an established business affordable. Owners who were in a hurry to eliminate the costs of conducting business, often due to illness, were sometimes amenable to extremely favorable terms for new owners.[114] Mr. Wyman, for example, agreed to give Mrs. McLeod a share in the ownership of his boardinghouse in exchange for her agreement to take over the monthly rent.[115] Other business owners were willing to provide long-term payment arrangements for buyers. Miss F. W. Reed's purchase agreement, for example, required that she put down only one-half of the sale price for Mrs. G. W. M. Croles's millinery store and pay the balance in one year's time.[116] Such arrangements could make a purchaser vulnerable since she would be in long-term debt to the business's former owner. In at least two cases, this vulnerability resulted in forced sales back to the businesses' original owners.[117] But for most, long-term payment plans made otherwise impossible business careers possible. Imitating an increasingly popular trend in late nineteenth- and early twentieth-century America, female proprietors utilized installment buying to purchase expensive businesses, just as American consumers used the strategy to purchase big-ticket items such as sewing machines and ice boxes.[118] Of course, amassing just half of a $1,000 purchase price, as Reed did, would have taken even a highly paid worker, such as a milliner laboring in another woman's store, many years and much diligence to save up from her weekly wages.[119] Yet the plethora of advertisements announcing that women had "taken over," "newly fitted," or "bought out" an established business indicates that this was a popular start-up strategy among San Francisco women in spite of its costs.

The particular vulnerabilities of a few of the women who chose to get started this way suggest why: buying or taking over an already established business was the strategy used by women with the most at stake. Mrs. Jane Thomas, for example, mentioned above, was a divorcée who turned to the millinery business as an escape from a bad marriage. Even before the divorce she sued for in Contra Costa County in 1875 was granted, she had made arrangements to purchase the business of Jeanie Evans. Mrs. Thomas may have had only one shot at economic independence. Purchasing an already established business may have been the surest path available to financial stability if not success.[120] Similarly, forty-six-year-old widow Mrs. Josephine Martineaut had to find a way to support herself. In 1875, after working as a dressmaker and barely making a living for two years, she purchased the stock of Charles Komfeld's business for $3,000 and added corsets and costumes to the small clothing retail business that she ran out of her home.[121] Smart commercial decisions were crucial for widowed businesswomen. For, as one historian of widows in the West has found, "in the final analysis, the widow's or children's economic management skills during this time of crisis determined how wealth would sustain the family."[122] Thus, women such as Thomas and Martineaut had to get it right the first time—that is, they did not have the luxury to experiment. Formerly married women who now found themselves on their own, perhaps with children to support, they turned to the most reliable way of starting a business—buying out an established one.

Single women too relied on already established businesses, since they had no one to fall back on if their foray into proprietorship failed. For example, Miss F. W. Reed, discussed above, purchased an established millinery business and renamed it F. W. Reed & Co.[123] In another month, she reported, she would be joined by her sister, Miss E. L. Reed, who, though "not . . . a regular partner of hers," would "take up Dress Making in the same store."[124]

Should the two sisters fail in business, they probably would be forced to take jobs plying their trade as laborers for another, more-successful proprietor, so the added confidence they must have gained from buying an established business was worthwhile.[125]

Women new to San Francisco who were trying to find a way to support themselves also bought out experienced proprietors. When they arrived from Paris in 1874, for example, Mme. Cantel and her daughter succeeded Mme. Fleurier in her lace-cleaning and -mending business. Miss C. L. Woods, a "stranger" to both the city and the business of millinery, started her first independent enterprise by buying out Mrs. F. Wheelan in 1877.[126] Like divorced, widowed, and single women, those completely unfamiliar with San Francisco's business world who tried to support themselves as independent proprietors probably had one shot at success. They had saved up enough to make the trip to California and set themselves up in business but probably did not have the financial resources to rebound if their businesses failed early on. For them, starting a business was not a commercial experiment, it was an economic strategy—one designed to gain them a foothold in the new city. Staking their claim in the unfamiliar marketplace was easier when they could rely on the foundations that their experienced and successful female colleagues laid down before them.

The reasons why women sold their businesses underscore that security rather than bargain prices motivated female purchasers. Women who sold their businesses did so not when they were in peril, but when they were financially healthy and had the best chance of attracting a purchaser. Mrs. Amalie Dannenberg, for example, sold her ladies' and children's goods store in 1866 because she had met with considerable success and made enough money to retire to Europe temporarily.[127] Few other sales transactions were precipitated by such unusual success, but those occasioned by failure were even scarcer. When crisis loomed behind the sale of an established business it was usually personal, not commercial. Mrs. Schaffer's saloon, for example, went on sale in August 1853 due to the proprietor's ill health—a circumstance echoed many times over in advertisements for business sales throughout the 1870s.[128] Individual as well as epidemic illness was, in fact, a common problem for San Franciscans, who suffered through deadly outbreaks of cholera, smallpox, and bubonic plague during the late nineteenth and early twentieth centuries. As Chapter 6 details, such illnesses were the cause of failure for more than one business. But again, this did not mean that such businesses were unprofitable, but simply unmanageable for their sickly proprietors. Similarly, while Mrs. Meta Kuck may have viewed the Menlo Park store she advertised for sale in 1877 as a much-needed source of cash during the depression, she sold it "at a bargain" not because it was failing but "on account of closing up the estate of Diedrich Kuck, deceased."[129] Businesses like these sold because they were good investments, not because they were bankruptcy bargains. When one considers why women purchased already established businesses—the benefits of a good name and reputation, a secure clientele, and lower risk of failure—this makes sense. Buyers were not interested in risky investments but in the closest thing they could find to a "sure bet."[130]

This fact is underscored by the behavior of business sales during economic downturns. As the national depression spread to San Francisco in 1877, for example, the number of businesses for sale did not increase dramatically, as might be expected. Advertisements in the *Daily Alta California*, in fact, which had been so prevalent earlier in the decade, slowed down and eventually ceased.[131] Similar notices for "business opportunities" in the *San Francisco Chronicle* remained constant but distanced business owners from the depression by emphasizing that their enterprises were being sold for reasons other than economic difficulty. Statements such as "satisfactory reasons given for selling," "ill health of proprietor only reason for selling," "owner leaving state," and, "doing a good paying trade" assured potential customers that the business being sold was financially viable and was not being sold because it had been bankrupt by the depression.[132]

Thus while one might expect to see a rising number of distress sales during such periods of economic hardship, buyers for small businesses in times of crisis declined. Many scholars have observed that the number of small-business proprietors usually goes up during periods of economic depression because people are driven out of other, more-reliable jobs and because they need to supplement family income to buffer themselves against other losses.[133] But such individuals would likely have been even more interested than usual in financial predictability and would have been loath to purchase a failing business. The financial crunch that forced one proprietor to sell, in other words, warned others away from entangling themselves in risky commercial obligations. Since the women who typically bought out established businesses were in search of "sure bets," they would not have been interested in businesses forced into sale by economic difficulty.

Through the remainder of the nineteenth and beginning of the twentieth centuries, San Francisco newspapers continued to carry notices by business agents announcing small businesses for sale. The second national depression of the century, during the 1890s, seemed to hardly affect the San Francisco marketplace, since newspapers continued to be filled with benign business advertisements.[134] From the 1890s through the 1910s, headlines such as "$1,000 [for an] extra fine candy and stationary store" and "Lady with

$300 can buy half interest in fine paying confectionery factory [and] ice cream parlors" continued to try to entice men and women into the world of small-business proprietorship. Assurances of "a good cash business" and "trial given" emphasized the peculiar merits of a particular commercial opportunity and the ease with which a new proprietor might enter the business; some ads continued to target women as potential business owners.[135]

If anything had changed about the way women bought and sold businesses between the 1870s and 1920, it was that transactions were being made across the nation and thus required even more careful investigation to ensure their merits. For example, one *San Francisco Chronicle* ad read: "$500 to $5,000 capital: lady or gentleman with money can secure magnificent business in any city paying handsome profit. Address P.O. Box 28, Station D, New York."[136] Thus, even small-scale proprietorship had entered the modern world of business, tied to national markets and dependent on distant and professional relationships, in this case with a nameless, faceless business promoter in New York. Like wholesalers who had to rely on information provided by R. G. Dun & Company to determine safe credit risks, business sellers and purchasers depended on the judgment of middlemen and their own good instincts to sniff out trustworthy deals.

When these safeguards failed, savvy businesswomen turned to the courts to right their wrongs. On July 2, 1891, for example, the *San Francisco Chronicle* reported that "after a few minutes deliberation," the jury in the case of the *People v. Irene S. Cowles* "returned a verdict of acquittal." "This was an action charging Mrs. Cowles with fraud in selling a lodging-house," the newspaper continued, but "the evidence indicated that the complaining witness, Mrs. Josie Schultz, was using the criminal department of the Superior Court to effect a civil suit growing out of the same transaction."[137] Evidently Schultz felt that Cowles had deceived her when she purchased Cowles's San Francisco lodging house. Whether she had actually been swindled or somehow misled or had just made a poor purchase is impossible to tell. But it is clear that Schultz felt that an injustice had transpired, and she knew enough about the judicial system to try to seek redress through the courts.

Mrs. Dazet is yet another example of a woman who used the court system to protest a business buyout that went awry. When Margaret Ennis went bankrupt in February 1906, she owed Dazet $2,471.85. Though this sum was not specifically identified as payment for a business, Dazet was likely the original owner of the dry goods and clothing store that Ennis operated in Vallejo, northeast of San Francisco. For when Ennis's belongings were inventoried for auction, officials discovered that several items actually belonged to Dazet: two plate-glass mirrors, one marble table with four chairs, and one millinery showcase containing a wax form and fixtures. This suggests that the money Ennis owed Dazet was in fact the purchase price (or some portion of it) for the business, perhaps originally spread over one to two years. That Ennis's bankruptcy could erode Dazet's profit underscores the degree to which *selling* an established business could be financially risky as well. It also demonstrates that buyers were protected by bankruptcy laws—yet another reason, no doubt, that buying out an established business was a start-up strategy favored by first-time businesswomen.

But Dazet's response to the case against Ennis illustrates yet another point: the degree to which women were financially and legally savvy enough to know how to maneuver in such situations. In addition to reclaiming her belongings, Dazet was determined to recoup as much of the money Ennis owed her as possible. Her first move, hiring an attorney to represent her interests in the case, was sensible. But her second move was clever. She wrote a letter to the bankruptcy judge presiding in the case arguing that the bid received for Ennis's inventory was too low: "The stock is clean, up to date stock, the fixtures new, and should bring $2,000 or at least $1,800, and we do not think it should be sacrificed for $950. If the store was properly advertised we are sure it would bring a good price, especially now when dry goods are hard to get. We ask that the sale of the store will not take place for that price, also that the place be advertised in San Francisco papers."[138] In her assessment of the worth of the inventory, Dazet displayed a clear knowledge of the dry goods and clothing business, further indication that she was probably a former clothing store owner herself. But it is her marketing knowhow that is most impressive here. It was not just "proper advertising" that Dazet pushed, but where the advertisements were placed. San Francisco was, of course, a much larger marketplace than Vallejo, with many more potential buyers for the inventory. More importantly, however, by May 2, 1906, the date of Dazet's letter, San Francisco was a ruined city. The April 18th earthquake and fire had wiped out the central business district and most wholesale houses with it. What Dazet understood, therefore, is that Ennis's inventory would have been especially valuable to dry goods and clothing proprietors in San Francisco. Compared to the Vallejo merchants who bid on the merchandise April 16, two days before the earthquake, San Francisco's businessmen and -women may have been willing to pay a higher price for the stock, furniture, and fixtures that would have enabled them to get back on their feet commercially.

Dazet's commercial know-how reminds us that the motivation behind buying out a business was financial. Sellers such as Dazet sought to make money out of the transactions, and buyers such as Margaret Ennis hoped for reduced business risk. For some men, decreasing the gamble of starting a business may have seemed like a move away from the masculine independence they sought. But for San Francisco's businesswomen, such emotional considerations were foolhardy. For the women who utilized this start-up strategy to launch their business enterprises were motivated by the kind of economic autonomy that required caution.

Buying out or taking over an already established business, therefore, was the most used start-up strategy by San Francisco's female proprietors because it provided the most secure way to launch a new business. These women were practical and cautious, concerned about reducing cost and risk, and thus eager to avail themselves of those opportunities that provided them and their potential success the greatest protection. Building a business on the strong foundation of a previously successful proprietor fit the bill better than any other start-up strategy women utilized.

San Francisco's female proprietors met the challenges of starting a business by utilizing the most conservative approaches available to them. For most women, restricted by economic and legal limits from relying on credit or savings, their options were borrowing, creating partnerships, and buying out or taking over an already established business. In line with their cautious manner, businesswomen rejected costly institutional loans and, when borrowing, relied instead on the financial aid of family and friends. The choice reflected an overall preference for less-expensive and often (but not always) more-forgiving loan terms, contracted with whomever was willing to offer them, whether male or female. When it came to partnerships, which enabled a woman to share the costs and liabilities of starting a business with an associate, women relied on this approach in only limited numbers because of the potential risk it added should a proprietor be unfortunate enough to chose a bad partner. These decisions clearly demonstrate that women were motivated above all else by a desire to limit their costs and liabilities, so it is no surprise that the most commonly utilized start-up strategy was buying out or taking over an already established business. This approach enabled would-be businesswomen to build their new enterprises on the sound foundation established by a previous owner. In most cases they started with a place, a product, and patrons in addition to the already sound reputation of the previous proprietor. The advantages were attractive to female business owners because they ensured a stronger start and thus a greater chance at success.

San Francisco's female proprietors were practical and penny pinching because they had so much at stake. For many, one shot at business ownership was all they could afford, so they did everything they could to ensure that their start was a strong one. Thus adopting cautious start-up strategies was a sound decision, one that reflected smart instincts when it came to managing capital. This was a good thing, because those who stayed in business quickly learned that drawing customers would involve many more-extravagant investments than they may have thought necessary. For as the next chapter shows, San Francisco's residents were decidedly picky patrons.

CHAPTER 4

WHAT IT TOOK TO

DRAW CUSTOMERS

————— ❋ —————

Starting their businesses was only the first of several hurdles that San Francisco businesswomen confronted at the end of the nineteenth and beginning of the twentieth centuries. The next challenge was to attract customers or, in the popular parlance of the day, to draw "a share of public patronage."

At first, doing so was relatively simple. In the 1850s, women in San Francisco enjoyed automatic appeal among male customers eager to lay their eyes on a woman. Whatever service she provided—whether it was cooking, laundering, or selling provisions—was inherently valuable in the society of single and unattached men who peopled the city in its early days. This made drawing customers relatively easy. A woman might found a successful business utilizing little more than a board laid over two barrels where she could sell her homemade biscuit. But attracting public patronage became more difficult as the city and its environs matured beyond the haphazard days of the gold rush decade.

As San Francisco began to resemble sophisticated urban centers of the East in the 1860s, its customers expected more. Businesswomen now competed on equal ground with male business owners and faced the same challenges in the city's newly urbane marketplace. For the middle class in particular, purchases were motivated not by simple needs but by the ability of the proprietor to inspire consumers to buy. Key to this formula was the art of display, requiring businesswomen and -men alike to invest not just in the able dispensation of their service or craft but in presentation and marketing as well. By the 1870s, consumption was a class signifier, and for the fortunate, which retailer to patronize had less to do with quality and convenience and more to do with where an establishment was located and whether or not it had the trappings of gentility. The city's department stores were at the forefront of such changes; thus, the apparel, retail, and beauty industries, where some 46–48 percent of women operated their businesses, were among those most affected by the changing standards of the consumer marketplace.[1] Female proprietors struggled to keep up with these new standards, since doing so required the kind of capital outlay and credit that few could muster.

By the end of the nineteenth century, proprietors competing for the "best trade" were obliged to provide the "modern improvements" that well-to-do customers had come to expect. Though at first only the largest businesses were forced to cater to such expectations, by the beginning of the 1900s even smaller establishments could be found investing in expensive improvements. Accommodations, apparel, and retail businesses alike were forced to comply with these new standards if they wanted to compete with the multitude of other proprietors in the city.

Finally, by the twentieth century, the increasing complications of attracting San Francisco customers had also changed the way in which women advertised their businesses. Simple, unillustrated newspaper ads had given way to decorative business cards, professional advertising agencies, and direct mail campaigns.

While these changes did not alter the experiences of businesswomen in all fields evenly, probably affecting the proprietors of hotels and apparel and retail stores the most, they nonetheless set the course for small-business ownership into the twentieth century. A new breed of picky consumers had changed dramatically what it took to draw a share of public patronage. The stakes had been raised; if San Francisco women wanted to play the game, they would have to ante up.

THE APPEAL OF A WOMAN:
OPERATING A BUSINESS IN GOLD RUSH CALIFORNIA

When Luzena Stanley Wilson and her family lost all they had in the Sacramento flood of 1849, she bounced back quickly with a plan to start a hotel in nearby Grass Valley. "When I was left alone in the afternoon," she recalled, "I cast my thoughts about me for some plan to assist in the recuperation of the family finances. As always occurs to the mind of a woman, I thought of taking boarders." With two young children to care for and no capital to invest, Wilson found herself in the same circumstances as countless other women throughout the country. Domestic skills were one of the few assets she could cash in on, so taking in boarders seemed natural. There was already one hotel down the road but she was "determined to set up a rival."[2]

Drawing customers required very little. Wilson bought two boards, chopped stakes, and drove them into the ground. Once her table was set up, she bought provisions at the neighboring store and began preparing a meal on the stove she had brought with her from Sacramento. "When [her] husband came back at night, he found, mid the weird light of pine torches, twenty miners eating at [her] table." In time, the El Dorado, as Wilson called her establishment, lost much of its rugged homeyness, gaining walls, a floor, and a roof. She built additional rooms as business grew, until eventually the hotel served from 75 to 200 borders paying $25 per week for their meals.[3]

While the rudimentary preparations with which Wilson commenced business took place in a small town north of the city, many San Francisco proprietors began their enterprises in a similar way. In fact, throughout northern California the path to business proprietorship in the 1840s and 1850s was simple no matter whether one was a man or a woman. "Half the inhabitants kept stores[, and] a board laid across the head of a barrel answered for a counter."[4] New business establishments went up so quickly, in fact, that residents sometimes found it hard to recognize their neighborhoods. In a letter home, William Schooling described the speed with which the commercial landscape changed. "Yesterday we drove our teams into the streets about 9 o'clock in the morning," he wrote, "[and] they stood there perhaps two hours. We then turned them round and drove them into the shade. In the evening of the same day," he continued, "I passed along and on the very ground there stood a Baker's shop in full operation selling bread and receiving money for it!" The changes were so dramatic and rapid that Schooling seemed not to trust his visual impressions anymore, claiming that the scene around him was "more like a romance or dream than reality."[5]

But when Luzena Stanley Wilson struck gold running the El Dorado, her success exemplified more than just the proliferation of commercial opportunities in gold rush California. Wilson's profits grew directly from the fact that she was a woman in a state overwhelmingly populated by men. The gold rush drew thousands of men from around the United States and other countries who traveled alone to California seeking their fortunes. In 1850, 90 percent of California's population was male, and in the mining camps the percentage was probably even higher.[6] Ten years later the male-to-female ratio in San Francisco, the state's cosmopolitan center, was still 158:100, or 61 percent male.[7] Because most men had always been dependent on women to provide their domestic needs, they found women's absence a day-to-day hardship. The rarity of female proprietors such as Wilson inflated the market value of their skills and services.[8]

Thus, every time women sold their domestic skills, they capitalized on their minority status and wagered that the single and unattached men who populated the region would pay money for the types of services they had received for free in the homes they had left behind. Sometimes women did not even have time to realize the opportunity before them but were drawn into commercializing their domestic skills by eager men. Luzena Stanley Wilson recalled, for example, how she first realized her worth as a service provider in gold rush California: "One morning an official of the town stopped at my fire and said in his pompous way, 'Madame, I want a good substantial breakfast cooked by a woman.' I asked him what he would have and he gave his order, 'Two onions, two eggs, a beef-steak and a cup of coffee.' He ate it, thanked me, and gave me five dollars. The sum seems large now for such a meal, but then it was not much above cost, and if I had asked ten dollars he would have paid it."[9] By demanding "a good substantial breakfast cooked by a woman" and demonstrating a willingness to pay substantial money for it, this town official managed, in one fell stroke, to transform Wilson into an entrepreneur. For it was the interest in her cooking expressed by him and one other miner that inspired her dreams of riches and perhaps provided the inspiration for her to start the El Dorado a short time later.

Oftentimes there were practical motivations behind such offers for women's services. Most forty-niners had one thing on their minds when they arrived in California, and that was gold. All mundane daily tasks, such as setting up a place to live, preparing meals, and cleaning clothes, paled in importance to devoting every waking hour to mining. The miners seldom took time out of their daily work routines to wash their clothes, for example, preferring instead to pay local Mexican women or Chinese men to do it for them.[10] The opportunity to pay someone else to cook their meals was similarly attractive to many miners, since it freed them from the time-consuming task of starting a fire, preparing food, and cleaning up afterward. Pent-up demand for such services made the men and women who supplied laundry, food, boarding, and other goods and services valuable and enabled them to charge higher prices than they would have been able to otherwise.[11]

For some, the preference for women's services may have had to do with quality. When it came to cooking, in particular, women's skills and the food they prepared may have been preferable to that provided by camp mates. Given their traditional dependence on women to prepare their meals, it is not surprising that some men in the diggings "had trouble even lighting a fire,

[to] say nothing of preparing meals." But others, such as Henry Garrison, cooked so well that his tent companion, William Miller, looked forward to his cooking and remarked on it in his journal. One week of Garrison's meals included what Miller called "the Best Pudding I had Eaten Since Leaving home" and a "Beautiful Stew" of squirrel meat.[12]

But men who paid for women's cooking were usually in search of more than just a good meal; they were looking for female companionship. "The paucity of women along with cultural constructions of male needs and desires," one historian argues, "meant that, for many men, contact with women was at a premium."[13] One miner detailed the extensive list of homemade food served him by a rancher's wife but commented that the landlady was "the rarest dish."[14] Another reportedly dreamed about having food served to him by a pretty, young, white woman—a fantasy that no doubt had more to do with feasting his eyes on a female face and figure than it did with food.[15]

Danger as well as privilege accompanied this heterosexual and sexist obsession with women and their services. This was particularly true for non-white women, who were the most likely to work as prostitutes in gold rush California, providing sexual services to men in exchange for typically paltry sums. The Native American, Chinese, Hawaiian, Mexican, and African American women who dominated the profession "lived desperate lives that were shadowed by violence, disease, alcoholism, and crime."[16] This was particularly true for Chinese women who "arrived in San Francisco already indentured or enslaved" and thereafter lived life under the "strict surveillance and control" of Chinese tongs, or secret societies, for whom prostitution was an extremely profitable business.[17] But even women who were not prostitutes "did not fully control" their bodies. In gold rush California a woman's body "was the object of desire, not only of her lover(s), but the many who were not." This led to violent and tragic deaths for some women who themselves looked for companionship and security in their sexual liaisons with men but instead found deception and domination.[18]

Many men, however, were content with "proximity to women" and made their purchase decisions accordingly.[19] Encouraged by the middle-class domestic ideology of the day, such men conflated nourishment with nurture, cooking with companionship, and sought out women service providers when they could afford to do so. As the authors of the *Annals of San Francisco* reported in 1854: "Women were scarce in those days, and men were frequently willing to pay largely for the slight privilege of addressing one even in the way of business."[20]

In the eyes of many male residents, therefore, it was the emotional value of women's work that was so precious.[21] Women who sold boarding and cooking services provided a kind of "commercial domesticity" that substituted for the more-personal kind of domestic nurturing that most men received from their sisters, mothers, or wives. This meant that most men probably preferred to pay a woman of their same nationality, ethnicity, and/or race for such services, but historians have documented multiple examples of white men paying nonwhite women to prepare their food or launder their clothes. In the male-dominated mining camps of the early 1850s, men willingly crossed racial and social boundaries that they would have considered barriers in their home communities.[22] For, as one historian has argued, in the nineteenth century, "home was anywhere women and children were."[23] So when women wielded their domestic charms, even if it was on the kinds of rustic, commercial terms common in gold rush California, "they not only tended to miners' physical well-being but also to their emotional well-being by creating the illusion of home."[24]

Thus, a skillet, a stove, a needle, or a washboard—and a woman who knew how to use it—was all it seemed to take in the early 1850s to create a profitable business selling domestic services to gold rush men. That plus a little ingenuity and a lot of hard work made many women more money than they probably had ever imagined their skills worth. The story of one female baker provides a dramatic example. In a letter home written sometime before 1852, an anonymous woman wrote the following account:

> I have made about $18,000 worth of pies—about one third of this has been clear profit. One year I dragged my own wood off the mountains and chopped it, and I have never had so much as a child to take a step for me in this country. $11,000 I baked in one little iron skillet, a considerable portion by a campfire, without the shelter of a tree from the broiling sun. But now I have a good many "Robinson Crusoe" comforts about me . . . I bake about 1,200 pies per month and clear $200 . . . I intend to leave off work the coming spring, and give my business into the hands of my sister-in-law. Not that I am rich, but I need little, and have none to toil for but myself.[25]

This baker seems to have viewed her "little iron skillet" as a kind of simple revenue-generating device, so profitable was her primitive, campfire bakery. Her description of the profit, in fact, suggests that her business success was so great and so steady that she saw herself as a kind of aproned Midas. That is, anything she put into the skillet turned into money; it was that easy. In her recollection, she baked $11,000, not pies.

But despite the relative simplicity of making money selling pies to miners, what this emigrant's letter home also tells us is that she clearly did not consider her life as a baker easy. Dragging and chopping wood and baking over a campfire in the heat of a bright sun made her life physically difficult. Nor was she eager to continue the work once she had obtained certain "Robinson Crusoe comforts." This too was characteristic of early California businesses. They were simple to set up, and basic domestic skills could be made extremely profitable, but what it took to draw customers was, in fact, hard labor.

Though they needed little in the way of start-up costs or materials, gold rush establishments of all kinds were labor intensive and became successful only by dint of the hard work put into them by proprietors. This was especially true of women's businesses that were concentrated in the physically demanding lodging and restaurant industries. The story of Mary Ballou, a woman employed by a boardinghouse keeper in California in 1852, illustrates the work involved in keeping customers happy: "Sometimes I am washing and ironing, sometimes I am making mince pie and apple pie and squash pies . . . sometimes making coffee for the French people strong enough for any man to walk on that has Faith as Peter had . . . sometimes I am taking care of babies and nursing at the rate of Fifty Dollars a week but I would not advise any Lady to come out here and suffer the toil and fatigue that I have suffered for the sake of a little gold."[26] For Ballou, who did not own the boardinghouse in which she labored, the rewards she earned hardly justified the work required. Considering the primitive conditions in which most food preparation and other domestic tasks occurred during the first few years after the gold rush, her frustration and exhaustion is not surprising. "Large metal stoves of the kind common in Eastern homes after the 1830s were far too heavy to carry in a wagon or ship any considerable distance," writes one historian, so few if any made it to California at midcentury. Without such nineteenth-century kitchen technology, making pies enough for a house full of boarders was even harder work than usual. In all likelihood, Ballou, like other women in the new western United States "cooked in an open fireplace or over an outdoor campfire," a process that "entailed a good deal more dexterity than the pictures of rosy-checked pioneer mothers stirring up a tasty kettle of soup would imply."[27] Turning out mince, apple, and squash pies on a regular basis, therefore, was feat enough to exhaust and discourage many a laboring woman.

Though the financial rewards were potentially greater for the female *owners* of boardinghouses and related businesses, the work was just as difficult. Even women who bragged about monetary success in their journals and letters also commented on the physical hardships their work entailed. For example, Mary Jane Megquier, a boardinghouse keeper in San Francisco during the early 1850s, wrote: "I do not sit down until after eight o' clock at night and three nights out of a week I have to iron. I do not go to bed until midnight and often until two o'clock . . . I am in hopes to be able to write more when I get a negro to do my work."[28] Megquier may have been disappointed in this respect, since African American cooks reportedly earned as much as $125 per month in San Francisco, more than ten times what black domestic workers made in Georgia at the turn of the century. Even servant women in San Francisco took in between $50 and $70 per month, ten times what they made in New York City.[29] But Megquier's fatigue was palpable. Chastina Rix too looked forward to the day when her long hours of labor would end. Her diary entry on September 1, 1853, read: "Ironing. I have to work pretty hard. Have seven in the family [including boarders] most of the time. I hope I shall not always have to work so hard."[30] Like Megquier, she worked at keeping boarders only as long as financial circumstances required. Even Luzena Stanley Wilson "retired from active business in the kitchen" at El Dorado as soon as she had the luxury of hiring a cook and waiters, although she continued working as "managing housekeeper."[31]

The point, therefore, is that while setting up a profitable business might be as simple as laying a board across two barrels and calling it a store or building a campfire and calling it a bakery, women's enterprises typically required grueling work to keep customers satisfied. Selling one's cooking, sewing, homemaking, or other skills for profit in the mid-nineteenth century multiplied the many domestic challenges that women faced in "frontier" households all over the West and was supremely difficult work.[32] In fact, for women, getting started was very likely the only easy part of operating a business in gold rush California.

Keeping customers coming in the door required long hours of intensely physical labor, yet, compared to what was to come, consumer demands were straightforward. Early San Francisco men wanted to be housed, fed, and clothed by women. What they longed for was what Mark Twain called "the score of little unclassifiable tricks and touches that a woman's hand distributes about a home, which one sees without knowing he sees them, yet would miss in a moment if they were taken away."[33]

CATERING TO CUSTOMER PRETENSIONS

Starting in the 1850s, the gold rush depot, where fly-by-night business ventures popped up on every street, began to change into the nineteenth-century commercial hub commemorated in numerous literary and journalistic accounts as the new "city on a hill." Thousands of tents pitched in Happy Valley by the most eager new residents in 1849 were soon replaced by more-permanent wooden structures containing lodging houses, restaurants, and sources of entertainment. Along the southeastern edge of the peninsula, sand dunes gave way to Market Street, site of the first horse-drawn railcar line a decade later and still San Francisco's central thoroughfare.[34] By 1860 the city's homes were equipped with gaslight fixtures and running water, and one year later, residents could make use of the transcontinental telegraph to wire business and personal information to colleagues, family, and friends around the country. All these developments prompted one 1865 visitor to comment that the city "look[ed] and seem[ed] very city-like, like Providence, for instance, but very unlike New York"; she was, she admitted, "very favorably impressed."[35]

What this meant for would-be female proprietors was that launching a small-business establishment and drawing a steady stream of customers ceased being such a straightforward task. As soon as San Francisco started to look like established eastern cities, commerce there began to resemble the more-complicated web of transactions that characterized the economy of its more-mature East Coast cousins. Real estate and rental prices in the city surged in the 1850s, making the procurement of a business location both more complicated and more costly.[36] Finally, enterprising women enticed by the "early illusion of making a quick fortune" saw those flush times vanish "in the face of disastrous economic conditions in the years immediately following the boom" of the early 1850s.[37] Once a remarkably easy place for a woman to operate a simple but successful small business, San Francisco had become a city, like so many others in the country, where commercial enterprise was increasingly costly and complicated and customers were demanding.

In particular, as San Francisco came to resemble large East Coast cities and embrace urban ways, its residents adopted "big city" airs and looked to proprietors to satisfy their newfound interest in urbane sophistication and opulence. Gold rushers previously accustomed to spending their money at haphazard, overnight successes such as Wilson's El Dorado Hotel now sought more-established and refined settings. The bigger and more elaborate, it seemed, the better.

Madame Mondelet's restaurant business is a good example of such an establishment. She entered into the fray in 1853 with a "new and elegant Coffee Saloon" where "ladies and gentlemen [would find] . . . all the luxuries of the most delicate taste." She banked on the ubiquitous appeal of all things French for San Franciscans and modeled her Cafe du Commerce after "the coffee saloons in Paris." In addition to cold and warm breakfasts and light broths and soups for supper, "all descriptions of ice cream" were available. An adjoining room housed two billiard tables where patrons could sip "Cognac de Sazerae of 1795," a well-known eighteenth-century French brandy that the cafe would "have constantly on hand." The opulence that Mondelet created in the Cafe du Commerce must have been in high demand. Nine months later she moved the business to a "magnificent building" on Postsmouth Square, expanding it into a restaurant with "private saloons on the second story," a "fresh oyster saloon," and facilities for balls, parties, and banquets. The grand opening was celebrated with a "Grand Dress and Masquerade Ball" to which ladies were admitted gratis and gentlemen for $5.[38] Mondelet's was no board-and-stake dining table experience like the one provided by Luzena Stanley Wilson at the El Dorado. Nor was its selling point a warm meal cooked by a woman. Cafe du Commerce sold sophistication, elegance, and exoticism. The fact that the café was run by a woman probably had less appeal than the fact that it was run by a *French* woman with the help of her French husband — an automatic badge of distinction in the minds of most San Franciscans.[39]

What Madame Mondelet's Cafe du Commerce makes clear is that during the 1850s, San Franciscans began to expect more. That she noted her restaurant's move to Portsmouth Square, "center of the city's casino life," underscores the significance of location and the fact that for the city's proprietors, certain parts of the city were more desirable then others, though which ones depended on the kind of business one operated.[40] In addition, Mondelet's announcement that the Cafe du Commerce would reopen in a "magnificent building" demonstrates the growing importance of first impressions and grand appearances in drawing customers. In this case, what made the building grand must, at least in part, have been its size, since it was two stories high and large enough to house both private saloons and facilities for balls and parties. Also clear is that by 1853 San Franciscans expected the accoutrements of East Coast cities and that the costs involved in providing them were deemed worthwhile investments by proprietors. Mondelet specifically celebrated the fact that the café would contain two billiard tables — large and expensive pieces of furniture to acquire in a city that did not have its first billiard-table manufacturing firm until two years later.[41] She must have arranged for the importation of both tables from a local merchant with distant connections. Finally, San Franciscans' tastes had clearly matured beyond skillet pies and campfire biscuits. To draw a steady stream of the sort of high-rollers they hoped to attract, the Mondelets promised a constant supply of both imported French brandy and fresh oysters. Though oysters were widely available, maintaining a constant supply of French brandy may have involved special relationships with city Frenchmen or overseas merchants, since "Cognac de Sazerae of 1795" was not produced domestically.[42]

By the mid-1850s, San Franciscans' taste for the elaborate, the elegant, and the eccentric had a broad impact on the city's suppliers. Small-scale, simple enterprises were not entirely replaced by establishments like the Cafe du Commerce. Women continued to rent out rooms in their homes to boarders, to take in sewing and washing for a fee, and even to run grocery stores out of the front rooms of their houses. But the new trend toward increasingly extravagant establishments such as Madame Mondelet's raised the bar for proprietors, making the costs and complications of attracting customers much greater. San Francisco customers now expected more than just comfort and quality and demanded instead that proprietors treat them like the cosmopolites they considered themselves to be. In response, a growing contingent of small-business owners engaged in the game of "one-upmanship" to draw a share of patronage from this newly urbane clientele.[43] San Francisco women considering proprietorship now had to plan several steps beyond securing a location and providing basic goods and services. They had to figure out how to keep up with and distinguish themselves from their commercial neighbors if they wanted to win any favor with the city's decidedly picky public. As a result, boardinghouses needed to be well situated *and* "elegantly furnished," dressmaking and millinery services had to be provided "on the most reasonable terms" *and* according to "the latest Parisian fashions," and restaurants and saloons were obliged to provide imported liquors, champagne, and cigars *and* fresh oyster bars.[44]

Such elaborate and expensive consumer tastes were no doubt fueled by the prosperity that San Franciscans enjoyed during the Civil War period. Isolated geographically from the battle front, the city faced none of the economic dislocations that eastern cities suffered and won the trade in agricultural products that Britain and others had previously placed through East Coast ports. At the same time, San Francisco was for the first time cut off from many of its suppliers, inspiring investment in the local manufacture of all sorts of new products and stimulating the creation of many new jobs.[45] Such prosperity during the 1860s made it possible for customers to splurge on niceties rather than necessities and made it impossible for proprietors to ignore their demands for fashionable and fancy places to spend money.[46] By the end of the decade, San Francisco had earned designation as "the Paris of America," cementing its destiny as a city of sophisticated tastes and tony stores, restaurants, and hotels.[47]

The city's growing sophistication was also reflected in businesswomen's advertisements. In the 1850s they tended to be simple and straightforward announcements of inventories and services. For example, Mrs. Johnson's 1852 ad for her store on Sacramento Street simply listed the twenty-odd items of children's and women's apparel that she had just received. Though she assured customers that it was a "splendid assortment," Johnson provided little else in the way of inducement; the point of the ad, is seems, was informational rather than inspirational.[48] Similarly, Mrs. E. Gerish's 1851 ad "respectfully inform[ed] her customers" that she had opened a millinery and dry goods store, where she would "be able to furnish every thing in her line to ladies on the most reasonable terms."[49] Though not as simple as a list of her inventory, Gerish's ad attempted to draw customers by promising "reasonable terms." Price, like product, was front and center in the simple ads of the 1850s. A final ingredient in businesswomen's ads during the decade was the draw of professional experience. The ad run by Mrs. C. Pierson, a national and fancy flag maker, is a good example. "Having been for a number of years extensively engaged in the above business in the city of New York," she announced, she was now prepared to take orders for all manner of flags and regalia in San Francisco.[50] Professional experience, price, and product, therefore, were the main attractions in the newspaper ads of the 1850s. Like the information such ads contained, their graphics were simple and straightforward, with little in the way of illustration or even artful design or formatting.

In contrast to the simple text messages described above, the ads that female proprietors placed in San Francisco newspapers during the 1860s demonstrated a sense of panache that underscores their growing appreciation for the need to market their businesses to customers. Mrs. E. Morris's advertisement in 1865 is a good example:

The Best Fitting Shirt at
   Mrs. E. Morris
No. 126 Kearny street.
Bet. Sutter and Post
   The Neatest Made
Shirt and Collar at
   Mrs. E. Morris
No. 126 Kearny Street.
   The Handsomest
Style Shirt at
   Mrs. W. Piper,
Formerly Mrs. E. Morris,
   No. 126 Kearny street.[51]

Text-wise, the first noticeable difference between this ad and those 1850s ads discussed above, is its use of multiple adjectives. "Best Fitting," "Neatest Made," and "Handsomest" together suggest that this ad is rhetorical, not just informational — meant to convince customers to utilize this businesswoman's services and to distinguish her from her competitors. Also new here is the use of repetition, both of Morris's name and her address, intended to help the pertinent details lodge in readers' minds and perhaps inspire gentlemen to make an impromptu stop at 126 Kearny Street on their way home from work. One might wonder why "Mrs. W. Piper," evidently the new name of the establishment and therefore the one that customers really needed to remember, is not repeated. For this message—her name change—she relies on layout rather than repetition. This is the aspect of the ad that stands out most: the way its design highlights key points, with the business's name and address as well as two superlatives aligned in the right-hand column. Certainly designed to be eye-catching, the advertisement made effective use of language as well as layout to draw a share of public patronage from San Francisco's increasingly sophisticated and picky consumers.[52]

While not all proprietors suddenly displayed such marketing savvy in their advertisements, those who did were participating in an advertising revolution that by the turn of the century had changed the face of urban American newspapers substantially. "Advertisements grew in size, and their use of white space embraced new design principles." In addition, their purpose changed. Whereas before, the "closely packed small ads" (resembling modern classified advertising) were meant simply to provide information about the goods and services available, the catchier ads that predominated by the beginning of the twentieth century were meant "to influence." That is, their purpose was to convince buyers to purchase—regardless of their needs.[53] The changes certainly indicate that a shift in commercial expectations had permeated the world of female business owners, pushing them to pursue rather than simply serve their customers.

LOCATION, LOCATION, LOCATION

Location held some value for San Francisco proprietors concerned about how best to draw customers to their establishments from the beginning. Luzena Stanley Wilson, for example, paid someone to take her from Sacramento to Grass Valley to start her hotel business. She was probably motivated by the small town's gender imbalance and focus on mining, which together created a greater market for women's domestic services than existed in large cities. Similarly, Madame Mondelet moved her café, bar, and billiards room to Portsmouth Square in 1854 because, as the center of the gambling industry in San Francisco, it offered the best opportunity to draw customers in search of a good time. Location mattered to many other female proprietors in the 1850s who, as discussed in Chapter 3, bought out established businesses and included the names of previous owners in their ads because it helped customers find their establishments in a city still devoid of a reliable numerical address system.

As female proprietors were forced to cater to customers' increasing pretensions, however, location took on new importance. Indeed, by the 1860s, the introduction of the cable car helped make Market Street the primary transportation artery of the city. To the south of this east-west trajectory lay the working-class haunts of countless San Francisco laborers and their families, while to the north lay the tonier homes of the city's wealthy. Such class distinctions were made even clearer by the construction of the railroad barons' mansions on Nob Hill, north of "the strip," once the transcontinental railroad was completed in 1869. Thus, the "fashionable thoroughfares" were Kearny and Montgomery Streets, both of which jutted up from Market, toward the homes of the city's wealthy residents. Businesswomen aspired to locations on one of these two streets, but only those with considerable capital or access to generous loans could afford to pay for the exposure they would get from such a location. As contemporary observer Benjamin E. Lloyd wrote, "A fashionable thoroughfare makes valuable property, and valuable property calls for high rents." In turn, customers who shopped on these exclusive avenues paid a pretty penny for their purchases. Merchants located on Market or nearby Third Street (Kearny Street below Market), instead paid lower rents and charged lower prices, drawing the patronage of laborers and mechanics who generally did their shopping after dark when the work day had come to a close.[54] Thus a woman's business location signaled the type of customer she hoped to draw and, to a significant degree, predicted the level of income she could earn. This must be why creditor reports were, as one scholar has found, "quite sensitive to the location of a business."[55]

Yet what was exclusive even about Market and Third Streets was that they were located in the primary commercial district of the city. As the map in Chapter 1 shows, Kearny, Montgomery, Second, and Third Streets all crossed Market at the center of the city, forming a highly contained zone of business enterprise. By the 1870s, this was the most desirable commercial location in the city, particularly for those who operated businesses in the apparel trades and certain types of retail. Remarkably, 40 to 70 percent of all female retailers in cloaks and suits, clothing, ladies' furnishings, human hair pieces, hair jewelry, and millinery goods and services were located on one of these five streets in 1878 (see table A12).[56] This trend suggests that location had everything to do with public image in the commercial world of fashion, and therefore everything to do with public patronage. As a result, businesswomen who could afford to invested considerable capital in procuring one of the coveted spots in the city's central commercial district.[57]

In businesses where women proprietors competed with a male majority, they appear to have been less able to procure such choice spots. Only 20 percent of female fancy goods retailers and 10 percent of female dry goods retailers had stores located on Kearny, Montgomery, Market, Second, or Third Streets. By contrast, approximately 50 percent of all male proprietors in both fields made it to the city center with their retail establishments. Both industries were dominated by men—65 percent in fancy goods and 85 percent in dry goods—who seemed to have had greater access to the capital required to start a business on the expensive but fashionable thoroughfares.[58]

The emphasis on location is evident in the business career of Mrs. Eva Goldstein, who sold ladies' and children's wear in the city from 1868 until 1879. Initially, she opened her business "in a very small way" on Second Street. But she "made headway fast" and in 1875 moved a few blocks across Market to 120 Kearny Street—one of the "fashionable thoroughfares"—near the outer limits of the central commercial district. The store size and customer traffic enabled her to carry a regular stock of clothing worth about $5,000. She did "a fair business on small expenses" and was "believed to be steadily gaining in a small way." One year later she announced her intention to move to a "much larger store near Sutter," where she intended to carry stock worth $15,000 to $20,000. Since Sutter Street crossed Kearny and Montgomery just before they intersected Market, the move would have put her in the commercial heart of the city. Nonetheless, the expansion and expensive move were risky, and her credit evaluator that year claimed "the trade generally considers that she is acting very unwisely in making the changes." While her expenses were light in the first two locations, in the new store rent would cost $500 per month, and all other expenses would be proportionally larger. Undeterred by dire predictions, however, Goldstein relocated to the city's core mercantile location. One year later, in 1877, credit reporters recorded: "Is in bankruptcy." Ducking creditors, she continued to conduct business in her son's name at 206 Kearny. By 1878 she was listed in the directory again as Goldstein, proprietor of an apparel business located at 130 Kearny and a ladies' furnishings business at 18 Kearny. Whether her business was going to live or die, Eva Goldstein seemed determined that it would happen on Kearny Street.[59]

Of course not all women located their businesses along the city's "fashionable thoroughfares." City-center businesses, in fact, were only one of "two distinct types of female petty entrepreneur geography." The other type was the neighborhood grocery, laundry, retail store, or restaurant located in one of the residential areas of the city in which female business owners and their customers "related to each other not simply on commercial terms but as neighbors, co-ethnics, and often as kin."[60] These widely dispersed shops, very often the combined living and working spaces of their proprietors' families, drew daily traffic from neighborhood residents. Customers stopped on their way to work to drop off dirty clothes, on the way home to get a drink or a bite to eat, and on the weekends to purchase ingredients for the Sunday stew. The female proprietors of such establishments likely knew not just the names of their customers but also the names of their customers' children, and may have even worshiped at the same church or contributed to the same mutual aid society. These neighborhood enterprises were an essential part of the fabric out of which city residents wove their own enclaves along ethnic, racial, and class lines.

This was particularly true for the Irish, who by 1880 dominated the city's primarily working-class neighborhood south of Market Street. Proximity to industrial jobs as well as affordable housing and domestic services drew immigrant men to the neighborhood. According to one study, "forty to fifty percent of the population [there] was of Irish parentage compared to ten to twenty percent north of Market."[61] Since the Irish showed a distinct preference for patronizing Irish-owned establishments, female proprietors there found an abundance of commercial opportunities. This was especially true in the boarding business, since almost 50 percent of first-generation Irish men and almost 25 percent of second-generation Irish men were boarders or lodgers.[62] Irish boardinghouse keepers such as Mrs. A. O'Brien, who operated an establishment at 630 Mission, and Mary O'Connor, who operated one at 115 First, capitalized on this, helping to make the South of Market region, known to city dwellers as the Seventh Ward, home to the majority of the city's accommodations businesses during the 1870s.[63] Since the South of Market neighborhood housed a significant proportion of all city residents, especially the working class, at the end of the nineteenth century, it is not surprising that many neighborhood shops were also located there. For example, according to the city directory for 1877/78, 53 percent of all female-owned bakeries were located on one of the streets south of Market.[64]

This differentiation between the central business district stores of middle-class, primarily native-born white women and the working-class neighborhood shops and boardinghouses of immigrant women underscores the degree to which class circumscribed the geography of female petty proprietorship. As one historian has argued, the "power women had to shape the city to their ends was limited and affected by class, race, ethnicity and geography."[65] Thus Market Street was not just the central artery of the city but also the dividing line demarcating the status of San Francisco's female proprietors and their clientele. Eventually residents would settle in more far-flung sections of the city, drawing women's businesses to new neighborhoods and secondary "main streets." But class would continue to determine where women operated their businesses.

Comparatively speaking, race never dissected the city the way that class did. African American and Chinese business owners could be found throughout the city. This was different than other late nineteenth-century cities such as New York or Chicago, where black residents and their economic enterprises "concentrated in one area like Harlem or Chicago's South Side." On the one hand this bespoke an openness to nonwhites uncharacteristic of cities further east. For example, few African American proprietors elsewhere were able to locate their businesses near the heart of the central commercial district, but that is precisely what the proprietors of the Harper and West Boarding House, a "colored" establishment at the corner of Kearny and Clay Streets, did.[66] On the other hand, as one scholar argues, "the physical dispersal" of African Americans throughout the city "made it difficult for small shops to monopolize the Negro trade." This in combination with the fact that many black city residents "chose to spend their money in non-Black establishments" meant that the city boasted fewer black-owned businesses than other cities with comparable African American populations at the end of the 1800s.[67] Those that did exist depended on the patronage of white customers to stay afloat. Business dispersal throughout the city could be a liability for other reasons as well. As one historian argues, because Chinese laundries were spread throughout white commercial and residential neighborhoods in San Francisco they were perceived as "infiltrators" and became the focus of the city's first anti-Chinese laws.[68] Nonetheless, the persistence of Chinese laundries in spite of these laws underscores the degree to which white San Franciscans did patronize these businesses. Thus while class could be a powerful predictor of location for the city's female proprietors, race did not have the same influence on commercial geography in San Francisco. Women business owners found this could be more of a setback than an advantage, since it meant they could not rely on the neighborly network of customers that sustained enterprises in densely populated immigrant neighborhoods such as the South of Market district.

THE ART OF DISPLAY

After 1870, the number of small commercial establishments grew dramatically in San Francisco, adding competition to the list of concerns that female proprietors in the city had to contend with in order to draw a share of public patronage. Between 1872 and 1877, for example, fancy goods retailers more than doubled, while grocers and dry goods retailers grew 64 and 41 percent, respectively.[69] Competition between this growing number of proprietors was probably all the more intense during the 1870s because of the depression plaguing the nation. As discussed in Chapter 2, instead of reducing the number of proprietors, the economic slump increased the number of women whose families relied on their ability to provide a decent income while at the same time fulfilling their domestic obligations.

Competition came from outside the world of small-business proprietorship as well. For at the same time that small-business ownership in the city was expanding, the establishments that would soon rise to preeminence as the city's first department-store-size retailers—Golden Rule Bazaar (which later became the Emporium), the City of Paris, I. Magnin, and Gump's— were being formed. By 1880 they had, in fact, established a stranglehold on downtown retailing.[70] Thus, as one scholar writes, "after 1870 the small grocery stores and the one-man shops were having to compete with the larger and more-efficient retail stores and also faced intense competition within their own ranks."[71] Coupled with the severe economic depression that hit San Francisco between 1876 and 1878,[72] sending the disposable incomes of working residents plummeting, this meant that an increasing number of small-business proprietors had to compete for a decreasing number of consumer dollars.[73] This increased competition meant that proprietors had to find ways to distinguish their businesses from the multitude of others in the city offering the same goods and services.

Because of the growing popularity of department stores—characterized by lavish displays of almost any product a customer might desire—one change that many small-business owners started to embrace by the last quarter of the nineteenth century was an increased attention to display. In San Francisco, where retail giants Gump's, I. Magnin, and City of Paris catered to exclusive tastes with expensive "orientalia," "exquisite lingerie," and French imports, emotional impact was what selling was all about, and artful presentation of such products was supremely important in achieving the desired effect. Though retailers nationwide did not embrace the "art" of display until the 1880s, the trend clearly began much earlier in San Francisco.[74]

Indeed, investing in interior display and design was a priority second only to location for any woman who wanted to attract a steady stream of "respectable" customers in 1870s San Francisco. Mrs. M. E. Doherty, for example, must have launched her business with this in mind. When she opened Mrs. Doherty's Hair Shop in 1867, she chose a location on Market Street just a few blocks west of Kearny. The store was big enough for her to carry $1,500 worth of hairpieces and still have room to add a millinery department five years after opening. What is remarkable about Doherty's business, however, is not her location or the size of her stock, but the amount of furniture and fixtures that filled her store. Records show that by 1871 she had amassed over $2,000 worth of furnishings. The fact that her husband had formerly been a furniture dealer probably had a lot to do with this accumulation, but the pieces were no doubt meant to attract customers to her store by presenting a refined setting for her products. Interior design may have been particularly important in a millinery and hair products store, where the simple white forms used to model hats and hairpieces took little room and added little elegance to an establishment's appeal.[75] Figuring out how to create an inviting interior was especially important among those apparel and retail establishments hoping to draw customers away from the increasingly spectacular department stores beginning to inhabit the city's central shopping district.

Competing with the architectural drama and merchandise excess of department stores required female proprietors to invest not just in lavish interiors but also in window displays. For it was through these, after all, that customers' first impression of a business would be formed. Whether or not to enter a small-scale establishment rather than a department store, or one establishment rather than another, was a consumer decision most likely based on the store's sidewalk appeal. Thus by the 1870s plate-glass windows dressed to lure customers into downtown stores were widespread along Montgomery and Kearny Streets, the fashionable thoroughfares of the city.[76] As Benjamin Lloyd observed,

> Each store of any pretensions has its broad plate-glass display window, and also a particular artist to decorate it. . . . About the principal dry-goods houses there is constantly a throng of curious persons, gazing with much interest at the beautiful fabrics that deck the windows. Everything is arranged for effect. . . . The windows of the notion stores are a scene of harmonious confusion. . . . The mantua-makers and milliners turn the heads of the ladies by the tempting suits or bonnets they show; and the ringlets, curls, and silken tresses that ornament the chalk craniums at the hair stores are objects of their admiration. The hatter, the toy-dealer, the druggist, the florist, the clothier, and the grocer, all vie with each other in style of display. . . . [It is] an ever-changing panorama of marketable commodities. . . in all its varied splendor.[77]

Merchandising in San Francisco had been elevated to a fine art by the 1870s—as befitted the Paris of America. It was no longer as simple as carrying an array of stock, and it did not seem to be enough for a craftsperson to ply her trade well. Drawing a share of customers now meant investing in presentation.

Even small stores had adopted the practice by the end of the century. As one scholar argues, "after technological improvements cheapened plate glass in the mid-1890s, even small stores had display space visible from the street."[78]

Widespread by the turn of the twentieth century, such window displays added a visibly more-complicated face to the job of customer satisfaction. The large-scale retailers continued to set the standard, giving attention even to ready-to-wear men's clothing, hats, and shoes (visually much less interesting than the colorful feather-, lace-, and ribbon-adorned garments of women and children). This "new emphasis on display unleashed economic pressures that few female proprietors could meet." And since the department store "achieved its greatest fame as a showcase for feminine finery," its impact was greatest on the female purveyors of women's apparel. Keeping up and or competing with retail giants on this front must have been impossible for most. Female proprietors operating modest neighborhood shops probably rejected such pretensions and bet on customer loyalty for their survival.[79] But women who aimed to draw the choicest customers into their expensive downtown stores competed directly with the larger stores and could not afford to ignore new merchandising trends. For these female business owners, staying in the game required that they comply with the new standards and expectations for investing in the art of display.

Once the mass retailers of brand-name products began investing in promotion at the end of the 1800s, display became important even to small-scale grocery retailers. As with the influence of department stores, this was a nationwide trend that impacted male and female owners of small businesses equally. How to utilize window display space was not a question that the manufacturers of Quaker Oats or Ivory Soap left up to the owners of the thousands of small neighborhood stores that continued to sell the majority of Americans their groceries.[80] Instead, "manufacturers hired designers to help retailers use that space." Payment arrangements for window displays varied. Companies such as Nabisco provided the "three-dimensional cardboard replica of its factory, with Niagara Falls and a field of grain in the background," for free. Other manufacturers paid retailers for display space. Such dealer "helps" were so ubiquitous that most retailers "threw out more . . . than they used."[81] By 1900 San Francisco's female grocers came from all ethnicities and could be found throughout the city. But because they comprised less than 10 percent of the field, they may have had to work especially hard to compete with their many male competitors as well as with the increasingly popular chain stores encroaching on their territory.[82] What this meant is that as soon as small businessmen in the field capitulated to the demands of mass retailers then women would have to, too. Whereas neighborhood stores selling apparel, toys, or stationery had several more decades before they would be beholden to the manufacturers of brand-name products, grocers already faced that challenge at the end of the nineteenth century. This meant that brand loyalty trumped customer loyalty even for those retailers who enjoyed friendly neighborhood and ethnic ties with the people who patronized their stores. As a result, grocery retailers were forced to carry the brands Americans came to expect and to display them prominently in their windows and on their shop floors to draw traffic. That this trend was complete in the San Francisco area by the early 1900s is made clear in the inventory of Cora Buck, a bankrupt general store owner, whose shelves were filled with Campbell's soup, Niagara corn starch, Shredded Wheat cereal, and Electric Spark soap when she went out of business.[83]

By the end of the nineteenth century, the art of display had permeated even the way in which women marketed their businesses in print. In addition to investing in more-sophisticated newspaper advertisements to draw customers, as discussed above, female proprietors began to rely on "trade cards" to circulate information about their businesses. Mrs. Mish's trade card, shown here, is a good example. Though it simply provided her name and the name and address of her 1890s business — "Bon Ton Millinery, 133 Kearny St" — it displayed this information on a card illustrated with a fanciful drawing of two cherubs fishing from lily pads.[84] The image seems to have had no particular relevance to a millinery business. Most likely the popular iconography was meant to encourage the recipient to display the card in her home or perhaps even to trade the card — as the nineteenth-century name for business cards implies — for one she had not yet collected, "a popular hobby during the 1880s and early 1890s."[85] The smudged writing on this card underscores the degree to which trade-card printing could be an informal endeavor in which proprietors might have simply stamped their business information on a preprinted card, as Mish appears to have done. Presumably this was a less-expensive way to produce cards than paying a printer to manufacture them. Though women business owners also utilized this latter strategy, many must have been forced to economize on such business expenses because of their low capitalization.[86]

Even more elaborate was the trade card of Mrs. Lester & Crawford, "dealers in Millinery and Fancy Goods" in Nevada City, California, no doubt illustrating a trend that was also popular in San Francisco.[87] While the back of the card featured a list of the types of goods and services offered at the establishment, similar to simple newspaper advertisements during the nineteenth century, the front of the card was a spectacular example of the art of display. The eight-and-a-half inch cut-out featured an elaborately dressed woman at

Mrs. Mish's trade card advertising her millinery store on Kearny Street, ca. 1890, shows the fanciful illustrations that were typical on women's business cards. (Huntington Library, San Marino, California)

the center of a colorful, seasonal tableau that included spring flowers and an Easter egg. The woman appears to be breaking out of the egg, perhaps symbolizing a fresh start in her new outfit. A tiny "copyrighted" printed in the lower right-hand corner of the picture suggests that the artwork was not original, but perhaps one of many such images proprietors chose from when hiring someone to print their cards. Clearly, Lester and Crawford had determined that the bigger and more elaborate a card the better. Like Mrs. Mish, they too calculated that potential customers would be most likely to hold on to, display, or trade a card if it offered some sort of value—in this case the value of "art" and seasonal celebration. A line at the top of the illustration read, "Compliments of Mrs. Lester & Crawford." This underscores the expectation that such a decorative trade card might function as a sort of greeting card for regular and potential customers—a nineteenth-century precursor to the plethora of "Season's Greetings" many of us receive today from our friendly realtors, accountants, and retailers.

Trade cards such as these paralleled the emphasis on interior and window display driving the marketing efforts of female proprietors by the end of the 1800s—particularly, but not exclusively, those who hoped to draw a share of public patronage from the city's genteel consumers. Vaunting one's goods

Mrs. Lester & Crawford's trade card included elaborate artwork, probably in hopes that customers would display it in their homes. (Huntington Library, San Marino, California)

and services was a new tool of the trade, necessary for any San Francisco businesswoman competing under the commercial big top.

ALL THE MODERN IMPROVEMENTS

Drawing consumers at the end of the nineteenth century also required female proprietors to focus on providing the latest modern improvements and conveniences. This strategy was, in fact, widely lauded by national retail experts as the best defense against competition from chain stores.[88] But in San Francisco the strategy was most pronounced among the female proprietors of accommodations businesses. Thus, while stores such as Mrs. Doherty's Hair Shop got more elegant, women's boardinghouses and hotels got more elaborate. Among those competing for the "genteel" trade in particular, customer satisfaction involved considerable capital investment in the latest domestic technologies and comforts and might also require the service of several staff members.

Mrs. Nancy Noyes was typical. She operated a large boardinghouse in 1878 and invested her earnings entirely in the improvement and operation of her establishment. Although she rented the house at 227 Geary Street that she used for the business, she owned the furniture for twenty-five rooms. In total her "stock in trade" was valued at $2,000. In addition, seven women were on her payroll for "work & labor," "cook[ing]," "sewing," and "general work."[89] The investment she made in furniture and labor speaks to their importance. Well-appointed rooms and good service were selling points and may have given Noyes an edge over her competition in the industry.

Not all accommodations businesses were complicated, of course. During the six months in 1878 that she operated a lodging house on Jones Street, Ellen Crocker accumulated only $500 worth of furnishings. Her focus, though, seemed less on building a business and more on building a fortune, since she invested, and lost, the majority of her money in mining stock.[90]

The preference for elaborate lodging establishments reached a high point at the turn of the century, when "the great hotel building boom" spread luxury—both in terms of size and amenities—to cities throughout the country.[91] Mrs. Hackmeier's "first-class hotel" exemplifies the trend, showing that San Francisco female proprietors participated in it too. Opened in 1890, the hotel occupied four lots on Eddy Street and contained 170 "finely furnished rooms, with all modern improvements."[92] Among the efforts at modernization in which Hackmeier invested was telephone service—a fifteen-year-old invention by then but one not widely installed in American homes until after 1915.[93]

Even those hotels and lodging businesses that did not aspire to "first-class" status invested in modern comforts for their guests. Some twenty years after Hackmeier fitted up her hotel, Olive Wells adopted similar improvements in her much smaller and more-modest lodging house. She furnished the twenty-plus rooms in the house with mattresses, carpets, lace curtains, and furniture made from leather and oak, cherry, or maple woods. In addition, to draw the male customers she relied on in her line of work, Wells invested in piped-in water and gas, a new four-burner gas kitchen range (with water heater), a washing machine and wringer, and two commodes: all symbols of the increasing demand for modern improvements.[94]

Of course many of these modernizations made women's work easier. Plumbing, gas stoves, and washing machines are all examples. Such tools revolutionized women's domestic labor and could reduce both the time and the physical exertion involved in daily household tasks.[95]

But such refinements were also key to drawing customers by the turn of the century. This point is underscored by the degree to which marketing efforts promoted them. Modernity was a common theme in early twentieth-century advertising generally.[96] But in the accommodations industry, where "modernization" could mean the difference between flush and pit toilets, such improvements took on particular importance. The 1900 brochure for the Ramona Hotel, managed by Mrs. Kate Hart, demonstrates this. Modern improvements were key selling points in the small, eleven-page booklet produced to market the hotel. "All rooms have hot and cold running water," it stated, "and the plumbing is 'open' of the most approved modern, sanitary style." In addition, the rooms had "electric bells with return calls" and were serviced by an electric elevator. Each of the suites was furnished with pieces made of "quartered oak and curly birch," and "the beds [were] of No. 1 curled hair." Finally, the hotel paid attention to improvements for safety as well as comfort: "Every window in the front and rear [was] provided with a fire escape, and a careful watchman patrol[led] the house at all hours of the night." Clearly such modern features were considered an important ingredient in customer satisfaction at fine hotels by 1900. And customer satisfaction, it seems, was by then the chief concern of large-scale accommodations businesses. For the brochure also promised that hotel manager Hart had prior experience at two hotels, was "thoroughly familiar with all branches of hotel business," and would "conduct the Ramona on the very highest lines." Even the "most punctilious person," it assured, "need have no hesitation" in choosing to stay at the hotel.[97]

Of course, simpler lodging establishments persisted into the twentieth century. Women continued to take boarders into their own homes and to run small-scale boardinghouses catering to working men and women. It is unlikely, for example, that the laborers who patronized South of Market establishments such as Mrs. Josephine Buss's boardinghouse at 434 Second Street, hesitated to check in if the house lacked running water or curled hair beds.[98] Yet Hackmeier's, Wells's, and Hart's attention to detail and emphasis on fine furnishings and modern improvements underscores that the trend in the accommodations sector, particularly among those businesses hoping to draw middle- and upper-class patrons, was toward the refined and up-to-date. Image, service, and "modernity"—characterized by plumbing, lighting, construction, and communication improvements—was what it would take to compete for a share of public patronage.

By the second decade of the twentieth century, businesswomen in the accommodations industry were spending more and more of their income on modernization in order to keep up with both improved technology and rising customer expectations. This trend was manifest in Ida Selig's 1918 Hotel O'Farrell. In addition to the kinds of fixtures and improvements provided by Hackmeier and Wells, Selig furnished her seventy-six-room hotel with electric lights throughout as well as an electric sign that cost her $120. She was also in debt $76.50 to the Federal Elevator Co.[99] Even restaurant proprietors, perhaps hoping to draw the same customers as hotels like Selig's, were likely to invest heavily in "modernity" by the 1910s. Ida Warren, for example, owned a $180 cash register that accounted for 13 percent of the appraised worth of her 1918 business.[100] Her early adoption of such new technology was, in fact, typical of many of the nation's small-business owners who were eager to keep up with their large-scale competitors.[101]

In San Francisco in the 1910s, there was particular cause for hotel and restaurant owners to invest in such modern improvements. For the city was one of several that by the early twentieth century could count on a steady stream of tourists. A heavily promoted vacation destination, San Francisco began drawing out-of-town visitors in the 1890s.[102] Those who could afford to make such trips would have been coveted customers because they arrived with considerable spending money. Such deep-pocketed visitors were a particular attraction for the city's business owners during the second decade of the twentieth century when San Francisco hosted the Panama Pacific Exposition. This 1915 event celebrating the completion of the Panama Canal drew scores of visitors from around the world. Aiming to announce to the world that San Francisco had fully recovered from the devastating 1906 earthquake and fire, city leaders invested heavily in "an enormous publicity campaign."[103] In part because of the anticipation of tourists expected for the fair, extensive rebuilding and renovation in the downtown area occurred during the years between 1906 and 1915. Present-day landmarks such as the Geary Theater on Geary Street (1909), the St. Francis Hotel at Union Square (1913), and the Palace Hotel on Market Street (1909) were completed in time for the exposition.[104] Female proprietors whose establishments were located near such exciting redevelopment stood to gain and had considerable incentive to invest in their own modernizations. Ida Selig's location at 140 O'Farrell Street, just blocks from the city's upscale theater and retail district, and Ida Warren's location at 747 Market Street, walking distance from the city's grandest hotel, the Palace, as well as its "fashionable thoroughfares," Kearny and Montgomery, put them in this category. Both seemed to justify liberal spending on improvements by their surroundings and confidently bet they would recoup the costs of their investments through the 1915 boom in tourism.[105]

Tourism also had a hand in transforming the way San Francisco accommodations businesses advertised. For in addition to keeping up with the trend toward the new, the novel, and the nouveau-riche, drawing tourists required that proprietors advertise in a regional rather than a local market. By the 1910s Californians were increasingly taking to the road for their leisure activities, helped along by affordable automobile prices and statewide investment in highways.[106] Local advertisements in one city newspaper were no longer enough because they would not draw this new pool of customers. Thus female proprietors, particularly at the larger hotels, were likely to keep open advertising accounts with several newspapers, perhaps in several different cities. Marketing to tourists might also require access to statewide venues. Mr. and Mrs. Bird, joint proprietors of the Palace Hotel in Benicia, just north of San Francisco, accomplished this by signing a contract allowing them to advertise in the California State Automobile Association Tour Book—to this day one of the premier resources for tourists throughout the state. Their $45 advertisement would likely have touted the same types of modern improvements seen in the enterprises above, as well as the hotel's special geographic attractions for California travelers.[107] Tour books were one more indication of how "modern" and "improved" the business of housing and feeding people had become in San Francisco by the beginning of the twentieth century. Advertising in such widely distributed materials offered proprietors broad geographic reach but also forced them to compete in a much larger marketplace.

LINGERING AND LONGING

In the retail and apparel trades the department stores had a similar impact, raising the bar for what it took to draw a share of public patronage; resisting their influence was, even by 1900, futile for small-scale proprietors, who were now obliged to capitulate to the retail giants' marketing tactics.[108] Small businessmen and -women did not give in without a fight, however. At the end of the nineteenth century, partly in reaction to the market compression of the 1893–97 depression, small-scale proprietors had joined forces to try to quell the powerful competition of large merchandisers by challenging them legally. In California they responded to the intrusion of giants such as the City of Paris, I. Magnin, the Joseph Magnin Company, Gump's, and the Emporium, all San Francisco–based stores, by introducing legislation to limit department store operations.[109] "The octopus. . . ha[d] stretched out its tentacles in every direction," small-business owners lamented, "grasping in its slimy folds the specialist or one-line man" who could not survive under the pressure.[110] But like states across the country, California sided with the giant retailers, concluding that they were "on the whole advantageous to the consuming public."[111] As the depression abated, many small retailers saw their business increase, and they too became complacent about the new kings in American retailing.[112] By the end of the decade, one historian writes, "the message to the public was . . . that department stores embodied all that was up to date and in urban bourgeois good taste, [and] that they were the exemplars of rising urban standards of beauty and convenience."[113] For proprietors in San Francisco and other urban centers in the state, this meant that since the department stores were there to stay, they might as well learn to live with them. Resistance gave way to imitation, and even small stores began to adopt the principle guiding the retail giants: encourage customers to respond to desire rather than need in their purchase decisions.

Because competition for customers was so great, after 1900 retailers set about to instigate spontaneous and unplanned purchasing. Espoused by L. Frank Baum, the man responsible for "uplifting mercantile decorating to the level of a profession," the new retail philosophy was to "use the best art to arouse in the observer the cupidity and longing to possess the goods" being sold.[114] One way to do this was to create sumptuous window displays —something small-scale business owners had already started doing by the end of the 1800s as discussed. But the new way to "arouse the longings" of potential customers was to create a store environment so appealing that those who ventured in chose to stay awhile. Big department stores encouraged shoppers to linger by providing fully outfitted lavatories, restaurants and cafes, and comfortable lounges.[115] In one large-scale New York establishment, for example, the corridor in the middle of the store "widen[ed] into an ample court," where "shoppers could recover equilibrium, relax, and look around."[116] Smaller retailers had no room for courts or lounges. But by the second decade of the twentieth century, the evidence shows that many tried to entice their customers to dally by decorating their whole stores like pri-

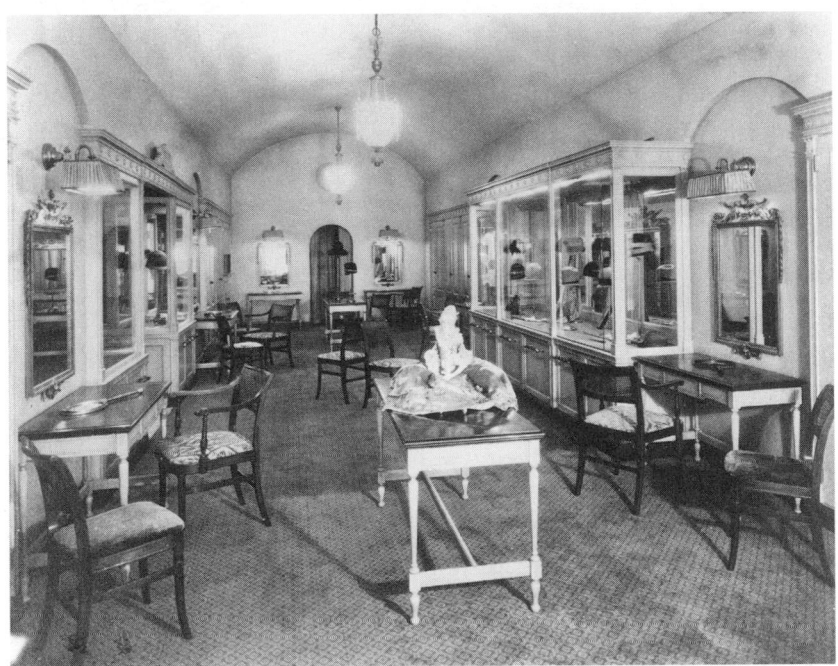

The ultimate standard for interior decor was I. Magnin. Its millinery department, shown here ca. 1900, boasted gilded mirrors, private dressing tables, ornate chandeliers, elaborate display cases, and comfortable chairs. Female customers, it was hoped, would linger in this elegant salon as they tried on the latest hat styles. (San Francisco History Center, San Francisco Public Library)

vate living spaces. The hope, it seems, was that if customers got comfortable enough to linger, they might finally give in to the urge to make a purchase.

Those female proprietors eager to compete with the department stores for genteel customers presided over luxuriously comfortable establishments. Setting up such an interior might first involve investing in structural improvements. Bertha Root, for example, paid $250 to have her ceiling repaired and a new hardwood floor installed in her millinery store at the San Francisco Hotel Company.[117] Elizabeth Ezell, also a milliner, paid $13 to a carpenter for the construction and painting of furniture and $53 to a decorator to repair the plaster and enamel work in her basement store and to paper its walls.[118] Once such background work was complete, proprietors set about filling their stores with homelike furnishings. Emily Gomez's millinery store, for example, was filled with ornamental figures, jars of artificial flowers, couches and cushioned chairs, and dozens of display stands.[119] Mrs. Annie Horstmann's ladies' apparel store must have been even more elaborate and comfortable. Though the store was located in Stockton, some seventy miles from San Francisco, its decor seems to have reflected the larger trend that gripped proprietors throughout the region and the country. Its furnishings included the welcoming sorts of pieces that one might find in the home of a friend, with a couch, a rocker, and an easy chair for lounging; an oak cloak case for stowing overcoats and personal belongings; and a washstand for splashing hot faces and cleaning soiled hands. Several expensive carpets and mirrors (one with a gilded frame) added to the elegance of the store. A phonograph, perhaps playing the popular tunes of the day, serenaded customers as they spent hard-earned money at the ten-foot sales counter and Mrs. Horstmann wrapped their new belongings in paper.[120] Clearly Horstmann, like Gomez, Ezell, and Root, understood that by 1915, no product sold itself. Her emphasis on customer comfort suggests that she believed if she was going to compete with the department stores that dominated the women's apparel industry, she had to create the sort of environment that encouraged customers to linger and to long for the items she sold.

San Francisco female proprietors were not alone in facing such new challenges. The trend could be found among women business owners throughout the country. One Boston store owner, for example, reportedly invested $2,000 in fixing up her interior decorating shop, "insisting that people in 'our district' demand fireplaces, plumbing, etc."[121] Nationally distributed trade journals such as the *Milliner* encouraged such excess by publishing laudatory descriptions of "de luxe" shops and praising those female proprietors who "adopted the tactics of their competitors [by] transforming their tiny shops into replicas of elegantly appointed millinery and dressmaking departments."[122] The influence of the department store, therefore, reached deep into the pockets of businesswomen throughout the country, especially those in any line of business that competed directly with the grand emporiums.

Beauty industry proprietors were another group to feel the effects of department stores. Weekly trips to the beauty salon were commonplace for many women at the beginning of the twentieth century. But while such excursions might have included the purchase of homemade cosmetics products in addition to hair styling decades earlier, by the early 1900s small, woman-owned and -operated salons "no longer provided the springboard into cosmetics manufacturing and sales" they once had. "Increased competition for consumers, commitment to costly national advertising, drug- and department-store distribution, and greater need for capital" made successful small-scale production virtually impossible. Thus while a handful of innovative women continued to enjoy spectacular success in the cosmetics market—Madame C. J. Walker, Annie Turnbo Malone, Helena Rubenstein, and Elizabeth Arden among them—most beauty culturists were forced to rely on hairdressing alone to turn a profit.[123] No wonder then that female proprietors who operated hair salons also mimicked the refinement and modernization associated with mass retailers. Thus Madame Phillips's San Francisco hairdressing establishment at 218 Post Street advertised that it was "very elaborately fitted up" and featured "all the modern conveniences—electric lighting, electric hair dryers, and private booths, five for hairdressing and two for manicuring." That an African American female proprietor underwrote such investments indicates the degree to which modernizing improvements were embraced widely by business owners of all backgrounds. The reason is because they attracted paying customers and helped ensure the level of success that Madame Phillips's tony address—in the middle of the most desirable retail and hotel district of the city—indicates she enjoyed.[124]

Changes in interior decor were accompanied by new marketing techniques also designed to draw customers in, encourage them to linger, and instill in them a longing for the goods and services female proprietors sold. To accomplish this, some female proprietors seem to have engaged in direct-mail campaigns. Bertha Root, for example, a San Francisco milliner during the 1910s, spent $64.50 on over 800 business announcements (some engraved) and engagement cards.[125] She might have used such printed business materials to write thank you notes to customers, to send out sale announcements, for use as appointment cards, or, finally, to send business advertisements to new potential customers. Her mailing list must have been long to warrant such extravagant spending on business stationery, an investment that underscores the lengths to which apparel retailers and other businesswomen were willing to go by the second decade of the twentieth century to draw customers.[126] If done well, such mailing campaigns could enhance the sense of friendliness and homey comfort that a store's interior instilled. Skillful descriptions of merchandise, received at home via mail, also might whet a customer's sense of longing before she even arrived at the store. In this respect, such direct-mail promotions emulated the advertisements from mass retailers that inundated Americans' mailboxes by the beginning of the twentieth century.[127]

While some businesswomen must have relied on their own marketing prowess to reel in customers with such mail campaigns, Bertha Root was one of a handful of early twentieth-century businesswomen who paid advertising agencies to help market their enterprises.[128] The advertisements generated by such professionals were probably modest, given the small costs incurred by proprietors for this service. Yet this investment demonstrates what some female proprietors were willing to do to draw a share of public patronage by the twentieth century. Glossy, photographic images such as the ones that bombard us today were still a long while away, but already small business-women, like small businessmen and large-scale retailers, were engaging in the psychology of desire to turn members of the San Francisco public into their patrons.[129]

<hr />

In just two generations, the customers of San Francisco businesswomen had evolved from biscuit-hungry forty-niners eager to pay for the "touch" of a woman to urbane men and women who expected to be enticed into consumption by display and modernity. Straightforward delivery of necessary goods and services was no longer enough; by the end of the nineteenth century customers wanted to be lured into spending their money on sophisticated foods, products, and accommodations by centrally located, lavishly decorated, and conveniently outfitted enterprises.

The city's female proprietors acceded to these changing demands by transforming the ways in which they pursued public patronage between 1850 and 1920. In the city's early years, drawing customers was of little concern because the appeal of a woman was typically enough to guarantee a business-woman a steady stream of patrons. Such gold rush entrepreneurs unquestionably worked hard, but they did not have to put much effort into making their product or service especially attractive to the mainly male San Franciscans who gladly patronized their establishments. Yet as the city began to acquire the trappings of East Coast urbanity, female proprietors were forced to step up the effort they put into jockeying for customers. By the 1870s, women business owners in the Paris of America located themselves in the most expensive commercial corridors of the city, showed off their wares in elaborate window displays, and took out adjective-filled advertisements to entice patrons to their doors. Throughout the next several decades, investing in technological and safety advancements became a priority, especially among accommodations proprietors, while mimicking the enticements to "linger" and "long" pioneered by department stores became the new objective of small-scale business owners in the apparel, retail, and beauty industries. Advertising techniques became more aggressive too, as female entrepreneurs turned to advertising agencies, direct-mail campaigns, and statewide promotion venues to draw customers.

These increasing complications made starting and operating a business more difficult, adding to the incentives twentieth-century San Francisco women found to leave proprietorship altogether. Such elaborate expenditures to draw customers also, of course, added to the already formidable job of financial management facing San Francisco's female proprietors—the subject we turn to in the next chapter.

CHAPTER 5

WOMEN AS FINANCIAL

MANAGERS

"Do a good job and the profits will take care of themselves." According to her son Grover, this was the philosophy of Mary Ann Magnin, founder of the elegant San Francisco–based department store, I. Magnin.[1] The formula seems to have worked, since the retail chain eventually opened stores in thirty different locations and maintained a reputation as the West's premier retailer until it was closed in 1995 more than one hundred years after its founding.[2] And yet, even Grover admitted that with this approach the company was "not run like a business" but was "more of a hobby."[3] Awash in the kind of success that no other San Francisco female proprietor enjoyed during the late nineteenth and early twentieth centuries, Mary Ann Magnin could afford such an indulgent view of business management.[4] Yet for most of the city's businesswomen, the profits did not "take care of themselves" but instead had to be carefully managed.

Such financial management had little to do with the sort of informal business instincts that guided many women through the start-up phase or helped them figure out how to draw customers. For to take charge of a business's financial affairs required learned skills rather than intuitive behaviors. Instinct alone was not enough. By the end of the nineteenth century financial management was a science, a matter few successful businesspeople left to fortune or feelings.

Business financial decisions were difficult and often meant the difference between keeping an enterprise profitable and driving it into the ground. Among the financial affairs connected with small-business management were record keeping, inventory, loans, debts, credit, insurance policies, and investments. Managing each one required a set of executional skills that needed to be employed every day. What merchandise was paid for and what was not, who still owed money for their hotel stay or new hat, and which policies were up-to-date and which ones past due were among the daily inquiries that occupied small-business proprietors. Successful management of such issues could easily mean the difference between making a profit or not. While these decisions were difficult ones for any proprietor, businesswomen in the late nineteenth and early twentieth centuries may have been especially ill equipped to handle them.

The reason was that the day-to-day financial management skills required in the operation of a business were best mastered through training and experience — precisely the sort of background that most female proprietors did not have. During the nineteenth century businessmen could take advantage of jobs as apprentices in other businesses where they learned hands-on what it took to manage a business financially, but women rarely had this opportunity. In the apparel trades, women often worked their way up to proprietorship after long periods of apprenticeship in another woman's millinery or dressmaking establishment, but such training supplied women with expertise as craftswomen, not necessarily as businesswomen.[5] In other fields of business, women more often struck out on their own without having been trained by a fellow businesswoman at all. And in contrast to businessmen, women business owners were less likely to enter a new enterprise of their own with previous experience operating a business. The management of households and charitable organizations provided limited training opportunities for some women but did not prepare them for the extensive and rigorous financial challenges of proprietorship. Best prepared of all were women who received training in family businesses. Yet evidence shows that many women ceded financial control of such businesses to male family members when possible, underscoring that those who learned to manage money constituted a minority of all female proprietors. All this meant that San Francisco's businesswomen were, as a group, much "greener" in their role as financial managers and, perhaps, less likely to manage the financial side of their businesses with skill and success.

Thus, to examine female proprietors as financial managers requires both that we recognize the degree to which they were economic actors, embroiled in complex financial decisions and transactions on a daily basis, and the extent to which they met these challenges without the training and experience that would have made them good at it. Their job was to protect the profits of their businesses, but often they did so with little skill.

FINANCIAL MANAGEMENT AND BUSINESS PROPRIETORSHIP

Business operation engaged female proprietors in tough financial decision making on a daily basis. Whether or not they were prepared, San Francisco's businesswomen found they had to don the cap of financial manager to make choices as debtors and creditors, purchasers and advertisers, investors and employers, lessees and policy holders, tax payers and licensees. Keeping records of such transactions was, in and of itself, a daunting task for many of San Francisco's female proprietors. But no matter the level of skill or experience they applied to the job, these women became financiers, forced to engage in the world of business as economic actors to a degree that few historical accounts of nineteenth-century businesswomen have captured.[6]

Among the first financial challenges facing female proprietors were the tax and licensing fees they were assessed as business owners. Evidence from the 1850s and 1860s indicates that such financial levies came early in the history of San Francisco. Municipal fees, which became law in the city as early as 1852, when they were written into its incorporation documents, presented the earliest challenge.[7] Knowing that they were required to apply for a business license, and which kind, was the first step. But businesswomen probably struggled even more with how to afford the potentially hefty assessments that accompanied such permits. For example, the city required that any business-woman who served alcohol with meals at her boardinghouse or lodging house purchase a liquor license, bar license, lodging house license, and restaurant or hotel license, all totaling $110 to $250 per quarter.[8] Balancing such costs against quarterly earnings to anticipate and afford these fees required careful money management. Municipal fees were matched by national assessments as well. An 1863 *Daily Alta California* ad for a "Pocket Edition of the Schedules of U.S. Stamp Duties and Federal Internal Taxes," for example, hints at the complicated tax and duty laws that businesswomen had to master.[9] Since between 1868 and 1913, "90 percent of all internal revenue collected in the United States came from excise taxes on distilled spirits, tobacco and fermented liquors," the owners of hotels, restaurants, and saloons would have been particularly affected by tax expenses.[10] Keeping up with government fees was difficult, and not all women embraced such public responsibilities. Mrs. M. E. Doherty, the owner of a hairpiece and millinery shop during the late 1860s and early 1870s, actually misrepresented her finances to R. G. Dun & Company credit reporters because she "feared [their] reporter was connected with the Internal Revenue Department."[11] In 1870s San Francisco, proprietors had reason to fear federal tax collectors. Collector William Higby, a former congressman, had been extraordinarily diligent in the administration of his job, prosecuting individuals to such a degree that he had aroused the animus of the San Francisco public. This prompted California governor George C. Perkins to request Higby's replacement, stating "seizures have been made and prosecutions instituted for trifling offenses to such an extent as to arouse public indignation."[12] Thus Doherty was probably one of many proprietors during the period who tried to duck tax collectors. But avoiding taxes was a strategy that would have worked for very few. Most were forced to confront these financial requirements head on or suffer serious consequences to their commercial livelihood.

Such license and tax fees continued into the twentieth century, of course. Evidence that they were still a part of businesswomen's day-to-day work as financial managers in the early 1900s is clear in bankruptcy court records. For example, when Frances Maita, a hotel owner, defended herself in court in 1918 on charges that she had committed an act of bankruptcy, a retail liquor dealer's permit was among the items considered of value in her business.[13] Maita's acquisition of such a permit was an important factor in her hotel's success. Taxes too were consistently a part of the financial puzzle businesswomen had to solve. After the Sixteenth Amendment to the Constitution was implemented in 1913, all U.S. residents and businesses were accountable for income taxes. But, as one scholar asserts, most small-scale proprietors did not make more than the $4,000 exemption for married persons, and thus probably did not pay income tax.[14] Yet Helen Tarbox, a San Francisco confectioner, found that in 1921, she was also accountable for a war tax on beverages, probably assessed as both a revenue and a conservation measure for the nation during World War I.[15] While the tax only amounted to $5.90, it was among the items Tarbox had not paid at the time of her bankruptcy. Similarly, Ida Selig owed a $27.50 corporation franchise tax to the State of California at the time of her bankruptcy.[16] Both debts suggest that such fees may have come as a surprise to the women and that they had not planned for the additional expense.

Purchasing decisions were also closely linked with businesswomen's ability to manage finances. Shopping for good prices was an important first step in containing costs. An early advertisement in the *Daily Dramatic Chronicle* indicates that wholesalers expected proprietors to haggle over prices. It stated: "Lunch Houses, Grocers, and Boarding Houses, Choice Cheese at your own Price."[17] At the very least, a female proprietor of such an establishment had to have a good grasp of how much she could afford to spend and what constituted a good price. Careful financial managers paid a great deal of attention to the cost of supplies, since stretching their business dollar as far as possible was the most prudent way to manage a budget.

Just how complicated purchasing decisions were depended on what type of business a woman owned and when she operated it. Ethel Watson's music store purchases, for example, were confined to sheet music, a relatively simple inventory to manage.[18] In contrast, any proprietor of an accommodations business where food was served had to manage perishables and thus was forced to consider when and how such purchases would be used to avoid investing in meats, produce, or dairy products that might expire before being consumed by customers. In the early days of the city's history, nonperishables such as dried meats, beans, and simple biscuits were standard fare, making the job of restaurateur or boardinghouse keeper easier. But as the city and its customers became more sophisticated, businesswomen in such establishments found themselves catering to a clientele that expected much more than just campfire food.

Clara Moody, owner of two San Francisco restaurants at the beginning of the twentieth century, is a good example. At the Cottage Restaurant, located on busy Market Street, she served popular delicacies such as roast leg of pork, crab, peaches, imported cheeses, and two flavors of ice cream. All, of course, were perishables, and expensive ones at that, requiring that she carefully manage her inventory. Not all the supplies she purchased were perishable, such as the sacks of sawdust, coal, and canned oil, lard, and ham she bought. But most were. And because she purchased fresh meat, poultry, seafood, produce, and dairy in massive quantities, managing her inventory well was imperative. Examining the foods that Moody purchased in a single month underscores this point. During the month of June in 1912, for example, she bought 102 pounds of pork leg, 77 pounds of veal, 175 pounds of ribs, 252 chickens, 4½ quarts of clams, 47 pounds of salmon, 57 pounds of fresh beans, 3 boxes of apples, 64 pounds of butter, 6 cans of ice cream, and 1,600 pounds of ice. And these supplies represent only a fraction of her total monthly grocery list, which included some 180 items totaling nearly $600. Managing the purchase, storage, and timely consumption of such items must have occupied the majority of Moody's time as a restaurant owner and required an ability to predict turnover that even a seasoned restaurant owner would have found difficult. For her the job was compounded by the fact that she had a second restaurant on Battery Street to contend with as well.[19]

Of course managing inventory was an important skill even for those businesswomen who did not sell food, because inventory was so closely tied to cash flow. If a woman spent too much money on the product(s) she sold and did not draw the share of public patronage she expected, she could easily find herself stuck with hundreds or even thousands of dollars worth of merchandise that, if liquidated, would bring in less than she had paid for it. This was clearly a consistent problem for female proprietors, as the bankruptcy court records are full of women who went out of business with large inventories that were eventually appraised at low auction prices rather than their potential retail value.

A particularly dramatic example of poor inventory management is the case of Annie Horstmann, the proprietor of a women's clothing business in neighboring Stockton, California, in 1915.[20] At the time of her bankruptcy, Horstmann's inventory included 10 furs, 48 skirts, 40 dresses and suits, 18 coats, 50 housedresses, 79 undergarments, 57 pairs of gloves, 262 pairs of stockings, 150 pieces of underwear, and 62 corsets. In conjunction with several other miscellaneous pieces of clothing, these items were appraised at $747.82, a fraction of the cost for which she might have sold them at retail.[21] Furthermore, in spite of Horstmann's extensive and elegant inventory, or more probably because of it, she signed an affidavit declaring herself a pauper, stating that she could not even afford the court costs associated with filing for bankruptcy. Clearly all of her money was wrapped up in the excessive purchases she had made to fill her store's shelves.[22]

Inventory management was also a concern because of what national retail experts called "stock turn." The Butler Brothers, for example, authors of several advice books for retailers at the beginning of the twentieth century, argued that the reason more merchants were not getting rich could be explained in just three words: "LACK OF TURNOVER."[23] The problem was that inventory tied up shelf space. If a $1 box of cereal sat on a shelf for five days before being purchased, for example, it prevented the store owner from filling that space with a 50¢ box of crackers that, thanks to popularity or price, she might sell daily. In the end, five 50¢ boxes of crackers would yield a profit of $1.50, 50¢ more than the proprietor would gain selling one box of the $1 cereal. Because shelf space was expensive real estate, experts argued, retailers were better off discounting stock that did not rapidly turn over and filling the space with something that would.[24] This was of particular concern by the beginning of the twentieth century when mass marketers, who "stressed high volumes of sales through quick stock turnovers and low unit costs" themselves, began making inroads in the retail sector.[25]

Of course, from the perspective of financial management, how a businesswoman paid for her inventory was even more important than how much she bought. For even more dangerous than spending all of one's cash on excessive amounts of inventory was making the purchases using credit or extended payment plans. Yet Americans used credit almost "universally." As one historian put it, "credit was a way of life everywhere."[26] Thus one of the most important aspects of financial management was maintaining a good credit history. As outlined in Chapter 3, with the exception of the short-lived gold rush period, credit was hard for San Francisco women to obtain in the second half of the nineteenth century. Few could rely on it as a start-up strategy because they had neither the assets nor the experience that credit evaluators looked for. After they had gotten started, however, most businesswomen did make their purchases using credit. The next challenge for them was paying back creditors in a timely fashion and managing a sensible debt-to-asset ratio to maintain a good credit rating.

The 1870s R. G. Dun & Company reports demonstrate what credit evaluators believed to be "good" debt management.[27] For example, Mrs. Mary Howard, a millinery store owner in 1875 was reported to be "in very fair credit locally for [her] wants," and a "prompt pay," both signs that she was considered a safe credit risk.[28] Mrs. Dannenberg, who ran a long-lived ladies' and children's goods store, was described as having "met her payments in fair time"; as a result she was "in good credit with the trade in general for modest accounts."[29] Mrs. Emmons maintained her credit rating by contracting with only one wholesale millinery house, who reported that her payments were satisfactory; to the rest of the trade she was "not well known."[30] Finally, Mrs. Charles Mercer, a manufacturer of confectionery, was described both as a solid businesswoman and as having a good credit rating. Dun reporters wrote: she "thoroughly understands her business and is in excellent credit, usually discounting her bills."[31]

By contrast, Dun reporters expressed concern about businesswomen who were in more debt than their businesses were worth and who took too long to repay their creditors. Miss May Thompson, for example, whose "assets would not more than cover her liabilities," was not a good credit risk in the eyes of company representatives. Should creditors have called in her debts, she would not have been able to pay them at the time of Dun's assessment.[32] Mrs. J. Martineaut, on the other hand, did such a small business selling corsets and costumes that in the opinion of Dun reporters, "the very limited extent of her business [did] not warrant her buying away from home." She was unlikely to even ask for credit, let alone get it.[33] And while Mme. Leroy, a San Francisco dressmaker, was reported to be a "well disposed woman," she was a "slow pay" and was "hardly desirable for credit outside of parties already interested."[34] In fact, as studies of businesswomen in other parts of the country have shown, "slow" was a common refrain in credit reporters' descriptions of female proprietors, since they were often hampered by low capital resources, thin profit margins, and tardy customers.[35]

Businesswomen were not entirely in control of how they were evaluated as credit risks, since Dun reporters seemed as interested in an individual's moral habits as they were in her business practices. Whether or not a businesswoman had given any cause for concern over her ability to repay her debts, her private life was fair game for examination and commentary. While the report on Mrs. G. W. M. Croles, a San Francisco milliner, was unusual in its findings — "her character will not bear investigation, [and] she drinks heavily and is somewhat lax in morals" — its invasive inquiry into her private life was not.[36] Marital status was of particular interest. In reports on both Jane Thomas and Esther Schloss, Dun agents went into considerable detail about each proprietor's divorce proceedings.[37] The behavior of family members was also scrutinized as a reflection of a businesswoman's own financial responsibility. Dun reporters commented that Mrs. C. Jordan "ha[d] a dissipated husband who retards her progress," while Frances Uznay "ha[d] a Son who spends a great deal of her money."[38] "The worst feature" about Mrs. Broderick, a credit reporter declared, "is that she allowed her husband to raise $2,000 on the house and lot already lost in stock."[39] It seems businesswomen responsible not only for their own financial management but for their family members' as well. "While male proprietors suffered similar indignities," writes one scholar, "these sorts of semipublic revelations must have been particularly painful to women in a culture that celebrated female delicacy and modesty."[40]

Credit and collection problems consumed enormous amounts of time, energy, and money, and if not managed carefully, could finish off a business. A businesswoman who was careful about borrowing conservatively, investing wisely, and making most purchases with cash mitigated the risks of being forced to pay debts she could not afford. But the challenges of money management proved too difficult for many women, and their businesses suffered accordingly.

The problem for most began with buying too much on credit. San Francisco milliner Minnie Borgstrom, for example, who declared bankruptcy in June of 1878, simply overspent. She showed her vulnerability as a businesswoman in the excessive amount of stock she purchased on credit. When she declared bankruptcy Borgstrom's "stock in trade" (the value of her inventory) was appraised at $1,500. Her substantial number of outstanding bills suggests that most of this merchandise must never have been paid for. Between 1877 and 1878 Borgstrom had contracted $3,000 worth of debts "for millinery goods," which she owed to six different merchant houses. To Toplitz

& Co. she owed $1,013.39; to Haker & Hinz, $500; to Mish & Son, $392.60; to Hinz & Weilin, $395.24; to Selig & Newman, $400; and to W. Butler, $267. The rest of Borgstrom's expenditures were moderate. She rented a store on Montgomery Street from Michael Reese for $125 per month, and her store fixtures were valued at $300. Her personal belongings were limited to $100 worth of "wearing apparel." She was not an extravagant woman; she just went into too much debt buying stock on credit for her millinery business.[41]

In contrast to those of Minnie Borgstrom, Bessie Hamilton's expenditures had been personal and frivolous. She had no "stock in trade" and no property when she declared bankruptcy in 1899. Her San Francisco boarding-house must have been either sparsely furnished or filled with rented furniture because she owned none. Nonetheless Hamilton, like Borgstrom, had overspent, but she had done so not on stock but on extravagant and seemingly unnecessary goods and services. Did she really need a carriage horse? Was maintaining an open account for dressmaking truly necessary? Perhaps to Hamilton such purchases seemed smart: the horse might help to distinguish her boardinghouse from those of her competitors, while routinely hiring a dressmaker rather than making her own clothes freed up her time for managing the business. But Hamilton must have regretted both decisions when she realized that she could not repay the $2,445 she owed to creditors for these and other purchases. When she declared bankruptcy in February 1899, her creditors probably received nothing, since she owned no inventory or property for them to auction off. And for the dressmakers, housekeepers, laundry proprietors, and milk and provision dealers she owed, businesspeople often on the margins of commercial viability themselves, Hamilton's bankruptcy may have caused the beginning of their own spirals of debt.[42]

Other businesswomen walked such a fine line between poverty and making a modest income that bankruptcy had nothing to do with extravagant decisions. When Bertha Baschan, an Oakland peddler, declared bankruptcy in 1900, it may have seemed like a long time in coming to her creditors. Her possessions were limited to a peddler's wagon and a horse, together worth $25, and personal effects (wearing apparel and furniture) also worth $25. She had no stock in trade and no property that could be sold to compensate her creditors, to whom she owed a total of $265. The $50 debt that Baschan owed Thomas Norffen of San Francisco for five months of rent seems to have been contracted in 1898. The $215 she owed to Edward Pierce of Oakland was an even older debt, the money having exchanged hands in 1896. The larger amount Baschan owed to Pierce was for a joint promissory note she had signed with Julia Brown to "secure the indebtedness of the latter." This kind gesture may have been the key to her downfall. For though peddling never made anyone a lot of money at the turn of the century, it could support a woman and the kind of modest monthly expenses that Baschan paid. Going out on a limb for a friend by securing her debt with an IOU, however, pushed her over the edge of economic security.[43]

Purchasing on credit continued to be standard practice into the twentieth century, challenging the city's businesswomen as financial managers. Overbuying was often the root of the problem. In fact, by the early 1900s, wholesale merchants had singled out women in the millinery business as particular offenders. Of concern for the suppliers was the tendency of millinery store proprietors to return merchandise. Although this practice was often prompted by practical concerns, the receipt of damaged goods, for example, wholesalers largely interpreted it as an indication of careless and excessive purchasing on credit. The *Milliner's Designer*, for example, an industry trade journal, argued that "it is a confession of weakness on the part of the milliner to buy a bill of merchandise and then return part of it. It shows lack of business judgment in that the purchaser does not know what can be sold and in the fact of her allowing herself to become overstocked."[44] Overstocking, however, was not a problem confined to businesswomen in the millinery trade but plagued female proprietors in all lines of work. Grocer Cora Buck, for example, owed $1,076.54 to a variety of wholesalers at the time of her bankruptcy in 1918 and had a store full of merchandise. In all likelihood this meant that she had not yet even paid for the 59 soaps, 17 cans of soup, 39 boxes of cornstarch, and 4 boxes of cereal among the items still on the shelves of her San Jose general store when she went out of business.[45] Even when a businesswoman planned for such purchases and executed regular payments, her efforts hardly had an impact if she had bought too much. A receipt issued to Lilly Stevens, a woman's clothier in San Francisco in 1918, shows that she typically carried a large balance for the items she bought wholesale, only occasionally making cash payments. When she did bring in cash to pay down her balance, the amount she produced was so small, $10 for example, that it hardly reduced the total amount she owed.[46] Helen Tarbox, too, invested in thousands of dollars worth of store fixtures for her O'Farrell Street confectionery business but could only pay small amounts of cash toward the debt, which accrued interest on a monthly basis.[47]

Extended payment plans for "big-ticket" items or "consumer durables, products designed to last for more than just a year or two," were also increasingly common at the beginning of the twentieth century.[48] By then the emphasis on modern improvements and conveniences had taken hold of the commercial marketplace, and female proprietors were purchasing expensive new appliances such as electric ranges, signs to light up their storefront win-

M Helen Tarbox,

497 O'Farrell Street, San Francisco, Cali

Eng-Skell Company

INCORPORATED
208-210 MISSION STREET

TERMS: 30 DAYS NET OR 2 PER CENT FOR CASH IN 10 DAYS

		Balance,						
		To Mdse. as per bill rend.						
May	19	Cash	500.00					
June	1	Mdse					3,225.00	
Aug	30	Cash	50.00					
Sept	13	"	50.00					
Oct	3	"	100.00					
Nov	29	"	50.00					
			750.00				750.00	
							2,475.00	
		Interest on the above					96.59	
							2,571.59	

This receipt, produced as evidence in the bankruptcy case of a confectionery store owner, demonstrates the difficulty some female proprietors had obtaining enough cash to pay off the sizable debts they incurred outfitting their businesses with fixtures and furniture. (National Archives, Pacific Region, San Bruno, California)

---

dows, and modern cash registers.[49] Easy payment plans lured women into such purchases because they made expensive items seem reasonably priced, even when interest was added. Western Butchers' Supply Company, for example, charged Ida Warner 7 percent interest for the "Cleveland Chopper" butcher block that graced her restaurant kitchen in 1918. But their lease agreement, which included low bimonthly payments of just $10 after her initial $100 down payment, made it seem affordable.[50] That entering into this contract had been a poor financial decision must have been clear to Warner when she declared bankruptcy several months later. For, like so many women before her, Warner neither owned nor retained possession of the butcher block and recouped none of the $100 she had spent to secure its lease.

As running a business became more complicated after the turn of the century, small proprietors' debts became more complex too. Now they not only had to pay local landlords and merchants for rent and stock, but they also owed money to large department stores, to wholesalers of brand-name goods, to utility companies, and to advertising agencies. When Eva Pommer, copartner with her husband of the Monarch Dry Goods Store, declared bankruptcy in July 1915, among the creditors they owed were Lord & Taylor, Levi Strauss & Company, the Pacific Telegraph and Telephone Company, and the Blum Advertising Agency.[51] Such large and impersonal companies were probably even less likely than local merchants—with whom businesswomen often had long-term relationships—to make allowances when a proprietor was unable to keep up with her bills.[52]

By the turn of the century, female store owners stretched their credit even further by negotiating trade back and forth between San Francisco and numerous American cities. "Newly established wholesaling centers in Chicago, St. Louis, Dallas, and San Francisco," writes one historian, "vied . . . for the business of tradeswomen."[53] Caroline Louise Leuenberger, for example, a corset maker and designer who declared bankruptcy in 1915, owed creditors in San Francisco, New York City, Chicago, Newark, New Jersey, and La Crosse, Wisconsin. Maintaining relationships with so many distant creditors proved so complicated that even her careful record keeping—two sales books, one order book, the store lease, and a stack of bills and receipts were among her possessions listed in the bankruptcy record—was not enough to keep her payments current.[54] "Spurred by the increasing physical distance that separated them from retailers, the depression of the 1890s, and the 'search for order' that infected much of American society, wholesalers struggled to do business according to 'businesslike' principles."[55] Such a matter-of-fact approach to the dispensation of credit and collection of debts must have meant that such distant wholesale merchants had little tolerance for women who, like Caroline Leuenberger, could not keep up with their payments.

Of course, whether or not a woman could pay her debts had everything to do with whether or not she could collect the debts owed her. Unreliable or fraudulent customers were a problem for business owners throughout the country. But even if such customers were not unique to any particular region, they do seem to have presented a problem that intensified in the late nineteenth century. "As cities grew and trade expanded," argues one historian, "credit became a more and more serious problem." In the public marketplace of the late 1800s, "goods were sold to people the merchant did not know personally, and whose credit was also unknown."[56] While wholesalers could rely on credit reports such as those provided by R. G. Dun & Company, retailers had only each other and their instincts to consult when it came to deciding whether or not to extend credit to a particular customer. An 1889 Illinois law designed to aid hotel and restaurant keepers suggests that this was not enough. The law made it a crime to enjoy "food, lodging, or other accommodation at any hotel, inn, boarding or eating house with intent to defraud the owner or keeper." Any "customer who left without paying his bill, or 'surreptitiously' removed his luggage, was prima facie guilty of fraud."[57] Such legal support for small-business owners was rare, but the fact that even one such law was passed underscores the difficulty some proprietors had extracting payment from their customers.

Because most women in business ran small enterprises that tended to teeter on the edge of economic failure, customers who did not pay often constituted the first step on a path toward commercial disaster. "Handicapped from the outset by scant capital and limited access to credit," one scholar contends, women's businesses "suffered disproportionately" from negligent consumers because they often had no financial resources to fall back on when their income ceased.[58] When a proprietor's business did not generate any profit, then she often had only two choices: go into debt to stay open or go out of business altogether. For Teresa Holden, her inability to collect the money owed her meant both. When she petitioned the District Court of Northern California for voluntary bankruptcy on March 7, 1873, she owed an estimated $3,000 to her creditors. It was the coal dealers from whom she had purchased fuel for her boardinghouse who had commenced the bankruptcy suit against her. But she owed others as well: a stock broker for losses on stock she had purchased from him, a capitalist for money she had borrowed, an attorney for legal services, and a variety of merchants for supplies she had purchased. Her debts would have been difficult to repay even if her business was making money. In the 1870s the finest hotels commanded $65 to $90 per month from single boarders, while a subsidized boardinghouse like the Women's Pioneer Hotel provided lodging for $15 to $50 per month.[59] If Holden charged $55 per month, an average of these prices, then even with twenty-five borders, a large-sized house, her monthly income would be $1,375. After paying expenses to keep the boardinghouse operating, she would have had very little left to pay her creditors.

Since at least some of Teresa Holden's boarders were not paying her for her services, she was quickly sucked into a spiral of debt that eventually put her out of business. On the day she petitioned the court for bankruptcy, Robert Haley, Samuel Leildays, Harry Aston, and B. Hewitt owed her a total of $622 "for Board and Lodging." Since her personal property was only valued at $110—$100 worth of household goods, furniture, and wearing apparel and $10 worth of books, prints, and pictures—she had nothing to sell to cover her costs and nothing to offer her debtors to repay her debts.[60] As a renter she had no property to seize, yet if she lost the rental contract she held as proprietor of the boardinghouse, she would have also lost her home.[61] Holden was forced to start over again, whether as a businesswoman or a laborer, with nothing but $110 worth of household objects, worthless stock, no cash to invest in a new enterprise, and no home to speak of. Turns of fortune such as that experienced by Teresa Holden were commonplace into the twentieth century. This was especially true among accommodations proprietors, who routinely appeared in the bankruptcy court records with long lists of customers who did not pay their bills.[62] One study of early nineteenth-century boardinghouses helps explain the prevalence of nonpaying lodgers. Providing a "home" for boarders required that landladies provide emotional as well as market-based services for their additional "family" members; it was an arrangement that might easily be exploited by lodgers when it came time to pay their bills.[63]

Female proprietors of retail businesses faced similar problems with customers unwilling or unable to pay them. But since they worked in an industry where granting credit, "often for a period as long as six months," was not just commonplace but expected, it was a problem that was difficult to avoid. One scholar who has studied the dressmaking and millinery trades in Boston between 1860 and 1930 suggests that businesswomen in these occupations may have had it the worst. "While the relatively lenient lending practices that governed nineteenth-century retailing created considerable uncertainty for [all] business people, they proved particularly troublesome for dressmakers and milliners." She argues that "a variety of sources indicate that their customers were especially tardy in settling their bills, suggesting that patrons recognized and exploited [these] businesswomen's pecuniary vulnerability."[64] This assertion is borne out by the bankruptcies of two of the Bay Area's female proprietors working in the women's apparel industry.

If Margaret Grisby, a women's clothing retailer, was typical of Bay Area women in this industry, then it should not be surprising that proprietors who could not collect their debts went into debt themselves and often out of business. When her case was filed in the District Court on May 20, 1915, Grisby was owed $187, the total of thirteen customers' debts for suits, coats, skirts, and other items purchased from her store at 523 12th Street in Oakland. What is noteworthy here is not the amount owed; $187 was a relatively small amount in comparison to the amount of money owed other female proprietors. It is the fact that Grisby had extended credit to thirteen different female customers who could not or would not pay for their merchandise. She had been careful to keep her own debt low, paying her creditors outright for about one-half of the stock she owned. This was no small feat since on May 20, 1915, her store displayed "80 suits valued at $840; 57 coats valued at $399; [and] 19 skirts valued at $49.50." For this stock she owed creditors $589.62, less than half of its appraised value. But while we can infer from her bankruptcy case that Grisby was a careful businesswoman who had tried to keep her debt-to-earnings ratio low, the record tells us nothing of why she could not collect her own debts. Why did Mrs. Quinn, Mrs. Clara Hinckley, Mrs. Smith, Miss Smith, Miss Langland, Miss McCloud, Mrs. Waltham, Mrs. Schugart, Mrs. Avery, Mrs. Moses, Mrs. Anderson, Miss Foster, and Miss Murphy fail to pay Grisby for the merchandise they had purchased from her?[65]

The bankruptcy case of Emily Gomez, a San Francisco millinery store owner, helps answer this question. It suggests that diligence in record keeping and in pursuing one's debtors could mitigate against circumstances such as Margaret Grisby's. Gomez owed $60 rent for two months when she filed for bankruptcy on June 28, 1915. But, like Grisby, she had been careful to pay for her stock—appraised at $250.16—at the time of purchase and so owed nothing to dry goods merchants. Yet because she could not collect her debts from customers, the $60 she owed her landlord pushed her over the edge. Gomez's list of debtors, five female customers owing a total of $91.50, was a lot smaller than Grisby's, but it contained additional information that provides clues to why her customers did not pay. Mrs. Currier, who owed $8, and Mrs. Blain, who owed $12, were both listed with no address and thus could not have been tracked down very easily—either by Gomez herself or by the court's collectors—to confront them about paying. While more careful record keeping might have solved these two cases, there were other instances where an account book would not have helped at all. The largest debt owed to Emily Gomez, for $40, was by the "Estate of Alma Welch." Whether or not Gomez could collect this debt depended entirely on how much property Welch left behind and on how the probate courts valued or rated her creditors. But deciding to pursue this delicate matter was another issue. Diligently following up on the debts of a dead woman may have seemed an unpleasant if not unethical task to a small-business proprietor such as Emily Gomez, who may have known this customer personally after years of interactions.[66]

In fact, relationships between female proprietors and their customers were often delicate, even when all parties were alive and well. "Etiquette prevented the tradeswoman from pressing her claims" against nonpaying customers, one scholar contends, because "the importance of word-of-mouth advertising placed a premium on retaining the allegiance of one's clientele."[67] Indeed, even the language female business owners used with their customers, especially female customers, reflected delicacy. One study of Boston, for example, demonstrates that women tended to couch difficult financial disputes in "personal and maternal rather than commercial language." Such affectionate language was a disguise, however. For even as they tried to placate with carefully chosen words, female proprietors often pursued nonpaying customers in court.[68]

As many of the cases discussed above make clear, careful record keeping was an essential part of good financial management. Yet it is rare to find any evidence of ledgers, sales books, or cash records among San Francisco businesswomen's belongings before the 1900s.[69] One exception was the millinery business of E. & M. Holahan. The women carefully recorded transactions associated with their Kearny Street business between 1863 and 1866 in a receipt book.[70] Like many antebellum business owners, they relied on simple, single-entry bookkeeping, documenting daily transactions as well as keeping track of customers' accounts on an individual basis.[71] But no other women in the extant records before 1900 exhibited the care with which the Holahans accounted for their commercial transactions. The degree to which R. G. Dun & Company credit reporters relied on estimates of women's business worth during the 1870s underscores this absence of commercial records among small-scale proprietors. Throughout their reports the term "w[o]r[th] ab[ou]t" indicates the extent to which a proprietor's verbal statements, substantiated by information obtained through interviews with wholesalers and other business persons in the field, were the foundation of their evaluations. Occasionally, reporters even admitted to being able to obtain little useful information. In their 1878 evaluation of confectioner Mrs. Charles Mercer, for example, reporters stated, "Her actual means in business are not known but are considered ample for her needs."[72] Clearly documentation of one's business worth and daily commercial transactions were not required or provided for such investigations. Instead, proprietors were expected to be able to give "ballpark" figures that captured the essence of their financial health. Even during bankruptcy proceedings such estimates were commonplace, corroborated by the claims creditors filed to recoup money owed them by the bankrupt petitioner. In spite of the fact that the standard bankruptcy proceedings form asked whether there were any books for the business, female proprietors in the records did not list commercial books among their possessions until 1915 and later.[73] In this respect, women in San Francisco conformed to the national norm. Small-business proprietors typically did not keep records. Even "begin[ing] at the most elementary level, [and] making some kind of notation about every transaction," retail reformers agreed, would be a giant step in the right direction for small merchants, most of whom "kept no records at all."[74] Thus while numerous financial transactions punctuated the daily routines of the city's businesswomen, few could have stated their monetary status with any precision.

Much more common than business records among proprietors' possessions were insurance policies. As early as the 1870s, female insurance agents in San Francisco were peddling policies to help protect business property.[75] The fire insurance industry was rapidly maturing by then, spurred on by the increasingly crowded conditions in which urban Americans worked and lived. In just forty years, the number of general insurance companies dispensing policies for fire protection grew from 81 in 1860 to almost 500 by the turn of the century.[76] They may have found a ready customer base among the city's businesswomen, who early on turned to fire insurance to protect their commercial investments.[77] The importance of such policies as risk-management tools will be discussed in greater detail in the next chapter. What is important here is that insurance agents were among the cast of characters vying for proprietors' money. Increasingly, the agents who solicited woman-owned businesses were women themselves. Insurance companies and the female agents they employed "believed that women could make female customers more receptive to the product," and some argued that selling life insurance, in particular, "was logically suited to women because of their concern for family and children."[78] Purchasing life insurance was a common trend by the late nineteenth century as the "growing impersonality of life in big cities" led Americans to turn to insurance companies for benefits that family members had formerly given each other.[79] Women, in particular, constituted a rapidly increasing customer base.[80] By the beginning of the twentieth century, the insurance industry had expanded markedly; in addition to fire and life insurance, accident, travelers, commercial, and health insurance policies could all be found among businesswomen's investments.[81] Mabel Ritchart, owner of the Garment Specialty Company, even carried "Workmen's Compensation and Public Liability Insurance."[82] While insuring one's stock and fixtures against ruin was a financial decision looked upon favorably by credit evaluators, some women were clearly overinsured, perhaps hoping that if they invested in multiple types of policies it would bring some sense of control to their fragile commercial lives. Thus, how much to spend on insurance and what type to buy were among the many important financial decisions that faced San Francisco's female proprietors. Spending too much on insurance tied up much-needed cash that was perhaps better spent on paying back creditors or purchasing more stock. Yet failing to invest in the most basic form of protection for their businesses, fire insurance, could be commercially devastating, as Chapter 6 will discuss.

While unnecessary insurance policies suggest that agents sometimes duped businesswomen into spending needless amounts of money, it was advertisers who drew the most attention as con artists who had to be carefully handled by the city's small-scale business owners.[83] An 1875 *Daily Alta California* article, entitled "The Perils of Advertising," for example, discussed the pushy tactics employed by advertising solicitors. The businessman author lamented,

> In an unguarded moment I sent a simple little ad to a morning and evening paper. This morning as I approached my office door I found it blockaded with advertisement solicitors. . . . I have not been able to attend to any other business. They have absorbed every moment. Talk about insurance solicitors—they are lilies to these cauliflowers, summer mornings to Arctic Winters, doves to eagles, by comparison. . . . Many a dollar I should expend in advertising if allowed to do it in my own way. I cannot *afford* to spend a hundred dollars where I only propose to spend ten. I may want to put my advertisement in one, two, or three papers at most, and I do not want to put it in every newspaper in the city, and bring an avalanche of country solicitations.[84]

The hard-sell approach of advertisement solicitors that this businessman identified was a problem that countless female proprietors must have faced. Not all women advertised their businesses in local newspapers.[85] Neighborhood grocery and restaurant proprietors, for example, likely had no use for ads. They were not interested in generating citywide attention for the goods and services they provided. Instead such establishments relied on daily foot traffic and personal and ethnic ties to keep a steady stream of customers coming in the door.[86] But the hundreds of notices in San Francisco's papers between 1850 and 1920 advertising the goods and services provided by female proprietors indicate that many businesswomen did advertise.[87] By the beginning of the twentieth century, certainly, experts considered newspaper notices indispensable in some fields. *American Dressmaker*, a trade journal for the dressmaking industry, for example, argued, "The time has long since gone by when business can be carried on in the slipshod manner of former years, when one customer would recommend another." Placing advertisements "in your best local newspapers" was the essential alternative.[88] How much to spend on such customer outreach was probably second only to pushy solicitors as the most vexing aspect of the process. Clearly, solicitors were interested in getting businesspeople to spend as much money as possible on their ads. These were not employees of the city newspapers, but independent agents who typically "bought blocks of space in newspapers and magazines, and sold them to advertisers who created and designed their own ads."[89] Be-

Women such as this San Francisco ladies' hairdresser advertised their businesses in city newspapers between 1850 and 1920, clearly hoping to increase their public patronage. (*San Francisco Sentinel*, September 20, 1890)

cause ads were priced by the square or line and by how long they ran, the object was to get proprietors to pay for long ads that ran for weeks or months at a time.[90]

The goal for business owners, of course, was to get a substantial return on their investment in advertising. That is, proprietors hoped not only to recoup the cost of placing an advertisement but to make a profit from the new business such a notice brought in. During the late nineteenth and early twentieth centuries, proprietors had only their experience and estimation skills to measure such outcomes.[91] The fact that several businesswomen were in debt for newspaper advertising at the time of their bankruptcies underscores that such marketing techniques involved a truly imprecise science. By the early twentieth century, some female proprietors turned the job of advertising over to professionals, a decision that of course involved more money but which they no doubt expected to yield them more satisfying results.[92] With the professionalization of advertising came added attention to elements of design, copy, and cost, all part of the shift "from an emphasis on providing information to an attempt to influence buyers by any means possible."[93] This would have been particularly important for the owners of city-center stores and hotels competing with upscale department stores and catering to an elite audience. As discussed in the previous chapter, those were the businesswomen who labored over how to get their customers to linger in their stores and long for their merchandise and services, a process that began for many with advertising and marketing campaigns. By the 1920s women had made some inroads as copywriters, researchers, and "woman's viewpoint" experts in large advertising agencies of the sort that were hired for corporate accounts.[94] And some even founded local advertising agencies.[95] The agents that small-scale proprietors hired when they turned to the city's advertising professionals, therefore, could have been either women or men. Even expert advice could not guarantee that women's advertising dollars would yield the results they desired, however. In fact, since some of the women who hired agents declared bankruptcy, the wisdom of their decisions regarding advertising is inconclusive. They may have been overly optimistic in employing such services.

Optimism may also have played a role in women's decisions as investors. For among several businesswomen's belongings were certificates of stock. As early as the 1870s, female proprietors became stockholders, caught up in the Comstock Lode madness that seized San Franciscans. Robert O'Brien, writer of the *San Francisco Chronicle*'s nostalgic Riptides column wrote: "By the thousands they jammed California street every morning of the early '70s to turn the blocks east of Montgomery into bedlam as they screamed their mining stock bids to the curbstone brokers. Overnight, the caprice of fortune made paupers millionaires and beggars out of rich men." As with the gold-mining stock frenzy of the 1860s, "bankers, merchants, lawyers, doctors, mechanics, laborers, [and] even washer-women and servant girls" could be counted among the silver speculators.[96] By 1880, women stockbrokers and agents populated the financial districts of American cities, specifically targeting women as potential customers.[97] Female stockholders grew apace and, according to one scholar, were an increasingly important source of revenue and influence for companies, especially in the kinds of retail establishments that women patronized as customers. Such female capitalists were as likely to be domestic servants, nurses, governesses, and schoolteachers as they were wealthy widows.[98] Yet profits from stock investments generally devolved on wealthy insiders, while smaller stockholders often lost everything they had invested. San Franciscan Robert Louis Stevenson was evidently fond of saying that the stock market was the "heart of San Francisco"; it continually pumped "the savings of the lower quarter into the pockets of millionaires upon the hill."[99] Indeed, a number of the city's failed small-scale businesswomen held stock that was declared of no value at the time of their bankruptcies.[100] That they invested in stock at all, though, suggests that these women saw themselves as financial managers. Following in the footsteps of many nineteenth-century women before them, these women attempted to "use the financial markets" to increase the value of their assets.[101] They were eager to grow their earnings any way they could and willing to take risks doing so, even if they may not have understood the degree of risk involved with some of the schemes in which they invested.[102]

Among the riskiest financial arrangements businesswomen entered into were lease agreements. This was because, like purchasing on credit, such contracts bound the lessee to a financial payment regardless of whether or not her business was profitable. Some women reduced the costs of their rent by subletting a portion of their store space, splitting the cost with another proprietor, or combining their business and residence.[103] But many others utilized no such money-saving strategies and found regular rent payments difficult to maintain, sometimes accumulating months and months of unpaid rent. Julia Lyons, for example, a lodging house keeper in the 1870s, owed her landlord $4,187.50 for more than two years' worth of back rent.[104] Decades later, Ida Largent, a San Francisco dressmaker, owed $600 for several months worth of rent she had failed to pay between 1916 and 1918. According to one scholar, such contractual violation could be a financial strategy: "pay what bills [one] could to keep . . . credit good and only when none were pressing, pay [the] landlady everything above [one's] living expenses."[105] But not all property managers tolerated such breaches of contract. Largent's new landlady, Annie Nathorst, filed a claim against her with the district court for $125, one month of past due rent accumulated just before Largent declared bankruptcy. Clearly Largent's circumstances highlight the degree to which rental payments alone could drive a woman's business into the ground. Of the $865.60 she owed at the time of her bankruptcy, $725, or 84 percent, was unpaid rent.[106] Thus, how much she could afford to pay to lease her business premises was among the most important financial management decisions a female proprietor had to make. This was especially true for those women catering to the "fashionable" crowd, for whom location mattered so much (Chapter 4). Some female proprietors must have been tempted to procure sites for their businesses that they could not reasonably afford. Once a woman signed a lease, however, she had to manage her cash flow in such a way that she could afford to pay her rent each month. For even if she erred on the conservative side and rented an inexpensive place of business, if she failed to maintain the terms of her lease and did not keep up with her monthly payments, she might find herself thrown into bankruptcy like Lyons and Largent described above.

Last but not least among the cast of characters with whom female proprietors negotiated financial decisions were their employees. For many hotelkeepers, dressmakers, and retailers, the work performed by one or several laborers was essential to their success. And yet financial records emphasize that the expense of hiring staff was a problem for many of San Francisco's female proprietors. Hiring cheap labor was one solution that businesswomen pursued. Among proprietors in the accommodations industry in particular, one finds Chinese laborers employed as house servants and cooks. Bessie Hamilton, for example, employed Ah Liu and Ah Yuhn as servants in her lodging house in 1899.[107] Because they were racially ostracized in California as early as the 1850s, Chinese San Franciscans often worked in the least desirable jobs and commanded some of the lowest wages in the city.[108] Women such as Hamilton who hired them likely did so knowing this was the case. Whether or not their laborers came cheap, however, female proprietors often had a difficult time paying them. In fact, the number of women in the bankruptcy records who owed outstanding wages to their employees is quite remarkable. Some debts were small. Margaret Stein, for example, owed May Baley $8 for labor performed in her dressmaking business in 1918.[109] But often businesswomen failed to pay their employees for lengthy periods of time, accumulating large debts. For example, Lilly Stevens, also a San Francisco dressmaker, owed one of her employees $100, an amount large enough to have created substantial hardship for the woman.[110] Because they themselves teetered on the margins of economic distress, dressmakers, in particular, had a history of shirking their duties to employees. The Women's Educational and Industrial Union in Boston, for example, found that over half of the caseload in its legal aid department consisted of "women dressmakers dunning women clients and dressmakers' employees struggling to get their wages from their employers."[111] The two problems were inextricably linked, of course, as unpaid proprietors begot unpaid labor. Overall, the number of laborers in the city who were stiffed by their female bosses must have been substantial because payroll costs were among the most consistent financial difficulties of San Francisco businesswomen beginning in the 1870s and continuing through the 1920s. Whether female business owners actually were unable to pay their employees or simply exploited their workers' vulnerability, as more than one scholar has suggested, is impossible to tell from these records.[112] But clearly the cost of employing laborers consumed considerable time and energy and was among the most important daily challenges women faced as financial managers. As the bankruptcy court records indicate, many failed the challenge.

To some degree taking fiscal responsibility for a small business grew more complicated over time. Female proprietors in San Francisco, like small businesswomen and -men in cities around the country, adapted to an increasingly complex and impersonal commercial marketplace. Retailers, for example, had to contend with thousands of brand-name products. "By 1915, the average grocery store carried between 750 and 1,000 different brands of merchandise."[113] The professionalization of advertising made this marketing tool more expensive and less accessible, yet for those contending with new competitors such as the department stores, probably even more important. And expensive new technologies encouraged more and more businesswomen to make purchases using extended payment plans. Changes such as these made financial management decisions more difficult in the beginning of the twentieth century than they had been in the mid-1800s. But while the *nature* of San Francisco female proprietors' engagement in fiscal affairs changed in some substantial ways, what remained more or less continuous throughout the seventy years between 1850 and 1920 was the *fact* of their engagement in money management. Female proprietors found themselves enmeshed in financial decisions on a daily basis because the exigencies of business required it.

If this in and of itself did not set businesswomen apart from other women at the end of the nineteenth and beginning of the twentieth centuries, then the *publicness* of their decisions certainly did. For while the female managers of households and charities may have managed money, their financial decisions were not scrutinized and monitored to the same degree by the public, and their decisions did not impact their lives and profits and those of other people to the same extent. Thus the challenges of the financial tasks associated with day-to-day management of a small business were not ones women expected to wrestle with, and so many came to the job poorly prepared.

FINANCIAL TRAINING, EXPERIENCE, AND ASSISTANCE FOR FEMALE PROPRIETORS

As late as 1926, when San Francisco women had already been operating their own businesses for more than seventy years, there was still considerable concern about women's financial management abilities. That year the Women's Banking Department at Bank of Italy published a series of "pursery rhymes" designed to portray women's common financial predicaments in a poetic, playful, and childlike fashion. "If women all were financiers," one began,

> And knew just how to spend,
> And what to buy and where and when
> To borrow and to lend . . .
> If energy and precious time

Were put to the finest use,
We'd need no jingled warnings
To the tune of Mother Goose.[114]

In this and other rhymes, the publication portrayed women as hysterical fools, helpless victims, and brainless Mother Geese when it came to managing money. Female household and business managers alike were financial naifs and, it implied, in desperate need of the bank's assistance.

Such patent examples of gender stereotyping and condescension must have kept some businesswomen away from institutional help, but others turned to experts such as those available at the Bank of Italy Women's Banking Department for help with financial decisions.[115] Within seven years of the department's establishment, it had 20,000 female customers—and seven million of their dollars in the bank's coffers.[116] It was a trend on which banks everywhere tried to capitalize. Starting in 1915, women's banking departments were established in New York, Chicago, Kansas City, and Dallas, and in Wyoming, Colorado, Iowa, and Kansas. They relied on all-female staff to cater to the needs of female customers. "Aiming at the specific interests of women, in addition to the usual bank or trust products, departments also offered instruction in 'budget-making and in children's accounts.'"[117] In San Francisco, businesswomen comprised a significant portion of the department's customers at Bank of Italy. Because they occupied "places of dominating financial importance" and frequently had "the complete responsibility for considerable sums of money," female proprietors were one of the groups targeted by the bank as potential customers.[118] In fact, when a representative from the bank's head office conducted his survey of the department in November 1925, he interviewed eighteen of the bank's "good [female] customers"; fourteen of them were the owners of small businesses.[119]

Evidence from businesswomen's own financial documents suggests that by the 1910s, they used banks for a variety of financial services. Lilly Stevens, for example, a dressmaker in San Francisco, employed the "professional services" of O. G. Foelker at the First Savings Bank Building.[120] Though the historical record does not reveal the nature of these services, they may have included investment help, debt management advice, or budget development —any would have been helpful to a business owner in 1918, and all were provided by banks at the beginning of the twentieth century. Other female proprietors seemed to utilize banks less for the expertise of their employees than for the money-management services they provided. Mabel Ritchart, for example, proprietor of the Garment Specialty Company, kept a checking account at the First National Bank of Oakland, while the owner of the Women's

Apparel Shop, Posey Agee, kept deposits totaling $32.50 at the Oakland Bank of Savings.[121] This was probably the most common use of banks by women. One study found, for example, that "women's deposits in uptown Manhattan banks in the early 1920s ranged from 50 to 85 percent of all deposits."[122] These women all displayed a certain degree of know-how just by turning to their local financial institution whether for information or to utilize one of its many financial services. But the Bank of Italy argued that businesswomen typically operated their enterprises "without proper training, equipment, or advice, especially in the field of finance."[123]

Of course having poor financial management skills was a problem that plagued male as well as female proprietors, and not just in San Francisco. Since most small-business owners relied on on-the-job training to learn everyday business finance, it is not surprising that so many struggled with this all-important facet of small-business management.[124] To many small-business owners during the late nineteenth and early twentieth centuries, in fact, finances were a mystery. According to one historian, "many merchants kept haphazard records or none at all; few recorded cash transactions; most knew nothing about taking inventory, figuring margins, defining stock turn, or calculating numerical measures of their business."[125] Even as large industrial companies such as the railroads were pioneering new forms of financial accounting and bureaucratic organization, simple and even primitive record keeping persisted for many small-scale operations until at least the middle of the nineteenth century.[126] The sophisticated cost accounting developed in bigger businesses by the beginning of the last century was beyond the abilities or needs of most small-business owners. In 1916 the Federal Trade Commission addressed this gap by introducing a simplified accounting system for small-scale retailers. At its public debut, the commission chairman warned that "the majority of retail merchants do not know accurately the cost of conducting their business."[127] The problem, clearly, was not confined to women or to San Francisco but plagued most small-business owners, who were typically inexperienced and untrained.

But businesswomen appear to have been particularly disadvantaged in this regard. In general, they entered the business world with even less financial experience than most men. Some women did gain experience under the tutelage of long-time female business owners before they launched their own businesses. Milliners and dressmakers, for example, typically learned their trades during years-long apprenticeships under master craftswomen. But their training was generally confined to the craft of custom hat and dressmaking and did not include financial training.[128] Men, by comparison, had long had access to clerk jobs in other businesses where they were trained in the rudiments of business management.[129] Such "clerical occupations . . . were traditionally considered to be the major training ground for the merchant occupations." Among the job responsibilities of a typical young male clerk were "delivering goods, maintaining accurate financial records . . . and copying letters and billing."[130] Such clerks or bookkeepers worked closely with the business's proprietor and tended to have responsibility for broad managerial duties as well as financial accounting, a sound preparation for future business ownership.[131] Indeed, one scholar argues that in the 1840s "clerking became . . . the most commonly followed road to store ownership . . . in the West," where "some 70 percent of the storekeepers in that region started as clerks in other people's stores."[132] Of course, starting in the 1870s, the feminization of clerical work began to change what it meant to be a clerk, devaluing the job for men and opening it up to women who previously had had little access to office jobs. Over time clerking ceased to be the manly road to independent business ownership it had been in the first half of the nineteenth century, when firms were small and family-run. But it took over a generation for this change to be complete.[133] Thus while men gradually lost this opportunity for supervised on-the-job training, women never had it.

In addition to this valuable commercial exposure, many male proprietors had substantial experience as business owners themselves. Among the San Francisco businessmen evaluated by R. G. Dun & Company credit reporters, 30 percent had previous experience as proprietors and thus had years of hands-on training to prepare themselves for the rigors of financial management. In contrast, only 6 percent of businesswomen evaluated by credit reporters had previous experience.[134]

Experts considered the kind of financial inexperience typical among women a grave concern because it suggested an overly casual attitude about the challenges of business management. Paul Nystrom, for example, an academic economist during the 1910s and 1920s, argued that "[a] very large number of those who go into retailing have neither experience nor knowledge of the business." To those on the outside looking in, he said, it appeared as though "anybody [could] keep store."[135] This haphazard attitude toward business management condemned by experts was likely the attitude adopted by countless female proprietors. Because for any woman barred from wage labor, teaching, and clerical work who was looking for an alternative source of income that accommodated her family responsibilities (see Chapter 2), operating a business may have appeared to require few new skills. A woman contemplating opening a boardinghouse, for example, thought first about her ability to capitalize on good cooking and homemaking skills; one who planned to open a retail clothing store turned her thoughts to her knowledge of fashion. Both had a sense for how they could turn the skills they already possessed into money-making ventures. But neither one may have considered the financial management skills required in operating such a business, or how she would go about acquiring them. Ironically, the fact that women's business enterprises were commercial and financial undertakings—precisely what this book argues—is what female proprietors seemed to overlook.

So how did women figure out how to conduct the financial affairs of their enterprises? Where did they learn their skills? Who did they turn to for help?

In all likelihood women turned first to family for help with financial management. Miss E. Van Winkle, for example, a first-time milliner, received assistance from her mother, who had several years of experience in the millinery business. Such assistance likely consisted of expertise in both hat making and money making, since the older Van Winkle had enjoyed her period of success due in part, no doubt, to successful fiscal management. If Van Winkle's mother had not been able to provide such instruction, her father, proprietor of the West End Distillery, may have. Clearly there was no shortage of opportunities for the young Van Winkle to learn the financial skills required of business proprietors.[136] One study of dressmakers and milliners, however, shows that proprietors from "artisan" families, in which a father or mother had expertise in the business and could pass the knowledge along, constituted only a very small proportion of all craftswomen.[137] Exposure to sound financial decision making did not always produce a master of such practices either. One study of female business owners in Boston, for example, examines a woman who "had grown up in a household that maintained meticulous monthly accounts" but whose own financially disastrous business career indicates that she "clearly never learned the art."[138] When family connections facilitated credit and capital resources as well as advice, as they may have for Mrs. Amalie Dannenberg, whose two sons-in-laws were New York wholesalers, they were an even surer bet for long-term financial success.[139]

Other women probably mastered financial management skills working alongside their businessmen husbands. This is especially clear in the case of widowed businesswomen, whom several studies have found to comprise a significant percentage of female proprietors.[140] In San Francisco, some 19 to 35 percent of female proprietors were widows, many of whom took over their husband's enterprises.[141] Mrs. Stone, a stationery and toy retailer; Mrs. Borchard, a wholesale grocery and confectionery dealer; Mrs. Quigley, a hardware store owner; and Mrs. Short, a Japanner (shellac artisan) were among those in the R. G. Dun & Company credit reports who inherited their husbands' businesses and continued to operate them on their own after they became widows.[142] These women's ability to take over the business, especially in fields such as wholesale grocery, hardware retailing, and japanning, which were almost exclusively the domain of men, suggests that they had been intimately involved with the day-to-day operations of the businesses while their husbands were alive. In fact, "mom-and-pop" stores, common across the United States well into the twentieth century, typified such arrangements and illustrated the degree to which married men relied on the help of their wives in the conduct of their businesses.[143] Often only the man's name was used in conjunction with the business, but customers, suppliers, and even creditors may have been just as likely to conduct their business with the wife of the proprietor as with the proprietor himself.[144] As one historian argues, "The death of male spouses simply exposes to the light of history the contributions their wives had been making all along, by removing the official, male name under which the company had been operating."[145]

Women's contributions to their families' businesses included everything from tending to customers to minding the books. Such tasks may have been informally assigned instead of formally designated, but they exposed women to a wide variety of management skills. In some family enterprises, one study has found, it was the wife who had the job of "looking after the finances."[146] Studies of women in colonial America suggest that, in fact, this may have been a long-standing tradition in family-run businesses. One eighteenth-century female retailer reportedly argued that "many familys are ruined by the women not understanding accounts." (She made sure this was not the case with her own daughters.[147] By the beginning of the nineteenth-century, women's educational opportunities had expanded, ensuring that a greater proportion of the women engaged in business would be knowledgeable in mathematics, as well as literate.[148] Yet since educational opportunities were unevenly distributed, some female proprietors—especially the Irish-born immigrants who predominated among San Francisco's businesswomen— would not have benefited from this change. Far more women probably "learned the ropes" of financial management under their husband's tutelage.[149] Either way, women with experience in the operation of family businesses were often well-prepared to carry on when left on their own.

Credit reporters investigating the businesses of married businessmen occasionally found that the men's wives were the ones who actually oversaw the management of the business. But such women were anomalies, remarkable for their atypical role in the business as well as their mastery of business finance. Mrs. Finke, for example, who succeeded her husband as proprietor of a small champagne business upon his death, was, in the words of reporters, "the real manager of the business." They concluded that she "understood it thoroughly [and was] quite competent to continue it successfully" without her spouse.[150] Similarly, Mrs. Mercer presided over "one of the best paying restaurant [and] confectionery stores" in the city, but only after taking over its management from her "extremely dissipated and neglect[ful]" husband, who had steered the business into trouble.[151] Both women seem to have had better business instincts than their husbands. Who the best suppliers were, what products sold most, and how to keep customers coming back may have been among the important aspects of the business that these women knew better than their husbands. But they must also have mastered financial management skills in order to earn such accolades from the R. G. Dun & Company credit evaluators. Both women, it seems, had the opportunity to learn from their husbands' mistakes before carrying the burden of ultimate financial responsibility themselves. This likely helped them to become prudent money managers.

Women such as those described above, who benefited from the business experience of family members either through instruction or observation, may have entered the field of proprietorship unusually well prepared to handle the fiscal side of entrepreneurship themselves. Yet such women were certainly in the minority. As the following discussion of married businesswomen shows, the job of financial manager often devolved on men. Women who had the option commonly ceded control of their business's financial affairs to family members—most often their husbands.[152]

Relying on the financial management of their husbands was often a sign of success among married businesswomen. For a family to be able to afford to have the husband assist in his wife's business full time most likely required that the business be successful enough to provide the equivalent of two incomes. Occasionally such an arrangement grew out of the incompetence of a man, as in the case of Mr. Mercer, discussed above, whose wife took over his business and thereafter relied on him merely as an assistant. In other cases, husbands joined their wives' businesses as buyers, bookkeepers, or financial administrators after failing in their own attempts at business ownership. This was the case with both Mr. Dannenberg and Mr. Soper. Dannenberg joined his wife's ladies' and children's clothing store after his own business failure and "on account of deafness"; he worked steadily thereafter as her buyer and record keeper locally and in New York.[153] Similarly, Mr. Soper worked as the chief clerk for his wife's successful millinery establishment for more than ten years after the couple "found he could do better by managing her books" than by clerking in another store; his own business had failed years earlier.[154] Like most men who assisted in their wives' businesses, both Dannenberg and Soper had specific skills to contribute. Most often this meant that a married man provided financial management assistance to his wife as a "clerk" or financial record keeper. Women who could rely on their husbands to provide such expertise, some 18 percent of all women in the R. G. Dun & Company credit reports, were a step ahead of competitors who had to struggle with this difficult aspect of proprietorship all alone and with little preparation.[155]

Mrs. Emma E. Caswell provides a good example. Her husband, George, had "formerly earned his living as a clerk," but as soon as Emma "had a good trade" in the millinery business he left the job to apply his skills to the management of his wife's enterprise. While some men in this position pushed their wives' authority aside and quickly superceded them as business managers, the Caswells' relationship was a manager-assistant relationship with Mrs. Caswell clearly in the superior role.[156] In 1876 credit reporters stated that George was "now assisting [Emma] but [with] very little ability and apparently but little voice in the management"; two years later the reporters concluded that he "does oo [zero] but keep her books and attend to the buying sometimes."[157] He was, in essence, her bookkeeper. Credit reporters' dismissive assessment of George Caswell's contribution to his wife's business underscores that fiscal management skills without business savvy to inspire a commercial vision could not lead a proprietor to success. But the reverse was also true: without at least elementary skill in administering a business's finances, a visionary proprietor was also unlikely to sustain a profitable enterprise. Thus George's experience and help as a clerk may have made the difference between the kind of tidy financial accounting that kept successful proprietors on target and the haphazard record management so common among those business owners who failed. Mrs. Caswell's ability to relocate her business to Los Angeles in 1885, some nineteen years after she had gotten started in San Francisco, suggests that her husband's financial guidance did, in fact, make that difference.[158]

While a husband's financial management assistance might have helped a married woman overcome one of women's greatest impediments to business success in the late nineteenth and early twentieth centuries, entering such a commercial relationship with her spouse must have provided new challenges. Linguistically, working as his wife's "assistant" placed a married man in the subordinate position—one that marital convention at the end of the nineteenth century typically reserved for a woman. But as one historian has argued, the work that husbands performed in their wives' businesses gave them the "economic upper hand [and was] . . . accorded a higher social value." In the role of financial manager, in other words, a man in fact took hold of the equivalent of the wholesaler or white-collar job in a business, while the woman was consigned to the status of retailer, manual laborer, or employee.[159] Yet relationships such as the one between Emma Caswell and her husband, clearly the inferior in the assessment of credit reporters, suggests that such hierarchical distinctions along gender lines were not always so distinguishable.

Such blurring of marital roles was precisely what made formal business partnerships between married men and women problematic.[160] There were very practical reasons for husbands and wives to formalize their business relationship.[161] By the early twentieth century operating a small business had grown both more complicated and more costly. In addition, commercial transactions were being conducted on a nationwide scale, involving retailers and wholesalers who were strangers to each other. Wholesalers may have insisted that husband-wife teams outline their relationship in law so that the woman's assets could be reached along with the man's in case of bankruptcy. Some observers worried that formalizing commercial relationships between husbands and wives threatened to pollute the "sacred" nature of the marital bond, but what about the business relationship between spouses?[162] Did formal partnership also alter it? Did "partnership" imply that women were equal to men in such a relationship? Were women who were business partners with their husbands financial managers too, or did they, like women in less-formal business relationships with their spouses, most often cede control of financial affairs to their husbands?

The unusual relationship between Antoinetta and Giuseppi Alessandro, a married couple who were copartners in a theater venture, demonstrates that there were exceptional cases in which a wife did not relinquish financial management to her husband when they were formally partnered in business together. The Alessandros' extensive testimony in the bankruptcy case filed against them in 1909 in fact revealed that it was Antoinetta and not Giuseppi who oversaw the couple's financial transactions. When asked if he had anything to do with the negotiation of the lease for the property on which the couple was erecting a theater, Mr. Alessandro responded, "I leave everything to my wife." When asked if he signed "without question" anything his wife presented him, he answered: "When my wife signed a contract and said 'sign the contract' I signed it." And when the examiner questioned whether he ever saw or questioned the money that his wife had in her possession, Giuseppi Alessandro said, "No I never saw. My wife say she spent so much money today, and paid this and that. The best thing where a man has his own business to attend to outside [he operated a grocery stand], I don't want to hear nothing at night, because I have got enough to see the people on the market. I told my wife do anything she pleased. I didn't want to know nothing."[163] His lack of interest in involving himself in the details of the theater's construction was striking. Under cross examination he readily admitted that he did whatever his wife asked or told him to do. Even the builder's contract, which secured the services of Gaspano Leone for the construction of the theater building, carried only Antoinetta Alessandro's signature and not her husband's, in spite of the fact that he was named as a party in the agreement.[164] Giuseppi Alessandro's "hands-off" approach to the business partnership with his wife must have been inspired in large part by her obvious knack for business affairs. While he himself was a businessman, his commercial instincts must have paled in comparison to Antoinetta's for, as one theater historian noted, she was a master at capitalizing on income opportunities at the multiple theater businesses she managed between 1905 and 1914. Not only did she sell advertising space on her programs and theater curtains, but she also distributed paper fans graced with ads from local shops, saloons, restaurants, and banks.[165] Antoinetta Alessandro's business-management skills were likely as exceptional as her marketing instincts. Clearly she was a remarkable woman who forged an unusual business partnership with her husband, one that provided her with the controlling role in the relationship.

In most cases, however, women who entered into formal partnership agreements with their husbands were unlikely to supervise the financial management of a business. One study of female proprietors in nineteenth-century Britain, in fact, demonstrates that formal partnership agreements between men and women were likely to stipulate that the man "shall keep books" for the company.[166] For American women in partnership with their husbands, such agreements may have guaranteed little more than a place for their signature on official business documents. Even equal participation in a business's day-to-day affairs may have eluded married women "partners." So if women could not gain experience as financial managers even when they entered formal business partnerships with their husbands, where did some of them learn to become skilled financial managers?

Certainly women handled money as the managers of their own households and must have developed some proficiency as financial managers in that role. Eastern European Jewish women, for example, who constituted a significant proportion of America's immigrants at the beginning of the last century, typically "handled household finances" in addition to participating in family businesses.[167] Similarly, Irish American and Irish immigrant women asserted "greater female authority in major life decisions . . . [than] most other immigrants." In fact, one scholar argues, "in much of the Irish popular literature . . . [women] bore the burden for the economic well-being of the family, hoarding the money their husbands would otherwise squander."[168] As household managers, women engaged in bartering, household production for the market, and purchase decisions, all of which engaged them in eco-

nomic activity and, to some degree, financial management.[169] A variety of
entities acknowledged this by the beginning of the twentieth century. The
Bank of Italy Women's Banking Department produced budget guides for
housewives, implicitly acknowledging the degree to which the job of household manager was a financial one.[170] Women's magazines published articles
about the importance of efficiency and economy in household management,
particularly emphasizing the importance of purchasing decisions.[171] Advertisements during the same period by a wide variety of companies emphasized
this point. "Scores of tableaux disclosed the housewife planning expenditures
or paying bills at her home desk and labeled her role 'manager' or 'executive.'" Not uncommon was an ad by N. W. Ayer and Son entitled "The Little
Woman, G.P.A.," or general purchasing agent. In such ads women were con-
gratulated for their "capacities for planning, efficiency, and expert decision-
making."[172] The rationalization of housework and the acknowledgement of
women as consumption managers contrasted with the fanciful scenes punc-
tuating American magazines and newspapers. Both developments, widely
documented by contemporaries and historians alike, provide some insight
into the ways that running a household would have prepared a woman to
operate a business. Attention to operational details as well as careful purchasing were both important aspects of sound business management.

But the role of housewife did not encompass the range of money-management tasks that female proprietors encountered in the late nineteenth and
early twentieth centuries. While she might have mastered hunting for bargain prices or even managing employees, other tasks such as negotiating with
creditors or debtors may have eluded her. This was true in terms of scale
as well as scope; a housewife could arguably be said to have engaged in inventory control in the course of feeding her family, but certainly not on the
scale that the proprietor of a restaurant, such as Clara Moody, whom we met
earlier, did. Thus, if a woman entered proprietorship with only her job as
mother and wife for preparation, she was probably better off than someone
with no experience, but she was nonetheless inadequately prepared for the
variety of financial challenges she would face in her new enterprise.

Volunteering in charitable and religious organizations also provided some
women with financial management skills that might have been transferred
successfully to the world of small-business ownership. As one historian argued, "The emphasis on benevolence as a peculiarly female 'impulse from
the heart,' removed from crass economic considerations, tended to conceal
the fact that benevolence and money went hand in hand." Thus "business
concerns played a central role" in the day-to-day operations of women who
volunteered their time for charitable organizations.[173] One history of the

woman's exchange movement, for example, documents the degree to which women who operated charitable consignment stores were engaged in many of the same day-to-day operations that consumed business owners (minus the risk to their personal fortunes). Though male board members ultimately controlled the purse strings of such organizations, female managers procured leases, supervised employees, recruited craftswomen to display their goods, managed stock turn, orchestrated presentation and marketing, established prices, attended to customers, and took responsibility for balancing profits and losses.[174] Such charitable work might have been an exceptionally comprehensive training ground for proprietorship, except for the fact that the female volunteers in organizations such as this were typically elite or at the very least middle-class Anglo-Americans.[175] In contrast, most female business owners in San Francisco were immigrants (Chapter 1) who had little time or energy for charitable work. This was especially true of Irish women. As one historian argues, "Irish women . . . could rarely turn to all-female Irish societies, because for all practical purposes, such groups did not exist."[176] Clearly there were some exceptions. African American women, for example, operated businesses and participated in benevolent organizations. This fact underscores the degree to which even middle-class black women had few income opportunities available to them and thus turned to risky independent enterprise rather than much less attractive options such as domestic service.[177] In businesses such as millinery, which tended to attract a greater number of native-born Anglo-American women, some even from the middle class, charitable organizations might also have provided a profitable training ground.[178] But overall, because the female managers of late nineteenth- and early twentieth-century charitable organizations and the female proprietors of small businesses during the same period typically came from different ethnic and class backgrounds, managing benevolent societies likely did not furnish many women business owners with the skills they needed to successfully manage the financial affairs of their enterprises.

Thus the answer to the question of how female proprietors learned the financial management skills required to operate a business is probably that most did not. That is, with the exception of those fortunate women who had family members willing to educate them and provide them with experience in the day-to-day challenges of financial management and a handful of women involved in charitable organizations, most female proprietors struggled through decisions regarding money management, inventory control, debt maintenance, and record keeping without training or know-how. This did not mean that San Francisco's businesswomen were so incapable that they needed Mother Goose–like rhymes to teach them the principles of finance. But it does mean that most probably entered the world of independent proprietorship poorly prepared for this aspect of the job. Like countless businessmen and -women before them, their only opportunity for training and experience was on the job. If they were prudent, they learned from their mistakes and did not repeat them. If they were careful, they were not extravagant in their expenditures and managed their relationships with the variety of money mongers they encountered conservatively. If they were lucky, they stayed in business—the subject of the final chapter.

CHAPTER 6

WHEN WOMEN WENT

OUT OF BUSINESS

lthough most female proprietors entered the world of business poorly prepared to take on the complicated job of financial management, the marketplace did not wait for them to catch up. Not only were they hurled into a frenzy of daily financial decisions, but many also faced the caprice of business ownership head-on when calamity struck and their fortunes took a turn for the worse. Economic depressions, fire, illness, and earthquakes were regular occurrences for proprietors in San Francisco. Such catastrophes complicated the already treacherous dependencies between business owners, their creditors, and customers discussed in the previous chapter, often causing women's tenuous hold on proprietorship to falter once and for all.

The result was that woman-owned businesses in San Francisco persisted for relatively short lengths of time, as was typical of small-scale enterprises around the country, and many were thrown into bankruptcy, a mortifyingly public position for female proprietors even if it was temporary. Sheriff seizures, inventory auctions, and liquidation sale advertisements all made the experience of going out of business especially difficult since it forced women to endure commercial ruin before the gaze of their neighbors and colleagues. Yet such public failures were often impermanent since a surprising number of the city's female proprietors orchestrated commercial rebounds. Anywhere from a few months to a few years later, women were often back in business, plying their trade in the same industry, perhaps a little bit wiser if not wealthier.

These stories of women who went out of business demonstrate that while surviving disasters such as economic depression, illness, fire, and earthquake often depended on luck, anticipation of such setbacks and careful business planning also contributed to who persisted and who did not. Those women who bounced back even after such calamities sent them out of business, however, were motivated by something more. For some, desperation was a taskmaster, driving them to pursue small-business ownership over and over again because they simply saw no other options for generating an income. Others seem to be have been driven by personal pluck, an intrepid entrepreneurial spirit that gave them the necessary daring to cast their lot with proprietorship a second or third time. Either way, weathering business failure, whether precipitated by natural, commercial, or personal disaster, required both planning and persistence.

THE LONGEVITY OF WOMEN'S BUSINESSES

The careers of San Francisco's businesswomen in the late nineteenth century were relatively short. Female proprietors there typically remained in business for an average of 5.3 years, and one-third closed their doors in less than two years. Only 13 percent of the city's female proprietors, in fact, kept their doors open for over ten years.[1]

Compared to women around the country, female San Franciscans' short hold on their businesses was typical. In nonurban Illinois, for example, women stayed in business approximately 1.5 years less than women in San Francisco. Similarly, Boston's female-run millinery and dressmaking businesses lasted only one year longer than women's businesses in San Francisco.[2]

Of course, not all short-lived enterprises were failures.[3] Like small businessmen, some women used their businesses as "stepping stones" to better opportunities, while many others probably saw them as "stop-gaps" between jobs or during particularly difficult economic periods.[4] The majority of business closures recorded in newspaper advertisements, credit reports, and bankruptcy records, however, were failures caused by calamity and bankruptcy, and most likely precipitated by poor planning.

But in this respect, too, the experiences of San Francisco female proprietors were indicative of small-business owners generally. A number of sources underscore how widespread business failure was among small-scale owners during the late nineteenth and early twentieth centuries. "Small businesses came and went with much greater frequency than big businesses," one scholar argues, "[and] even in the fields in which they successfully competed or coexisted with big businesses, small firms formed and dissolved more often."[5] In one Poughkeepsie, N.Y., study, for example, nearly one-third of all retail businesses started between 1844 and 1926 closed in less than a year, and less than half lasted over three years.[6] Confectionery stores—a business popular with female proprietors—fared the worst: only 27.7 percent survived more than three years.[7] In Oshkosh, Wis., two-thirds of the businesses started between 1890 and 1912 failed within three years.[8] The large numbers of San Francisco businesswomen forced to close their doors, therefore, do not stand out.[9]

In fact, compared to the city's male-owned businesses, the enterprises operated by female proprietors failed at typically high rates. Evidence from the 1870s, the one decade for which comparative information is available, demonstrates this.[10] Of the ninety-two women who appeared in the R. G. Dun & Company records, twenty-three businesswomen, or 25 percent, had a history of business failure. During the same period, a comparable 21 percent of San Francisco's male merchants (both large- and small-scale business owners) exhibited the same pattern.[11] When the population of businessmen is reconfigured using only the owners of *small* businesses, the percentage of men who failed in business during the period goes up. Some 30 percent of small-scale businessmen in the R. G. Dun & Company reports had a history of commercial failure—comparable to the population of businesswomen in the same source.[12]

Because these figures are from the 1870s, a decade tainted by the dislocations of economic depression, they are inflated. Male merchants in San Francisco during the early 1850s, for example, had a failure rate of 7 percent, only one-third as high as their successors in the 1870s.[13] Economic hardship compounded debt and collection problems. It drove paying as well as non-paying ("owing") customers away and consequently caused income levels to plunge. At the same time, depression forced financially stretched creditors to call in their debts. Import merchants called on wholesalers, who called on retailers, who called on customers—all demanding that any merchandise bought on credit be paid for up front. Like dominoes, all came tumbling down. But while business failures were multiplied by depressions such as the one in 1877, fires, earthquakes, and illness made commercial ruin a distinct possibility even during periods of economic prosperity.[14]

DISASTERS BOTH NATURAL AND COMMERCIAL

Good money management could prevent some harbingers of business failure, as discussed in Chapter 5, but depressions, illness, fires, and earthquakes were impossible for a businesswoman to control. Such sudden reversals of fortune did not negotiate like creditors, courts, and customers might but spread adversity and destruction indiscriminately. A business owner's only chance of surviving such a calamity was anticipating its possibility and planning for it. The first step was maintaining a financially healthy enterprise, because businesses teetering on the brink of bankruptcy, such as those discussed in the previous chapter, were the least likely to survive major setbacks. Risk management went beyond this though. It involved purchasing insurance to protect one's stock and place of business and aggressively recuperating losses whenever possible. Perhaps hardest of all, it required the ability to close one's doors when that was the only option left to avoid financial ruin. But as the following stories illustrate, surviving a disaster also came down to luck and sometimes was beyond the control of even the most savvy businesswomen.

Mrs. Mary A. Soper's career illustrates how careful planning could help a small-business owner survive. She kept her liabilities low (under $1,500), bought merchandise on credit from only three houses (though she "principally paid cash"), and often discounted her bills by paying them earlier than they were due. When she closed her twelve-year-old millinery business in Leavenworth, Kans., in order to open one in San Francisco, she "did not owe a Dollar," and "it [was] claimed that she left . . . with $15,000."[15] Soper was, in the words of one credit reporter, "worthy of all the credit [she] will ask."[16] Such an enthusiastic recommendation for credit was rare, especially for a businesswoman, and underscores the degree of success she enjoyed. But while exemplary financial management kept proprietors such as Soper in business, it could not always keep them out of economic trouble.

When Mary Soper decided to relocate her millinery store to San Francisco in 1875, she was probably responding to the weakening economy spreading across the country. The depression that plagued the United States between 1873 and 1879 was unlike any that Americans had experienced before. By the time it was over, many had suffered reversals of fortune as millions became unemployed and thousands of businesses failed. But the depression affected the country unevenly. While shopkeepers in Kansas may have suffered a business slump starting in 1873, San Franciscans were still experiencing expansion through 1875. Population growth during the first five years of the decade exceeded all other periods since the gold rush, and by 1875 "new buildings were going up at the rate of 2000 a year."[17] During the same period, the city dispatched the first cable car, opening up Nob Hill to ostentatious shows of wealth by the railroad barons, and the city gained a new U.S. mint, a bigger city hall, the luxurious Palace Hotel, and Wade's Opera House, "the third largest opera house in the United States."[18] Anyone who looked toward San Francisco in 1875 might have assumed that this city was going to be spared the effects of the depression altogether. No wonder Mrs. Soper packed up for California.

But the depression did hit the city by the bay. Once applications to the San Francisco Benevolent Association for food and relief "soared . . . to 2000 a day in 1878," even Soper's careful financial management could not entirely shield her from the depression's effects.[19] In 1876 the R. G. Dun & Company credit reporter wrote, "Since starting here she has only met with modest success." And by 1878, when the last entry on Soper was recorded, the reporters wrote that she "decline[ed] giving any information" but added that "she has not been as prompt as formerly in paying for her local purchases."[20] Mary Soper was not forced out of business by the depression of 1877, but she was certainly affected by it.

When depression hit San Francisco again in the 1890s, Mary Soper "retired" from business for good. Having lived through one devastating national depression already, she knew what to expect and must have determined that she would be unable to survive another. While the depression's effects were not felt in San Francisco until 1896, stories of hardship in other parts of the country augured certain economic disaster for Californians sooner or later. Newspaper articles about Coxey's Army, the struggles between "Labor and Capital" in the middle of the country, and the desperate measures taken by East Coast residents to put bread on the table told Soper, a woman experienced with national depression, what she could expect in the next couple of years.[21] Along with old age (by now she was sixty-seven) and declining health, the impending economic hardship made closing her business the best option.[22] This was how a careful businesswoman planned for disaster: she managed risk and avoided financial ruin. For even if it meant the end of a career, economic depression only became a business disaster when a proprietor insisted on continuing in spite of declining income and in defiance of recalled debts. At that juncture, poor planning became the calamity.

Economic downturns such as the ones that affected Mrs. Soper's business in 1877 and 1894 were only the first of many misfortunes with which female proprietors had to contend. Repeated illnesses, fires, and earthquakes plagued thousands of large- and small-business owners in San Francisco during that period. Because they were even less predictable than economic depressions, which might be anticipated as they moved westward across the nation, such disasters could be even harder to manage.

Like other American cities, San Francisco was host to deadly cholera, smallpox, and other outbreaks during the late nineteenth century, and thus small-business owners there had to take illness seriously. San Francisco newspapers document the history of proprietors desperate to save themselves financially as well as physically. In a single day during the month of September 1869, for example, the *San Francisco Chronicle* ran two ads for businesses being sold in haste by proprietors who had become ill. One read: "$1,200 MILLINERY STORE for sale, located near Montgomery and Market streets; will sell at half cost of stock on account of sickness; has a fine established trade among the first class ladies in this city."[23] Both its location on Montgomery Street, widely known as one of the most fashionable streets in San Francisco during the 1860s and 1870s, and its price tag suggest that this millinery establishment was a highly successful one.[24] So why could the proprietor not "afford" to be sick and still maintain her business? Again, as in the case of Mrs. Soper's business closure, the decision was prompted in all likelihood by fiscal responsibility. By selling the business while still intact, the proprietor was attempting to avoid the fate that often befell less fortunate invalids: bankruptcy.

The story of yet another milliner forced to go out of business "on account of sickness" illustrates the spiral of debt that the ill often accrued and which could have ended the career of just about any small-business proprietor. In 1873 Lizzie Carter, a millinery store owner for at least two years prior, was forced to declare bankruptcy as a result of what must have been a very serious and incapacitating illness. In May of that year, a court clerk recorded that Carter owed $45 for the rent of her store, an unrecorded amount for various goods she had purchased and had delivered to the store, plus a sizable $2,612 in medical bills. Of this last debt, $2,000 was due to Dr. Sherb for "medical attendance to the petitioner" and $25 was due to Ann Garlting, a nurse, for "nursing [the] petitioner while sick." Lizzie Carter also owed $250 to Dr. Wecks, $45 to Dr. Green (a druggist), $142 to Wakelee's Drug Store for drugs and medicine, and $150 to the drug store on the corner of Third and Howard Streets for the same.[25] Even if she had been fortunate enough to have a family member or friend willing to run her business in her absence, the debts Lizzie Carter had accrued were so high they could have put out of business even an extremely successful millinery store such as the one advertised for sale above.[26]

Health issues beyond the personal could also affect a woman's business. Fear of contagious diseases, for example, could keep customers away. In a letter home to her sister, Sallie Snow wrote that while she felt isolated from "society" in her out-of-the-way boarding house, she preferred it to one more centrally located because she felt "safe from fires and small pox."[27] It was exactly this kind of consumer whom the proprietor of the Union Laundry feared. In response to the city's smallpox epidemic of 1868,[28] M. Michelsen placed an ad in the *Daily Alta California* announcing that "on account of the small-pox raging in th[e] city," he would no longer accept clothes from "all classes of people" and would from that day forward confine his business "ONLY to Private Families and such orders which [he could] . . . [him]self inspect."[29] By making this drastic change, Michelsen probably aimed to contain public hysteria about the risks of sending out one's laundry—leaving it to be mingled with that of hundreds of others of "all classes"—as much as he hoped to protect himself from contagion. His advertisement was a preemptive strike meant to save Union Laundry. It was a tactic emulated by the city itself decades later when faced with the greatest public health crisis in its history.

Between 1900 and 1908, San Francisco waged a heroic and divisive battle against the "black death," or bubonic plague. It was the first location in the continental United States to have to contend with the frightening epidemic that at the end of the nineteenth century had wreaked havoc in Asian cities such as Hong Kong. Because of its important role as a Pacific port, San Francisco was vulnerable to the disease from the outset. But it was the city's obsessive commitment to trade that forced the hand of quarantine officials on Angel Island in spite of their suspicions about the *Australia*.[30] In from Honolulu, Hawaii, a city that had just survived a terrible outbreak of the disease, the ship worried inspectors. But unable to find any evidence to condemn it and under pressure to keep commerce moving, island officials flagged the ship through to the city's port, where plague infested rats scampered on shore along with its cargo. Within two months, the city's first human casualty of the disease, Wong Chut King, a Chinese lumber salesman, was discovered in a Chinatown rooming house. In the minds of white city officials, the location of the outbreak was no accident. Chinatown and its immigrant residents had long been associated with disease and danger; it was one more way that they served as scapegoats for San Franciscans' problems. As a result, public health officers quarantined the area, immediately roping off its borders and stationing city police on its perimeter to keep whites out and Chinese in. Thereafter the Chinese suffered inspections, inoculation, and incarceration, since they continued to be incorrectly identified as the source of the disease. Yet bowing to pressure from city business leaders to counter the negative publicity, Mayor James Phelan went on record falsely stating that the plague had been contained to one case and the scare was over. A similar denial by Governor Gage and the deans of several local medical schools followed. Even if it temporarily quelled fears abroad, the announcements could not contain the epidemic that raged on in the city, on and off, until 1908. After 280 confirmed cases, 172 deaths, and the destruction of over 2 million rats, the primary carrier of the disease, the U.S. surgeon general declared San Francisco officially free of plague.[31]

Female proprietors must have felt the impact of such health scares. Certainly those who drew their pay from the tourist trade did. As news of the city's epidemic spread, "westbound trains traveled empty . . . [and] vacationers favored safer destinations."[32] Hoteliers suffered, no doubt, unable to draw the crowds to which they had grown accustomed. Most proprietors of such establishments were men, but, as discussed in Chapter 4, a handful were women who oversaw luxurious establishments designed to draw traveling customers. In addition to losing patrons during the plague outbreak, such businesses almost certainly lost employees too. Chinese men typically filled jobs as servants inside private homes, boardinghouses, and hotels, but the quarantines imposed on Chinatown, where the city's Chinese were segregated, kept them away from their jobs. Some whites were desperate for normal business to resume. The *San Francisco Chronicle* reported that one white woman was seen trying to pass garments to a Chinese tailor across the quarantine blockade before a police officer stopped her. Laundrymen were prevented from delivering clean bundles of clothes to white customers outside of Chinatown as well.[33]

This may, in fact, have created opportunities for some white women, especially those in the laundry industry. If quick to respond, they might capitalize on the gap in services caused by the Chinese quarantine. Others probably found that hysteria about the epidemic made it prudent to distinguish themselves from Asian service providers. Capitalizing on the "purity" of white womanhood, the strategy used by Caucasian laundry providers in the 1870s, took on new meaning this time around; such providers could use the argument that white meant clean, in the sense of disease-free. By 1908, Japanese immigrants operated eight successful laundries in the city and attracted much of the animosity that Chinese laundries had in the nineteenth century. Throughout the bubonic plague scare, Japanese businesses and residents were slandered along with the Chinese as the likely source of the disease. White female laundry workers used both these facts to orchestrate a movement against Japanese businesses in their industry. The "Anti-Jap Laundry League," in fact, distanced white women from Asian laundrymen with pamphlets such as "Protect Your Homes from Loathsome Oriental Diseases!" and "By patronizing a Jap you help reduce the White Girls' Standard of Living."[34] Of course, the fact that the Chinese won when they took their protest of the quarantine to court underscores the degree to which white San Franciscans were initially unconvinced of the severity of the epidemic and unwilling to let it interrupt their day-to-day lives, including where they took their laundry.[35]

The city's final triumph over the dreaded disease, however, came only with the full cooperation of city residents. This included the proprietors of small food shops and stands that were targeted by health officers as breeding grounds for rats because of the scraps they left behind. "Fruit sellers and vegetable dealers were complacent about tossing banana peels, rotten apples, and wilted produce in the street. The produce district, as a consequence, was second only to Butchertown as a rodent restaurant."[36] Publicity about the problem caused women consumers to threaten a boycott against the offenders. Scared straight, business owners complied with the new hygiene mandates, and the Front Street market was declared "clean enough to eat off."[37] Female grocers, fruit and vegetable vendors, food hawkers, and restaurant owners, all of whom abounded in early twentieth-century San Francisco, faced a clear mandate: invest the time and money required to dispose of their refuse properly or they would be put out of business. Like women residents themselves, woman-owned businesses were certainly among the casualties of the city's war against the plague.

If high fever or red rashes did not "burn up" a proprietor and her business between 1850 and 1920, then fire just might. In the early days of the city this was a particular risk. San Francisco burned down six times before 1851 just because no one would stop the hunt for gold long enough to organize a city fire department.[38] Writing home to her mother in 1849, Margaret De Witt wrote, "There has been a large fire here and I expect one of these days this place [the boarding house she conducted] will burn down. It is a great risk to have property here as there can be no insurance and no way of extinguishing a fire should it take place."[39] But even after fire-fighting institutions had been established, failure by incineration was a possibility with which all business owners had to contend.[40] Once a fire got going, firemen might be able to stop it from spreading to the whole city, but they could not always stop it from ruining one person's entire stock and place of business. So many San Francisco businesses were burned down, in fact, that in 1874 a credit reporter particularly noted that Mrs. A. H. Stoppelkamp, a grocer, "Has not been burned out since in business here."[41] In this city, being burned out seems to have been the norm rather than the exception.

While fire could destroy any proprietor's enterprise, certain types of businesses carried a greater risk of being burned out. The Home Mutual Insurance Company, for example, charged higher premiums in 1865 for any business that utilized cooking or heating equipment or whose stock was considered highly flammable. Among the enterprises singled out were bakeries, confectioneries, crockery and drug stores, hotels, restaurants, laundries, tobacco and cigar retailers, toy stores, and millinery shops—all businesses that were frequently operated by women.[42]

Those in the apparel industry may have been at the greatest risk of seeing their stores go up in smoke. In contrast to proprietors in other industries whose provisions turned over quickly, women who conducted dry goods, fancy goods, and millinery enterprises often stored large quantities of highly combustible inventory for months at a time. Fabric, lace, ribbon, feathers, artificial flowers (made of paper or silk), and even willow shoots and straw for summer hats turned these places of business into virtual tinderboxes waiting to be ignited.[43]

Miss Baker's story seems to provide convincing evidence of this. On September 12, 1871, under the subtitle "Fires Last Evening," the *Daily Alta California* reported:

> About a quarter past eleven o'clock last evening a fire was discovered in the rear of Miss J. A. Baker's millinery store, No. 426 Kearny street, but before an alarm was sounded the store was enveloped in flames. Though the Department was promptly on the ground, the flames had spread to the upper stories. The building, a three story brick, is owned by H. Proll. . . . The third floor is occupied by Reiss' family. The fire is supposed to have originated in a kitchen underneath Miss Baker's millinery store. Her stock was entirely destroyed, but is said to be insured. The loss will reach several thousand dollars.[44]

Although the fire reportedly started in the kitchen beneath Baker's shop, her stock must have quickly coaxed the flames upstairs and provided enough fuel for them to spread rapidly. Notice that "the store was enveloped in flames . . . before an alarm was sounded," in spite of the fact that the third floor was occupied by the Reiss family. Baker's fate may have been shared by other apparel industry proprietors who could do little to stop their stock from fueling the flames that burned them out.

Whether or not a businesswoman could recover from such a setback often depended on whether she had protected her commercial assets in advance. Proprietors of large establishments usually had the "capital resources to recoup or to make new investments elsewhere," but female as well as male small-business owners usually did not.[45] A businesswoman who insured her merchandise against ruin, however, was likely to survive a fire financially even without additional monetary reserves.

Miss Baker was probably one of these survivors. She had taken two precautions that suggest she anticipated the possibility of fire. First, she had rented store space in a brick building with the hope that she would reduce the risk of being burned out. Described as "fireproof" in San Francisco newspaper ads in the second half of the nineteenth century, brick buildings were believed to provide a virtual barrier to conflagration.[46] Proprietors who located their businesses in such buildings made a point of advertising it, suggesting that this choice was a deliberate one for renters such as Baker.[47] The second precaution she had taken to protect herself from this calamity was to insure her stock. Even though her inventory "was entirely destroyed" by the fire that night, Miss Baker probably could have recovered from the fire if her insurance coverage was extensive enough. While there was really no way to "fireproof" one's business, Baker had come about as close as possible and as a result of her preventive and precautionary measures, probably recovered from the disaster.[48] Many other businesswomen visited by fire were, of course, not so fortunate.

While fires plagued city residents and business owners throughout the nation in the late 1800s and early 1900s, earthquakes were a problem unique to Californians. In 1868 forty-niners got their first significant shake when San Francisco was struck by a quake large enough to send "a timid few packing to firmer ground across the Bay."[49] Since the tremors reportedly caused more of an effect "upon the heart and feeling" than they did "material damage," their influence on commerce must have been relatively mild.[50]

But the 1868 earthquake did affect female proprietors in the accommodations industry, since safety was a preeminent concern for customers when it came to choosing a place to live. One boarder, for example, declared in a letter home that "since the earthquake I have been much better contented with my home here because I am in a frame building and on solid [as opposed to land-fill] ground." "Many of the houses here are of brick," Sallie Snow continued, "and on 'made land.' These of course felt the earthquake most."[51] By the time San Franciscans had experienced their first major earthquake, boardinghouse keepers could make a case for the superior safety of either a brick building or a wooden frame building, depending on the latest catastrophe. In the 1850s the main concern was fire, after 1868 it was earthquakes. City dwellers probably debated endlessly whether brick or wood made a safer place to live and work. Either way, consumer interest in safety must have stopped more than one San Francisco female proprietor and forced her to consider which type of structure would be the more-profitable location for her business.

Neither brick nor frame buildings were spared, however, when earthquake and fire swept through San Francisco in April 1906, killing hundreds and leveling thousands of businesses.[52] The few proprietors who were spared its effects had luck, not their own anticipation and preparation, to thank for

Damage from the 1868 earthquake, shown here in dramatic detail, convinced some San Franciscans to reject brick structures built on "made land." Such preferences affected businesswomen in the accommodations industry who struggled to convince their customers that their hotels and boardinghouses were safe places to reside. (California Historical Society, FN-22923)

their good fortune. Ella Leigh, for example, owner of Stoneleigh Flats, an apartment house she was having built on Hayes and Scott Streets beginning in December 1905, hardly had reason to comment on the disaster. The project went forward as planned, but cost $26,500 instead of the $25,000 she expected to pay "on account of [the] earthquake and fires."[53] Leigh's property was safe simply because it was being built in the Western Addition, a neighborhood located above Van Ness Avenue which escaped the earthquake and fire virtually unscathed.[54]

Location, not surprisingly, had everything to do with surviving the 1906 disaster. Like all tremors before and since, the earthquake struck landfill areas the hardest and was felt the least in the sections of the city built on hilly rock foundation. This meant that the Financial District (east of Montgomery), the waterfront, and a large portion of the region south of Market, all landfill, were largely destroyed on April 18.

Inexpensive frame boardinghouses and family dwellings, hundreds of which housed the city's working class south of Market, were said to fare the worst. Since the quake struck at just past 5:00 AM, residents asleep in such buildings were buried in rubble by the hundreds, along with their landladies and landlords.[55] One rooming house owner in the neighborhood narrowly escaped with her life by climbing out of her window onto the street as soon as the "swaying and creaking" began. "The house collapsed a second afterward and was on fire immediately," killing all forty people in it, including her husband. The story was, according to its author, "one case out of dozens of others."[56]

The fires, which began on April 18 immediately following the quake and burned for four days, incinerated downtown, Chinatown, North Beach, Russian Hill, Telegraph Hill, and Nob Hill, essentially the original city site, leaving all in ruins. In the Mission District, the fire was contained in a finite area bordered by Howard Street in the east, Dolores in the west, 19th in the south, and 15th in the north—roughly twenty square city blocks. The rest of the area was untouched by fire and felt safe enough that the district's park, Mission Dolores, served as a refuge for those who had been burned out.[57]

Human error compounded the disaster. Occasioned by the centennial anniversary of the earthquake and fire, recent revisionist examinations emphasize, for example, the degree to which dynamiters, intent on carving a firebreak along Van Ness Avenue, "destroyed their city to save it."[58] In addition, self-interested political and business leaders abounded, new scholarship asserts, derailing humanitarian efforts in the city.[59]

Because the central business district was entirely destroyed, proprietors located on the outskirts of the city center stand out among the survivors. In fact, for grocers a location in one of the exterior regions known today as the upper or lower Mission, the Haight, the Castro, the Richmond, the Sunset, Western Addition, or Bernal Heights nearly predicted commercial persistence. There were 119 female grocers listed in the 1905 city directory, and 26 of them (22 percent) were listed in either the 1907 or 1908 directory, having rebounded in 1 to 2 years. Of the survivors, 18 (69 percent) were located in one of the regions described above. Among female dry goods retailers, 10 out of 30 rebounded in 1 to 2 years, and of the 10 survivors, 6 were located in the Mission District or Western Addition. Milliners and dressmakers rebounded from the earthquake at similar rates, with 23 percent (42 out of 184) of milliners and 22 percent (60 out of 276) of dressmakers from the 1905 directory appearing in the 1907 or 1908 directories, but show no similar geographic trend.[60]

Women must have operated many of the inexpensive boardinghouses and lodging houses south of Market Street that were destroyed by the earthquake and fire, because even fewer of them bounced back. None of the 12 female boardinghouse keepers listed in the 1905 directory appeared in either the 1907 or 1908 directories, and only 5 of the 307 (2 percent) women who operated lodging houses in 1905 rebounded within 1 to 2 years.[61] The problem was not limited to businesswomen, however, since the total number of proprietors in the industry shrank from approximately 1,288 in 1905 to about 298 in 1907 and less than 650 in 1908.[62] As the city began to rebuild, the influx of carpenters, masons, and general laborers breathed new life into the accommodations industry. Most were single men who sought their meals and a good night's rest in inexpensive boardinghouses and lodging houses—the kind women were likely to operate. This drove the number of women in the industry to a peak in 1910, as already discussed in previous chapters, but it was an increase that evidently started gradually and did not show its strength until after 1908.

The barriers to recovery for business owners were numerous. While looters were virtually eliminated by Mayor Schmitz's proclamation of martial law immediately following the earthquake (police officers were authorized to kill looters and other criminals on sight), procuring an inventory worthy of sale remained a challenge.[63] Even if their stock had survived the tremors and fires, grocers found their stores raided by soldiers "so as to get food for the people" until relief trains arrived. Food stores in nearby Oakland and Berkeley were "under martial law, [with] no provisions allowed to be sold" in order to prevent hoarders.[64] But of course, those who had lost everything had the hardest time rebounding. Locating new products to sell was particularly difficult since the entire wholesale district of the city had been destroyed. However, residents were allowed to pick over the remains of crumbled buildings in search of canned goods and replacement housewares; perhaps such scavenging produced the first post-earthquake retailers.[65] Beyond that, San Francisco banks and merchants were issuing no credit and cashing no checks in order "to raise money necessary for supplies," so even proprietors with cash reserves or well-established credit may have been unable to access them.[66]

In spite of the obstacles, however, those determined to reopen their businesses did so. By May 3, just two weeks after the disaster, one city resident reported that "the stores are commencing to open again," even though buildings were still without gas and electricity and many lacked a supply of water.[67] Most enterprises were likely simple, makeshift affairs thrown together with whatever a proprietor could find. The I. Magnin store, for example, reportedly reopened in the family home at Masonic Avenue and Page, where its founder, Mary Ann Magnin, and her family sold handmade laces and French imports to wealthy city residents who had managed to escape the fire financially unscathed.[68] Before rebuilding began, commercial endeavors could be located wherever traffic was greatest, and so Market Street, formerly one of the most expensive real estate locations, became home to a plethora of humble retail stands. "Already shacks are spring[ing] up all over the place," wrote Edith Bonnell. "Market Street is one line of booths, like an enormous country fair. They were selling all sorts of things."[69] But rebuilding began quickly. Once it did, landlords could charge "enormous rents" since the supply of permanent structures was so low and the demand for them so high.[70] Businesswomen had limited options for funding such expenses. Still off-limits to most women, bank loans likely helped few, if any, female proprietors.[71] Even the informal loan network, discussed in Chapter 3, which helped launch so many women's businesses, probably was unavailable since so many lost everything in the earthquake and fire. Relief funds, distributed by a committee of city and Red Cross officials to former proprietors with a viable business plan but no funds to implement it, helped some women, as discussed in Chapter 3.[72] Few would have benefited from fire insurance payments since so many companies defaulted on their obligations.[73]

Those who overcame the plethora of barriers to reentry, however, were likely the most seasoned of the city's businesswomen. Such long-term and successful proprietors may have had larger capital resources to call on, but even more importantly, they could rely on years of experience and good business planning skills. Maria J. Stacom, for example, knew how to steer a business through disaster. She had been a milliner in San Francisco since before 1876 and had survived business failure, two economic depressions, and now, the city's biggest calamity of all.[74] She was a proactive manager, one more likely to wrestle a problem to the ground than let it overtake her.[75] It was an approach that clearly served her commercial interests well. Two years after the earthquake, she reopened her millinery store on Ellis Street, just blocks from her former Market Street location.

The degree to which economic depressions, illness, fires, and earthquakes precipitated commercial failure underscores that going out of business was not a gender-specific fate that only women faced. Certainly, uneven access to capital and credit hampered businesswomen's ability to weather financial storms, whatever the cause, and may have deepened their difficulties during challenging times. But small businessmen too struggled under the burden of national economic dislocations, personal and family health tragedies, and natural disasters. Thus not only did male and female proprietors fail at similar rates, but their businesses failed for similar reasons as well.

BUSINESS FAILURE

Whether caused by depression, illness, fire, or earthquake, business failures could often be worked out privately between proprietors and their creditors. According to Peter Decker, "most merchants who failed in business sought private settlements with their creditors who, wishing to avoid the delays and expense of the courts, usually accepted between 30 and 50 percent of their outstanding bills." The advantage of such a settlement for the debtor was that it could be handled quietly and discretely, without "attract[ing] public notice" in the way that appearing in court would do.[76] Still, business failure was business failure. Even if such career lows were not recorded in court records, they were certainly remembered by credit reporters and creditors. It did not necessarily take a court order to brand a businesswoman "untrustworthy" or "unsafe" for credit.

When a businesswoman was unable to settle with her creditors and was forced into bankruptcy the ensuing process was both exposing and humiliating. Since a "declaration of bankruptcy was . . . a public advertisement to the community that all future business transactions with that person . . . would have to be conducted with extreme caution," the onslaught of attention that a female bankrupt received was less a branding than a public trial in which the defendant had no recourse.[77] On November 25, 1872, a Dun reporter wrote that Madame C. Goldberg "has been attacked by an Eastern creditor [and] probably will be put into Bankruptcy." Four days later she filed for bankruptcy.[78] That Goldberg's pursuit by a creditor was perceived as (and probably felt like) an attack points to how vicious bankruptcy proceedings could be. Discretion and propriety were discarded in favor of efficiency and inquisition while creditors and their agents sought to recoup as much of their outstanding bills from the bankrupt individual as possible. How they claimed those debts was often a matter of public interest. Possession of a proprietor's place of business by the sheriff, inventory of its contents by officially appointed appraisers, confiscation and storage of her property in city warehouses, and public auction of her stock in trade and the fixtures of her business were often a part of the process. Each of the individuals involved in this process stood to gain from the bankrupt's losses, engaging in what one scholar has called "vulture capitalism." The feeding frenzy that followed a woman's declaration of bankruptcy must have added to the difficulty of the experience, especially since it was often those who knew her inventory best—customers, lawyers, and appraisers with whom she had had personal interactions—who capitalized on the opportunity to benefit from her loss.[79] When carried out in this fashion, bankruptcy proceedings invited the public as well as self-interested acquaintances into a woman's business affairs in a way she surely never intended.

Once the proceedings got under way, businesswomen became truly public figures. When Mrs. Chapman was attached for rent in 1877, for example, the sheriff took possession of her human hair, lace, and millinery store and she was forced out of business. She must have been relieved that less than a year earlier she had left her former business location in the very popular Palace Hotel. A possession there—the hotel frequented by the 'creme de la creme'—might have made it into the society pages of the local papers.[80] Three years after she took over her deceased husband's saloon and grocery store, Mrs. McCarthy lost it in 1879. The sheriff advertised the sale of her store and placed the transaction in the hands of one Sam Harding, probably a business agent.[81] Luckily, notices for public auctions tended not to mention the bankrupt proprietor's name. But if the sheriff's ad looked anything like the one that appeared in the *Daily Alta California* on September 2, 1870, it would have been hard for Mrs. McCarthy to hide her fate. All anyone needed to know was where her grocery store was located and they would know that her business was being shut down. The September ad took nearly a foot of column space at the top of the page and read:

> This day, Friday, September 2, 1870, at 11 o'clock, A.M. on the southeast corner of Battery and Pacific Streets, we will sell the stock and fixtures of a grocery store, consisting of flour, sugar, teas, wines, liquors, pickles, can fruits, scales and weights, counters, shelving, and fixtures. To be sold without reserve. Terms—Cash in U.S. gold coin, and goods to be removed on day of sale. James Evrard & Co. Auctioneers.[82]

Since groceries in late nineteenth-century San Francisco were usually corner stores, the location of this sale was most likely where the proprietor had formerly conducted business.[83] Mrs. McCarthy and others like her may have been similarly exposed in notices like this that advertised business liquidations at proprietors' places of business. While patrons would have learned of a woman's business failure eventually, friends and colleagues might have been spared the embarrassment had it not been for such declarations. Women who had their businesses disposed of in this way must have felt that their failure was being advertised to the entire city. Such public humiliation was a high price to pay.

Women and men may have experienced this aspect of business failure differently. For a female proprietor, scrutiny of her financial affairs opened her private life to the public in a way that many nineteenth-century women would have been uncomfortable with given the high value placed on female modesty. Men, on the other hand, labored under a dominant belief that business failure was akin to personal failure. As one recent book on failure in America has documented, by the end of the nineteenth century the triumph of business culture caused Americans to conflate identity with achievement. Instead of describing business enterprises as failures, Americans began describing businessmen themselves as failures, applying "the language of business . . . to the soul." This weighed particularly heavily on businessmen whose personal identify, masculinity, social value, and family fortunes all were threatened by going out of business even if it was clearly caused by a disaster such as depression, illness, fire, or earthquake.[84]

BUSINESS REBOUNDS

Whether they were forced out by calamity or shut down by debt or credit problems, women often found their way back into business. Their resolve to do so may underscore how scarce alternative employment opportunities were for many women, as discussed in Chapter 2. Desperation could be a powerful motivator and may have driven some women to submit to the vagaries of proprietorship over and over again. But it also shows how deeply San Francisco women believed in the city's opportunities and how strongly they were motivated by the pluck to persist in spite of serious setbacks.

Thus while small business proprietorship was not an indication of permanent upward mobility, closing or failing in business was also not the end of an individual's attempts at or possibilities for independent economic enterprise.[85] In the words of one scholar, "reversal was business as usual" for women in small business.[86] This was true for male proprietors from the city's early days when "many failed as many as three times and started anew."[87] San Francisco may not have been "a land of opportunity," but it was a "place for another economic chance with a clean slate."[88] Women also took advantage of the city's liberal commercial environment, and many who failed in business reopened, sometimes as often as three times, as well. Thus the door that closed so frequently on business opportunities in San Francisco seems to have been a revolving door for many, one that rarely actually kept women out permanently.

In this respect, San Francisco female proprietors at the end of the nineteenth century may have been unique compared to businesswomen elsewhere. For example, one study finds that when milliners and dressmakers in Boston went out of business they stayed out. "Failed businessmen might reenter the marketplace—sometimes many times," the author writes, "but most women had neither the resources nor perhaps the resolve to begin anew. Once they left the business world they rarely returned."[89]

By comparison, San Francisco businesswomen almost look like commercial recidivists. While their economic circumstances may have been precarious, they held onto the promise of success with tenacity. Roughly one-fifth (21 percent) of women in the Dun reports reentered the business world after failing at least once (see table A13).[90] Even more remarkable, of the twenty-four women whose businesses failed, 79 percent were back in business within a few years. Whether they were forced out, shut down, or closed their businesses themselves, San Francisco women seem to have found both the resolve and the resources to return to the world of commerce. Some did so over and over again—failing as many as three times and still finding a way to reopen their businesses. For these female proprietors, proprietorship seems to have been precious indeed.

The individual story of one female proprietor demonstrates this point even more strongly. Lizzie Carter, who went bankrupt in 1873 on account of all the doctor and drug bills she accrued, was back in business selling millinery goods again by 1878. On February 20 of that year a Dun credit reporter wrote: "She says that she has her discharge in bankruptcy and does business in her own name. . . . She is fairly prompt in her payments and with some houses is given a modest credit for that reason but others decline selling [to] her except for cash. Her previous record and her general reputation is such that not much confidence would be placed in her statement should she make one."[91] Obviously Carter had recovered from her illness and worked to pay back her creditors. That she succeeded in this endeavor is demonstrated in her "discharge in bankruptcy." Then, fighting a bad reputation and restricted credit opportunities, Carter somehow managed to acquire the necessary capital and stock to reopen for business. Her determination points to how much some women cherished the opportunity to manage their own businesses and how resistant they were to calamity. It probably also underscores how desperately some women needed the chance proprietorship gave them to make a living.

As remains true of small-business owners even today, San Francisco's female proprietors were forced out of business by financial disaster often brought on by physical and economic calamity. Those that stayed in business did so largely because of careful planning. Business owners had to manage their finances conservatively to protect their inventory from risk, and they had to know when to fold if the hand they had been dealt could offer no better play.

Those who survived such setbacks, and especially those able to reenter the world of proprietorship after failing, also demonstrated a persistence, whether motivated by pluck or desperation, that set them apart. Rather than capitulate to calamities such as depression, illness, fire, and earthquake, such women rallied their resources and resolve to start anew. Their commitment to independent business ownership, though, was not just a display of tenacity but also an indication of their limited options. For these women, the unique ability to balance economic and domestic responsibilities as proprietors made business ownership an opportunity worth pursuing over and over again.

Lest planning, persistence and pluck be mistaken for financial security, however, this story ends with the demise of Mary A. Soper, one of the most successful of the San Francisco proprietors discussed here. After retiring from a millinery career that lasted nearly a generation, longer than any other woman located in the historical record, Soper died poor and alone. Her death on August 21, 1911, at the San Francisco Old People's Home was attended only by Dr. M. E. Rumwell, her physician; no family members were present.[92] She was buried the next day at Cypress Lawn Cemetery in an unmarked grave site along with over twenty other inmates from the same institution. The only public monument to Soper that remains is a stone reading: "Old Peoples Home."[93] At the end of her life, the only clue about Soper's remarkable persistence as a businesswoman was filed away in a dusty archive full of city death certificates: "Mary A. Soper, Milliner, Retired."[94]

CONCLUSION

Capital intentions steered San Francisco's female proprietors through the vagaries of small-business ownership between 1850 and 1920. This is not to say that women operated their businesses unhampered. In fact, women's choices as female proprietors, from start to end, were shaped by legal, economic, and family restrictions, sometimes in ways that distinguished these women from their male counterparts, who were often freer in their commercial maneuvers. Yet within the confines of these boundaries, women business owners displayed sensitivity to market forces. This was as true in their decision *to* start a business as it was in *how* they started and maintained the business, and even in how they grappled with commercial failure. Even when they operated businesses in industries traditionally associated with "women's work," female proprietors are best understood as commercial actors, women who capitalized on their domestic (and other) skills by responding to a market impulse that such services would draw paying customers and generate a profit.

The world in which such businesswomen operated was not a "female economy," as others have argued, but a heterosocial, commercial world. Men and women both could be found among their customers, creditors, and employees. This was especially true in late nineteenth- and early twentieth-century San Francisco since so many women found opportunity in the accommodations industry, providing lodging and cooking services to the city's disproportionate number of male residents. Immigrant and native-born, white, black, and Chinese women alike pursued proprietorship in the city, finding special opportunity catering to the domestic needs of the men who substantially outnumbered women in the city from 1850 to 1910. However, Irish immigrant women in particular and foreign-born white women more generally stand out as the majority of San Francisco's female proprietors, cashing in on long-standing traditions of female economic independence as well as cultural prescriptions that they reject paid labor outside the home after marriage and motherhood.

Married women's business laws as well as divorce laws in California underscore that, in fact, all married women were tied to their homes and their husbands; female proprietorship, therefore, was a particularly attractive option for women with families because it could be combined with household responsibilities and even operated out of or adjacent to their homes. In conjunction with the formal and informal barriers keeping married women and women with children out of many of the best employment opportunities, this drew nineteenth-century women into proprietorship in large numbers (10 percent of all women in the paid labor force), peaking in 1880. Female business ownership in San Francisco continued into the twentieth century, though the increasing costs and complications of proprietorship and expanded job accessibility in lucrative fields such as clerical work made it a less-attractive solution to women's personal and economic problems. By 1930 even married and formerly married women—the largest group of female proprietors throughout the seventy-year period studied—found alternatives to proprietorship, following in the footsteps of American women and men generally whose small-business aspirations fell victim to the consolidation of mass marketing and incorporation.

These were among the forces that made managing a small business difficult for women. During the gold rush, San Francisco women were successful operating simple, even primitive businesses and took advantage of unusually favorable credit opportunities. But as the city grew more settled and sophisticated, its customers demanded more. Female proprietors complied by investing in modern improvements and technology, more sophisticated advertising and marketing, and the trappings of gentility in their interior décor. This was especially true for women in the apparel, beauty, and accommodations industries who catered to the most urbane customers in city-center stores, salons, and hotels. These were the businesswomen who labored under new competitive pressures from department stores and tourism. But even neighborhood laundry providers had to face the growing influence of power laundries, while local retail dealers had to confront the spread of brand-name products and new machinery such as cash registers. All these developments could make operating even a modest business both more costly and more complicated. Adding to this was the fact that credit became less accessible for women and purchases were made from greater distances, involving less personal, and thus less negotiable, terms. The risks of proprietorship drove women to adopt more cautious start-up strategies than men. Most eschewed partnership in spite of the benefits of shared cost and liability, so attractive to male proprietors, because it entangled their fortunes with those of another. Far more popular was buying out an already established business because it provided a solid and predictable foundation and might be negotiated with an extended payment plan. Women's financing indicates both conservatism and lack of choice: they rarely utilized institutional loans or savings but turned instead to family, friends, and acquaintances for loans that offered the lowest costs and most favorable terms.

Small-business ownership engaged women in difficult financial decisions on a daily basis. In fact, fiscal management tested all small-business owners, male and female, since most came to the task poorly prepared, forced to learn the necessary skills on the job or not at all. Yet women may have been particularly disadvantaged in this regard since few had access to the business training and experience some men utilized to launch their own businesses. Participation in household management, no doubt, was the only experience of most, and while it provided some financial management skills and preparation, it did not expose women to the range or degree of financial challenge that faced female proprietors. Others may have "learned the ropes" as superintendents of charitable organizations, where fund-raising, budgeting, and supervision were often necessary skills. But since middle-class and elite women—the kinds of women most likely to find themselves in such responsible roles in charitable organizations—were a minority among the city's female small-business owners, such exposure helped but a few. Most likely, women mastered the financial management side of their businesses under tutelage of family members, on the job, or not at all. The widespread lack of record keeping as well as the high rate of business failure among male and female proprietors suggests that the latter was probably true for significant numbers of small-business owners.

The failure of a business, however, was sometimes due to factors beyond a proprietor's control. This may have been especially true in San Francisco, where two destructive earthquakes as well as an outbreak of bubonic plague added to the repetitive fires and epidemic illnesses that plagued all cities during the late nineteenth and early twentieth centuries. These were among the "natural" forces that drove business owners into failure throughout the period. Such factors simply compounded the more-controllable but no-less-ruinous debtor and creditor relationships that undermined proprietors' commercial persistence. Women in San Francisco's laundry industry faced one more deleterious factor: the high number of Chinese immigrant men competing for market share as laundry service providers. The competition drove most white women out of the business. Those who stayed hoped to benefit from anti-Chinese marketing campaigns but ultimately found the only opportunities that remained for them were as waged laborers, working alongside machines in the growing number of power laundries.

While a handful of factors made operating a small business in San Francisco unique for women between 1850 and 1920, female proprietorship in the city was not an exceptional case. Gold rush–era credit availability and business simplicity, augmented opportunity for accommodations proprietors, Chinese competition in the laundry industry, earthquakes, and bubonic plague all were uniquely San Franciscan. Probably unusual too were the number of accounts by city residents about women's economic opportunities and activities, stimulated in large part by San Francisco's rapid demographic and economic expansion—also unique in contrast to other cities that took hundreds of years to achieve the same growth. Yet a comparison with other cities in the United States shows that San Francisco female proprietors were typical in most ways. Scholarly literature confirms, in fact, that the story of women's small-business ownership in San Francisco during the late nineteenth and early twentieth centuries is not a story of western exceptionalism but one of female determination and innovation more generally. Because this study considers female proprietors in several industries (in contrast to earlier published studies of women in the apparel trades), however, it does offer several new insights. Among these is the heterosocial nature of women's commercial engagement. Another is the preponderance of Irish immigrant women, a group of female proprietors largely missed in scholarly accounts by women's business historians.

By placing the day-to-day lives of female small-business owners at the center of this study, I have insisted on viewing them as economic actors, embroiled in complex financial, commercial, and familial decision making. Here is a group of women, I have argued, who turned toward those areas in the marketplace that provided them with the best opportunities to care for their families. Prying open business records they probably would have preferred remain private, I have shown that female proprietors engaged in daily transactions with a variety of city residents that tied them to San Francisco's marketplace, its neighborhoods, its city center, and, ultimately, its fortunes and fables. Late nineteenth- and early twentieth-century female proprietors in the city matter, therefore, because they force a reaccounting of women's history, of business history, and of San Francisco history. Through the lens of female proprietorship, women become more trenchant commercial risk-takers and innovators, businesses become smaller and more family oriented, and San Francisco becomes repopulated by women who capitalized on the city's masculine proclivities. This study, therefore, adds to the scholarly transformations already underway in each of these fields.

But late nineteenth- and early twentieth-century female proprietors have lessons for contemporaries as well.

The lack of alternative opportunities to generate an income while maintaining responsibilities at home still drives large numbers of women into starting their own businesses. Research confirms that balancing work and family demands is a primary motivation for female self-employment.[1] One study found that one-fourth of women who started their own businesses had never planned for it but were driven into it by a traumatic event such as the death of a spouse or a dramatic change to their financial status such as divorce or the retirement of their spouse.[2]

And like their late nineteenth- and early twentieth-century predecessors, female small-business owners today still find the greatest opportunities in retail, food, fashion, cosmetics, and personal care as well as other service sector industries.[3] This remains true in San Francisco, where most of the over 150,000 female proprietors are concentrated in service. A handful of these enterprises have accomplished substantial success, becoming household names—Jessica McClintock, Inc., and Esprit de Corp, both manufacturers of women's apparel, for example.[4] But most are small-scale establishments, precisely the types of businesses that can be successfully combined with personal responsibilities. Some are even operated as home-based businesses, which account for a growing proportion of all women-owned enterprises today.

Female proprietors at the beginning of the twenty-first century also face some of the same financial challenges that their forerunners did one hundred years ago. Procuring start-up capital is the greatest obstacle. As late as 1972, most women capitalized their businesses with money from personal or joint savings. Only 31 percent used bank loans to fund their businesses, and those who did generally borrowed very small amounts.[5] Today, businesswomen are more likely to rely on loans, but the amounts banks lend them are still smaller than the loans granted to men.[6] In addition, women are more likely to have to put up collateral than men and tend to pay higher interest rates.[7] And a surprising proportion of women still use credit cards to fund their business start-ups. While this figure is declining—women using credit cards as a source of capital declined from 52 percent to 23 percent of first-time business owners between 1992 and 1996—women continue to use credit cards for this purpose more than men. This is especially true in small businesses that employ less than 25 people.[8]

Where women have made gains is in their numbers. In 2000, for example, the National Foundation for Women Business Owners reported 9.1 million woman-owned businesses that employed 27.5 million people and generated $3.6 trillion in sales annually. These establishments comprised 38 percent of all U.S. businesses that year.[9] Since only 10 percent of people engaged in business in urban areas during the nineteenth century were women, this illustrates the dramatic increase in women's business ownership over the course of the twentieth century.[10] But the change came late, for only after the feminist movement wrenched open the doors of opportunity did the proportion of female-owned businesses rise above the nineteenth-century apex. In 1970, for example, before the movement's impact had taken effect, only 5 percent of U.S. businesses were woman-owned.[11] For most of the 1900s, therefore, there were proportionally fewer female proprietors than there were in the 1800s. Nonetheless, twenty-first-century women business owners far outstrip their predecessors when it comes to gross population figures.

But even as their numbers rise, businesswomen's continuing struggles to balance work and family responsibilities, to find start-up capital, and to escape their historic concentration in the service sector demonstrate that there are more continuities than contrasts between businesswomen at the end of the nineteenth century and today. While women's commercial opportunities are certainly improving, they continue to be hampered by many of the same challenges that women faced one hundred years ago.[12]

What this tells me is that if we continue to measure women's gains in the business world via business magazine exposés on the richest or most powerful female entrepreneurs in corporate America then we are looking in the wrong place and will not see the real story. Instead we should be visiting the restaurants, book stores, dress shops, nail salons, and dry cleaners that dot our neighborhoods to ask their female proprietors whether the businesswomen of the 1800s look familiar. I suspect their answer would be a resounding yes!

APPENDIX 1

NOTE ON SOURCES

This history of female proprietors in San Francisco relies on a great deal of statistical data culled from a variety of sources. The creation of this data deserves further explanation than was possible within the note citations.

THE R. G. DUN & COMPANY CREDIT REPORTS

My use of the R. G. Dun & Company credit reports was limited by the fact that the records only exist for San Francisco for the 1870s. Nonetheless, these records were invaluable for this study, as for numerous previous studies of women business owners. In total, 92 women are included in the records for San Francisco. A few reports did not provide enough information to be of use, but they were still included in the total for my calculations. My use of the records to comment on San Francisco's small businessmen deserves more comment as well. To derive the comparative figures I use throughout the book, I derived a simple and unscientific sample. I singled out those male business owners in the reports who operated the types of enterprises I judged to be comparable in size to those owned by the businesswomen in the reports. The types of businesses men in the sample operated included boardinghouses and lodging houses as well as small hotels, groceries, tailor shops, pawn shops, saloons, restaurants, and retail stores that sold jewelry, drugs, crockery, furniture, cigars, hats, clothing, fancy/dry goods, carpets, toys, and candy/confectionery. I did not use a sampling technique. I simply leafed through the pages of the credit reports until I had accumulated a sufficient number of proprietors (155 businessmen who operated 135 establishments) to compare with the female proprietors I had gathered from the reports. I used the sample to develop all of my comparative statistics on men who clerked, men who had a history of failure, and men who relied on savings, borrowing, partnership, or buying out/taking over another's business. I also used the sample to develop comparative statistics on marital status and ethnicity among the city's male proprietors.

BANKRUPTCY COURT RECORDS

Bankruptcy court cases from the Northern California District for 1873–75, 1878, 1898–1900, 1903, 1906, 1909, 1912, 1915, 1918, and 1921 were examined (no national bankruptcy law was in effect between 1878 and 1898, and thus no bankruptcy cases were filed during those years), yielding a total of 96 bankrupt businesswomen in the northern California area. The sample includes all cities covered by the Northern District Court of California. Thus while San Francisco predominates in the records, other cities are also included in my figures. When I discuss a particular bankruptcy case in the text, I have supplied the city as well as the date and name of the bankrupt in the Notes.

The bankruptcy court records I use comprise a small but extremely valuable sample. It is valuable partly because conducting research with the bankruptcy records is laborious and time consuming. Since the bankruptcy court cases for 1872–1921 are not indexed, creating the sample discussed here involved looking over every case in each year I studied to locate the names of women. Even more important, though, the sample is valuable because I know of no other source that provides such extensive information about women's borrowing or spending habits. The court records typically listed all creditors to whom a bankrupt woman owed money and all debtors who owed money to her—often listing a description of why, when, where, and for how much a debt was incurred. In addition, several records contain detailed inventories, revealing precisely what sorts of merchandise businesswomen purchased as well as the kinds of furniture and fixtures they used to set up their establishments. On rare occasions, the records contain actual testimony from the bankrupt, rare first-hand accounts of women's roles as proprietors. Overall, the bankruptcy court records provide a riveting view into the ups and downs of late nineteenth- and early twentieth-century women's fortunes as business owners.

Because there is no index indicating the type of business a person operated, and because it is a difficult, delicate, and time-consuming process just to open one of the records (they have been trifolded since their creation), it was not practical to create a comparative sample of businessmen in the records.

Because I examined female proprietors in multiple industries and across seventy years, it would have been too time consuming to utilize the manuscript census. Its use would have provided valuable data on class and family composition, factors that no other source examines adequately. But since I chose not to use it, this study does not investigate either in a systematic or detailed way.

As an alternative, the printed census has been enormously helpful. I have used it to create comparative data on women and men in San Francisco and on women in San Francisco and women in other cities across time. As anyone who has worked with the census knows, not all years are the same. So I have relied particularly on the 1890 census because it is the only census during the seventy-year period I study that correlates occupation with gender, marital status, ethnicity/race, and nativity. I also rely on the 1930 census to measure change over time in relationship to female proprietorship and marital status but not ethnicity or nativity.

Determining "proprietorship" in the printed census, however, is an imprecise science. Not only do census categories change over time, but they are also different for men and women. Thus I have noted when my data is not entirely comparable and have described what categories have been included in my calculations for female and male proprietorship.

When comparing female proprietorship in San Francisco and other cities, I have relied on the same sample of six cities throughout the study. New York, Boston, and Chicago were selected because they were the great commercial leaders during the period, and Buffalo, N.Y.; Cincinnati, Ohio; and New Orleans, La., were comparable in size to San Francisco more or less throughout the seventy-year period studied. Together these cities also represent some geographic diversity. Most far-western cities were too small to provide a reasonable comparison for San Francisco during the period.

The printed census records also make it difficult to discuss racial background with any precision, especially for African American and Asian women. This is because black, Chinese, Japanese, and "civilized Indian" women (and men) are combined into one category for much of the period covered. The census takers designated this category "colored." Where applicable I have supplemented my use of the printed census with the city directory (though it stops designating race after 1875), newspaper ads, and secondary literature to try to create a fuller picture of the experience of female proprietorship for nonwhite women. Because they comprised a tiny 2 percent of all female proprietors in the city, however, I do not think this shortcoming detracts significantly from my findings. On the other hand, because other scholars have determined that black women, in particular, did find opportunities as business owners in late nineteenth- and early twentieth-century San Francisco, I have decided that when a record does not designate race, I can not assume that the proprietor is white. Throughout the text, therefore, I often use the term "women" to refer to the general experience of female proprietorship in the city. For example, when it came to an aspect of business ownership such as financial management, I do not think it is reasonable to assume that small numbers of nonwhite female proprietors did not have the same experience as white women. Thus, I purposely do not designate race much of the time throughout the text. Although the vast majority of the city's female proprietors were white, black women and to a much more limited degree Chinese women had many of the same experiences as white women when it came to proprietorship.

APPENDIX 2

FIGURES AND TABLES

FIGURE A1. Percentage of All Gainfully Occupied Women in the Hospitality Industry

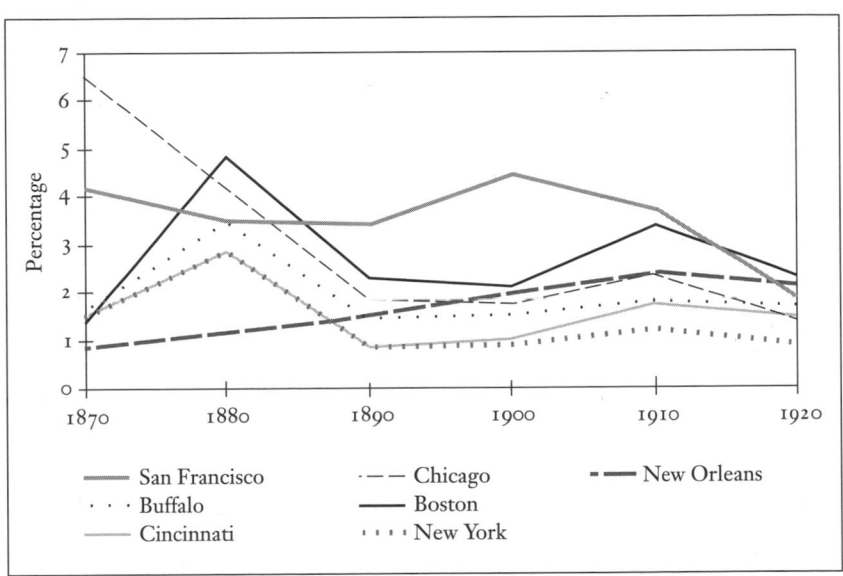

SOURCES: U.S. Census Bureau, *Ninth Census: The Statistics of the Population of the United States*, vol. 1 (Washington, D.C.: Government Printing Office, 1872); *Compendium of the Tenth Census*, part 1 (Washington, D.C.: Government Printing Office, 1883); *Report on the Population of the United States at the Eleventh Census*, part 1 (Washington, D.C.: Government Printing Office, 1895); *The Twelfth Census of the United States Taken in the Year 1900: Population*, vol. 1, part 1 (Washington, D.C.: Government Printing Office, 1901); *Thirteenth Census of the United States Taken in the Year 1910: Population, Occupation Statistics*, vol. 2 (Washington, D.C.: Government Printing Office, 1914); and *Fourteenth Census of the United States*

Taken in the Year 1920: Population, vol. 2 (Washington, D.C.: Government Printing Office, 1921).

NOTE: "Hospitality" includes women in boarding, lodging, and hotel businesses, as well as those listed under restaurants and saloons.

FIGURE A2. Number of San Francisco Female Proprietors in the Hospitality Industry

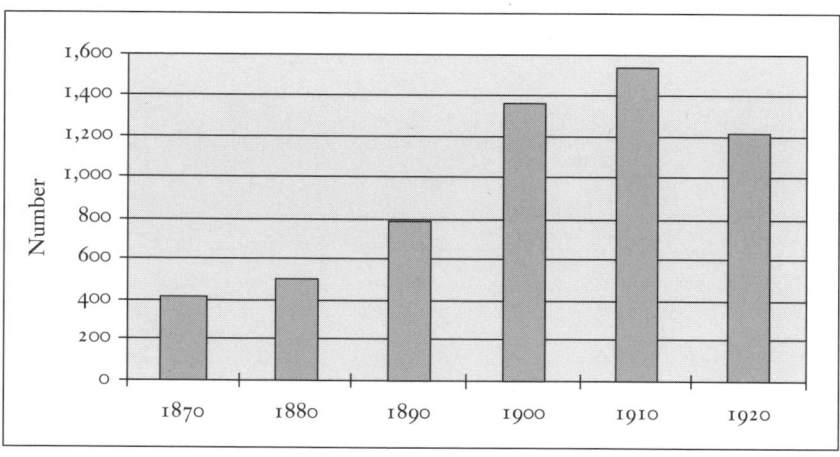

SOURCES: U.S. Census Bureau, *Population of the United States in 1860* (Washington, D.C.: Government Printing Office, 1864), 22–27; *Ninth Census: The Statistics of the Population of the United States*, vol. 1 (Washington, D.C.: Government Printing Office, 1872), 799; *Compendium of the Tenth Census*, part 1 (Washington, D.C.: Government Printing Office, 1883), 564; *Report on the Population of the United States at the Eleventh Census*, part 1 (Washington, D.C.: Government Printing Office, 1895), 452; *The Twelfth Census of the United States Taken in the Year 1900: Population*, vol. 1, part 1 (Washington, D.C.: Government Printing Office, 1901), 495; *Thirteenth Census of the United States Taken in the Year 1910: Population, Occupation Statistics*, vol. 2 (Washington, D.C.: Government Printing Office, 1914), 163; and *Fourteenth Census of the United States Taken in the Year 1920: Population*, vol. 2 (Washington, D.C.: Government Printing Office, 1921), 115.

NOTE: "Hospitality" includes women in boarding, lodging, and hotel businesses, as well as those listed under restaurants and saloons.

TABLE A1. Female Proprietors in San Francisco as a Percentage of All Gainfully Occupied Women

Type of Business	1870	1880	1920
Dressmakers and milliners	198[a]	754[b]	333[c]
Hairdressers	13	96	533
Traders and dealers	58	165[d]	837[e]
Hucksters and peddlers	10		
Boarding and lodging	299	291	773
Hotelkeepers	102	191	320[f]
Laundresses	487	478	244[g]
Total (excluding laundresses)	680	1,497	2,796
Total (including laundresses)	1,167	1,975	3,040
Women over the age of 10 in all occupations	9,634	14,142	62,318
Proprietors as % of women in all occupations excluding laundresses	7	10	4
Proprietors as % of women in all occupations including laundresses	12	14	5

SOURCES: U.S. Census Bureau, *Ninth Census: The Statistics of the Population of the United States*, vol. 1 (Washington, D.C.: Government Printing Office, 1872); *Compendium of the Tenth Census*, part 1 (Washington, D.C.: Government Printing Office, 1883); and *Fourteenth Census of the United States Taken in the Year 1920: Population*, vol. 2 (Washington, D.C.: Government Printing Office, 1921).

NOTE: Laundry is separated out because it generally included laundry employees as well as independent enterprisers in the industry and thus inflates the figures for female proprietors.

a. This figure includes dressmakers and milliners only. Proprietors are computed as 19 percent of all women working in the industry. Computation derived from comparison of relevant business directory listings (proprietors) figured as percentage of all women the printed census lists in the industry (proprietors plus laborers). This approach conforms with Wendy Gamber's computations for milliners and dressmakers in Boston in *The Female Economy: The Millinery and Dressmaking Trades, 1860–1930* (Urbana: University of Illinois Press, 1997).

b. This figure includes dressmakers, milliners, and tailoresses and thus artificially inflates the figures since "tailoress" generally described sweated laborers. Proprietors are computed as 19 percent of all women working in the industry.

c. This figure includes dressmakers/seamstresses and milliners/millinery dealers and thus inflates the figures since "seamstress" generally described sweated laborers. Proprietors for this year are computed as 10 percent of all working women in the industry.

d. Includes hucksters and peddlers.

e. Includes hucksters and peddlers.

f. This figure includes hotelkeepers and hotel managers.

g. This year the category was listed as "laundress, not in laundry" and thus this figure probably more accurately reflects the number of independent proprietors in the industry as opposed to waged laborers. This contrasts with the other two years represented here when all women in the laundry industry were combined.

TABLE A2. San Francisco Male and Female Populations

Population	1860	1870	1880	1890	1900	1910	1920
Total	56,802	149,473	233,959	298,997	342,782	416,912	506,676
Male	34,776	86,182	132,608	169,800	184,866	236,901	272,703
Female	22,026	63,291	101,351	129,197	157,916	180,011	233,973
% M/% F	61/39	58/42	57/43	57/43	54/46	57/43	54/46
M/F ratio	158:100	136:100	131:100	132:100	117:100	132:100	117:100

SOURCES: U.S. Census Bureau, *Population of the United States in 1860* (Washington, D.C.: Government Printing Office, 1864), 22–27; *Ninth Census: The Statistics of the Population of the United States*, vol. 1 (Washington, D.C.: Government Printing Office, 1872), 799; *Compendium of the Tenth Census*, part 1 (Washington, D.C.: Government Printing Office, 1883), 564; *Report on the Population of the United States at the Eleventh Census*, part 1 (Washington, D.C.: Government Printing Office, 1895), 452; *The Twelfth Census of the United States Taken in the Year 1900: Population*, vol. 1, part 1 (Washington, D.C.: Government Printing Office, 1901), 495; *Thirteenth Census of the United States Taken in the Year 1910: Population, Occupation Statistics*, vol. 2 (Washington, D.C.: Government Printing Office, 1914), 163; and *Fourteenth Census of the United States Taken in the Year 1920: Population*, vol. 2 (Washington, D.C.: Government Printing Office, 1921), 115.

TABLE A3. Women in the San Francisco Directory Employed in Hospitality

Occupation	1850	1860	1877/78	1889	1900	1915
Boarding	18	70	111	36	18	3
Lodging	0	38	469	176	432	0
Hotel	3	2	1	n/a	1	3
Restaurant	1	4	5	20	35	33
Total	22	114	586	232	486	39

SOURCES: *San Francisco City Directory, 1850* (San Francisco: Kimball, 1850); *San Francisco City Directory, 1860* (San Francisco: Kimball, 1859/60); *San Francisco City Directory, 1877/78* (San Francisco: Polk, 1877/78); *San Francisco City Directory, 1889* (San Francisco: Crocker-Langley, 1889); *San Francisco City Directory, 1900* (San Francisco: Crocker-Langley, 1900); and *San Francisco City Directory, 1915* (San Francisco: Crocker-Langley, 1915).

TABLE A4. Retail Dealers in San Francisco in 1920

Retail Dealers	Male	Female
Agricultural implements	39	0
Art stores, supplies	59	16
Automobiles, accessories	399	2
Bicycles	17	0
Books	27	8
Boots, shoes	149	5
Butchers, meat dealers	1,401	9
Grain buyers/shippers	51	0
Livestock buyers/shippers	63	0
Farm produce buyers/shippers	31	0
Candy, confectionery	202	70
Cigars, tobacco	390	8
Carpets, rugs	25	0
Clothing, men's furnishings	408	53
Coal, wood	108	6
Coffee, tea	69	4
Crockery, glassware	25	4
Curios, antiques, novelties	55	10
Delicatessen stores	54	12
Department stores	61	17
Drugs, medicines	648	47
Dry goods, fancy goods, notions	414	85
Florists (dealers)	90	15
Fruit	438	12
Furniture	190	12
Furs	45	11
Gas fixtures, electrical supplies	52	1
General stores	106	8

Retail Dealers	Male	Female
Groceries	1,491	190
Hardware, stove, cutlery	181	8
Hucksters, peddlers	385	8
Jewelry	223	8
Junk	127	3
Lumber	110	6
Milk	72	14
Music, instruments	61	8
News dealers	114	4
Oil, paint, wallpaper	62	3
Opticians	165	13
Produce, provisions	323	5
Stationery	101	28
Other specified retail	904	56
Not specified retail	418	68
Total	10,303	840

SOURCE: *San Francisco City Directory, 1920* (San Francisco: Crocker-Langley, 1920).

TABLE A5. Race and Nativity of Female Proprietors and of Total San Francisco Female Population, 1890

Race and Nativity	As % of All Female Proprietors[a]	As % of Total Gainfully Employed Female Population	Proprietors as % of Gainfully Employed Women in Specific Ethnic Group
Foreign-born white	57	41	14
Native-born, foreign parents	25	39	6
Native-born, native parents	16	17	9
"Colored"[b]	2	3	9

SOURCE: U.S. Census Bureau, *Report on the Population of the United States at the Eleventh Census*, part 1 (Washington, D.C.: Government Printing Office, 1895).

a. Female proprietors here include those listed in the following printed census categories: hotel and boardinghouse keepers; laundresses; restaurant and saloon keepers; merchants, dealers, and peddlers; dressmakers, milliners, seamstresses, etc. Only 9 percent of those listed as dressmakers, milliners, and seamstresses were included here, since proprietors accounted for only 9 percent of all women employed in the category by 1900. Laundry proprietors are overrepresented since there is no similar formula to capture proprietors only.

b. Census category included "persons of negro descent, Chinese, Japanese, and civilized Indians."

TABLE A6. San Francisco Female Proprietors in Types of Businesses as Percentage of All Proprietors from Racial/Ethnic Background, 1890

Race and Nativity	Boarding	Laundry	Restaurant/ Saloon	Retail	Apparel[a]
Foreign-born white	402 (31%)	418 (32%)	88 (7%)	268 (20%)	132 (10%)
Native-born, foreign parents	95 (16%)	116 (20%)	10 (2%)	83 (14%)	270 (47%)
Native-born, native parents	173 (48%)	37 (10%)	11 (3%)	40 (11%)	97 (27%)
"Colored"[b]	12 (22%)	14 (25%)	3 (5%)	13 (24%)	13 (24%)

SOURCE: U.S. Census Bureau, *Report on the Population of the United States at the Eleventh Census*, part 1 (Washington, D.C.: Government Printing Office, 1895).

NOTE: Female proprietors here include those listed in the following printed census categories: hotel and boardinghouse keepers (here listed as "Boarding"); laundresses; restaurant and saloon keepers; merchants, dealers, and peddlers (here listed as "Retail"); dressmakers, milliners, seamstresses, etc. (here listed as "Apparel").

a. Figured as 9 percent of all women in category in order to control for proprietors only. See text for further explanation.

b. Census category included "persons of negro descent, Chinese, Japanese, and civilized Indians."

TABLE A7. San Francisco Female Proprietors in Types of Businesses as Percentage of All Proprietors in Each Category, 1890

Race and Nativity	Boarding	Laundry	Restaurant/ Saloon	Retail	Apparel[a]
Foreign-born white	402 (59%)	418 (71%)	88 (79%)	268 (66%)	132 (26%)
Native-born, foreign parents	95 (14%)	116 (20%)	10 (9%)	83 (20%)	270 (53%)
Native-born, native parents	173 (25%)	37 (6%)	11 (10%)	40 (10%)	97 (19%)
"Colored"[b]	12 (2%)	14 (2%)	3 (3%)	13 (3%)	13 (2%)
Total	682	585	112	404	514

SOURCE: U.S. Census Bureau, *Report on the Population of the United States at the Eleventh Census*, part 1 (Washington, D.C.: Government Printing Office, 1895).

NOTE: Female proprietors here include those listed in the following printed census categories: hotel and boardinghouse keepers (here listed as "Boarding"); laundresses; restaurant and saloon keepers; merchants, dealers, and peddlers (here listed as "Retail"); dressmakers, milliners, seamstresses, etc. (here listed as "Apparel").

a. Figured as 9 percent of all women in category in order to control for proprietors only. See text for further explanation.

b. Census category included "persons of negro descent, Chinese, Japanese, and civilized Indians."

TABLE A8. San Francisco Foreign-Born White (FBW) Female Proprietors (FP) by Origin and Type of Business, 1890

Type of Business	Ireland	Germany	Great Britain	Scandinavia[a]
Boarding	195	59	52	26
Laundry	155	27	10	43
Restaurant/ saloon	43	24	6	3
Retail	101	83	29	5
Apparel[b]	37	23	19	8
Total	531 (39% all FBW FP)	216 (16% all FBW FP)	116 (8% all FBW FP)	85 (6% all FBW FP)

SOURCE: Census Bureau, *Report on the Population of the United States at the Eleventh Census*, part 1 (Washington, D.C.: Government Printing Office, 1895).

NOTE: Female proprietors here include those listed in the following printed census categories: hotel and boardinghouse keepers (here listed as "Boarding"); laundresses; restaurant and saloon keepers; merchants, dealers, and peddlers (here listed as "Retail"); dressmakers, milliners, seamstresses, etc. (here listed as "Apparel").

a. Census category included immigrants from Sweden, Norway, and Denmark.

b. Figured as 9 percent of all women in category in order to control for proprietors only. See text for further explanation.

TABLE A9. Race and Nativity of Male Proprietors and of Total San Francisco Male Population, 1890

Race and Nativity	As % of All Male Proprietors[a]	As % of Total Gainfully Employed Male Population	Proprietors as % of Gainfully Employed Men in Specific Ethnic Group
Foreign-born white	47	43	15
Native-born, foreign parents	12	21	8
Native-born, native parents	11	17	9
"Colored"[b]	29	19	20

SOURCE: U.S. Census Bureau, *Report on the Population of the United States at the Eleventh Census*, part 1 (Washington, D.C.: Government Printing Office, 1895).

a. Male proprietors here include those listed in the following printed census categories: barbers and hairdressers; hotel and boardinghouse keepers; launderers; restaurant and saloon keepers; merchants, dealers, and peddlers. These figures do not include the 659 men listed as "dressmakers, milliners, seamstresses, etc." because I did not know how to calculate the percentage of proprietors. Although one study has suggested that many men in this category operated large, successful shops, in San Francisco 539 (82 percent) of those listed were "colored," suggesting that Chinese immigrant men in the city found employment as sweated laborers in the sewing trades. See Wendy Gamber, *The Female Economy: The Millinery and Dressmaking Trades, 1860–1930* (Urbana: University of Illinois Press, 1997), 160, 175, for the argument that men in this category were likely to be proprietors. I have not included the much larger number of men listed as "tailors" either because, like female dressmakers and milliners, so many worked as waged workers rather than proprietors. Of course, male "launderers" also included large numbers of waged laborers, so these figures overestimate the number of proprietors in the city, especially "colored" male proprietors. Yet because so many Chinese men did operate small-scale enterprises in this industry, their inclusion here is important.

b. Census category included "persons of negro descent, Chinese, Japanese, and civilized Indians."

TABLE A10. San Francisco Male Proprietors in Types of Businesses as Percentage of All Proprietors in Each Category, 1890

Race and Nativity	Barber/Hair	Hotel/ Boarding	Launderers	Restaurant/ Saloon	Retail
Foreign-born white	513 (41%)	358 (67%)	464 (15%)	1,571 (77%)	5,020 (50%)
Native-born, foreign parents	247 (20%)	49 (9%)	82 (3%)	231 (11%)	1,484 (15%)
Native-born, native parents	114 (9%)	77 (14%)	92 (3%)	184 (9%)	1,418 (14%)
"Colored"[a]	377 (30%)	51 (9%)	2,354 (79%)	49 (2%)	2,006 (20%)
Total	1,251	535	2,992	2,035	9,928

SOURCE: U.S. Census Bureau, *Report on the Population of the United States at the Eleventh Census*, part 1 (Washington, D.C.: Government Printing Office, 1895).

NOTE: Male proprietors here include those listed in the following printed census categories: barbers and hairdressers; hotel and boardinghouse keepers; launderers; restaurant and saloon keepers; merchants, dealers, and peddlers. These figures do not include the 659 men listed as "dressmakers, milliners, seamstresses, etc." because I did not know how to calculate the percentage of proprietors. Although one study has suggested that many men in this category operated large, successful shops, in San Francisco 539 (82 percent) of those listed were "colored," suggesting that Chinese immigrant men in the city found employment as sweated laborers in the sewing trades. See Wendy Gamber, *The Female Economy: The Millinery and Dressmaking Trades, 1860–1930* (Urbana: University of Illinois Press, 1997), 160, 175, for the argument that men in this category were likely to be proprietors. I have not included the much larger number of men listed as "tailors" either because, like female dressmakers and milliners, so many worked as waged workers rather than proprietors. Of course, male "launderers" also included large numbers of waged laborers, so these figures overestimate the number of proprietors in the city, especially "colored" male proprietors. Yet because so many Chinese men did operate small-scale enterprises in this industry, their inclusion here is important.

a. Census category included "persons of negro descent, Chinese, Japanese, and civilized Indians."

TABLE A11. San Francisco Foreign-Born White (FBW) Male Proprietors (MP) by Origin and Type of Business, 1890

Type of Business	Germany	Ireland	Great Britain	Scandinavia[a]
Barber/hair	260	16	33	9
Hotel/boarding	119	70	35	24
Launderers	25	54	40	40
Restaurant/saloon	616	294	87	151
Retail[b]	2,188	754	427	131
Total	3,208 (40% all FBW MP)	1,188 (15% all FBW MP)	622 (8% all FBW MP)	440 (6% all FBW MP)

SOURCE: U.S. Census Bureau, *Report on the Population of the United States at the Eleventh Census*, part 1 (Washington, D.C.: Government Printing Office, 1895).

NOTE: Male proprietors here include those listed in the following printed census categories: barbers and hairdressers; hotel and boardinghouse keepers; launderers; restaurant and saloon keepers; merchants, dealers, and peddlers. These figures do not include the 659 men listed as "dressmakers, milliners, seamstresses, etc." because I did not know how to calculate the percentage of proprietors. Although one study has suggested that many men in this category operated large, successful shops, in San Francisco 539 (82 percent) of those listed were "colored," suggesting that Chinese immigrant men in the city found employment as sweated laborers in the sewing trades. See Wendy Gamber, *The Female Economy: The Millinery and Dressmaking Trades, 1860–1930* (Urbana: University of Illinois Press, 1997), 160, 175, for the argument that men in this category were likely to be proprietors. I have not included the much larger number of men listed as "tailors" either because, like female dressmakers and milliners, so many worked as waged workers rather than proprietors. Of course, male "launderers" also included large numbers of waged laborers, so these figures overestimate the number of proprietors in the city, especially "colored" male proprietors. Yet because so many Chinese men did operate small-scale enterprises in this industry, their inclusion here is important.

a. Census category included immigrants from Sweden, Norway, and Denmark.

b. Male proprietors listed here appeared in the census category labeled "merchants, dealers, peddlers."

TABLE A12. Percentage of Women's Businesses Located on Kearny, Montgomery, Second, Third, and Market Streets

Type of Business	Ratio	Percentage
Cloaks and suits	5/11	45
Clothing	2/5	40
Furnishings—ladies	8/13	62
Hair—human	4/9	44
Hair—jewelry	2/4	50
Milliners	36/78	46
Millinery—retail	7/10	70

SOURCE: *San Francisco City Directory, 1877/78* (San Francisco: Polk, 1877).

NOTE: Because dressmakers did not sell ready-made clothing and often toiled in second-floor studios with no store-front windows, their location was less important. Many made house calls as well and so could do their work out of their homes. Groceries were, for the most part, located in residential neighborhoods, as were liquor stores, boardinghouses, small hotels, laundries, variety stores, and produce vendors. For the proprietors of these kinds of establishments, proximity to customers' homes, not the central commercial zone, was what mattered most.

TABLE A13. Business Failure among San Francisco Female Proprietors

Type of Proprietor	Ratio	Percentage
Women with history of business failure	24/92	26
Women who reentered business after failing (as proportion of total)	19/92	21
Women who reentered business after failing (as proportion of those who failed)	19/24	79

SOURCE: These figures are based on the 92 San Francisco businesswomen who appear in the R. G. Dun & Company credit reports for the 1870s, RGDC.

NOTES

ABBREVIATIONS

The following abbreviations are used throughout the notes.

BCF   Bankruptcy Case Files, Records of the U.S. District Court, Northern District of California, Northern Division, San Francisco, Records of U.S. District Courts (Record Group 21), National Archives and Records Administration, Pacific Region, San Bruno, Calif.

BOAA   Women's Banking Department, Bank of Italy Collection, Bank of America Archives, San Francisco, Calif.

CHS   California Historical Society, San Francisco, Calif.

IMC   I. Magnin Collection, SFH 2, San Francisco History Center, San Francisco Public Library, San Francisco, Calif.

RCS   Riptides Column Scrapbook, California Historical Society, San Francisco, Calif.

RGDC   R. G. Dun & Company Collection, Baker Library, Harvard Business School, Cambridge, Mass.

SFEFC   San Francisco Earthquake and Fire Collection, California Historical Society, San Francisco, Calif.

SSP   Sallie Snow Papers, Bancroft Library, University of California, Berkeley, Calif.

1. At the end of the 1990s, the Small Business Administration reported that 80 percent of small businesses fail within the first five years. "Success on a Small Scale Celebrated," *San Francisco Chronicle*, January 26, 1998, B-1. Even when businesses do not fail, they usually succeed on only a "small scale." In one San Francisco newspaper article, the reporter interviewed the owner of a research firm who stated that most small businesses "do not generate wealth, just independence"; he referred to the businesses as "mice," "because they start small and never grow." Peter Sinton, *San Francisco Chronicle*, June 10, 1997, C-1.

2. One study reported that self-employment was an attractive option for women "as a means of balancing work and family demands" and a way "to avoid discrimination in the workplace." Daniel C. Feldman and Mark C. Bolino, "Career Patterns of the Self-Employed: Career Motivations and Career Outcomes," *Journal of Small Business Management* 38 (July 2000): 3, 53–67. Anecdotal evidence confirms the finding. See, for example, Laura Castaneda, "More Women Venture Forth on Their Own," *San Francisco Chronicle*, October 29, 1996, B-1. On the growth of women's business ownership see Candida G. Brush, "Research on Women Business Owners: Past Trends, a New Perspective, and Future Directions," *Entrepreneurship: Theory and Practice* 16 (Summer 1992): 5–31; and the Web site for the National Foundation for Women Business Owners, <http://www.nfwbo.org> (October 15, 2000).

3. Wendy Gamber argues that "unless one concentrates on the exceptional—the woman bank president, the rare female millionaire—studying the history of women in business (especially in the nineteenth century) means studying the history of small business, indeed the history of very small business." She later uses the terms "tiny, even minuscule and ephemeral" to make the same point. Wendy Gamber, "A Gendered Enterprise: Placing Nineteenth-Century Businesswomen in History," *Business History Review* 72 (Summer 1998): 189, 191, 200.

4. Of course there are exceptions. Madame C. J. Walker, early twentieth-century beauty industry entrepreneur, is a good example. The national network of agents who distributed her beauty products and trained women to use and sell them was probably the earliest, or at least one of the earliest, examples of network marketing. Kathy Peiss argues that Walker, along with the other most successful businesswomen in the beauty industry, "pioneered in the development of modern franchising and direct-sales marketing strategies." See Peiss, *Hope in a Jar: The Making of America's Beauty Culture* (New York: Henry Holt, 1998); quote is on p. 5. Virginia G. Drachman, *Enterprising Women: 250 Years of American Business* (Chapel Hill: University of North Carolina Press, 2002) contains additional examples of "exceptional" businesswomen.

5. This term comes from Wendy Gamber, *The Female Economy: The Millinery and Dressmaking Trades, 1860–1930* (Urbana: University of Illinois Press, 1997).

6. I am using very traditional concepts of "failure" and "success" here. See Susan Ingalls Lewis, "Women in the Marketplace: Female Entrepreneurship, Business Patterns, and Working Families in Mid-Nineteenth-Century Albany, New York, 1830–1885," (Ph.D. diss., State University of New York, Binghamton, 2002), especially

Chapter 6, "Beyond Horatia Alger: Breaking through Gendered Assumptions about Business 'Success' in Mid-Nineteenth-Century America."

7. Mrs. Stites Miller's Boarding House, Ephemera File, North Baker Research Library, CHS. Miller does not appear in any other sources.

8. In her article on antebellum boardinghouses, Wendy Gamber writes: "Shrewdly aware of domesticity's market value, boardinghouse keepers advertised their establishments as 'homes.'" Gamber, "Tarnished Labor: The Home, the Market, and the Boardinghouse in Antebellum America," *Journal of the Early Republic* 22 (Summer 2002): 185.

9. "Entrepreneurship" has been a contested term among historians. Harold Livesay, for example, defines it as "the art of aggressive management, practiced by an innovative, growth-oriented manager." Livesay, "Entrepreneurial Dominance in Businesses Large and Small, Past and Present," *Business History Review*, 63 (Spring 1989), 4. Angel Kwolek-Folland, among others, criticizes definitions such as Livesay's for emphasizing "socially and historically constructed economic or behavioral values (risk and initiative)." She argues for using the term "business" instead of "entrepreneurship" and redefining it as simply "engaging in economic activity in a market to seek profit and assuming the financial responsibility for that activity," a definition that she asserts is "as value neutral as possible." Kwolek-Folland, *Incorporating Women: A History of Women and Business in the United States* (New York: Twayne Publishers, 1998), 5. Margaret Levenstein's redefinition of "entrepreneur" embodies this approach. She defines it as "the proportion of the labor force which was either an employer or working on one's own account." Levenstein, "African American Entrepreneurship: The View from the 1910 Census," *Business and Economic History*, 24 (Fall 1995), 108. I favor Kwolek-Folland's and Levenstein's approach, though I am not adverse to the use of the terms "risk" and "innovation" when discussing the female owners of small and even "very small" businesses. Arguably, investing even a very small amount of money in a business or just putting one's good reputation on the line as a debtor demonstrated significant risk taking for a person with few resources. "Innovative," too, aptly describes the steps that female proprietors took when they turned to business ownership to solve the conflict between a need for income and responsibility as a parent or homemaker. "Growth," on the other hand, describes few of the female proprietors in this study.

10. Gamber, "A Gendered Enterprise." For her more-comprehensive treatment of this subject see Gamber, *The Female Economy*.

11. Alice Kessler-Harris's work is a good starting place for anyone interested in learning more about this abundant body of literature. See Kessler-Harris, *A Woman's Wage: Historical Meanings and Social Consequences* (Lexington: University Press of Kentucky, 1990), a classic; and her more-recent book, *In Pursuit of Equity: Women, Men, and the Quest for Economic Citizenship in 20th-Century America* (New York: Oxford University Press, 2001).

12. See, for example, Mansel Blackford, *A History of Small Business in America*, 2nd ed. (Chapel Hill: University of North Carolina Press, 2003), 37; and Rowland Berthoff, "Independence and Enterprise: Small Business in the American Dream,"

in *Small Business in American Life*, ed. Stuart W. Bruchey (New York: Columbia University Press, 1980), 41. The quotes are from Blackford.

13. Susan Ingalls Lewis's findings differ from mine on this point. Lewis, "Women in the Marketplace."

14. For example see Berthoff, "Independence and Enterprise," 41.

15. Bruchey, introduction to *Small Business in American Life*, 17; and Blackford, *A History of Small Business*, 18, respectively. Bruchey argues that low labor costs "have tended to offset" the high risk of failure.

16. Women's history scholars agree that wives constituted a vast, unreported, and thus undercounted, army of unpaid workers whose labor directly (and indirectly through their "reproductive" labor managing the household) contributed to the operation of their husbands' businesses. The ubiquitous term "mom-and-pop" store captures how essential the labor of married women was to small retail businesses at the end of the nineteenth and beginning of the twentieth centuries, yet employment figures vastly underestimate women's participation in such work. A classic study documenting the undercounting of women's labor force participation is Claudia Goldin, *Understanding the Gender Gap: An Economic History of American Women* (New York: Oxford University Press, 1990.)

17. For scholarship that addresses women's difficulty in obtaining credit and capital see, for example, Kwolek-Folland, *Incorporating Women*; Gamber, *The Female Economy*; and Juliet E. K. Walker, *The History of Black Business in America: Capitalism, Race, Entrepreneurship* (New York: Macmillan Library Reference USA, 1998).

18. Angel Kwolek-Folland's study of the banking and life insurance industries is a great example. See Kwolek-Folland, *Engendering Business: Men and Women in the Corporate Office, 1870–1930* (Baltimore: Johns Hopkins University Press, 1994).

19. According to printed census records San Francisco was ranked the eighth-largest city in the country in 1880 and twelfth-largest city in 1920. It was not surpassed in population by Los Angeles until 1920 after that city experienced an explosive 80 percent population increase in one decade and became the nation's tenth-largest city. U.S. Census Bureau, *Compendium of the Tenth Census* (Washington, D.C.: Government Printing Office, 1883); *Fourteenth Census of the United States Taken in the Year 1920: Population* (Washington, D.C.: Government Printing Office, 1921).

20. The literature on the Chinese in America is, by now, voluminous. See, for example, Erika Lee, *At America's Gate: Chinese Immigration during the Exclusion Era, 1882–1943* (Chapel Hill: University of North Carolina Press, 2003), who emphasizes the ways in which race, class, gender, and citizenship intersected in the implementation of the nation's exclusion laws; and Yong Chen, *Chinese San Francisco, 1850–1943: A Trans-Pacific Community* (Palo Alto, Calif.: Stanford University Press, 2000), who, among other things, provides an inside view of day-to-day life in San Francisco's Chinatown from the perspective of the Chinese, including their work experiences.

21. My comparative analysis of the printed census records between 1860 and 1920 included the nation's largest cities—New York, Boston, and Chicago—and three cities with populations similar in size to San Francisco's: Buffalo, Cincinnati, and New Orleans. I chose cities for their regional diversity as well as their population numbers. These numbers varied over time, of course, but for most of the period ex-

amined the three latter cities remained San Francisco's peers in terms of size and the three former cities were among the nation's five largest.

22. Peter Decker came to the same conclusion about businessmen, arguing that San Francisco did not offer more occupational opportunity than other cities in the nation at the end of the nineteenth century. Decker, *Fortunes and Failures: White-Collar Mobility in Nineteenth-Century San Francisco* (Cambridge: Harvard University Press, 1978), 260.

23. Population statistic is from ibid., 28.

24. U.S. Census Bureau, *Compendium of the Tenth Census* (Washington, D.C.: Government Printing Office, 1883).

25. The term "incorporation of America" is, of course, Alan Trachtenberg's. See Trachtenberg, *The Incorporation of America: Culture and Society in the Gilded Age* (New York: Hill and Wang, 1982).

26. Scholars have attributed the tendency toward big business history in large part to Alfred Chandler, whose foundational scholarship (*The Visible Hand: The Managerial Revolution in American Business* [Cambridge: Harvard University Press, 1977]; and *Scale and Scope: The Dynamics of Industrial Capitalism* [Cambridge: Harvard University Press, 1990]) and leadership in the field have made him enormously influential. See, for example, two excellent historiographical overviews: Gamber, "A Gendered Enterprise"; and Mansel Blackford, "Small Business in America: A Historiographical Survey," *Business History Review* 65 (Spring 1991): 1–26. Mary Yeager's introduction to *Women in Business* also does an interesting and impressive job of contextualizing women in business history generally, not just small-business history. Yeager, ed., *Women in Business*, 3 vols. (Cheltenham, U.K.: Edward Elgar, 1997).

27. For starters see the essays in Bruchey, *Small Business in American Life*; and Blackford, *A History of Small Business*.

28. Livesay, "Entrepreneurial Dominance," is one example.

29. One exception is Blackford, *A History of Small Business*. By including some discussion of women in business throughout the book Blackford acknowledges that they are an important part of the story of small business in America. Most of the evidence he presents is based on a synthesis of original research completed by women's historians. His excellent case study of K&M Books, a small, independent book store in Cleveland, Ohio, owned and operated by a woman during the 1990s, is the exception as it reflects his own original research (Chapter 9). Blackford calls for more research on businesswomen, arguing that "we need to know more about . . . the entire topic of the roles small businesses have played for women over time."(203)

30. See ibid. for a discussion of the different definitions of the term "small business." Blackford argues, "Firms that are today seen as small businesses by the SBA [Small Business Administration] would have been viewed as large by most mid-nineteenth-century Americans." Even those firms viewed by historians such as Blackford as "small" have had as many as 119 workers, as in his case study of iron and steel companies at the end of the nineteenth century. Ibid., 2, 82.

31. Livesay, "Entrepreneurial Dominance"; Blackford, *A History of Small Business*, especially Chapter 9, on independent bookstores in the 1990s; James H. Soltow, "Origins of Small Business and the Relationships between Large and Small Firms:

Metal Fabricating and Machinery Making in New England, 1890–1957," in Bruchey, *Small Business in American Life*, 192–211. Quote is from Blackford, *A History of Small Business*, 183.

32. Mary A. Yeager, "Making a Difference: Women and Business History," review of *Incorporating Women: A History of Women and Business in the United States*, by Angel Kwolek-Folland, H-Business (April 1999), <www.h-net.org/reviews/show reve.cgi?path=30313927576847> (May 28, 2004). Mary Yeager is a self-proclaimed "business historian and free-farm feminist, with one eye on men and business institutions, and the other on businesswomen and the world." I categorize her here as a business historian both according to this definition and because, in my opinion, she brings to bear a different set of questions than women's historians when she considers women in business. Because her work on the topic has been editorial and synthetic rather than the result of empirical research, however, her thoughts are helpful conceptually but do not counter what I have already stated. That is, that business historians have generally overlooked female proprietors. For Yeager's fuller treatment of the topic of women and business see Yeager, "General Introduction," in vol. 1 of *Women in Business*, viii–xciii. Yeager is critical of the way Kwolek-Folland examines businesswomen and accuses her of homogenizing a group that is, in fact, quite diverse.

33. See, for example, Elisabeth A. Dexter, *Colonial Women of Affairs: A Study of Women in Business and the Professions in America before 1776* (Boston: Houghton Mifflin, 1924); Caroline Bird, *Enterprising Women* (New York: W. W. Norton, 1976); and Bird, *Notable American Women* (1971). Virginia G. Drachman, *Enterprising Women: 250 Years of American Business* (Chapel Hill: University of North Carolina Press, 2002) is arguably a modern-day version of the same thing. Susan Ingalls Lewis argued just that in her paper "Beyond 'Enterprising Women': The Importance of Networks for Female Microentrepreneurs in Mid-Nineteenth-Century Albany, New York" (presented at the annual meeting of the Business History Conference in Le Creusot, France, June 2004). But while most of the businesswomen featured in Drachman's book are indeed unusual for their success and their experience not typical of female proprietorship in U.S. history, the text of the book presents a much more nuanced analysis and certainly warns the reader (or viewer, since the book is based on a traveling exhibit) that most women in business did not achieve such heights.

34. Gerda Lerner, "Placing Women in History: Definitions and Challenges," *Feminist Studies* 3 (Fall 1975): 5–14.

35. See, for example, Lucy Eldersveld Murphy, "Her Own Boss: Businesswomen and Separate Spheres in the Midwest, 1850–1880," *Illinois Historical Journal* 80 (Autumn 1987): 155–76, which emphasizes women's shops as "comfortable female preserves."

36. Gamber, "A Gendered Enterprise," 188.

37. Gamber, *The Female Economy*.

38. Sarah Deutsch, *Women and the City: Gender, Space, and Power in Boston, 1870–1940* (New York: Oxford University Press, 2000).

39. Kwolek-Folland, *Incorporating Women*, 1. See Yeager review, cited above, for critical insight into shortcomings of this approach.

40. Lewis, "Women in the Marketplace."

41. Gamber, *The Female Economy*, 60–62. The term "female aristocracy of labor" is Gamber's.

42. See, for example, Kwolek-Folland, *Incorporating Women*, 118–19; Gerald Sorin, *Tradition Transformed: The Jewish Experience in America* (Baltimore: Johns Hopkins University Press, 1997), 36; and Irene D. Neu, "The Jewish Businesswoman in America," *American Jewish Historical Quarterly*, 66, no. 1 (1976): 137–54.

43. Peiss, *Hope in a Jar*; Walker, *The History of Black Business*; Levenstein, "African American Entrepreneurship"; Tiffany Melissa Gill, "'I Had My Own Business . . . So I Didn't Have to Worry': Beauty Salons, Beauty Culturists, and the Politics of African-American Female Entrepreneurship," in *Beauty and Business: Commerce, Gender, and Culture in Modern America*, ed. Philip Scranton (New York: Routledge, 2001); and Suzanne Lebsock, *The Free Women of Petersburg: Status and Culture in a Southern Town, 1784–1860* (New York: W. W. Norton, 1984). Kwolek-Folland, *Incorporating Women*, typically emphasizes the same points since her survey of the history of women and business is primarily a synthesis of published research. Drachman, *Enterprising Women*, cites neither immigrants nor Irish women in the index, though both African American and Jewish women can be found.

44. The scholarly neglect of the accommodations industry will come to an end with the publication of Wendy Gamber's highly anticipated book on the antebellum boarding house. But since she focuses her attention on the pre–Civil War period, our knowledge of the late nineteenth- and early twentieth-century accommodations industry will still require further investigation. In her article "Tarnished Labor," a publication of her preliminary research findings, Gamber herself asserts that the antebellum and postbellum periods were characterized by notably different popular attitudes toward the boarding house, and we may assume, therefore, different commercial conditions. Susan Ingalls Lewis's work is an exception to this rule, as mentioned earlier. The laundry industry, to be sure, has been studied, but not in a detailed way as a site for female proprietorship. For studies that do include women see Ronald M. James, Richard D. Adkins, and Rachel J. Hartigan, "Competition and Coexistence in the Laundry: A View of the Comstock," *Western Historical Quarterly* 25, no. 2 (1994): 164–84; Constance Backhouse, "White Women's Labor Laws: Anti-Chinese Racism in Early Twentieth-Century Canada," *Law and History Review* 14, no. 2 (1996): 315–68; Patricia Malcolmson, *English Laundresses: A Social History, 1850–1930* (Urbana: University of Illinois Press, 1986); and Arwen P. Mohun, *Steam Laundries: Gender, Technology, and Work in the United States and Great Britain, 1880–1940* (Baltimore: Johns Hopkins University Press, 1999).

45. See Hasia R. Diner, *Erin's Daughters in America: Irish Immigrant Women in the Nineteenth Century* (Baltimore: Johns Hopkins University Press, 1983); and *Hungering for America: Italian, Irish, and Jewish Foodways in the Age of Migration* (Cambridge: Harvard University Press, 2001). Irish women only appear as laborers in Kwolek-Folland's survey of women in business, *Incorporating Women*, and only as the second-generation daughters of immigrants in Gamber's *The Female Economy*, since native-born women dominated the needle trades.

46. For example, while Gamber writes of Boston that there were only "a tiny

number of African American businesswomen [in the apparel trades] in the city," Walker found that the dressmaking and millinery trades provided free black women, especially in southern cities such as New Orleans, with ample opportunity. Gamber, *The Female Economy*, 51; and Walker, *The History of Black Business*, 137–38, respectively.

47. Though Gamber's *The Female Economy* is marketed as a national survey of the industry, some of its conclusions—again, especially about race and ethnicity—are specific to the Northeastern seaboard, from which she culled much of her data. She writes, "The geographical focus of my work, which confines itself to the urban Northeast and Midwest, further limits my analysis to white women of native and Irish origins." Gamber, "A Gendered Enterprise," 3.

48. My research with the printed census records, for example, shows that Chicago seems to have had an unusually high level of female proprietorship. I hope there is a Chicago historian somewhere who will one day tell us why.

49. I am thinking here particularly of Mary P. Ryan, *Women in Public: Between Banners and Ballots, 1825–1880* (Baltimore: Johns Hopkins University Press, 1990). Like her, I am defining "politically" in the broadest possible sense, to include women involved in social reform as well.

50. See, for example, Susan Lee Johnson, *Roaring Camp: The Social World of the California Gold Rush* (New York: W. W. Norton, 2000). The suggestion that gender was a "useful category of analysis" of course comes from Joan Scott, "Gender: A Useful Category of Historical Analysis," *American Historical Review* 91 (December 1986): 1053–75.

51. Michelle E. Jolly, "Inventing the City: Gender and the Politics of Everyday Life in Gold Rush San Francisco, 1848–1869," Ph.D. diss, University of California, San Diego, 1998); Martha Mabie Gardner, "Working on White Womanhood: White Working Women in the San Francisco Anti-Chinese Movement, 1877–1890," *Journal of Social History* 33, no. 1 (1999): 73–95; and Lynn M. Hudson, *The Making of "Mammy Pleasant": A Black Entrepreneur in Nineteenth-Century San Francisco* (Urbana: University of Illinois Press, 2003).

52. General studies of San Francisco tend to overlook women almost completely. Decker, *Fortunes and Failures*, does not discuss women at all; Robert W. Cherny and William Issel, *San Francisco, 1865–1932: Politics, Power, and Urban Development* (Berkeley: University of California Press, 1986), provides minimal coverage; and in Gray Brechin, *Imperial San Francisco: Urban Power, Earthly Ruin* (Berkeley: University of California Press, 1999), only heiresses to vast fortunes in the Hearst and de Young families have a significant role.

53. Joan Jensen and Gloria Lathrop, *California Women: A History* (San Francisco: Boyd and Fraser, 1987), is a good example. The book's treatment of businesswomen in early Los Angeles diminishes their importance. JoAnn Levy's *They Saw the Elephant: Women in the California Gold Rush* (Hamden, Conn.: Archon Books, 1990), the only book written explicitly about women in California during the 1840s and 1850s, is one exception. An entire chapter is devoted to the story of businesswomen in mining camps. Yet because it is not always possible to trace the source of Levy's information, the book is less useful to scholars. Malcolm J. Rohrbaugh's study of the gold rush also includes businesswomen, who are treated in a chapter on women generally.

His emphasis is, appropriately, on the remarkable opportunities many women found in the diggings, especially providing laundry and cooking services. Rohrbaugh, *Days of Gold: The California Gold Rush and the American Nation* (Berkeley: University of California Press, 1997). In *Westering Women and the Frontier Experience, 1800–1915* (Albuquerque: University of New Mexico Press, 1982), Sandra L. Myres recasts the separate spheres argument, stating that since female members of society really belonged in the home sphere, such pursuits were not always accepted as "feminine."

54. Angel Kwolek-Folland, "Customers and Neighbors: Women in the Economy of Lawrence, Kansas, 1870–1885," *Business and Economic History*, 27 (Fall 1998): 129–39; Paula M. Nelson, " 'Do Everything' — Women in Small Prairie Towns, 1870–1920," *Journal of the West*, 36 (October 1997): 52–60.

55. One study that does consider women as influential city shapers in the West is Lee M. A. Simpson, *Selling the City: Gender, Class and the California Growth Machine, 1880–1940* (Palo Alto, Calif.: Stanford University Press, 2004). Simpson documents the ways in which white, middle-class women participated in California urban development, a field previously characterized as exclusively male. However the women she discusses are not, of course, female proprietors.

CHAPTER 1

1. Mrs. Ann Hudson, proprietor of a second-hand clothing store, is listed in the 1888 San Francisco city directory in both the alphabetized and business classified sections with an address at 1077 Market Street. No separate residential address is listed. *San Francisco City Directory, 1888* (San Francisco: Crocker-Langley, 1888). See also photograph of Odd Fellows' Building, Seventh and Market Streets, circa 1888, CHS FN-32508. Its details could not be captured clearly in the reproduction, and thus it is not reproduced here.

2. "Report of Survey of Department, including statistical data on loans and deposits, list of and comments on employees, customers' comments on service provided by department, statistical data on women workers in various fields of business," December 1925, BOAA.

3. This walking tour of San Francisco is inspired by Billy G. Smith's *The "Lower Sort": Philadelphia's Laboring People, 1750–1800* (Ithaca, N.Y.: Cornell University Press, 1990), especially Chapter 1, entitled "Walking the Streets."

4. Mrs. G. W. M. Croles, California v. 14, p. 155, RGDC. The credit report specifically mentions Mrs. Crole's store sign.

5. *San Francisco Chronicle*, September 14, 1869.

6. Mrs. F. McAuliff, California v. 14, p. 362, RGDC.

7. *San Francisco Chronicle*, June 7, 1870.

8. *San Francisco City Directory, 1869* (San Francisco: Towne and Bacon Printers, 1869). The directory stopped designating residents as "colored" in 1875, so its usefulness is limited for identifying the city's population of black female business owners. In her discussion of the hair care and beauty aid industry, Juliet E. K. Walker says that African American female proprietors "participat[ed] in the black hair care business," suggesting that they did not provide hair care services for nonblack cus-

tomers. One of the reasons so many black women in the industry enjoyed so much success is because the care of black women's hair was entirely overlooked by white, mainstream hair product companies and salons. Walker, *The History of Black Business in America: Capitalism, Race, Entrepreneurship* (New York: Macmillan Library Reference USA, 1998), 208.

9. *San Francisco Chronicle*, June 7, 1870.

10. Ibid., September 1, 1870.

11. *Daily Alta California*, December 19, 1870.

12. Ibid. Mrs. Worth rented the house and furniture from Stern in 1877 for $1,100 per month. Mrs. Worth, California v. 19, p. 278, RGDC.

13. Sue Long, California v. 14, p. 25, RGDC.

14. Mrs. A. H. Stoppelkamp, California v. 17, p. 104, RGDC; *San Francisco City Directory, 1877/78* (San Francisco: Polk, 1877).

15. Because over 70 percent of all Chinese women in the city reportedly worked as prostitutes in 1870, Chinese wives were rare. But for those that did exist, paid labor was familiar. Judy Yung argues, for example, that the low wages of Chinese male laborers generally necessitated that their wives supplement their incomes. Typically they did so by spinning, weaving, sewing, washing, and sometimes taking in boarders. In contrast to the wives of merchants, more predominant after Chinese exclusion laws prevented all laborers and their families from entering the United States, working-class women were permitted to leave their homes to purchase supplies, but these transactions were generally confined to Chinatown. Yung, *Unbound Feet: A Social History of Chinese Women in San Francisco* (Berkeley: University of California Press, 1995), 19, 25, 29. For more on how anti-Chinese laws privileged the wives of merchants, see George Anthony Peffer, *If They Don't Bring Their Women Here: Chinese Female Immigration before Exclusion* (Urbana: University of Illinois Press, 1999). Erika Lee also emphasizes that after 1882, when the country became a "gate-keeping" nation, Chinese women's admission or exclusion was predicated on both gender (they were only admitted as dependents of male relatives) and class (the United States relied on "bound feet" as the primary indication that a woman was from the merchant class). She argues, "many women—especially those who were not members of the merchant class—continued to be routinely suspected of being potential prostitutes and were often unfairly detained and/or denied entry." This, of course, kept small the population of women who might otherwise have engaged in the family economy as immigrant enterprisers. Erika Lee, *At America's Gates: Chinese Immigration during the Exclusion Era, 1882–1943* (Chapel Hill: University of North Carolina Press, 2003), 95.

16. *Daily Alta California*, December 19, 1870.

17. *San Francisco Chronicle*, December 3, 1870.

18. *San Francisco City Directory, 1920* (San Francisco: Crocker-Langley, 1920). There were 68 proprietors listed under ladies' furnishing goods in the business section of the 1920 directory. Fifteen were women, and nearly half of their establishments were located on Geary or Fillmore, both less centrally located than Market, Montgomery, Kearny, Third, or Second. Ten out of the fifty-three male proprietors were located on one of the central and more-desirable streets.

19. U.S. Census Bureau, *Fourteenth Census of the United States Taken in the Year 1920: Population*, vol. 2 (Washington, D.C.: Government Printing Office, 1921).

20. *San Francisco City Directory, 1920*.

21. Ibid.

22. Angel Kwolek-Folland, *Engendering Business: Men and Women in the Corporate Office, 1870–1930* (Baltimore: Johns Hopkins University Press, 1994), 190.

23. U.S. Census Bureau, *Ninth Census: The Statistics of the Population of the United States*, vol. 1 (Washington, D.C.: Government Printing Office, 1872); *Compendium of the Tenth Census*, part 1 (Washington, D.C.: Government Printing Office, 1883); and *Fourteenth Census*.

24. These figures are derived from the 1890 and 1920 printed census. The 1890 figure includes merchants, dealers, peddlers, hotelkeepers and boardinghouse keepers, restaurant and saloon owners, and barbers. The 1920 figure includes retail dealers, hotelkeepers/managers, restaurant and café owners, and barbers. These categories were singled out because they are comparable to those used for women and because they were largely comprised of small-business owners. U.S. Census Bureau, *Report on the Population of the United States at the Eleventh Census*, part 1 (Washington, D.C.: Government Printing Office, 1895); and *Fourteenth Census*.

25. U.S. Census Bureau, *Compendium of the Tenth Census*. The exceptions are Buffalo and New Orleans, which peaked a decade earlier and a decade later, respectively.

26. U.S. Census Bureau, *Fourteenth Census*. By 1920 New Orleans had the highest proportion of women in proprietorship (6 percent), and the proportion of Chicago proprietors (4.5 percent) no longer stood out.

27. Valerie Steel, *Fashion and Eroticism: Ideals of Feminine Beauty from the Victorian Era to the Jazz Age* (New York: Oxford University Press, 1985), 51–71, quoted in Wendy Gamber, *The Female Economy: The Millinery and Dressmaking Trades, 1860–1930* (Urbana: University of Illinois Press, 1997), 109. Steel argues that such fashions prevailed between 1820 and 1910.

28. This figure was derived from calculating the proprietors of dressmaking and millinery establishments listed in the business directory as a percentage of all women listed in the industry in the printed census. U.S. Census Bureau, *Ninth Census*; and *San Francisco Business Directory, 1872–73* (San Francisco: A. W. Morgan, 1873). This approach conforms with Wendy Gamber's computations for milliners and dressmakers in Boston in *The Female Economy*.

29. See Gamber, *The Female Economy*.

30. Ibid., 191.

31. This figure was calculated by figuring the number of women who appear in the city directory as the proprietors of millinery and dressmaking establishments as a percentage of all women listed in the industry according to the printed census, per explanation in n. 28 above. U.S. Census Bureau, *The Twelfth Census of the United States Taken In the Year 1900: Population*, vol. 1, part 1 (Washington, D.C.: Government Printing Office, 1901); and *San Francisco City Directory, 1900* (San Francisco: Crocker-Langley, 1900).

32. The printed census confirms a decrease in the number of women in the industry generally, and Wendy Gamber's study of the dressmaking and millinery trades documents the change as a nationwide transformation brought on by the introduction of new technologies in clothes production and the onslaught of department stores. U.S. Census Bureau, *The Twelfth Census*; and Gamber, *The Female Economy*.

33. A classic study of deskilling and industrialization of women's work is Mary H. Blewett, *Men, Women, and Work: Class, Gender, and Protest in the New England Shoe Industry, 1780–1910* (Urbana: University of Illinois Press, 1988).

34. A mangle was an apparatus "designed for pressing linen flat between two rollers [and] was frequently used instead of ironing for large flat items." Patricia Malcolmson, *English Laundresses: A Social History, 1850–1930* (Urbana: University of Illinois Press, 1986), 27.

35. Arwen P. Mohun, *Steam Laundries: Gender, Technology, and Work in the United States and Great Britain, 1880–1940* (Baltimore: Johns Hopkins University Press, 1999), 71.

36. Lillian R. Matthews, "Women in Trade Unions in San Francisco," in *University of California Publications in Economics*, vol. 3, no. 1, ed. Adolph C. Miller (Berkeley: University of California Press, 1913), 10.

37. In 1880, 85 percent of all laundry operators in the city were Chinese men. That year only 9 percent of all gainfully employed women were listed as laundresses, down from 18 percent ten years earlier. The concentration of women in the laundry industry that year (1870)—above average compared to other U.S. cities (New York, Boston, Chicago, Cincinnati, and Buffalo) save for New Orleans, which had a preponderance of washerwomen—underscores the unusually high demand for laundry services in San Francisco. This conclusion conforms with the finding of other scholars, such as Malcolmson, cited above, that port cities and other locations that attracted large numbers of unattached and single men, typically had significantly higher demands for laundry services. U.S. Census Bureau, *Compendium of the Tenth Census*, 902.

38. For the antagonistic and violent reception the Chinese received in nineteenth-century California see Alexander Saxton, *The Indispensable Enemy: Labor and the Anti-Chinese Movement in California* (Berkeley: University of California Press, 1971); Ronald Takaki, *Strangers from a Different Shore: A History of Asian Americans*, (Boston: Little, Brown, 1989); Susan Lee Johnson, *Roaring Camp: The Social World of the California Gold Rush* (New York: W. W. Norton, 2000); Charles J. McClain, *In Search of Equality: The Chinese Struggle against Discrimination in Nineteenth-Century America* (Berkeley: University of California Press, 1994); and Erika Lee, *At America's Gates*. Lee argues that it was in the western United States, and San Francisco in particular, that the racist response to Chinese immigrants helped shape the country into a "gate-keeping" nation which regulated both its borders and its immigrants.

39. Sinophobic city leaders responded to the perceived incursion of Chinese immigrants after 1870 by passing laws which specifically targeted Chinese-operated laundries. In 1873 and 1876, for example, the city passed ordinances taxing all laundries which did not own a horse-drawn cart for laundry pick-ups. While some claimed the law unfairly targeted the small-scale concerns of laundresses as well, it was only enforced against Chinese proprietors. Both laws, however, were overturned in court. Such legal battles between city lawmakers and Chinese immigrant leaders

continued into the 1880s with more city ordinances and more legal challenges until the issue finally reached the U.S. Supreme Court in 1886 in *Yick Wo v. Hopkins*, when the court again overturned the city's law. "In sum," argues legal scholar Charles J. McClain, "when the Chinese laundrymen argued in court that California municipalities were interfering with their right to pursue a livelihood or to advance themselves economically, they could count on a sympathetic hearing from the judges." McClain, *In Search of Equality*, 47–54, 98–132. For more on the Chinese in California's laundry industry see also Paul Ong, "An Ethnic Trade: The Chinese Laundries in Early California," *Journal of Ethnic Studies* 8 (Winter 1981), 95–113; for comparative examples of the Chinese in laundry industries elsewhere see Ronald M. James, Richard D. Adkins, and Rachel J. Hartigan, "Competition and Coexistence in the Laundry: A View of the Comstock," *Western Historical Quarterly* 25, no. 2 (1994): 164–84; Renquiu Yu, *To Save China, to Save Ourselves: The Chinese Hand Laundry Alliance of New York* (Philadelphia: Temple University Press, 1992); and Constance Backhouse, "White Women's Labor Laws: Anti-Chinese Racism in Early Twentieth-Century Canada," *Law and History Review* 14, no. 2 (1996): 315–68.

40. *San Francisco Chronicle*, September 1, 1870.

41. Takaki, *Strangers from a Different Shore*, 181. Six pamphlets from the "Anti-Jap Laundry League" are included in the appendix of Matthews, "Women in Trade Unions," 95–100.

42. In the 1920 census only 39.2 percent of San Francisco women and 42.1 percent of Oakland women in the paid labor force were listed in the category "domestic and personal service," which included laundry and domestic service, both areas where women competed with Asian men. In contrast, in other western cities such as Seattle, Portland, and Los Angeles, women in this category constituted 51.5, 55.7, and 56 percent of all gainfully employed women, respectively. In southern cities, such as Richmond, Virginia, more than 70 percent of all gainfully employed women were concentrated in "domestic and personal service." Domestic and personal service workers in midwestern and northeastern cities typically constituted 50 to 65 percent of all gainfully employed women. The only other city in the census table with a strikingly low percentage of gainfully employed women in this category was Akron, Ohio; I do not know how to explain the anomaly. U.S. Census Bureau, *Fourteenth Census*, 129.

43. Lois W. Banner, *American Beauty* (New York: Alfred A. Knopf, 1983), 40.

44. *San Francisco City Directory, 1877/78*.

45. These figures are derived from the printed census records. U.S. Census Bureau, *Compendium of the Tenth Census*, part 1.

46. Ibid. The cities used for comparison were New York, Boston, and Chicago—all large commercial marketplaces with lively small-business economies—and Buffalo, New Orleans, and Cincinnati—all cities comparable in size to San Francisco between 1870 and 1920.

47. Kathy Peiss, *Hope in a Jar: The Making of America's Beauty Culture* (New York: Henry Holt, 1998), 4–5, 84.

48. Peter R. Decker, *Fortunes and Failures: White-Collar Mobility in Nineteenth-Century San Francisco* (Cambridge: Harvard University Press, 1978), 83.

49. These figures are derived from *San Francisco City Directory, 1877/78*; and the printed census, U.S. Census Bureau, *Ninth Census*, 799.

50. Numbers from San Francisco City Directory, 1920 (San Francisco: Crocker-Langley, 1920). Percentage from U.S. Census Bureau, *Fourteenth Census*.

51. U.S. Census Bureau, *Ninth Census*; *Tenth Census*; *Eleventh Census*; *Twelfth Census*; *Thirteenth Census of the United States Taken in the Year 1910: Population, Occupation Statistics*, vol. 2 (Washington, D.C.: Government Printing Office, 1914); *Fourteenth Census*.

52. See n. 51. For more on the cities selected for comparison see n. 46.

53. U.S. Census Bureau, *Twelfth Census*.

54. *San Francisco Business Directory, 1877–78* (San Francisco: Polk, 1878).

55. Gamber, *The Female Economy*, 28–29. This figure is for 1876.

56. This figure taken from a comparison of the San Francisco business directories for 1860, 1877–78, and 1900. Because it is assumed that those listed in the laundry industry include workers and not just proprietors (a difficult population to distinguish in all historical records for this industry), it is assumed that the directory overrepresents the proportion of female proprietors working in the laundry industry. Thus while the 1870 directory listed 42 percent of proprietors in laundry and 35 percent in accommodations, an adjustment for *proprietors only* in the laundry industry would make accommodations proprietors the largest group.

57. Charles P. Kimball, *The San Francisco City Directory* (San Francisco: Journal of Commerce Press, 1850), preface.

58. Wilson Wright, ed., *Luzena Stanley Wilson '49er: Memories Recalled Years Later for Her Daughter* (Oakland: Eucalyptus Press, 1937), 27–28.

59. Julie Roy Jeffrey, *Frontier Women: The Trans-Mississippi West, 1840–1880* (New York: Hill and Wang, 1979), 115.

60. Decker, *Fortunes and Failures*, 202.

61. A company agent to Mssrs. Joseph G. Bearly & Co., May 30, 1850, Edward D. Weld Papers, CHS.

62. Decker, *Fortunes and Failures*, 44.

63. Robert Glass Cleland, ed., *Apron Full of Gold: The Letters of Mary Jane Megquier from San Francisco* (San Marino, Calif.: Huntington Library, 1949), 25. This astronomical figure reflects a booming rate of inflation that drove up the price of everything from onions to housing in early San Francisco.

64. Mel Scott, *The San Francisco Bay Area: A Metropolis in Perspective* (Berkeley: University of California Press, 1959), 26, quoted in Alvin Averbach, "San Francisco's South of Market District, 1850–1950: The Emergence of a Skid Row," *California Historical Quarterly* 52 (Fall 1973): 201.

65. Decker, *Fortunes and Failures*, 33.

66. Benjamin E. Lloyd, *Lights and Shades of San Francisco* (San Francisco: A. L. Bancroft, 1876), 449.

67. A historian who has traced San Francisco's early merchant population has determined that "initially only 15 percent of the merchants and 16 percent of the general population brought their wives with them to the West Coast. Even fewer (10 percent) transported their children." Decker, *Fortunes and Failures*, 33.

68. This was not a trend common to all of California. Among the eight cities in the state with populations of 25,000 or more, Sacramento was the only other city with a noteworthy gender imbalance of 130.8 men to every 100 women. In 1910, Los Angeles, Oakland, and San Diego had male-to-female ratios of 103.9:100, 108.7:100, and 109.9:100, respectively. The other three large cities—Berkeley, Pasadena, and San Jose—each had more women than men. U.S. Census Bureau, *Thirteenth Census*, 164.

69. William Laird MacGregor, *Hotels and Hotel Life at San Francisco California in 1876* (San Francisco: San Francisco News Company, 1877), 36–37.

70. Lloyd, *Lights and Shades*, 449–52.

71. Averbach, "South of Market," 198–201. "Modiste" was another word used for "dressmaker."

72. Ibid., 198–201.

73. *San Francisco City Directory, 1879–80*, 943–45, 989. Quoted in Averbach, "South of Market," 205.

74. Robert W. Cherny and William Issel, *San Francisco, 1865–1932: Politics, Power, and Urban Development* (Berkeley: University of California Press, 1986), 61.

75. Claudia Goldin, *Understanding the Gender Gap: An Economic History of American Women* (New York: Oxford University Press, 1990), 42–50.

76. Cherny and Issel, *San Francisco*, 61–62.

77. Ibid.

78. Ibid., 59–60.

79. Kimball, *The San Francisco Directory, 1850*.

80. Letter from "A Storeman in San Francisco," published in the *St. Joseph (Mo.) Adventure*, October 10, 1851, collected in Walker D. Wyman, ed., *California Emigrant Letters* (New York: Bookman Associates, 1952), 169.

81. *San Francisco City Directory, 1860* (San Francisco: Kimball, 1860); *San Francisco City Directory, 1877–78*.

82. Scott A. Sandage relates that Mark Twain's enduring and widely used term "Gilded Age" to describe the end of the nineteenth century was coined in 1874 in the midst of the depression with ironic intent, meant to capture the degree to which most Americans suffered economically even as the privileged few got wealthy. Sandage, *Born Losers: A History of Failure in America* (Cambridge: Harvard University Press, 2005), 228.

83. Mansel Blackford, *A History of Small Business in America*, 2nd ed. (Chapel Hill: University of North Carolina Press, 2003), 105.

84. John Modell and Tamara K. Hareven, "Urbanization and the Malleable Household: An Examination of Boarding and Lodging in American Families," *Journal of Marriage and the Family* 35 (August 1973): 467–79.

85. Gray Brechin, *Imperial San Francisco: Urban Power, Earthly Ruin* (Berkeley: University of California Press, 1999), 135, and the rest of Chapter 3 more generally. For more on the role that race played in the Filipino-American War, see the fascinating account by Kristin L. Hoganson, *Fighting for American Manhood: How Gender Politics Provoked the Spanish-American and Philippine-American Wars* (New Haven: Yale University Press, 1998).

86. Roger W. Lotchin, *Fortress California, 1910–1960: From Warfare to Welfare* (New York: Oxford University Press, 1992).

87. Brechin, *Imperial San Francisco*, 135.

88. For documentation of San Francisco's role in the war as a port of leave, see Sara Bunnett, ed., *Manila Envelopes: Oregon Volunteer Lt. George F. Telfer's Spanish-American War Letters* (Portland: Oregon Historical Society Press, 1987). For troop and casualty figures, Gary B. Nash et al., *The American People: Creating a Nation and a Society* (New York: Harper Collins College Publishers, 1994), 685.

89. Printed census records show the rise and fall of female proprietors in the hospitality industry in San Francisco (see figs. A1 and A2).

90. Russell Quinn, "The San Francisco Press and the Fire of 1906," monograph 5 of *The History of San Francisco Journalism* (San Francisco: Works Project Administration of Northern California, 1940), quoted in Kevin Starr, *Americans and the California Dream, 1850–1915* (New York: Oxford University Press, 1973), 293.

91. Starr, *Americans and the California Dream*, 294.

92. For more on the new jobs in clerical work see Chapter 2.

93. In her study of antebellum New York, Elizabeth Blackmar argues that boardinghouses "suffer[ed] censure from their association with sailors and wharf-district epidemics." Blackmar, *Manhattan for Rent, 1785–1850* (Ithaca, N.Y.: Cornell University Press, 1989), 134.

94. "Fifty-Third Annual *San Francisco Chronicle* California Efficiency Edition," *San Francisco Chronicle*, January 16, 1918, 59.

95. "Charlie's Side-Walk Acquaintances," *Harper's New Monthly Magazine* 15 (1857), 861–62, quoted in Stuart M. Blumin, *The Emergence of the Middle Class: Social Experience in the American City, 1760–1900* (New York: Cambridge University Press, 1989), 179.

96. Blumin, *Emergence of the Middle Class*, 182.

97. Because this study does not make use of manuscript census records it was impossible to calculate the class status of San Francisco female proprietors with accuracy. Other studies have made use of samples from the manuscript census to calculate real and personal property and living arrangements—two indicators of class status. Wendy Gamber's study of milliners and dressmakers is a good example. See her Tables 6 and 7, which provide these calculations for Boston proprietors in one industry during one year. Gamber, *The Female Economy*, 36 and 41. Another example can be found in Susan Ingalls Lewis, "Women in the Marketplace: Female Entrepreneurship, Business Patterns, and Working Families in Mid-Nineteenth-Century Albany, New York, 1830–1885" (Ph.D. diss, State University of New York, Binghamton, 2002). This study's examination of women business owners in multiple industries and occupations traced over seventy years precluded such calculations. Bankruptcy court records, city directories, credit reports, and even newspapers do give occasional insight into the class status of female proprietors. Whenever that is true, it has generally been noted in the text. The examples discussed in this paragraph are drawn from such sources. But this kind of anecdotal evidence does not provide a systematic or quantifiable way to assess class.

98. For more on the invisibility of some women's economic enterprise see

Kwolek-Folland, *Incorporating Women: A History of Women and Business in the United States* (New York: Twayne Publishers, 1998); and Goldin, *Understanding the Gender Gap*.

99. Kwolek-Folland, *Incorporating Women*, 118–19.

100. See Hasia R. Diner, *Erin's Daughters in America: Irish Immigrant Women in the Nineteenth Century* (Baltimore: John Hopkins University Press, 1983), for more on this.

101. See Lewis, "Women in the Marketplace."

102. The one stand-out exception to this trend in San Francisco was Mary Ann Magnin, founder of I. Magnin department store, who built a retail empire that generated enduring success and wealth for approximately one hundred years. She will be discussed briefly in subsequent chapters but deserves a study all her own.

103. Blackford, *A History of Small Business*, 105.

104. Several scholars have examined the tendency of immigrants toward small-business proprietorship. See, for example, Scott Cummings, ed., *Self-Help in Urban America: Patterns of Minority Business Enterprise* (Port Washington, N.Y.: Kennikat, 1980); Ivan H. Light, *Ethnic Enterprise in America: Business and Welfare among Chinese, Japanese, and Blacks* (Berkeley: University of California Press, 1972); Jan Rath, ed., *Immigrant Businesses: The Economic, Political, and Social Environment* (New York: St. Martin's, 2000); and Philip Scranton, "Moving Outside Manufacturing: Research Perspectives on Small Business in Twentieth-Century America," in *Small Firms, Large Concerns*, ed. Konosuke Odaka and Minoru Sawai (Oxford: Oxford University Press, 1999), 19–46.

105. Edmund D. McGarry, *Mortality in Retail Trade* (Buffalo: University of Buffalo Bureau of Business and Social Research, 1930), 71–80; cited in Roland Berthoff, "Independence and Enterprise: Small Business in the American Dream," in *Small Business in American Life*, ed. Stuart W. Bruchey (New York: Columbia University Press, 1980), 41.

106. Clyde Griffen and Sally Griffen, *Natives and Newcomers: The Ordering of Opportunity in Mid-Nineteenth-Century Poughkeepsie* (Cambridge: Harvard University Press, 1978), 119, 130, 147–4; cited in Berthoff, "Independence and Enterprise," 34.

107. These figures capture the apparel, accommodations, retail, and laundry industries but not the beauty industry. Conclusions drawn from U.S. Census Bureau, *Eleventh Census*. Two computations were completed. Male and female proprietors from each nativity were computed as a percentage of all laborers in each nativity. And male and female proprietors from each nativity were computed as a percentage of all proprietors. See Appendix 2 for more data.

108. In comparison, foreign-born white men comprised 43 percent of all gainfully occupied men in the city, much closer to their representation in the field of small-business proprietorship.

109. The figures discussed in this section on the ethnicity and race of male and female proprietors in San Francisco are all based on the 1890 printed census records. U.S. Census Bureau, *Eleventh Census*.

110. Diner, *Erin's Daughters in America*, 96.

111. Diner, *Hungering for America: Italian, Irish, and Jewish Foodways in the Age of*

Migration (Cambridge: Harvard University Press, 2001), emphasizes, in particular, the ubiquity of boarding establishments operated by Irish women throughout urban America during the nineteenth century. Lewis, "Women in the Marketplace," corroborates this finding for Albany, New York.

112. Kwolek-Folland, *Incorporating Women*, 118.

113. Shelly Tenenbaum, "Borrowers or Lenders Be: Jewish Immigrant Women's Credit Networks," in *American Jewish Women's History, A Reader*, ed. Pamela S. Nadell (New York: New York University Press, 2003): 79–90.

114. Aidan Hollis, "Women and Microcredit in History: Gender in the Irish Loan Funds," <www.econ.ucalgary.ca/fac-files/ah/womenandloanfunds.pdf> (May 2004).

115. U.S. Census Bureau, *Eleventh Census*. See Appendix.

116. Cherny and Issel, *San Francisco*, 56. The figures cited here from Cherny and Issel are based on an examination of the *Twelfth Census of the United States, 1900*. Percentages are the portion of all female laborers who were Irish, the portion of all female laundry workers who were Irish, etc.

117. Angel Kwolek-Folland, *Engendering Business*.

118. For Irish labor leader Dennis Kearney's claims that "our women are degraded by Coolie labor," see Lucille Eaves, *A History of California Labor Legislation: With an Introductory Sketch of the San Francisco Labor Movement* (Berkeley: University of California Press, 1910), 136, 311–17, quoted in Diner, *Erin's Daughters*, 92–93. For the Anti-Coolie Co-operative Laundry Association, see advertisement in the *San Francisco Chronicle*, September 1, 1870. The organization was an incorporated enterprise, complete with constitution and by-laws. Canvassers assigned to each city district passed out cards at the residences of citizens advertising the co-operative and offering stock subscriptions for sale. Their reliance on consumer boycotts, precinct level organization, and invocations of racial privilege mirrored tactics used by white, male workers against the Chinese in San Francisco. For more, see Saxton, *The Indispensable Enemy*, 65. At this time, I can not say with certainty that white women were among the members of the anti-Chinese laundry organization. Yet scholarship documenting white women's active resistance against the perceived Chinese male encroachment on domestic service suggests that they were. See, for example, Mary P. Ryan, *Women in Public: Between Banners and Ballots, 1825–1880* (Baltimore: Johns Hopkins University Press, 1990); and Martha Mabie Gardner, "Working on White Womanhood: White Working Women in the San Francisco Anti-Chinese Movement, 1877–1890," *Journal of Social History* 33, no. 1 (1999): 73–95.

119. Ong, "An Ethnic Trade," 95–113.

120. Immigrants from Great Britain and Scandinavia (Sweden, Norway, and Denmark) ranked third and fourth among foreign-born businessmen in all industry categories, with 10 percent and 6 percent respectively. U.S. Census Bureau, *Eleventh Census*.

121. RGDC. These findings are based on my sample of men from the 1870s credit reports (the only years the reports are available for San Francisco) who oper-

ated saloons, groceries, tailor shops, and the like, typically small businesses of a size comparable to the enterprises operated by women. In this sample, Jews comprise the second-largest ethnic group (8 percent of total). Sometimes the reporter listed "Polish Jew" in the reports, otherwise the country of origin remains unnamed.

122. U.S. Census Bureau, *Eleventh Census*.

123. See Diner, *Erin's Daughters*, for starters. Others have documented the ways in which the difficult circumstances of Irish laborers drove them to the front of the anti-Chinese labor movements in San Francisco. See Saxton, *The Indispensable Enemy*.

124. Robert A. Burchell, *The San Francisco Irish, 1848–1880* (Manchester, U.K.: Manchester University Press, 1979), 64.

125. U.S. Census Bureau, *Eleventh Census*.

126. See Mohun, *Steam Laundries* for more on the transformation of the industry. See also Joan Wang, "Gender, Race and Civilization: The Competition between American Power Laundries and Chinese Steam Laundries, 1870s–1920s," *American Studies International*, 40 (February 2002): 52–73, which demonstrates how American Power Laundry owners described themselves in terms of white masculinity/civilization and the Chinese in terms of femininity/primitivity to try to subvert Chinese competition in the industry. The greatest difference between the two types of laundries was technology.

127. U.S. Census Bureau, *Eleventh Census*. These figures provide an important counterbalance to Gamber's figures on Boston's dressmaking and millinery proprietors who were predominantly (78 percent) native-born Americans. Gamber, *The Female Economy*, 35. Examining proprietorship beyond the sewing trades reveals that nativity did not exclude women from proprietorship but in fact that those of foreign origins were most likely to find proprietorship an attractive option.

128. Six percent of gainfully occupied native-born, white women with immigrant parents were proprietors, compared to 9 percent for native-born, white women with native parents. Fourteen percent of white immigrant women in the paid labor force pursued proprietorship. U.S. Census Bureau, *Eleventh Census*. See Table A5.

129. Of course a bias toward more-substantial businesses with the greatest capital investment could also explain the omission of nonwhite women from the credit records. Wendy Gamber discusses this bias in *The Female Economy*, 235, in her "Essay on Primary Sources."

130. Albert S. Broussard, *Black San Francisco: The Struggle for Racial Equality in the West, 1900–1954* (Lawrence: University Press of Kansas, 1993), 21.

131. Yung, *Unbound Feet*, 24.

132. Scholarship on Mexican and Californio women in nineteenth-century California focuses on Los Angeles. One such study found that native women in Los Angeles after the American conquest of California "took on unskilled jobs, working as seamstresses, washerwomen, housekeepers, and farm laborers, enabling them, alongside their spouses, brothers and fathers, to eke out an existence for themselves and their families." Perhaps some were enterprising women who operated businesses out of their homes since, like Irish immigrant women, such married women lived cir-

cumscribed lives, controlled by cultural expectations that they remain in the home once married. Miroslava Chávez-García, *Negotiating Conquest: Gender and Power in California, 1770s to 1880s* (Tucson: University of Arizona Press, 2004), 149.

133. Records on San Francisco black women show them engaging in a variety of business occupations, including hair care, custom clothing production, retail, laundry, and boarding. But scholars emphasize, in particular, opportunity in the boarding business. See, for example, Douglas Henry Daniels, *Pioneer Urbanites: A Social and Cultural History of Black San Francisco* (Philadelphia: Temple University Press, 1980), 57.

134. Loren Schweninger, "Property Owning Free African-American Women in the South." *Journal of Women's History* 1 (Winter 1990): 17; Walker, *The History of Black Business*, 143.

135. Margaret Levenstein, "African American Entrepreneurship: The View from the 1910 Census," *Business and Economic History* 24 (Fall 1995): 106–22.

136. Daniels, *Pioneer Urbanites*, 57.

137. Juliet Walker argues that after 1900, in particular, "black business activity became more dependent on the development of a separate black economy." Walker, *The History of Black Business*, 215.

138. Schweninger, "Property Owning," 17.

139. Lynn M. Hudson, *The Making of "Mammy Pleasant": A Black Entrepreneur in Nineteenth-Century San Francisco* (Urbana: University of Illinois Press, 2003).

140. Delilah Beasley, *Negro Trail Blazers of California* (Los Angeles: James Stevenson, 1919), 95; cited in Walker, *The History of Black Business*, 142.

141. 1900 Manuscript Census, District 37, Sheet 10, National Archives and Records Administration, Pacific Region, San Bruno, Calif.

142. Donna J. Guy, "The Economics of Widowhood in Arizona, 1880–1940," in *On Their Own: Widows and Widowhood in the American Southwest, 1848–1939*, ed. Arlene Scadron (Urbana: University of Illinois Press, 1988): 195–223.

143. Yung, *Unbound Feet*, 46.

144. Because the numbers of businesswomen in the beauty industry were so small, I did not include the industry in my computations here. For "colored" women's industry concentration the figures were apparel (24 percent), laundry (25 percent), retail (24 percent), and hospitality (27 percent). U.S. Census Bureau, *Eleventh Census*.

145. For more on the importance of balancing income opportunities with household work see Chapter 2.

146. Gamber, *The Female Economy*, discusses proprietorship in the custom clothing trade as upward mobility for immigrant women.

147. U.S. Census Bureau, *Eleventh Census*.

148. Ibid. Large numbers of nonwhite men also worked as tailors and retail dealers, boosting the population of African American and Asian American men in the ranks of proprietorship.

149. High numbers of nonwhite male business owners, of course, meant that white men were less significant proportionally. Thus native-born white men with foreign-born parents and native-born white men with native-born parents comprised 12 and 11 percent, respectively, of all small-scale business owners in the city, a much smaller proportion than that of women from the same background.

CHAPTER 2

1. Wilson Wright, ed., *Luzena Stanley Wilson '49er: Memories Recalled Years Later for Her Daughter* (Oakland, Calif.: Eucalyptus Press, 1937), 9.

2. Unsigned letter to Catherine D. Oliver of Boston, 1850, written by a female friend recently arrived in San Francisco. Collection MS 1596, CHS.

3. Robert Glass Cleland, ed., *Apron Full of Gold: The Letters of Mary Jane Megquier from San Francisco* (San Marino, Calif.: Huntington Library, 1949), 23.

4. Ibid., 30.

5. Ibid., 28, 17.

6. This term describes those who arrived in northern California with the first wave of the gold rush in 1849.

7. Julie Roy Jeffrey, *Frontier Women: The Trans-Mississippi West, 1840–1880* (New York: Hill and Wang, 1979), 108, 116.

8. Lynn M. Hudson, *The Making of "Mammy Pleasant": A Black Entrepreneur in Nineteenth-Century San Francisco* (Urbana: University of Illinois Press, 2003), 8.

9. For more on women's legal status in the United States see Joan Hoff, *Law, Gender, and Injustice: A Legal History of U.S. Women* (New York: New York University Press, 1991); and Norma Basch, *In the Eyes of the Law: Women, Marriage, and Property in Nineteenth-Century New York* (Ithaca, N.Y.: Cornell University Press, 1982).

10. Hudson, *The Making of "Mammy Pleasant,"* 59.

11. JoAnn Levy, *They Saw the Elephant: Women in the California Gold Rush* (Hamden, Conn.: Archon Books, 1990), 100.

12. Cleland, *Apron Full of Gold*, 30.

13. Joseph R. Conlin, *Bacon, Beans, and Galantines: Food and Foodways on the Western Mining Frontier* (Reno: University of Nevada Press, 1986), 91.

14. Charles P. Kimball, *The San Francisco City Directory* (San Francisco: Journal of Commerce Press, 1850).

15. U.S. Census Bureau, *Report on the Population of the United States at the Eighth Census*, part 1 (Washington, D.C.: Government Printing Office, 1860), Table 6: Statistics of Population. The Boston figure is taken from Wendy Gamber, *The Female Economy: The Millinery and Dressmaking Trades, 1860–1930* (Urbana: University of Illinois Press, 1997), 28–29. Gamber does not compute the total number of proprietors as a proportion of all gainfully occupied women in the city that year.

16. Peter R. Decker, *Fortunes and Failures: White-Collar Mobility in Nineteenth-Century San Francisco* (Cambridge: Harvard University Press, 1978), 278 n. 45, 30, 73–74.

17. While prostitutes can certainly be characterized as "businesswomen," they are not covered in this study in any detail both because they have been examined extensively elsewhere and because they can not be studied utilizing the same original source material that is used here to capture the history of female proprietors in the accommodations, apparel, retail, beauty, and laundry industries.

18. For more on Chinese prostitutes in San Francisco see, for example, Benson Tong, *Unsubmissive Women: Chinese Prostitutes in Nineteenth-Century San Francisco* (Norman: University of Oklahoma Press, 1994).

19. Decker, *Fortunes and Failures*, 89. One study of businesswomen in Albany, New York, found at least one madam who operated a cash-based business so profitable that she was deemed good for credit by R. G. Dun & Company credit reporters. Other madams appeared in the credit reports for Albany, New York, clearly identified as operating houses of "ill fame." Susan Ingalls Lewis, "Women in the Marketplace: Female Entrepreneurship, Business Patterns, and Working Families in Mid-Nineteenth-Century Albany, New York, 1830–1885" (Ph.D. diss., State University New York, Binghamton, 2002), 276. In contrast, no prostitutes were identified by the credit reporters who evaluated San Francisco's businesswomen, in spite of the clear success of some.

20. Jacqueline Baker Barnhart, *The Fair but Frail: Prostitution in San Francisco, 1849–1900* (Reno: University of Nevada Press, 1986), 81.

21. Benjamin E. Lloyd, *Lights and Shades of San Francisco* (San Francisco: A. L. Bancroft, 1876), 80.

22. Upon her death, one Sacramento madam left a "resplendent wardrobe" consisting of thirty-one dresses, twenty-one skirts, eleven chemises, a red jacket, and a white silk cape. This underscores that she had provided a lot of business for local apparel proprietors. W. N. Davis Jr., "Research Uses of County Court Records, 1850–1879, and Incidental Intimate Glimpses of California Life and Society, Part I," *California Historical Quarterly* 52 (Fall 1973): 260. Barnhart also makes this point in *The Fair but Frail*, 81.

23. Decker, *Fortunes and Failures*, 31.

24. Jane F. Hale, advertisement in the Princeton, Illinois, *Bureau County Republican*, January 10, 1861, quoted in Lucy Eldersveld Murphy, "Her Own Boss: Businesswomen and Separate Spheres in the Midwest, 1850–1880," *Illinois Historical Journal* 80 (Autumn 1987), 164.

25. Gray Brechin, *Imperial San Francisco: Urban Power, Earthly Ruin* (Berkeley: University of California Press, 1999), 32.

26. Decker, *Fortunes and Failures*, 34.

27. At the National Gold Rush Symposium held at the Oakland Museum in January of 1998, western historian Patricia Nelson Limerick declared that despite some contemporaries' insistence that gold rush California was a world turned on its head, "the interlude of 'economic democracy' [was] very brief, very passing." "The rapidity by which conventional arrangements of power and privilege reconstituted themselves," she argued, "seems to be the story that emerges for the long haul." Patricia Nelson Limerick, "The Gold Rush and the Shaping of the American West," *California History* 77 (Spring 1998): 35.

28. *San Francisco City Directory, 1859–1860* (San Francisco: Kimball, 1860).

29. Mansel Blackford, *A History of Small Business in America*, 2nd ed. (Chapel Hill: University of North Carolina Press, 2003), 105. Blackford makes this point for the colonial, antebellum, and postbellum periods as well.

30. As far as I am aware, no one has examined marital status as a significant factor in male small-business proprietorship. I would not be surprised if a divergence between never married and married/formerly married men with regard to small-business ownership was discovered as well.

31. Blackford, *A History of Small Business*, 74.

32. In her 1916 study of Boston and Philadelphia milliners, Lorinda Perry argued that "sometimes a salesgirl [or millinery worker] will take with her no small amount of her employer's business." One employer, she continued, "estimated that one of his salesgirls took from him $5,000 worth of trade into her own business." Lorinda Perry, *The Millinery Trade in Boston and Philadelphia: A Study of Women in Industry* (Binghamton, N.Y.: Vail-Ballou Company Press, 1916), 31.

33. Miss Eliza McGearny, California vol. 19, p. 316, RGDC.

34. Gamber, *The Female Economy*, 1.

35. Ibid., 42.

36. Blackford, *A History of Small Business*, 104.

37. Figure composed using the 1890 printed census. U.S. Census Bureau, *Report on the Population of the United States at the Eleventh Census* (Washington, D.C.: Government Printing Office, 1895), part 1, 890; and part 2, 728–29. This statistic was originally created for my dissertation, where it appears in Table 2:4, "Percent of Gainfully Occupied Women Working as Business Proprietors by Marital Status in 1890." See Edith Sparks, "Capital Instincts: The Economics of Female Proprietorship in San Francisco, 1850–1920" (Ph.D. diss., University of California, Los Angeles, 1999), 121.

38. These figures were composed using the 1890 and 1930 printed census. U.S. Census Bureau, *Eleventh Census*, part 2, 728–29; *Fifteenth Census of the United States, 1930: Population*, (Washington, D.C.: Government Printing Office, 1933), 4:218; and 2:949. These statistics were originally created for my dissertation and appear there in Table 2:1, "Businesswomen By Marital Status, 1890"; Table 2:7, "Businesswomen by Marital Status, 1930"; and Table 2:6, "Percent of Gainfully Occupied Women Working as Business Proprietors by Marital Status, 1890 and 1930." See Sparks, "Capital Instincts," 115, 136–37.

39. Chinese "house boys" and cooks often took the place of female servants in San Francisco. Until 1880, they constituted a majority of all domestic servants in California. David M. Katzman, *Seven Days a Week: Women and Domestic Service in Industrializing America* (New York: Oxford University Press, 1978), 55.

40. It was reported that during the same period, domestic servants in New York earned $4 to $7 per month. Hasia Diner, *Erin's Daughters in America: Irish Immigrant Women in the Nineteenth Century* (Baltimore: Johns Hopkins University Press, 1983), 90.

41. U.S. Census Office, *Ninth Census: The Statistics of the Population of the United States* (Washington, D.C.: Government Printing Office, 1872), 1:799.

42. Robert A. Burchell, *The San Francisco Irish, 1848–1880* (Manchester, U.K.: Manchester University Press, 1979), 55.

43. Evelyn Nakano Glenn, "From Servitude to Service Work: Historical Con-

tinuities in the Racial Division of Paid Reproductive Labor," in *Unequal Sisters: A Multi-Cultural Reader In U.S. Women's History*, 2nd ed., ed. Vicki L. Ruiz and Ellen Carol DuBois (New York: Routledge, 1994), 405–35.

44. Journal of Alfred and Chastina Rix, January 1, 1854, CHS.

45. Claudia Goldin, *Understanding the Gender Gap: An Economic History of American Women* (New York: Oxford University Press, 1990), 162–63.

46. Female teachers in the city were paid an average monthly salary of $68 in 1875 while male teachers earned $84.93. In administrative positions, women were typically confined to the primary school level and found little opportunity among the higher grades. In a casual survey of San Francisco school principals in 1875, for example, there were twice as many female principals in primary schools as there were male principals, and men outnumbered women 8 to 1 in administrative positions at middle schools. John Swett, *History of the Public School System of California* (San Francisco: A. L. Bancroft, 1876), 233, 91.

47. Between 1870 and 1910, the percentage of all employed women working as domestic servants in San Francisco decreased from 40 percent to 15 percent, while the percentage of all employed women working as teachers stayed the same: 4 percent. U.S. Census Bureau, *Ninth Census*, 799; and *Thirteenth Census of the United States Taken in the Year 1910: Population, Occupation Statistics* (Washington, D.C.: Government Printing Office, 1914), 194.

48. See photo of Hazel Gibson Bookman in Sharon Strom, *Beyond the Typewriter: Gender, Class, and the Origins of Modern American Office Work, 1900–1930* (Urbana: University of Illinois Press, 1992). In the caption Strom explains that "African American clerks found limited employment in their own communities and helped to anchor the growing black middle class in the 1920s." For more see 209–303.

49. Olivier Zunz, *Making America Corporate, 1870–1920* (Chicago: University of Chicago Press, 1990), 12.

50. Margery W. Davies, *Woman's Place Is at the Typewriter: Office Work and Office Workers, 1870–1930* (Philadelphia: Temple University Press, 1982), 28.

51. This idea is discussed in ibid.

52. Strom, *Beyond the Typewriter*, especially Chapter 4, "'Light Manufacturing': The Feminization of Clerical Work."

53. See, for example, Angel Kwolek-Folland, *Engendering Business: Men and Women in the Corporate Office, 1870–1930* (Baltimore: Johns Hopkins University Press, 1994). She discusses all of the points cited here in Strom and Davies and goes into considerable depth about the gendered culture of the office place, especially in Chapter 4, "The Domestic Office: Space, Status, and the Gendered Workplace."

54. Strom, *Beyond the Typewriter*, 334.

55. See ad in *Daily Alta California*, June 24, 1876.

56. See ad in ibid., March 8, 1890.

57. U.S. Census Bureau, *Ninth Census*, 799; *Eleventh Census*, 728; and *Thirteenth Census*, 194–207.

58. These figures are taken from Table 23 in Joseph A. Hill, *Women in Gainful Occupations*, Census Monographs 9 (Washington, D.C.: Government Printing Office, 1929), 33–34.

59. See photograph of such a sign at 268 Market Street, California Historical Society, FN-32515. The details were too small to be captured in a reprint here.

60. Blackford, *A History of Small Business*, 43.

61. Ibid., 99, Table 3.

62. These figures were developed using the 1890 printed census for San Francisco. U.S. Census Bureau, *Eleventh Census*, part 2, 728.

63. Goldin, *Understanding the Gender Gap*, 163–64.

64. These figures are derived from the 1890 printed census. U.S. Census Bureau, *Eleventh Census*, part 1, 890; and part 2, 728–29.

65. In her study of San Francisco, Los Angeles, and Portland women, Mary Lou Locke found that 61 percent of married working women and 53 percent of widowed working women in 1880 had children at home. Locke, "'Like a Machine or an Animal': Working Women of the Late Nineteenth-Century Urban Far West, in San Francisco, Portland, and Los Angeles" (Ph.D. diss., University of California, San Diego, 1982).

66. See Goldin, *Understanding the Gender Gap*; and Angel Kwolek-Folland, *Incorporating Women: A History of Women and Business in the United States* (New York: Twayne Publishers, 1998), for more on women's part-time work.

67. Lewis, "Women in the Marketplace," 106–7.

68. Kwolek-Folland, *Incorporating Women*, 96, 126.

69. Julia Lyons, case #1296, San Francisco, 1873, BCF.

70. The information on alimony presented here is from *Index to the Laws of California, 1850–1920* (Sacramento: California State Printing Office, 1921). For alimony suits, see the notice regarding Mrs. Wolff's case against her husband, Henry, a jewelry store owner who had been ordered to pay her $150 a month alimony. *San Francisco Chronicle*, August 7, 1894, 6. When a woman had property of her own, she too could become the recipient of an order for alimony. One man pursuing such a case against his wife was smart enough to hire Clara Foltz—the first female lawyer in the state of California—as his attorney in the matter. *San Francisco Chronicle*, December 5, 1894, 12.

71. Robert L. Griswold, *Family and Divorce in California, 1850–1890: Victorian Illusions and Everyday Realities* (Albany: State University of New York Press, 1982).

72. Kwolek-Folland, *Incorporating Women*, 56. Remarkably, these motivations for female proprietorship remained more or less continuous from colonial America through the nineteenth and twentieth centuries and even into today. For continuity, see ibid., 192.

73. Mrs. A. Finke, California vol. 14, p. 106, RGDC.

74. Elizabeth Dexter, *Colonial Women of Affairs: A Study of Women in Business and the Professions in America before 1776* (Boston: Houghton Mifflin, 1924), 14–15, quoted in Julie E. Matthei, *An Economic History of Women in America: Women's Work, the Sexual Division of Labor, and the Development of Capitalism* (New York: Schocken Books, 1982), 67.

75. Mrs. Rosanna Short, California vol. 18, p. 215, RGDC. See also Mrs. P. Quigley, California vol. 17, p. 250, RGDC.

76. In Boston such women turned to the Bureau for Handicapped Women (their

handicap being both their age and their alleged lack of experience), which was operated by the Women's Educational and Industrial Union. Corinne T. Field, "'Handicapped by Age': Women Over Forty-Five and the Employment Bureaus of the Women's Educational and Industrial Union, 1877–1933" (paper presented at the annual meeting of the Organization of American Historians, Indianapolis, Ind., April 2, 1998).

77. Mrs. Michael C. Murphy, California vol. 15, p. 38, RGDC. Gamber, *The Female Economy*, 46.

78. *Daily Alta California*, March 14, 1867.

79. Frances Fuller Victor, *The New Penelope, A Novella* (San Francisco: A. L. Bancroft, 1877), 27.

80. Mrs. L. H. Lichtenstein, California vol. 20, p. 350, RGDC.

81. Based on figures derived from the 1890 and 1930 printed census reports. U.S. Census Bureau, *Eleventh Census*, part 1, 890; and part 2, 728; and *Fifteenth Census*, 4:218; and 2:949. The figures were originally composed for my dissertation and appear there in Table 2:6 "Percent of Gainfully Occupied Women Working as Business Proprietors by Marital Status, 1890 and 1930." See Sparks, "Capital Instincts," 136.

82. See Kwolek-Folland, *Incorporating Women*, cited above; and Donna J. Guy, "The Economics of Widowhood in Arizona, 1880–1940," in *On Their Own: Widows and Widowhood in the American Southwest, 1848–1939*, ed. Arlene Scadron (Urbana: University of Illinois Press, 1988), 195–223, who examines boarding, in particular, as an important strategy for widows in Arizona.

83. Alice Kessler-Harris, *A Woman's Wage: Historical Meanings and Social Consequences* (Lexington: University Press of Kentucky, 1990), 121.

84. Kwolek-Folland, *Incorporating Women*, 8–9.

85. Alan Trachtenberg, *The Incorporation of America: Culture and Society in the Gilded Age* (New York: Hill and Wang, 1982).

86. These figures developed from the printed census for San Francisco. U.S. Census Office, *Eleventh Census*, part 1; and *Fifteenth Census*, vol. 2.

87. U.S. Census Office, *Eleventh Census*, part 1; and *Fifteenth Census*, vol. 2.

88. Blackford, *A History of Small Business*, 91–92.

89. U.S. Census Office, *Fifteenth Census*, vol. 2.

90. Goldin, *Understanding the Gender Gap*, 140.

91. Robert L. Griswold, *Family and Divorce in California*, 29, 69, 79.

92. "Autobiographical Notes by Mrs. Joseph S. Newmark, Translated from the German by her daughter, Amelia H. Newmark, December 1939," 7–8, Mrs. Joseph Newmark Papers, Bancroft Library, University of California, Berkeley, Calif.

93. Ibid., 8.

94. Ibid.

95. Donna Schuele argues that "by 1870, the marital property system, intended as a reform, actually rendered California wives worse off than their eastern sisters, who were protected in their dower rights and were increasingly benefiting from the enactment of MWPAs [Married Women's Property Acts] that served to segregate other property from the husband's control. California's system," she continues, "did nothing to empower wives, did little to protect families, and in fact, [through the inter-

ventions of the courts] blatantly violated the state's constitution." Schuele, "'None Could Deny the Eloquence of This Lady': Women, Law, and Government in California, 1850–1890," in *Taming the Elephant: Politics, Government, and Law in Pioneer California*, ed. John F. Burns and Richard J. Orsi (Berkeley: University of California Press, 2003), 176.

96. Kwolek-Folland, *Incorporating Women*, 52, 96.

97. In their fight to pass an Earnings Act in 1860 guaranteeing, among other things, their right to make business contracts, New York women had noted women's limitations in this capacity. One speaker described a friend in the boardinghouse business "who could not rent premises without her husband's signature" because landlords "insisted that her husband could claim her earnings and refuse to pay the rent on the grounds that the contract was made without his permission. "Proceedings of the Women's Rights Convention Held at the Broadway Tabernacle in the City of New York on Tuesday and Wednesday, September 6th and 7th, 1853," quoted in Basch, *In the Eyes of the Law*, 165.

98. "Autobiographical Notes by Mrs. Joseph S. Newmark," 8, 11.

99. These figures are composed from an analysis of the women in the R. G. Dun & Company credit reports for the 1870s, the only years for which the reports are available for San Francisco. RGDC.

100. See, for example, Gamber, *The Female Economy*; and Kwolek-Folland, *Incorporating Women*.

101. Miroslava Chávez-García argues that married women in California earned the right to register as sole traders and "conduct business in [their] own name[s]" earlier, citing the California statutes of 1850. My evidence is based on the publications in San Francisco newspapers that stipulated that the women filing their claims did so under an 1852 law. Chávez-García, *Negotiating Conquest: Gender and Power in California, 1770s to 1880s* (Tucson: University of Arizona Press, 2004), 126.

102. *Statutes of California, passed at the Third Session of the Legislature* (San Francisco: G. K. Fitch and V. E. Geiger, State Printers, 1852). In eastern states women battled for legal protection of their earnings after marriage up to 1860 and continued to fight for the right of contract into the 1880s. The Massachusetts law guaranteeing married women's right to engage in business independently of their husbands, therefore, was progressive compared to other states, though it was passed three years after California's law. Even among western territories California's law stood out; Colorado's territorial law, for example, led the rest of the western region in guaranteeing women's right of contract but was passed nearly a decade after California's married women's business law. Ultimately, however, the California law authorizing married women to conduct business in their own names was a conservative precedent in that it led to additional controls over how and why women could operate a business. More discussion of this fact follows in the text. For the information on other states cited here see Basch, *In the Eyes of the Law*, 165, 224; Gamber, *The Female Economy*, 50; Gordon Morris Bakken, *The Development of Law on the Rocky Mountain Frontier: Civil Law and Society, 1850–1912* (Westport, Conn.: Greenwood Press, 1983), 30–32.

103. While a husband's "insolvency" was not an acceptable reason for a married woman to declare sole trader status (suggesting that the bankruptcy of a man's busi-

ness could not win his wife the right to protect the family's assets in her name), a man's inability to support his family was the primary reason the courts expected to hear for why a married woman wanted to operate a business in her own name. *The Statutes of California, passed at the Thirteenth Session of the Legislature, 1862* (Sacramento, Calif.: Benj. P. Avery, State Printer, 1862), 108.

104. Only one-fifth of all married women's businesses reviewed by R. G. Dun & Company credit reporters throughout the 1870s in San Francisco were actually used to shield assets. This statement is based on the percentage (18 percent) of women's businesses that were in fact carried on by their husbands according to credit reporters. RGDC.

105. Gamber, *The Female Economy*, 50. Gamber does not discuss the specifics of the law.

106. Kwolek-Folland, *Incorporating Women*, 52–53.

107. I have not been able to locate any discussion of such laws in either Basch, *In the Eyes of the Law*; or Hoff, *Law, Gender, and Injustice*.

108. *Statutes of California and Digests of Measures . . . General Laws, Amendments to the Codes, Resolutions, and Constitutional Amendments passed by the California Legislature, 1979–80 Regular Session*, vol. 1 (St. Paul, Minn.: West Publishing, 1980), 293.

CHAPTER 3

1. Because gender, as opposed to sex, is culturally determined, the advantages of being a woman in gold rush California were racially specific. As already mentioned, the domestic services most desired by white men were the services of white women. Sexual desirability, too, was ranked according to race, with white prostitutes earning the most money and enjoying the greatest status. Many scholars have convincingly shown that nonwhite women, in contrast, enjoyed no advantages during California's early history as an American state and frequently were subjected to violence and sexual abuse—both emblematic of their powerlessness and lack of status. See, for example, Albert L. Hurtado, *Intimate Frontiers: Sex, Gender, and Culture in Old California* (Albuquerque: University of New Mexico, 1999). African American women experienced significant challenges in early California, particularly during the 1850s, when the property status of slaves brought to the mines by gold-hungry masters underwent several conflicting interpretations—this in spite of the state's entry into the union as a "free" state. African Americans continued to battle for their civil rights thereafter, enjoying some significant early successes in San Francisco. Discussing the "advantages" of the gold rush era for women can suggest an inaccurately rosy picture of black women's experiences during the period. Yet while credit likely remained elusive for them, black women and, to a small degree, Chinese women also capitalized on the gender imbalance by operating businesses, particularly lodging houses and hotels. See, for example, Willi Coleman, "African American Women and Community Development in California, 1848-1900," in *Seeking El Dorado: African Americans in California*, ed. Lawrence B. de Graaf, Kevin Mulroy, and Quintard Taylor (Seattle: University of Washington Press, 2001), 98–125; and Judy Yung, *Unbound*

Feet: A Social History of Chinese Women in San Francisco (Berkeley: University of California Press, 1995).

2. Wilson Wright, ed., *Luzena Stanley Wilson '49er: Memories Recalled Years Later for Her Daughter* (Oakland, Calif.: Eucalyptus Press, 1937), 24.

3. Walker D. Wyman, ed. *California Emigrant Letters* (New York: Bookman Associates, 1952), 159–60. This figure attests to labor conditions in San Francisco in 1849. Wages in Nevada City the same year may have been even lower.

4. Wright, *Luzena Stanley Wilson '49er*, 28. For income comparison, see Sean Wilentz, *Chants Democratic: New York City and the Rise of the American Working Class, 1788–1850* (New York: Oxford University Press, 1984), 117 and 405 (Table 14); and Thomas Dublin, *Women at Work: The Transformation of Work and Community in Lowell, Massachusetts, 1826–1860* (New York: Columbia University Press, 1979), 159, 185, 186, and 195; both quoted in Jeanne Boydston, *Home and Work: Housework, Wages, and the Ideology of Labor in the Early Republic* (New York: Oxford University Press, 1990), 62.

5. Susan Lee Johnson, *Roaring Camp: The Social World of the California Gold Rush* (New York: W. W. Norton, 2000), 163.

6. Joan Jensen is one of several scholars who examines the movement of "women's work" into the marketplace during the nineteenth century. She argues that "the goal of women's household production for the marketplace [whether they were producing butter or boarding services] remained . . . to raise a family, if the woman was a widow, or to contribute to the household income." Thus, this type of work did not overturn long-standing expectations that women remain tied to their households. She emphasizes that once the work traditionally performed by women served interests other than the family or gained potential as a highly capitalized, profit-generating business, then it was taken over by men. Jensen, "Cloth, Butter and Boarders: Women's Household Production for the Market," in *Promise to the Land: Essays on Rural Women* (Albuquerque: University of New Mexico Press, 1991), 202. This perspective helps explain the loosening of credit for women during the early years of the gold rush in California. Even as female proprietors, they still served the interests of men and the family. On the other hand, as Reva Siegel has shown, being able to operate independently in the economic marketplace was a right that nineteenth-century feminist reformers fought for, arguing before Congress that it ought to be encoded in law. This fact underscores how radical women's independent economic activity in the marketplace was for mid-nineteenth-century women. That male creditors helped enable this activity is perhaps remarkable yet likely demonstrates male self-interest rather than charitable benevolence. See Reva B. Siegel, "Home as Work: The First Woman's Rights Claims Concerning Wives' Household Labor, 1850–1880," *Yale Law Journal* 103 (March 1994): 1073–1217.

7. White and nonwhite women might both have enjoyed this position, since, according to one scholar, during the gold rush Mexican women "specialized in selling prepared foods." In describing the entrepreneurial Mexicans in Sonora, California, Susan Johnson writes, "There is no way to quantify how much gold dust passed from men's hands to women's hands in this domestic marketplace, but it must have been

considerable." Johnson, *Roaring Camp*, 167 and 120. But no first-hand accounts document the spectacular success of nonwhite women whose cooking lacked the emotional appeal of white women's for Anglo men. On the particular appeal of white women's cooking, see ibid., 116.

8. William Perkins, *Three Years in California: William Perkins' Journal of Life at Sonora, 1849–1852*, ed. Dale L. Morgan and James R. Scobie (Berkeley: University of California Press, 1964), 268, in Johnson, *Roaring Camp*, 166.

9. Wendy Gamber also discusses the importance of concealing profit for antebellum boardinghouse keepers. Women in that venue too drew criticism from boarders if they were openly acquisitive about the services they provided; boarders wanted to view their mistresses as lovingly motivated instead of profit motivated. In order to avoid the taint of self-interest, some boardinghouse keepers went so far as to leave envelopes outside boarders doors when it came time to pay rent so that money never actually crossed hands. Gamber, "Tarnished Labor: The Home, the Market, and the Boardinghouse in Antebellum America," *Journal of the Early Republic* 22 (Summer 2002), 177–204.

10. Wright, *Luzena Stanley Wilson '49er*, 11.

11. In fact, there are lots of examples of the association with motherhood being an asset in the business world that women are able to exploit to their own advantage. See, for example, Sarah Stage, *Female Complaints: Lydia Pinkham and the Business of Women's Medicine* (New York: W. W. Norton, 1979), which explores the way Pinkham marketed her homemade "medicine" to American women by exploiting her motherly image as a nurturer. Angel Kwolek-Folland's *Engendering Business: Men and Women in the Corporate Office, 1870–1930* (Baltimore: Johns Hopkins University Press, 1994) explores the ways in which female insurance agents helped create a special role for themselves in the life insurance industry because of their close association with motherhood and children. More recently, Deborah Fields, founder of Mrs. Field's Cookies, and Martha Stewart, founder of a multimillion dollar homemaking empire which includes magazines, television, and branded product lines, are both examples of the same phenomenon. This has also been a theme in American popular culture. See, for example, the 1980s film *Baby Boom* (Charles Shyer, MGM, 1987), in which a new mother leaves corporate America and starts her own, very successful line of baby food.

12. For San Francisco's gender imbalance see the Appendix.

13. Lyle W. Dorsett, "Equality of Opportunity on the Urban Frontier: Access to Credit in Denver, Colorado Territory, 1858–1876," *Journal of the West* 18 (1979): 78.

14. Angel Kwolek-Folland, *Incorporating Women: A History of Women and Business in the United States* (New York: Twayne Publishers, 1998), 52–53.

15. See, for example, Wendy Gamber, *The Female Economy: The Millinery and Dressmaking Trades, 1860–1930* (Urbana: University of Illinois Press, 1997); Kwolek-Folland, *Incorporating Women*; Susan Ingalls Lewis, "Beyond Horatia Alger: Breaking through Gendered Assumptions about Business 'Success' in Mid-Nineteenth-Century America," *Business and Economic History* 24 (Fall 1995).

16. Peter R. Decker, *Fortunes and Failures: White-Collar Mobility in Nineteenth-Century San Francisco* (Cambridge: Harvard University Press, 1978), 97.

17. The figure for female proprietors was computed using all 92 entries in the R. G. Dun & Company credit reports for women during the 1870s, the only decade for which the reports exist for San Francisco. The figure on men was computed using a sample of 155 male small-business owners from the credit reports. Their businesses included tailor shops, restaurants, saloons, and apparel stores—those types of establishments comparable to the ones women operated. California vol. 14–19, RGDC.

18. William M. Searby, California vol. 14, p. 9, RGDC.

19. *Milliner* 26 (February 1915): 76; quoted in Gamber, *The Female Economy*, 171.

20. On the paternalism of creditors in their dealings with female proprietors, see Gamber, *The Female Economy*, 159–68.

21. Mrs. H. Jacobs, California vol. 17, p. 85, RGDC.

22. Gerald Sorin, for example, argues that "the Jews, with the same Old World cohesion and penchant for small-business enterprise and with similar credit associations, created an ethnic economy in many American cities which provided wide opportunities for Jews." Sorin, *Tradition Transformed: The Jewish Experience in America* (Baltimore: Johns Hopkins University Press, 1997), 67.

23. Shelly Tenenbaum, "Borrowers or Lenders Be: Jewish Immigrant Women's Credit Networks," in *American Jewish Women's History, A Reader*, ed. Pamela S. Nadell (New York: New York University Press, 2003).

24. Peter Decker writes that "'personal character' . . . the most subjective of all the criteria, . . . received greatest importance." Decker, *Fortunes and Failures*, 258. Wendy Gamber found Dun assessments of Boston's female proprietors in the apparel trades to be similarly influenced by the concern for "character." Gamber, *The Female Economy*, 235. The classic study of ethnic/racial bias in the reports is David Gerber, "Cutting Out Shylock: Elite Anti-Semitism and the Quest for Moral Order in the Mid-Nineteenth-Century American Marketplace," *Journal of American History*, 69 (Summer 1982): 615–37. The most recent work on this topic is Rowena Olegario, *A Culture of Credit: Embedding Trust and Transparency in American Business* (Cambridge: Harvard University Press, 2007).

25. Juliet E. K. Walker, *The History of Black Business in America: Capitalism, Race, Entrepreneurship* (New York: Macmillan Library Reference USA, 1998), 129, 148, 158–63.

26. These generalizations are based on the author's examination of R. G. Dun & Company reports for San Francisco during the 1870s. RGDC.

27. Business historian Thomas Cochran argues that this was one of the most common ways that business owners around the country in the nineteenth and early twentieth centuries got started. Thomas Cochran, *200 Years of American Business* (New York: Basic Books, 1977), 129.

28. David Safferhill and Louis Beyersdorf, California vol. 18, p. 26, RGDC.

29. N. J. Wyman, California vol. 18, p. 39, RGDC.

30. Mansel Blackford, *A History of Small Business in America*, 2nd ed. (Chapel Hill: University of North Carolina Press, 2003), 105. Blackford does not distinguish between male and female proprietors in this regard, asserting that utilizing savings was a common strategy among small-business proprietors generally. Yet in other sections of the book he emphasizes women's difficulty accessing capital and credit.

31. These conclusions are taken from a sample of male small-business owners in the R. G. Dun & Company credit reports for the 1870s who were in comparable industries to the city's female proprietors, RGDC.

32. E. Anthony Rotundo, *American Manhood: Transformation in Masculinity from the Revolution to the Modern Era* (New York: Basic Books, 1993), 248–49.

33. Of course all this changed with the feminization of clerical work, a shift that was just getting underway in the 1870s. By the end of the nineteenth century the job of clerk would be a woman's role in the minds of most Americans. See Kwolek-Folland, *Engendering Business*.

34. Gamber, *The Female Economy*, 42–43.

35. For an examination of wage differentials between men and women and the purposes they served see Alice Kessler-Harris, *A Woman's Wage: Historical Meanings and Social Consequences* (Lexington: University Press of Kentucky, 1990).

36. While several states passed laws protecting the wages of women from their husbands in the nineteenth century, married women in California still did not enjoy such rights at the dawn of the twentieth century. See Kwolek-Folland, *Incorporating Women*, 95–96.

37. Mrs. Jane Thomas, California vol. 14, p. 100, RGDC.

38. Miss E. Van Winkle, California vol. 18, p. 347, RGDC.

39. Mrs. L. H. Lichtenstein, California vol. 20, p. 350, RGDC.

40. Gamber, *The Female Economy*, 45; Sarah Deutsch, *Women and the City: Gender, Space, and Power in Boston, 1870–1940* (New York: Oxford University Press, 2000), 117; Susan Ingalls Lewis, "'Beyond Enterprising Women': The Importance of Networks for Female Microentrepreneurs in Mid-Nineteenth-Century Albany, New York" (presented at the Annual Meeting of the Business History Conference in Le Creusot, France, June 2004), 11; Kwolek-Folland, *Incorporating Women*, 27–28. Lewis and Kwolek-Folland emphasize the help of female family members; Deutsch specifically mentions the help of male family members. My records do not suggest a similar connection between female proprietors and female family members when it came to start-up capital. Perhaps that is not surprising given that San Francisco's population was still overwhelmingly male during the 1870s, the decade from which my data on start-up capital is derived. Still, one might expect such circumstances to have engendered a heightened degree of female solidarity, but I did not find evidence of that.

41. In his history of small business, Mansel Blackford discusses the difficulty in accessing capital for small-business owners and emphasizes that immigrants in particular called on family and friends to raise the necessary money to create their own enterprises. Blackford, *A History of Small Business*, 71 and 105.

42. Mrs. S. Fiala, California vol. 19, p. 348, RGDC. Fiala invested $1,000 to start her business, substantially more than the law allowed for married women who operated businesses in their own names. Fiala's business must have been in her husband's name.

43. Gamber, *The Female Economy*, 47.

44. Gamber also cites husbands' "modest" income as a motivation for female proprietorship. Ibid., 46.

45. By the beginning of the twentieth century, California was among twelve

states that still did not protect married women's wages. In these states married men were considered the rightful owners of any employment income earned by their wives. Kwolek-Folland, *Incorporating Women*, 96.

46. *The Statutes of California, passed at the Thirteenth Session of the Legislature, 1862* (Sacramento, Calif.: Benj. P. Avery, State Printer, 1862). See also Orrin K. McMurray, *Community Property, Contributed to California Jurisprudence, 1930 Supplement* (Berkeley, Calif.: Bancroft-Whitney, 1930), 113.

47. This underscores why the Married Women's Property Acts, passed in most states during the nineteenth century, were, ultimately, so radical. Women who retained their property after marriage gained a great deal of economic independence otherwise not enjoyed by married women. Those who benefited were, admittedly, a privileged group, but the changes they effected by passing property on to their daughters were long lasting. For more on the radical effects of this change in women's legal and economic status see Carole Shammas, "Re-Assessing the Married Women's Property Acts," *Journal of Women's History* 6 (Spring 1994): 9–30. Richard Chused lays out a more-conservative interpretation of the acts, arguing that "married women's separate domestic sphere was not seriously challenged" by the adoption of these laws, and thus the laws "should not be perceived as an attack on coverture laws." Chused, "Married Women's Property Law: 1800–1850," *Georgetown Law Journal* 71 (June 1983): 1425.

48. Many scholars have examined married women's legal dependence on their husbands throughout American history. For a good synthesis of this literature as it connects to women's economic enterprise, see Kwolek-Folland, *Incorporating Women*. For more on the feminist fight to expand married women's legal status, including their right to "contract" as business owners, and the ways in which lawmakers sometimes hijacked the original purpose of the laws with provisions such as those discussed above, see Siegel, "Home as Work."

49. In *Gray v. Perlis*, a California court found that because the wife had "established [her business] with money raised from pledging her personal effects," and because she was a sole trader, her business was protected from the claims of her husband's creditors in spite of the fact that her husband "devoted his time, skill and industry to the business." McMurray, *Community Property*, 54. While this case is interesting for several reasons, it is cited here to illustrate one strategy used by women to raise the money necessary to start their own businesses.

50. *San Francisco Chronicle*, April 2, 1894.

51. Johanna Pulfer, case #12256, San Francisco, 1921, BCF.

52. These figures compare all women business owners found in the R. G. Dun & Company reports for San Francisco in the 1870s and a sample of small-scale businessmen in the same reports. RGDC.

53. See Blackford, *A History of Small Business*, 105, for the general case.

54. Mrs. Nancy C. Noyes, case #1878, San Francisco, 1878, BCF.

55. Teresa Holden, case #1283, San Francisco, 1873, BCF; *Daily Alta California*, September 8, 1863.

56. Diana O. Anderson, case #1728, Sacramento, 1875, BCF.

57. Bankruptcy court cases from the Northern California District for 1873–75,

1878, 1898–1900, 1903, 1906, 1909, 1915, 1918, and 1921 were examined (no national bankruptcy law was in effect between 1878 and 1898 and thus no bankruptcy cases were filed during those years), yielding a total of ninety-six bankrupt businesswomen in the northern California area. Of this total, twenty-two (or 23 percent) listed loans among their outstanding debts at the time they declared insolvency. Together, these women listed a total of fifty loans they had contracted individually or as partners. This is a small but extremely valuable sample. It is valuable partly because conducting research with the bankruptcy records is extremely laborious and time consuming. Creating the sample discussed here involved culling through well over 2,000 cases; none are indexed. Even more important, though, the sample is valuable because I know of no other source that provides such extensive information about women's borrowing habits.

58. Report on a visit to the Women's Banking Department, November 4–6, 9–10, 1925 (RG 2.10.571.24), BOAA. There is evidence of one woman in the bankruptcy court records who borrowed money from the Bank of Italy. But there is no evidence that the loan was contracted through the women's banking department, and more importantly, the money was borrowed jointly with her husband, co-owner of a retail tire business. It is possible, therefore, that she had no influence on the decision to borrow from the Bank of Italy. Johanna Pufter, case #12256, San Francisco, 1921, BCF.

59. Charles J. O'Connor et al., *San Francisco Relief Survey: The Organization and Methods of Relief Used after the Earthquake and Fire of April 18, 1906* (San Francisco: Russell Sage Foundation, 1913), 171–211.

60. Cochran, *200 Years of American Business*, 129.

61. Blackford, *A History of Small Business*, 105.

62. Forty-six percent of the loans in my sample from the bankruptcy records came from women and 42 percent from men. The remaining 12 percent came from "capitalists" and institutions. Twenty-five percent of the loans in my sample from the bankruptcy court records charged interest. For an explanation of my sample from the bankruptcy court records, spanning 1873–1921, see Appendix 1, Note on Sources.

63. Nancy Noyes, case #2457, San Francisco, 1878, BCF; Bertha Root, case #9364, San Francisco, 1915, BCF.

64. Martha Ballinger, case #6400, San Jose, 1909, BCF. This, and not the fact that Ballinger was still alive, was the explanation in the documents for why Evarts could not recoup her money.

65. Ibid. This information is taken from testimony by Mr. W. R. Gallagher, the broker mentioned here, in the Martha Ballinger bankruptcy case. Ballinger was the one to whom Vioget's money was loaned. When Vioget cashed out of the transaction with a profit, the broker sold Ballinger's debt (secured by a mortgage) to another woman, Mrs. Garman. This is a remarkable piece of evidence that I have not found repeated elsewhere. But I suspect that such transactions were in fact numerous, if not widespread, and simply were not recorded in extant records.

66. Of the thirteen loans in the sample listed with interest, female lenders had contracted eight (62 percent), male lenders only five (38 percent). Of the seven lawsuits evidenced in the bankruptcy case sample, women filed five (70 percent). For more on these interesting findings, see Edith Sparks, "Terms of Endearment: Informal Borrowing Networks among Northern California Businesswomen, 1870–1920," *Business and Economic History On-Line* 2 (Winter 2004), <www.h-net.org/~business/bhcweb/publications/BEHonline/beh.html>, where I discuss in greater detail the participants in businesswomen's informal borrowing networks.

67. Robert E. Wright, "Women and Finance in the Early National U.S.," in *Essays in History* 42 (2000), <http://etext.lib.virginia.edu/journals/EH/EH42/Wright42.html> (May 2004); and Kwolek-Folland, *Incorporating Women*. Quote is from Wright.

68. Beverly Lemire, "Petty Pawns and Informal Lending: Gender and the Transformation of Small-Scale Credit in England, circa 1600–1800," in *From Family Firms to Corporate Capitalism: Essays in Business and Industrial History in Honour of Peter Mathias*, ed. Kristine Bruland and Patrick O'Brien (Oxford, U.K.: Clarendon Press, 1998): 112–38.

69. Aidan Hollis, "Women and Microcredit in History: Gender in the Irish Loan Funds," <http:www.econ.ucalgary.ca/fac-files/ah/womenandloanfunds.pdf> (May 2004).

70. Tenenbaum, "Borrowers or Lenders Be," 79–90.

71. Kwolek-Folland, *Incorporating Women*, 68, see also 27–28.

72. One study of women inventors shows that "who they knew, and how they networked in social and political circles (or related to the general public)," often determined their success. For inventors, certainly, this included interactions with men. Lisa A. Marovich, "'Let Her Have Brains Too': Commercial Networks, Public Relations, and the Business of Invention," *Business and Economic History* 27 (Fall 1998): 140–61. For arguments that businesswomen circulated in a "female" world, see Gamber, *The Female Economy*; Deutsch, *Women and the City*, and Lucy Eldersveld Murphy, "Her Own Boss: Businesswomen and Separate Spheres in the Midwest, 1850–1880," *Illinois Historical Journal* 80 (Autumn 1987): 155–76.

73. Away from the male-dominated main room of the bank, located in "cheerful surroundings, where harmony of color and furnishings unite for comfort," female bank customers, it was thought, would find it much easier to ask for financial help. In such an environment, the department's brochure asserted, San Francisco women would find that "the problems of business and finance find ready solution." "Women's Banking Department, Bank of Italy," brochure, 1921, BOAA. For more on women's banking departments elsewhere see Kwolek-Folland, *Engendering Business*. Nancy Marie Robertson is also working on the topic. See Robertson, "'The Disagreeable Experience of Handling Soiled Money': Women and Banking in the U.S. at the Turn of the Twentieth Century" (presented at the Thirteenth Berkshire Conference on the History of Women at Scripps College, Claremont, Calif., June 2005).

74. Decker, *Fortunes and Failures*, 230. Gray Brechin's more-recent book, *Imperial San Francisco: Urban Power, Earthly Ruin* (Berkeley: University of California Press, 1999), makes a similar argument, emphasizing the power that elite San Franciscans held over the city, the surrounding environment, and the region's history.

75. Ellen Crocker, case #2464, San Francisco, 1878, BCF; Martha Herriman, case #2776, San Jose, 1898, BCF; Ellen Parker, case #11133, Oakland, 1918, BCF; Johann Pufter, case #12256, San Francisco, 1921, BCF.

76. This assertion is based on the author's review of seventy years of newspaper advertisements (1850–1920), one decade of credit reports (1870s), and ten years worth of bankruptcy records (spread between 1874 and 1921). See Appendix 1, Note on Sources for more information.

77. Gamber, *The Female Economy*, 32; Lewis, "Beyond 'Enterprising Women.'"

78. These figures are compiled from a survey of all 92 entries for women business owners evaluated in the R. G. Dun & Company credit reports for the 1870s, California vols. 14–20, RGDC.

79. Gamber makes the opposite point about Boston's milliners and dressmakers, arguing that it was less common for unrelated women to "join forces." Gamber, *The Female Economy*, 31.

80. *Daily Alta California*, July 15, 1851.

81. For more on the early San Francisco housing market, see Chapter 1.

82. *Daily Alta California*, February 3, 1857.

83. Lewis, in fact, argues that "most partnerships [between women] dissolved within a few years." Lewis, "Beyond 'Enterprising Women,'" 15.

84. See the *Daily Alta California*, May 3, 1855; November 3, 1855; and February 3, 1857 (the text of Mr. Butler's ad states that Clarke & Co. was established in 1850).

85. Ibid., May 3, 1855.

86. Archibald H. Stocker, *Business Ownership Organization* (New York: Henry Holt, 1922), 52–59.

87. Miss May Thompson, California vol. 14, p. 303, RGDC; Mrs. A. Dannenberg, California vol. 14, p. 318 and 319, RGDC.

88. Mrs. H. E. Booker, California vol. 16, p. 400, RGDC.

89. Decker, *Fortunes and Failures*, 79–80.

90. Ethel Watson, case #9417, Oakland, 1915, BCF; Bessie Newman, case #9521, San Francisco, 1915, BCF.

91. This figure is based on a sample of small-scale businessmen in the R. G. Dun & Company credit reports for the 1870s, RGDC.

92. Naomi Lamoreaux, "Constructing Firms: Partnerships and Alternative Contractual Arrangements in Early Nineteenth-Century American Business," *Business and Economic History* 24 (Winter 1995): 43–71.

93. This benefit would not have devolved to female proprietors who took on partners unless their business partnerships involved men, since, as already discussed, women generally lacked access to credit after the unique days of the early gold rush.

94. Decker, *Fortunes and Failures*, 97.

95. See, for example, Gail Bederman, *Manliness and Civilization: A Cultural History of Gender and Race in the United States, 1880–1917* (Chicago: University of Chicago Press, 1995); and Kristin L. Hoganson, *Fighting for American Manhood: How Gender Politics Provoked the Spanish-American and Philippine-American Wars* (New Haven: Yale University Press, 1998).

96. Susan Yohn, "Crippled Capitalists: The Inscription of Economic Dependence and the Challenge of Female Entrepreneurship in Nineteenth-Century America," *Feminist Economics* 12 (April 2006): 85–109.

97. These figures are compiled from a survey of all 92 entries for women business owners evaluated in the R. G. Dun & Company credit reports for the 1870s, the only decade for which the reports are available for San Francisco. California vols. 14-20, RGDC.

98. This figure was compiled from a sample of 155 male owners of small businesses such as tailor shops, restaurants, saloons, and apparel stores—those types of establishments comparable to the ones women operated, California vols. 14-20, RGDC.

99. Rotundo, *American Manhood*, 236.

100. *Daily Dramatic Chronicle*, September 19, 1866.

101. *Daily Alta California*, November 1, 1851; January 11, 1852; February 3, 1855.

102. Ibid., August 3, 1853.

103. Alan Trachtenberg, *The Incorporation of America: Culture and Society in the Gilded Age* (New York: Hill and Wang, 1982).

104. *San Francisco Chronicle*, June 7, 1870.

105. Ibid.

106. Thomas S. Dicke, *Franchising in America: The Development of a Business Method, 1840–1980* (Chapel Hill: University of North Carolina Press, 1992), 4.

107. *Daily Morning Chronicle*, December 13, 1868. The ad never actually stipulates what type of business is for sale.

108. *San Francisco Chronicle*, September 14, 1869.

109. *Daily Alta California*, March 13, 1869.

110. Credit reports indicate a similar range of prices. Miss C. L. Woods bought out her new millinery business for $1,500, as did Mrs. Jane Thomas; while Mrs. Martineaut bought the stock alone of Charles Komfeld's retail clothing business for $3,000. Miss C. L. Woods, California vol. 19, p. 321, RGDC; Mrs. Jane Thomas, California vol. 14, p. 100, RGDC; Mrs. J. Martineaut, California vol. 16, p. 349, RGDC.

111. Mrs. Jane Thomas, California vol. 14, p. 100, RGDC. This case is discussed at greater length in Chapter 2 in the section on divorced women who started their own businesses and is discussed again below.

112. *Daily Alta California*, February 3, 1854.

113. Ibid., December 19, 1870.

114. See, for example, the ads from the *San Francisco Chronicle*, September 14, 1869: a produce, fruit, and provision store "for sale at a sacrifice" for $500 and a millinery store listed for $1,200 at "half cost of [the stock]." Both were sold on account of illness.

115. Cornwall & McLeod, California vol. 17, p. 318, RGDC.

116. F. W. Reed & Co., California vol. 19, p. 314, RGDC.

117. Mrs. Amalie Dannenberg sold and then repurchased her business from Ellen Milligan in 1870. Mrs. A. Dannenberg, California vol. 14, p. 318 and 319, RGDC. In 1894 Mr. and Madame Ferran repurchased their French laundry business from the Trouillets due to "business differences." *San Francisco Chronicle*, April 2, 1894, p. 6, col. 1.

118. See Blackford, *A History of Small Business*; and Susan Strasser, *Satisfaction*

Guaranteed: The Making of the American Mass Market (Washington, D.C.: Smithsonian Institution Press, 1989). Installment buying in the general consumer marketplace is discussed in more detail in the following chapter. Female proprietors utilized the strategy to participate in the purchase of "big-ticket" items as well.

119. According to Wendy Gamber, weekly wages for Boston garment workers in 1870 ranged from $2.50 to $20 depending on the job performed. These figures are taken from the table entitled "Weekly Wages of Women Workers, 1859–1916," compiled from several printed sources in Gamber, *The Female Economy*, 78.

120. On the importance of divorced women in nineteenth-century California finding a reliable way to support themselves economically, see Robert L. Griswold, *Family and Divorce in California, 1850–1890: Victorian Illusions and Everyday Realities* (Albany: State University of New York Press, 1982).

121. Mrs. Jane Thomas, California vol. 14, p. 100, RGDC; Mrs. J. Martineaut, California vol. 16, p. 349, RGDC.

122. Donna J. Guy, "The Economics of Widowhood in Arizona, 1880–1940," in *On Their Own: Widows and Widowhood in the American Southwest, 1848–1939*, ed. Arlene Scadron (Urbana: University of Illinois Press, 1988), 196. Kwolek-Folland, *Incorporating Women*, also has a lot to say about the particular vulnerabilities of widows.

123. It was not uncommon for women to leave the title "Mrs." or "Miss" out of the names of their businesses. By doing so they may have hoped to protect themselves from customer prejudices or to make their businesses sound less personal and more official, as here, where what might have been called "Miss Reed's Millinery" became "F. W. Reed & Co." For historians this practice is frustrating because it obscures the gender of the business owner. The only reason it is possible to determine the gender of the proprietor in this case is because the information about Miss Reed's business comes from the credit reports, where a proprietor's personal story, including gender, marital status, etc., was recorded. F. W. Reed & Co., California vol. 19, p. 314, RGDC.

124. Ibid.

125. See Gamber, *The Female Economy*, for more on the degree to which female proprietors in the millinery and dressmaking trades reverted to wage labor.

126. "Mme. Cantel, From Paris," *Daily Alta California*, March 11, 1874; and Miss C. L. Woods, California vol. 19, p. 321, RGDC.

127. Mrs. A. Dannenberg, California vol. 14, p. 318 and 319, RGDC.

128. *Daily Alta California*, August 3, 1853.

129. Ibid., February 21, 1877.

130. Of course, if a business *was* being sold because of financial difficulties, it behooved the seller to conceal that information rather than advertise it, so locating such examples is difficult. But when small businesses faced serious financial difficulties, they were usually sold in pieces, not whole. As the bankruptcy court records demonstrate, if a business was in enough trouble that creditors feared losing money, they could file a claim, and the owners' stock, fixtures, and real estate would be auctioned off, piece by piece, to raise money for paying debts. Snapping up auctioned items was not the way most first-time businesswomen got started, but the practice of profiting off others' failure, termed "vulture capitalism" by one historian, was common during the nineteenth century. See Edward J. Balleisen, "Vulture Capitalism in Antebellum America: The 1841 Federal Bankruptcy Act and the Exploitation of Financial Distress," *Business History Review* 70 (Winter 1996): 473–516.

131. This argument is based on the author's examination of newspaper advertisements in the *Daily Alta California* during the 1870s. The paper was examined at three-month intervals in March, June, September, and December, as well as some additional months, during each year of the 1870s. Advertisements and articles pertaining to female proprietors were photocopied and catalogued.

132. *San Francisco Chronicle*, April 22, 1877; September 6, 1879; January 7, 1880; and September 19, 1877. Entries under the paper's "Business Opportunities" heading numbered around twenty-five daily from 1877 through 1879, essentially the same number as had appeared in the paper during the early 1870s before the depression hit San Francisco.

133. See, for example, Blackford, *A History of Small Business*, 105.

134. When depression came to San Francisco a second time in the 1890s, its effect was much less noticeable. The city's newspapers no doubt contributed to history's oversight. For while the *San Francisco Chronicle* covered its 1896 front page with headlines such as "Aid and Comfort for the City's Deserving Poor," and "Aid [to] Persons Seeking Employment," by 1897 such stories had been relegated to the interior pages of the paper, and the city seemed to go about its business with little notice. *San Francisco Chronicle*, December 2, 1896; January 1, 1896; and "Uneventful Sunday for the Unemployed," March 1, 1897, p. 16, col. 3–4. History textbooks also suggest that California more or less skated by during the 1890s depression. Walton Bean and James J. Rawls devote a few sentences to the depression, remarking particularly on the collapse of the wheat industry and on the slowed growth of California's population—"the lowest rate for any decade between the 1830s and the 1930s"—but do not discuss it at any length. Bean and Rawls, *California: An Interpretive History*, 5th ed. (New York: McGraw-Hill, 1988), 186–87. In Andrew Rolle's survey, "unemployment" is indexed for the depressions of the 1870s and 1930s but not that of the 1890s. Rolle, *California: A History*, 4th ed. (Arlington Heights, Ill.: Harlan Davidson, 1987). There appears to be no mention of it either in David Lavender, *California: A Bicentennial History* (New York: W. W. Norton, 1976); and Kevin Starr, *Americans and the California Dream, 1850–1915* (New York: Oxford University Press, 1973).

135. *San Francisco Chronicle*, July 2, 1890, p. 8, col. 1, under "Business Opportunities"; *The Bulletin*, June 4, 1902, p. 10, col. 1, under "Business Chances." Several ads specifically targeted potential female proprietors with lines such as "$2,500 Ladies Attention: An elegant genteel established business paying $250 to $500 per month" and "Lady with $2,000 is offered one of the nicest businesses in the city." *San Francisco Chronicle*, July 2, 1891, p. 9, col. 7.

136. *San Francisco Chronicle*, January 21, 1894, p. 20, col. 1.

137. Ibid., January 2, 1891, p. 6, col. 6.

138. Margaret Ennis, case #5068, Vallejo, 1906, BCF.

1. These figures combine data from the 1880 and 1890 printed census reports. (1890 data did not cite beauty industry proprietors, so I use 1880 figures for that industry; figures for the other industries come from 1890.) Apparel industry proprietors are measured here as 11 percent of the total number of women listed in the industry (see section on the apparel industry later in the chapter for an explanation). U.S. Census Office, *Compendium of the Tenth Census*, part 1 (Washington, D.C.: Government Printing Office, 1883); U.S. Census Office, *Report on the Population of the United States at the Eleventh Census*, part 1 (Washington, D.C.: Government Printing Office, 1895).

2. Wilson Wright, ed., *Luzena Stanley Wilson '49er: Memories Recalled Years Later for Her Daughter* (Oakland, Calif.: Eucalyptus Press, 1937), 27.

3. Ibid., 28.

4. Ibid., 12. This quote refers to Sacramento.

5. Walker D. Wyman, ed., *California Emigrant Letters* (New York: Bookman Associates, 1952), 164.

6. Julie Roy Jeffrey, *Frontier Women: The Trans-Mississippi West, 1840–1880* (New York: Hill and Wang, 1979), 109.

7. U.S. Census Office, *Population of the United States in 1860* (Washington, D.C.: Government Printing Office, 1864), 22–27.

8. Similar arguments about the impact of the gender imbalance on western women's economic opportunities in the second half of the nineteenth century may be found in Paula Petrik, *No Step Backward: Women and Family on the Rocky Mountain Mining Frontier, Helena, Montana, 1865–1900* (Helena: Montana Historical Society Press, 1987); and JoAnn Levy, *They Saw the Elephant: Women in the California Gold Rush* (Hamden, Conn.: Archon Books, 1990); and Malcolm J. Rohrbaugh, *Days of Gold: The California Gold Rush and the American Nation* (Berkelely: University of California Press, 1997).

9. Wilson, *Luzena Stanley Wilson '49er*, 12.

10. Susan Lee Johnson, *Roaring Camp: The Social World of the California Gold Rush* (New York: W. W. Norton, 2000), Chapter 2; and Alexander Saxton, *The Indispensable Enemy: Labor and the Anti-Chinese Movement in California* (Berkeley: University of California Press, 1971), 53.

11. Julie Roy Jeffrey argues that "even in the most feverish moments of the '49 gold rush, only about half of California's residents were involved in mining. The rest serviced the miners." Jeffrey, *Frontier Women*, 112.

12. Journal entries, December 22 and 30, 1849; January 1, 4, and 5, 1850, William Miller Journal, Beinecke Library, Yale University, New Haven, Conn.; quoted in Johnson, *Roaring Camp*, 111.

13. Johnson, *Roaring Camp*, 163.

14. Journal entry, April 18, 1852, P. V. Fox Journals, Beinecke Library, Yale University, New Haven, Conn.; quoted in Johnson, *Roaring Camp*, 116.

15. Joseph R. Conlin, *Bacons, Beans, and Galantines: Food and Foodways on the Western Mining Frontier* (Reno: University of Nevada Press, 1986), 117.

16. Albert L. Hurtado, *Intimate Frontiers: Sex, Gender and Culture in Old California* (Albuquerque: University of New Mexico Press, 1999), 82.

17. Johnson, *Roaring Camp*, 298–99. Chinese women did not earn money for their labor as prostitutes, only food, clothing, and shelter. For more on Chinese prostitutes, see Benson Tong, *Unsubmissive Women: Chinese Prostitutes in Nineteenth-Century San Francisco* (Norman: University of Oklahoma Press, 1994).

18. Hurtado, *Intimate Frontiers*, 125–26.

19. Johnson, *Roaring Camp*, 163.

20. Frank Soulé, John H. Gihon, and James Nisbet, *The Annals of San Francisco* (New York: D. Appleton, 1854); cited in Conlin, *Bacons, Beans, and Galantines*, 157.

21. Wendy Gamber argues that in the antebellum United States, boardinghouse keepers' obvious profit motivation troubled many observers who persisted in their belief that women should provide such domestic services out of an emotional desire to nurture rather than an instinct for self-preservation. See Gamber, "Tarnished Labor: The Home, the Market, and the Boardinghouse in Antebellum America," *Journal of the Early Republic* 22 (Summer 2002): 177–204.

22. Susan Johnson documents several examples. See Johnson, *Roaring Camp*, especially Chapter 2.

23. Paula Baker, "The Domestication of Politics: Women and American Political Society, 1780–1920," in *Unequal Sisters: A Multicultural Reader in U.S. Women's History*, 2nd ed., ed. Vicki L. Ruiz and Ellen Carol DuBois (New York: Routledge, 1994), 91; essay originally published in *American Historical Review* 89 (June 1984).

24. Jeffrey, *Frontier Women*, 125.

25. Wyman, *California Emigrant Letters*, 149. The pies this baker made were probably individual dried fruit pies that were generally prepared by folding the dough over the filling, like a turnover, and frying them. These are still popular today in some regions of the South.

26. Mary Ballou, *"I Hear Hogs in My Kitchen": A Woman's View of the Gold Rush* (New Haven: Yale University Press, 1962), 8–9.

27. Sandra L. Myres, *Westering Women and the Frontier Experience, 1800–1915* (Albuquerque: University of New Mexico Press, 1982), 147.

28. Robert Glass Cleland, ed. *Apron Full of Gold: The Letters of Mary Jane Megquier from San Francisco* (San Marino, Calif.: Huntington Library, 1949), 33.

29. Wyman, *California Emigrant Letters*, 159–60; Jacqueline Jones, *Labor of Love, Labor of Sorrow: Black Women, Work and the Family, from Slavery to the Present* (New York: Vintage Books, 1986), 133; Hasia R. Diner, *Erin's Daughters in America: Irish Immigrant Women in the Nineteenth Century* (Baltimore: Johns Hopkins Press, 1983), 90.

30. Journal of Alfred and Chastina Rix, September 1, 1853, CHS.

31. Wright, *Luzena Stanley Wilson '49er*, 28.

32. See Myres, *Westering Women*, especially Chapter 6, "A New Home—Who'll Follow: Women and Frontier Homemaking," 141–66.

33. Mark Twain, "The Californian's Tale," in *Stories of the Old West: Tales of the Mining Camp, Cavalry Troop, and Cattle Ranch*, ed. John Seelye (New York: Penguin Books, 1994), 80–86.

34. Robert O'Brien, "Pageant of the Years—'50s: The Truly Golden Days," and "Pageant of the Years—'60s: Grain, Grapes," *San Francisco Chronicle*, September 9, 1950, Book 6, no. 665–66, RCS.

35. Lura Case Smith to Helen Hunting, June 19, 1860. Lura Case Smith Papers, 1852–1865, Huntington Library, San Marino, Calif.; quote from Hannah Bourn Ingalls to her husband, October 27, 1865, Bourn and Ingalls Family Papers, 1865–1965, CHS.

36. Roger W. Lotchin writes that "steadily rising real estate costs were a strong centrifugal force, expelling people and businesses from the heart of the city." Lotchin, *San Francisco, 1846–1856: From Hamlet to City* (New York: Oxford University Press, 1974), 21.

37. Peter R. Decker, *Fortunes and Failures: White-Collar Mobility in Nineteenth-Century San Francisco* (Cambridge: Harvard University Press, 1978), 252.

38. *Daily Alta California*, May 3, 1853; and ibid., February 3, 1854.

39. Marie Mondelet's maiden name was Marie Duchene, also a French name. The couple was married in Valparaiso, Chile, in August of 1848. See Marie Mondelet's announcement of her intention to operate a business in her own name, published in the *Daily Alta California*, October 1, 1853. On the appeal of all things French, Joseph Conlin writes: "Dining on fancy 'frenchy' or 'keskydee' food was not only then emerging as an index of wealth and status in the U.S., but it was also the one item in addition to warm baths, shaves, and whiskey that was immediately available in the diggings." Conlin, *Bacon, Beans, and Galantines*, 130. In addition, early French emigre Francis L. A. Pioche reportedly imported forty Parisian chefs and set them up in business in San Francisco sometime during the 1850s and 1860s. Robert O'Brien, Riptides, *San Francisco Chronicle*, June 3, 1946, Book 1, no. 64, RCS.

40. Kevin Starr, *Americans and the California Dream, 1850–1915* (New York: Oxford University Press, 1973), 81.

41. Hubert Howe Bancroft asserts that "the manufacture of billiard-tables was early encouraged by the great demand" but that the "earliest existing firm" in California, P. Liesenfeld, did not commence business until 1855. Bancroft, *History of California* (1890; reprint, Santa Barbara, Calif.: Wallace Hebberd, 1970), 7:81.

42. According to Bancroft, fresh oysters were first imported successfully to San Francisco from Shoalwater Bay in 1851, after which "the supply became regular." Ibid., 7:83.

43. California historian Kevin Starr writes: "California developed as much as a maritime colony as a frontier—that is to say, within twenty years it developed a type and style of civilization, especially in San Francisco and adjacent areas, resembling nothing else in the Far West: urban, cosmopolitan, reminiscent in a provincial sort of way of the Atlantic states and parts of Southern Europe." Starr, *Americans and the California Dream*, 49.

44. See Mrs. S. A. Leland's advertisement, *Daily Alta California*, August 1, 1851; Mesdames Gillam & Touchard's advertisement, ibid., July 15, 1851; and Miss Helen's Arbor Saloon advertisement, ibid., September 29, 1851, respectively.

45. Decker, *Fortunes and Failures*, 1487–88; Bancroft, *History of California*, 7:683.

46. This does not mean, of course, that all San Francisco female proprietors pros-

pered during the 1860s. Madame Fairbanks, for example, advertised that "greenbacks at par" would be accepted at her millinery establishment in 1870. The notice suggests she was desperate for business, willing to trade in paper currency when the rest of San Francisco adhered to a gold standard. Most city merchants shunned greenbacks altogether, but when they did accept them it was at the more-profitable "merchant value" (what the market would bear) not "par" (the established or recognized value of one currency, in this case greenbacks, in terms of another currency, gold). *San Francisco Chronicle*, March 22, 1870; Decker, *Fortunes and Failures*, 150.

47. For two examples of San Francisco's reputation as the "Paris of America," see Starr, *Americans and the California Dream*, 75; and Benjamin E. Lloyd, *Lights and Shades of California* (San Francisco: A. L. Bancroft, 1876), Chapter 1.

48. *Daily Alta California*, August 15, 1852.

49. Ibid., June 28, 1851.

50. Ibid., July 31, 1852.

51. *Daily Dramatic Chronicle*, September 28, 1865.

52. Richard W. Pollay identifies all of these features as characteristic of the changes afoot in print advertising at the end of the nineteenth century. Pollay, "The Subsiding Sizzle: A Descriptive History of Print Advertising, 1900–1980," *Journal of Marketing* 49 (Summer 1985): 24–37.

53. Susan Strasser, *Satisfaction Guaranteed: The Making of the American Mass Market* (Washington: Smithsonian Institute Press, 1989), 90–91.

54. Lloyd, *Lights and Shades*, 490–91.

55. Susan Ingalls Lewis, "Women in the Marketplace: Female Entrepreneurship, Business Patterns, and Working Families in Mid-Nineteenth-Century Albany, New York, 1830–1885" (Ph.D. diss, State University New York, Binghamton, 2002), 240.

56. *San Francisco City Directory, 1877/78* (San Francisco: Polk, 1877).

57. Peter Decker defined the city's central business district along similar boundaries: Market Street was the southern boundary, Broadway the northern boundary, Dupont (present-day Grant) the western boundary, and the waterfront along East Street the eastern boundary. But the area south of Market Street between the waterfront and Seventh (east to west) and as far south as Harrison or Brannan had a merchant occupation rate (more likely petty entrepreneurs than general or import wholesale merchants) of 1–3 percent, demonstrating that securing a retail spot in the region was still highly desirable. Decker, *Fortunes and Failures*, 216, Map 5: "Density of San Francisco Merchant Business Establishments, 1880."

58. *San Francisco City Directory, 1977/88*.

59. Mrs. Eva Goldstein, California vol. 18, p. 46, RGDC; *San Francisco City Directory, 1877/78*. For more on bankruptcy, its causes and effects, and the persistence of bankrupt female proprietors who reentered the commercial world, see Chapter 6.

60. Sarah Deutsch, *Women and the City: Gender, Space, and Power in Boston, 1870–1940* (New York: Oxford University Press, 2000), 132.

61. Robert W. Cherny and William Issel, *San Francisco: Presidio, Port and Pacific Metropolis* (Sparks, Nev.: Materials For Today's Learning, 1988), 29.

62. Robert A. Burchell, *The San Francisco Irish, 1848–1880* (Manchester, U.K.: Manchester University Press, 1979), 74.

63. *San Francisco City Directory, 1877/78*; Alvin Averbach, "San Francisco's South of Market District, 1850–1950; The Emergence of a Skid Row," *California Historical Quarterly* 52 (Fall 1973), 200–201.

64. *San Francisco City Directory, 1877/78*. This calculation is based on a summary of all female-owned businesses located on the following streets: First, Third, Fourth, Fifth, Sixth, Seventh, Mission, Folsom, and Howard.

65. Deutsch, *Women and the City*, 22.

66. Delilah Beasley, *Negro Trail Blazers of California* (Los Angeles: James Stevenson, 1919), 92.

67. African American dispersal throughout the city was a function of the community's small size. Once sizable numbers of new black residents moved into San Francisco during World War II, the city was segregated along racial lines. "Racist attitudes, restrictive covenants, and the sudden influx of Black migrants created the ghettos near the San Francisco shipyards at Hunter's Point and along Fillmore Street." Douglas Henry Daniels, *Pioneer Urbanites: A Social and Cultural History of Black San Francisco* (Philadelphia: Temple University Press, 1980), 47, 169.

68. Paul Ong, "An Ethnic Trade: The Chinese Laundries in Early California," *Journal of Ethnic Studies*, 8 (Winter 1981): 95–113. Whereas African American residences *and* businesses were dispersed throughout the city, only Chinese businesses — and particularly laundries since they served non-Chinese customers — could be found outside of the compact Chinese residential community in Chinatown. The same tactics that created the black ghetto following World War II were employed to keep the Chinese in Chinatown from the beginning.

69. *San Francisco City Directory, 1872–73* (San Francisco: Gilman and Swanwick, 1873); *San Francisco City Directory, 1877/78*.

70. I. Magnin opened its first downtown store in 1880. The Golden Rule Bazaar, founded in 1850 on Kearny Street, grew in size and profits during its first five decades. By 1880 it must have dominated much of the retailing scene because in the next decade its founders had enough capital to purchase a Market Street competitor — the Emporium. Robert Hendrickson, *The Grand Emporium: The Illustrated History of America's Great Department Stores* (New York: Stein and Day, 1979), 140–42, 158–59, 162–67, 365–67.

71. Decker, *Fortunes and Failures*, 189.

72. By all accounts, the depression that began in the rest of the country in 1873 did not hit San Francisco in earnest until 1877, when a major drought brought agricultural and mine production to a standstill and a crash in mining stock values bankrupted thousands. According to Peter Decker, "it was estimated that about 15 percent of the city's labor force was unemployed in 1878." Ibid., 194. A sudden "trade revival" in 1881, helped "to impart a healthy tone to the returning prosperity" and brought the workingmen's movement, which the depression had aroused, to an end. Bancroft, *History of California*, 689.

73. That the economic depression of the 1870s primarily affected the wallets of the city's working class rather than the wealthy is underscored by the rise of I. Magnin during the same period. The first department store established by a woman, I. Magnin began as a humble, home-based business in 1876 selling the hand-crafted

lingerie of Mary Ann Magnin. According to Robert Hendrickson, Magnin was inspired to start the business when her husband, Isaac, a woodcarver and gold leaf layer
for Gump's, was put to work gilding the ceiling of a San Francisco church. Worried
that he would injure himself on the job, she suggested they start a business together
instead. Mary Ann reportedly named the business after Isaac as soon as her customers
were numerous enough to open a downtown store in 1880. In that four-year period,
the Magnins survived economic conditions that put numerous other retailers out of
business because they catered to the city's elite. Hendrickson, *The Grand Emporium*,
163.

74. Ibid., 158, 163, 365.

75. Mrs. M. E. Doherty, California vol. 14, p. 291, RGDC. *San Francisco City
Directory, 1877/78*, 968, under "Hair-Human." In the 1870s, such forms were made
of chalk, referred to as "chalk craniums," and may have decomposed over time. See
Lloyd, *Lights and Shades*, 489–90, quoted in text below.

76. William Leach argues that "modern display can be traced specifically to 1889,
when the *Dry Goods Economist*, the most influential voice in late nineteenth-century
merchandising . . . decisively embraced merchandising." "Show your goods," it told
merchants, "even if you show only a small quantity, for the sale of goods will certainly
be in proportion to the amount of goods exhibited." Also, one year earlier, the first
issue of the *Show Window* was published by L. Frank Baum, though the publication
did not gain true notoriety until 1900, when it was lauded by Marshall Field's superintendent H. Gordon Selfridge as "indispensable." Leach also points out, however,
that nineteenth-century retailers had to import plate glass from France for the creation of show windows. It was not until 1900 that American factories began producing enough quality plate glass to satisfy domestic demand. This makes the plethora
of show windows in San Francisco in the 1870s all the more remarkable. Leach, *Land
of Desire: Merchants, Power, and the Rise of a New American Culture* (New York: Pantheon Books, 1993), 55–56, 59–61.

77. Lloyd, *Lights and Shades*, 489–90.

78. Strasser, *Satisfaction Guaranteed*, 189.

79. Wendy Gamber, *The Female Economy: The Millinery and Dressmaking Trades,
1860–1930* (Urbana: University of Illinois Press, 1997), 202, 193.

80. Mansel Blackford argues that in spite of encroachments by chain stores and
department stores, "as late as World War I, most sales, especially at the retail level,
continued to be made by small neighborhood stores." Blackford, *A History of Small
Business in America*, 2nd ed. (Chapel Hill: University of North Carolina Press, 2003),
65.

81. Strasser, *Satisfaction Guaranteed*, 189–93.

82. *San Francisco City Directory, 1900* (San Francisco: Crocker-Langley, 1900).
Italian, Irish, German, Spanish, and Anglo names can all be found among the 139
female grocers listed in the classified business directory that year. Although small-
scale retailers continued to dominate sales, they faced stiffened competition from
chain stores, which, by the middle of the twentieth century, accounted for one-third
of the nation's retail sales. Blackford, *A History of Small Business*, 108.

83. Cora Buck, case #1172, San Jose, 1918, BCF.

84. Ephemera File entitled "Business-Clothing," Box F4, Folder 11: Business, Clothing, Hats, California, Huntington Library, San Marino, Calif. Mrs. Sarah Mish was listed as a milliner located at 133 Kearny St. in the 1892 city directory. *San Francisco City Directory, 1892* (San Francisco: Crocker-Langley, 1892).

85. Strasser, *Satisfaction Guaranteed*, 164.

86. For examples of preprinted trade cards, see "Mrs. R. G. Lewis, Dressmaking Parlors," and "Madame Robison, Manicure," both in the Trade Card Collection, San Francisco History Center, San Francisco Public Library, San Francisco, Calif.

87. Ephemera File entitled "Business-Clothing (Hats, Shoes, Pefumes, Powder) —Oversize Trade Cards," Box F4, Folder Ephemera F4C-O, Huntington Library, San Marino, Calif. This card is not dated, but conforms to the elaborate style typical of late nineteenth-century trade cards.

88. The Butler Brothers, authors of several advice books for retailers at the beginning of the twentieth century, told the proprietors of established variety and general stores that "the very first thing" to do when the "syndicate" five-and-ten store came to town was to "modernize your store room, fixtures and front. Unless your store compares favorably in appearance with the syndicate's, you will be badly handicapped from the start." Quoted in Strasser, *Satisfaction Guaranteed*, 246.

89. Mrs. Nancy C. Noyes, case #2457, San Francisco, 1878, BCF.

90. Ellen Crocker, case #2464, San Francisco, 1878, BCF.

91. Catherine Cocks, *Doing the Town: The Rise of Urban Tourism in the United States, 1850–1915* (Berkeley: University of California Press, 2001), 84.

92. *Daily Alta California*, January 1, 1890.

93. Gary B. Nash et al., *The American People: Creating a Nation and a Society*, 3rd ed. (New York: Harper Collins College Publishers, 1994), 2:784.

94. Olive Wells, case #6344, San Francisco, 1909, BCF.

95. For the ways in which modern improvements could also complicate, even multiply, women's household tasks see Ruth Schwartz Cowan, *More Work for Mother: The Ironies of Household Technology from the Open Hearth to the Microwave* (New York: Basic Books, 1983).

96. See, for example, Strasser, *Satisfaction Guaranteed*; as well as Roland Marchand, *Advertising the American Dream* (Berkeley: University of California Press, 1985).

97. "The Ramona," in Broadsides no. 13207 PAM, North Baker Research Library, CHS. The Ramona is listed in the city's directory for 1900.

98. *San Francisco City Directory, 1900*.

99. Ida Selig, case #11034, San Francisco, 1918, BCF.

100. Ida Warren, case #11288, San Francisco, 1918, BCF.

101. Blackford, *A History of Small Business*, 66. Blackford asserts that "cash registers made by the National Cash Register Company were cheap enough for even small retailers to purchase and came into common use throughout the nation by around 1900." But Strasser's examples of pushy cash register salesmen who exploited the ignorance and gullibility of small-scale retailers suggests that there were additional forces at work in this trend. Strasser, *Satisfaction Guaranteed*, 235–36.

102. Promotion by the Southern Pacific Railroad company and others brought

scores of visitors to California at the end of the nineteenth and beginning of the twentieth centuries. For examples of the artful promotion of California during this era, see K. D. Kurutz and Gary F. Kurutz, *California Calls You: The Art of Promoting the Golden State, 1870–1940* (Sausalito, Calif.: Windgate Press, 2000). For more on the importance of first-class hotels in the rise of urban tourism, as well as San Francisco as a tourist destination, during this period, see Cocks, *Doing the Town*.

103. Cocks, *Doing the Town*, 175. See Kurutz and Kurutz, *California Calls You*, for examples of the publicity posters.

104. Peter Booth Wiley, *National Trust Guide to San Francisco: America's Guide for Architecture and History Travelers* (New York: Preservation Press, 2000). Both hotels were destroyed in the earthquake and fire and rebuilt.

105. Both women started their businesses before 1915. Since both filed for bankruptcy protection in 1918, their bet on the lucrative tourist trade was clearly a riskier gamble than it appeared in 1915.

106. See, for example, Kurutz and Kurutz, *California Calls You*, 121–29; and Kevin Starr, *Inventing the Dream: California through the Progressive Era* (New York: Oxford University Press, 1985), *and Material Dreams: Southern California through the 1920s* (New York: Oxford University Press, 1990).

107. R. and M. Bird, case #7829, Benicia, 1912, BCF.

108. Angel Kwolek-Folland argues that department stores' "triumph over small retailers was nearly complete by 1920." Kwolek-Folland, *Incorporating Women: A History of Women and Business in the United States* (New York: Twayne Publishers, 1998), 116.

109. Hendrickson, *The Grand Emporium*, 140–42, 158–59, 162–67, 365–67.

110. "Fighting That Octopus," *Dry Goods Economist*, May 15, 1897; quoted in Leach, *Land of Desire*, 27.

111. This was the ruling of the U.S. Industrial Commission, whose decision culminated years of unfair competition charges lodged by states throughout the country. Susan Porter Benson, *Counter Cultures: Saleswomen, Managers, and Customers in American Department Stores, 1890–1940* (Urbana: University of Illinois Press, 1986), 31.

112. Leach, *Land of Desire*, 30.

113. Benson, *Counter Cultures*, 19.

114. Quoted in Leach, *Land of Desire*, 60.

115. Benson, *Counter Cultures*, 20.

116. The Siegel-Cooper Scrapbook, quoted in Leach, *Land of Desire*, 73.

117. Bertha F. Root, case #9364, San Francisco, 1915, BCF.

118. Elizabeth Ezell, case #275, San Francisco, 1918, BCF.

119. An official inventory of Gomez's store was submitted as evidence to the U.S. District Court for her bankruptcy case. Emily Gomez, case #9432, San Francisco, 1915, BCF.

120. Mrs. Annie Horstmann, case #9277, Stockton, 1915, BCF. Earlier, the Merced Securities and Savings Bank had accepted Horstmann's store furniture as security for a loan, valuing it at $700. The carpets too must have been worth a great

deal because they were valuable enough to secure a loan from one Lauxen & Catts, most likely a wholesale company from which Horstmann purchased her stock of ladies' apparel.

121. Deutsch, *Women and the City*, 121 and n. 34. Deutsch interprets such lavish spending as an "exultation in spatial autonomy" and suggests that the risk of female petty entrepreneurship was an incentive in and of itself for women to spend so lavishly. My argument in the previous chapter about women's careful start-up strategies suggests otherwise. I believe many women believed they had little choice in the matter given the trend in retailing.

122. Gamber, *The Female Economy*, 190–91. Millinery and dressmaking departments here refers to the specialized custom hat and clothing departments developed in department stores to draw customers away from small-scale milliners and dressmakers.

123. Kathy Peiss, *Hope in a Jar: The Making of America's Beauty Culture* (New York: Henry Holt, 1998), 106. For more on businesswomen in the cosmetics industry, see Chapter 3: Beauty Culture and Women's Commerce.

124. *San Francisco Pacific Coast Appeal*, January 17, 1902, p. 1; and May 3, 1902, p. 4; cited in Daniels, *Pioneer Urbanites*, 46. Daniels argues that Phillips and her husband, who operated a successful barbershop, owned property valued at $3,000 in 1902. It is not clear whether beauty salons such as Phillips's served white or black clientele. Historically, black beauty salons were among the only "free" and "black" spaces that women enjoyed in the twentieth century. This provided black beauty culturists with enormous social and political influence in their communities. Tiffany Gill, "Civic Beauty: Beauty Culturists and the Politics of African American Female Entrepreneurship, 1900–1965," *Enterprise and Society: The International Journal of Business History* 5 (December 2004), 583–93. Yet because San Francisco historians such as Daniels argue that black business owners in the city did not typically rely on exclusively black patronage (because of the relatively small and dispersed black population), it is possible that female beauty salon owners there instead followed the trend of black barbers, who historically competed with white barbers for white customers. Douglas Bristol Jr., "From Outposts to Enclaves: A Social History of Black Barbers from 1750–1915," *Enterprise and Society: The International Journal of Business History* 5 (December 2004), 594–606.

125. This computes to approximately $1,800 in 1999 dollars if inflation is calculated at 4 percent a year. Bertha Root, case #9364, San Francisco, 1915, BCF.

126. Additional examples of substantial investments in stationery can be found in the bankruptcy case files for Ida Selig, a hotel proprietor (case #11034, San Francisco, 1918, BCF), and Ida Warren, a restaurant proprietor (case #1288, San Francisco, 1918, BCF).

127. Strasser, *Satisfaction Guaranteed*, especially Chapter 6, "Sales and Promotions." See also Marchand, *Advertising the American Dream*.

128. For additional examples, see Ethel Watson, case #9417, Oakland, 1915, BCF; and Paul C. Pommer and Eva Pommer, copartners, case #9455, San Francisco, 1915, BCF.

129. In *Advertising the American Dream*, Roland Marchand evaluates the content

of advertisements in order to examine how advertising professionals manipulated consumer tastes and pocketbooks.

CHAPTER 5

1. "Call Me Mr. Grover," p. 3, Memoir of Grover Magnin, Box C, IMC.

2. "Significant Dates in I. Magnin Store History," "Close Out," *Los Angeles Magazine*, January 1995, 50–57, IMC.

3. "Call Me Mr. Grover," 3.

4. Grover Magnin, who became general manager of the company in 1908, reported that "one day after returning from New York, where she saw the beautiful white marble floor at B. Altman's," Mary Ann Magnin asked her son, "Why don't you put a marble floor on the First Floor?" When Grover told her that it would cost ten to fifteen thousand dollars, "a large sum of money for Magnin's," Mary Ann responded, "I know it is, but if the Company can't afford it, put it in and I'll pay for it." "Cal Me Mr. Grover, p. 9, IMC.

5. Wendy Gamber, *The Female Economy: The Millinery and Dressmaking Trades, 1860–1930* (Urbana: University of Illinois Press, 1997), 12–14.

6. Angel Kwolek-Folland's synthesis of the literature on women and economic enterprise in *Incorporating Women: A History of Women and Business in the United States* (New York: Twayne Publishers, 1998) does a good job showing women's role as economic actors, but does so (of necessity) in a general way. Most original research on particular populations of women business owners has not examined their role as financial managers in great detail. See, for example, Gamber, *The Female Economy*.

7. *Manual of the Corporation of the City of San Francisco* (San Francisco: G. K. Fitch, 1852); cited in Michelle E. Jolly, "Inventing the City: Gender and the Politics of Everyday Life in Gold Rush San Francisco, 1848–1869" (Ph.D. diss., University of California, San Diego, 1998), 132.

8. Jolly, "Inventing the City," 131–32.

9. *Daily Alta California*, March 18, 1863.

10. *History of the San Francisco District: Challenge and Change, 1862–1990*, p. 21, IRS Historical Studies, Department of the Treasury, Internal Revenue Service, National Archives and Records Administration, Pacific Region, San Bruno, Calif.

11. Mrs. M. E. Doherty, California v. 14, p. 291, RGDC.

12. *History of the San Francisco District*, 25. Higby's removal from the position was, in part, a political move, since the Republican governor went on to warn about the ways in which the tax collector's actions might "jeopardize" the success of the party in California at the upcoming elections. This was before the institution of the Civil Service Reform Law, when federal government employees still enjoyed political appointments as part of the "spoils" system.

13. Frances Maita, case #11259, San Francisco, 1918, BCF.

14. John F. Witte, *The Politics and Development of the Federal Income Tax* (Madison: University of Wisconsin Press, 1985), 77; cited in Susan Strasser, *Satisfaction Guaranteed: The Making of the American Mass Market* (Washington, D.C.: Smithsonian Institution Press, 1989), 72–73.

15. Helen Tarbox, case #12339, San Francisco, 1921, BCF.

16. Ida Selig, case #11034, San Francisco, 1918, BCF. Few female proprietors incorporated, however, so few would have paid this tax.

17. *Daily Dramatic Chronicle* (precursor to the *San Francisco Chronicle*), March 9, 1867.

18. Ethel Watson, case #9417, Oakland, 1915, BCF.

19. Clara Moody, case #7579, San Francisco, 1912, BCF. Moody's bankruptcy was unique because referees for the case decided it was financially beneficial to continue to operate the business for several months to generate revenue for creditors. As a result, the records include a full accounting of the business expenditures for three months, permitting the detailed discussion of costs and inventory here.

20. Some seventy miles east, Stockton was a substantially smaller city but one with extensive commercial ties to and commonalities with San Francisco.

21. This comparative statement is based on contemporary newspaper advertisements for women's clothes. See, for example, *The Bulletin*, March 2, 1910, 3–7.

22. Mrs. Annie Horstmann, case #9277, Stockton, 1915, BCF.

23. Quoted in Strasser, *Satisfaction Guaranteed*, 231.

24. Ibid., 231.

25. Mansel Blackford, *A History of Small Business in America*, 2nd ed. (Chapel Hill: University of North Carolina Press, 2003), 66.

26. Strasser, *Satisfaction Guaranteed*, 69.

27. The credit reports only exist for San Francisco for the 1870s.

28. Mrs. Mary Howard, California v. 14, p. 76, RGDC.

29. Mrs. Dannenberg, California v. 14, p. 318 and 319, RGDC.

30. Mrs. Emmons, California v. 17, p. 233, RGDC.

31. Mrs. Charles Mercer, California v. 14, p. 337, RGDC.

32. Miss May Thompson, California v. 14, p. 303, RGDC.

33. Mrs. J. Martineau, California v. 16, p. 349, RGDC.

34. Mme. Leroy, California v. 16, p. 119, RGDC.

35. Gamber, *The Female Economy*, 161.

36. Mrs. G. W. M. Croles, California v. 14, p. 155, RGDC.

37. Mrs. Jane Thomas, California v. 14, p. 100, RGDC; Mme. Esther Schloss, California v. 16, p. 215, RGDC.

38. Mrs. C. Jordan, California v. 14, p. 155, RGDC; and Frances Uznay, California v. 17, p. 89, RGDC.

39. Mrs. Broderick, California v. 19, p. 336, RGDC.

40. Gamber, *The Female Economy*, 160.

41. Minnie Borgstrom, case #2490, San Francisco, 1878, BCF.

42. Bessie Hamilton, case #2847, San Francisco, 1899, BCF.

43. Bertha Baschan, case #3211, Oakland, 1900, BCF.

44. *Milliner's Designer, Illustrated* 4 (September 1908), 6; quoted in Gamber, *The Female Economy*, 174.

45. Cora Buck, case #11172, San Jose, 1918, BCF.

46. Lily Stevens, case #11022, Oakland, 1918, BCF.

47. Helen Tarbox, case #12339, San Francisco, 1921, BCF.

48. Blackford, *A History of Small Business*, 103.

49. Olive Wells agreed to a payment schedule for her electric range, while Helen Tarbox signed a long-term contract for the purchase of an electric sign and a cash register. Olive Wells, case #6344, San Francisco, 1909, BCF; and Helen Tarbox, case #12339, San Francisco, 1921, BCF.

50. Ida Warner, case #11288, San Francisco, 1918, BCF.

51. Paul C. and Eva Pommer, case #9455, San Francisco, 1915, BCF.

52. Gamber discusses, for example, the degree to which benevolent paternalism characterized many of the credit negotiations between wholesalers and female proprietors in the millinery and dressmaking trades. Gamber, *The Female Economy*, 159–68.

53. Ibid., 169.

54. Caroline Louise Leuenberger, case #9144, San Francisco, 1915, BCF. Leuenberger's careful record keeping was unusual, as discussed in the following paragraphs.

55. Gamber, *The Female Economy*, 168.

56. Lawrence Friedman, "Law and Small Business in the United States: One Hundred Years of Struggle and Accommodation," in *Small Business in American Life* ed. Stuart Bruchey (New York: Columbia University Press, 1980), 312.

57. Ibid., 312.

58. Gamber, *The Female Economy*, 122.

59. William Laird MacGregor, *Hotels and Hotel Life at San Francisco California in 1876* (San Francisco: San Francisco News Company, 1877), 36–37; and *Daily Alta California*, February 22, 1877.

60. All household goods, personal apparel, and items determined to be for personal use were exempt from the 1867 Bankruptcy Act that was in effect in the United States until 1878.

61. Teresa Holden was not alone in this respect. Many businesswomen combined their place of business with their residences. This was as true for some dressmakers and milliners as it was for those women running businesses in the lodging industry. For boardinghouse and lodging house keepers, as well as hotel proprietors, the nature of the work demanded this of them. For others, this combination strategy may have been necessitated by restricted finances that did not allow them to pay rent for both a business and a home. Of course for proprietors who combined their home and place of work, going into business, and consequently taking the risk of going *out* of business, was an even higher stakes endeavor. For such women commercial failure not only put them out of business, but also put them out on the street with nowhere to live.

62. For more-recent examples, see Olive Wells, case #6344, San Francisco, 1909, BCF, who was owed more than $1,000 by lodgers; J. B. and Mrs. J. B. Palmer, case #6033, Camp Seco, 1909, BCF, who were owed by thirty-seven customers in their boardinghouse/grocery store; and Ellen Parker, case #11133, Oakland, 1918, BCF, who had ten male customers who owed her a total of $533 at the time of her bankruptcy.

63. Wendy Gamber, "Tarnished Labor: The Home, the Market, and the Boardinghouse in Antebellum America," *Journal of the Early Republic* 22 (Summer 2002), 177–204.

64. Gamber, *The Female Economy*, 116–17.

65. Margaret Grisby, case #9357, Oakland, 1915, BCF.

66. Emily Gomez, case #9432, San Francisco, 1915, BCF.

67. Gamber, *The Female Economy*, 117.

68. Sarah Deutsch, *Women and the City: Gender, Space, and Power in Boston, 1870–1940* (New York: Oxford University Press, 2000), 123–26.

69. This statement is based both on an examination of the R. G. Dun & Company credit reports for 1870s San Francisco (the only ones that still exist) and on the bankruptcy court records examined for the 1870s and 1890s.

70. "E. & M. Holahan, Milliners receipt book, 1863–1866," Bancroft Library, University of California, Berkeley, Calif.

71. Blackford, *A History of Small Business*, 18–19.

72. Mrs. Charles Mercer, California v. 14, p. 337, RGDC.

73. See, for example, Caroline Leuenberger, case #9144, San Francisco, 1915, BCF; Daisy Brink, case #11197, San Francisco, 1918, BCF; and Posey Agee, case #12337, Oakland, 1921, BCF.

74. Strasser, *Satisfaction Guaranteed*, 231–232.

75. See, for example, the *Daily Alta California* advertisement for March 11, 1874, placed by Mrs. M. R. Mercado.

76. Blackford, *A History of Small Business*, 67.

77. See, for example, Ellen Crocker, case #2464, San Francisco, 1878, BCF. There are also numerous mentions of fire insurance in the R. G. Dun & Company credit reports for San Francisco businesswomen during the 1870s.

78. Kwolek-Folland, *Incorporating Women*, 108–9, 200–201. See Kwolek-Folland, *Engendering Business: Men and Women in the Corporate Office, 1870–1930* (Baltimore: Johns Hopkins University Press, 1994) for the author's more-comprehensive treatment of the industry.

79. Blackford, *A History of Small Business*, 67.

80. Kwolek-Folland, *Engendering Business*, 3.

81. See, for example, Clara Moody, case #7579, 1912, San Francisco, BCF; Annie Horstmann, case #9277, Stockton, 1915, BCF; and Louis and Estella Spiro, case #9475, San Francisco, 1915, BCF.

82. Mabel Ritchart, case #12198, Oakland, 1921, BCF.

83. Lydia Pinkham, owner of a large patent medicine company, had similar concerns about working with advertisers in the nineteenth century. See Sarah Stage, *Female Complaints: Lydia Pinkham and the Business of Women's Medicine* (New York: W. W. Norton, 1979), 95.

84. *Daily Alta California*, June 20, 1875.

85. Gamber argues that female proprietors in the millinery and dressmaking trades only occasionally placed ads in newspapers and otherwise depended on trade cards and word-of-mouth recommendations from happy customers. Gamber, *The Female Economy*, 202.

86. See Deutsch, *Women and the City*. This idea was discussed in more detail in Chapter 4.

87. This statement is based on a sample of ads located in the *Daily Alta California* and the *San Francisco Chronicle* (in all of its forms). Both papers were examined every third month (March, June, September, December), every year between 1850 and 1920, or in the case of the *Daily Alta California*, for as long as it was in print. In some of the later years, I used the *San Francisco Call*, too.

88. *American Dressmaker* 3 (January 1912), 45; cited in Gamber, *The Female Economy*, 203.

89. Strasser, *Satisfaction Guaranteed*, 93.

90. See, for example, *Daily Alta California*, March 12, 1872; and June 21, 1881. Both entries list the newspaper's prices for advertising. Thomas Cochran argues that such advertising agents were "influenced no doubt more by their profits as space sellers than by any careful plan of campaign." Cochran, *200 Years of American Business* (New York: Basic Books, 1977), 125.

91. At the end of the nineteenth century, "Market testing amounted to asking a few questions of dealers in the commodity." Cochran, *200 Years of American Business*, 125. Today, in contrast, consumer products companies have sophisticated tools, such as supermarket scanners, to help them measure the impact of their advertisements. Most small-scale business proprietors even today, however, probably rely on less-scientific methods of evaluation to determine the profitability of their advertising.

92. See Bertha Root, case #9364, San Francisco, 1915, BCF; Ethel Watson, case #9417, Oakland, 1915, BCF; and Paul C. Pommer and Eva Pommer, copartners, case #9455, San Francisco, 1915, BCF.

93. Strasser, *Satisfaction Guaranteed*, 91. Roland Marchand argues that while it was not until the 1920s that advertising professionals' techniques matured, the professional advertising industry had already "prove[d] its worth on pragmatic economic grounds" by the end of the 1910s. Marchand, *Advertising the American Dream* (Berkeley: University of California Press, 1985), 5.

94. Marchand, *Advertising the American Dream*, 34–35.

95. Sara Alpern, "In the Beginning: A History of Women in Management," in *Women in Business*, ed. Mary Yeager (Cheltenham, U.K.: Edward Elgar, 1997), 34.

96. Robert O'Brien, Riptides, *San Francisco Chronicle*, September 9, 1950, RCS.

97. Kwolek-Folland, *Incorporating Women*, 78.

98. Erika Rappaport, *Shopping for Pleasure* (Princeton: Princeton University Press, 2000), 170. This study examines women in London in the early 1900s, taking Selfridge's department store as its example.

99. Peter R. Decker, *Fortunes and Failures: White-Collar Mobility in Nineteenth-Century San Francisco* (Cambridge: Harvard University Press, 1978), 151, 183.

100. See, for example, Teresa Holden, case #1283, San Francisco, 1873, BCF; Ellen Crocker, case #2464, San Francisco, 1878, BCF; Clara Moody, case #7577, San Francisco, 1912, BCF; and Louis Spiro and Estella Spiro, case #9475, San Francisco, 1915, BCF.

101. Robert E. Wright, "Women and Finance in the Early National U.S.," *Essays*

in History 42 (2000), <http://etext.lib.virginia.edu/journals/EH/EH42/Wright42 .html> (December 5, 2003).

102. At least one woman hired an investment firm to handle such decisions for her. See Ellen Parker, case #11133, Oakland, 1918, BCF.

103. See, for example, Mrs. Arnold, California v. 18, p. 378, RGDC; and Mrs. Dannenberg, California v. 14, p. 318 and 319, RGDC. Dressmakers and boarding- house- or hotelkeepers were most likely to combine their personal and professional addresses.

104. Julia Lyons, case #1296, San Francisco, 1873, BCF.

105. Deutsch, *Women and the City*, 125.

106. Ida Largent, case #11097, San Francisco, 1918, BCF.

107. Bessie Hamilton, case #2847, San Francisco, 1899, BCF. See also Ida Selig, case #11034, San Francisco, 1918, BCF.

108. Judy Yung argues that "Chinese men [in nineteenth-century San Francisco] concentrated in three low-wage industries (cigars, woolen goods, and boots and shoes), engaged in Chinatown enterprises that serviced their own community, or did menial work as domestic servants and laundrymen." Little had changed by 1920, when "most worked in ethnic enterprises in Chinatowns, as domestic servants for European American families, or opened small laundries, grocery stores, and restau- rants in out-of-the-way places." Yung, *Unbound Feet: A Social History of Chinese Women in San Francisco* (Berkeley: University of California Press, 1995), 25 and 36.

109. Margaret Stein, case #11187, San Francisco, 1918, BCF.

110. Lilly Stevens, case #11022, Oakland, 1918, BCF.

111. Deutsch, *Women and the City*, 126.

112. See Gamber, *The Female Economy*, Chapter 3; and Deutsch, *Women and the City*, 124–26.

113. Strasser, *Satisfaction Guaranteed*, 231.

114. "Mother Goose Pursery Rhymes," BOAA.

115. Nancy Robertson argues that in fact it was this sort of condescending view of women's money management skills that drove them to seek out female tellers and advisers in women's banking departments in the first place. The perception was that they had less to be embarrassed about around other women who perhaps only re- cently had mastered the skill of finance. Nancy Marie Robertson, "'The Disagree- able Experience of Handling Soiled Money': Women and Banking in the U.S. at the Turn of the Twentieth Century" (presented at the Thirteenth Berkshire Conference on the History of Women at Scripps College, Claremont, Calif., June 2005).

116. The Bank of Italy's first Women's Banking Department was established in San Francisco in 1921. A second one followed in the main Los Angeles branch of the bank in 1924. But in 1930, due to the economic pressures of the depression, both were abolished in favor of a "Women's Department" that required fewer staff because it did not duplicate any of the bank's functions (teller services, for example), as did the Women's Banking Department.

117. Kwolek-Folland, *Engendering Business*, 171–72.

118. "Women's Banking Department, Bank of Italy, San Francisco," brochure, 1921, BOAA.

119. "Report of Survey of Department, including statistical data on loans and deposits, list of and comments on employees, customers' comments on service provided by department, statistical data on women workers in various fields of business," December 1925, BOAA. Among the female-owned businesses listed in the report were the Children's Book Shop (Mrs. Powell), Flo Rie Beauty Shop (Miss Rolin), Candle Glow (Miss Cook), Courtyard Tea Rooms (Miss de Gomez), the Butterfly Sweet Shop (Mrs. Carlson), the Fashion Beauty Shop (Miss Buck), Tiny's Beauty Studio (Miss Berio), the Berry Corset Company (Mrs. Berry), the Columbia Hat Shop (Mrs. Williams), Alcaza Hair Store (Mrs. Farrell), Panchon Hat Shop (Miss Ready), Kentucky Tavern (Mrs. Washington), Mignon Privette Millinery Store, and Milady's [Gown] Shop (Miss Harding).

120. Lily Stevens, case #11022, Oakland, 1918, BCF.

121. Mabel Ritchart, case #12198, Oakland, 1921, BCF; see the check she wrote for wages to Mrs. Silva. Posey Agee, case #12337, Oakland, 1921, BCF.

122. Kwolek-Folland, *Engendering Business*, 171.

123. "Women's Banking Department" brochure, BOAA.

124. Cochran argues that "trial and error was the general guide" when it came to business management generally in the nineteenth century, though "some exchange of information" between proprietors also helped. Cochran, *200 Years of American Business*, 55.

125. Strasser, *Satisfaction Guaranteed*, 72.

126. Blackford, *A History of Small Business*, 18–19, 46–47.

127. Introductory letter from Edward N. Herley, chairman, in Federal Trade Commission, *A System of Accounts for Retail Merchants* (Washington, D.C.: Government Printing Office, 1916), 3; quoted in Strasser, *Satisfaction Guaranteed*, 72.

128. Gamber argues that, in fact, "complaints that apprentices learned nothing but plain sewing" and not even the more-complicated aspects of dress or hat construction were common. The hiring of apprentices under false pretenses, too, was widespread, resulting in the exploitation of cheap laborers who gained no training at all. Regarding "the rudimentary reading, writing, and bookkeeping skills that would enable them one day to run their own businesses," Gamber argues that only "in the best of circumstances" did aspiring milliners and dressmakers gain such training. Gamber, *The Female Economy*, 149, 87, 13.

129. Eleven percent of small-scale businessmen in San Francisco during the 1870s who appeared in the credit reports had worked as clerks before becoming businessmen. This figure was computed from the R. G. Dun & Company credit reports for the 1870s using a sample of male small-business owners, RGDC.

130. Decker, *Fortunes and Failures*, 67 and 79.

131. One study differentiates between bookkeeping before 1870, when the job involved general managerial tasks as well as specific bookkeeping/accounting tasks, and after 1870, when it divided into routine, mechanized record keeping (what we now know as bookkeeping), a job starting to be filled by women, and accounting (financial advising), which remained in the hands of men. Charles W. Wootton and Barbara E. Kemmerer, "The Changing Genderization of Bookkeeping in the United States, 1870–1930," *Business History Review* 70 (Winter 1996): 541–86.

132. Blackford, *A History of Small Business*, 18.

133. Kwolek-Folland, *Engendering Business*, 29. Men still constituted the majority of clerks in the banking industry until 1930 and in the insurance industry until 1910. See Table 2 in Kwolek-Folland's Introduction.

134. These figures were computed from the R. G. Dun & Company credit reports using all female proprietors listed in the ledgers and a sample of male small-business owners, RGDC. See the Note on Sources for an explanation of sample.

135. Paul H. Nystrom, *The Economics of Retailing: A Textbook for Colleges and Schools of Business Administration*. 2nd ed. (New York: Ronald Press, 1920), 313.

136. Miss E. VanWinkle, California v. 18, p. 347, RGDC. There are several famous cases of women learning business management under the tutelage of parents. See, for example, Constance B. Schulz, "Eliza Lucas Pinckney," in *Portraits of American Women*, ed. G. J. Barker-Benfield and Catherine Clinton (New York: St. Martin's Press, 1991), 65–84.

137. Gamber, *The Female Economy*, 71. In contrast, one study of female proprietors in nineteenth-century Britain argues that "most women entrepreneurs came from a small business background." Stana Nenadic, "The Social Shaping of Business Behaviour in the Nineteenth-Century Women's Garment Trades," *Journal of Social History* 31 (Spring 1998), 635.

138. Deutsch, *Women and the City*, 122.

139. Mrs. A. Dannenberg, California v. 14, p. 318 and 319, RGDC.

140. Gamber found that 20–32 percent of female proprietors in the millinery and dressmaking trades in the second half of the nineteenth century were widows. Gamber, *The Female Economy*, 33. Deutsch argues that the female proprietors of neighborhood shops were predominantly widows. Deutsch, *Women and the City*, 117. Kwolek-Folland seconds these findings, arguing throughout her history of women in business that widows were consistent participants in economic enterprise. Kwolek-Folland, *Incorporating Women*.

141. Widows accounted for 19 percent of all San Francisco female proprietors in the R. G. Dun & Company credit reports during the 1870s, RGDC. In the printed census, they account for 35 percent of all businesswomen in 1890. U.S. Census Bureau, *Report on the Population of the United States at the Eleventh Census*, part 2 (Washington, D.C.: Government Printing Office, 1895), 728–29.

142. Mrs. H. S. Stone, California v. 14, p. 113, RGDC; Mrs. Charles Borchard, California v. 14, p. 280, RGDC; Mrs. Quigley, California v. 17, p. 250, RGDC; Mrs. Rosanna Short, California v. 18, p. 215, RGDC.

143. Strasser, *Satisfaction Guaranteed*, 65. Strasser argues that "as late as 1923, over two-thirds of American retail business was done as these 'mom-and-pop' stores." A good example of the phenomenon can be found in Deutsch, *Women and the City*, Chapter 1, which highlights the story of Mrs. Brest, who helped her husband operate a neighborhood business in Boston. The low number of widowers among businessmen (less than 2 percent of the R. G. Dun & Company sample) also highlights the trend. Among the city's widowers there must have been hundreds who shuttered their businesses upon the loss of the wives who had played such an integral part in

their operations. Statistic composed from a sample of male small-business proprietors in the R. G. Dun & Company credit reports, RGDC.

144. Lucy Eldersveld Murphy discusses this idea in "Business Ladies: Midwestern Women and Enterprise, 1850–1880," *Journal of Women's History* 3 (Spring 1991), 65–89.

145. Susan Ingalls Lewis, "Beyond Horatia Alger: Breaking through Gendered Assumptions about Business 'Success' in Mid-Nineteenth-Century America," *Business and Economic History* 24 (Fall 1995): 101. Another pair of historians describes women's labor in family enterprises as "the hidden investment." See Leonore Davidoff and Catherine Hall, eds., *Family Fortunes: Men and Women of the English Middle Class, 1780–1850* (New York: Routledge, 1987), Chapter 6; reprinted in *Women in Business*, ed. Mary Yeager (Cheltenham, U.K.: Edward Elgar, 1997): 352–401.

146. Blackford, *A History of Small Business*, 105.

147. Quoted in Mary Beth Norton, "A Cherished Spirit of Independence: The Life of an Eighteenth-Century Boston Businesswoman"; as cited in Patricia Cleary, "'She Will Be in the Shop': Women's Sphere of Trade in Eighteenth-Century Philadelphia and New York," *Pennsylvania Magazine of History and Biography* 119 (July 1995), 199. Other studies suggest that wives were conversant with financial management far earlier in history. See Gayle K. Brunelle, "Wives as Business Partners in Early Modern France" (presented at the Business History Conference at Florida International University, Miami, Fla., April 2001).

148. Kwolek-Folland, *Incorporating Women*, 59. Rebecca Lukens, she points out, could read and compute and was skilled in accounting. This area of women's education needs further exploration. I believe there is still much to be learned about where and how women became financially literate. Education is one place to look for more clues.

149. Suzanne Lebsock, *The Free Women of Petersburg: Status and Culture in a Southern Town, 1784–1860* (New York: W. W. Norton, 1984), 191.

150. Mrs. A. Finke, California v. 14, p. 106, RGDC.

151. Mrs. Charles H. Mercer, California v. 14, p. 337, RGDC.

152. I found only one example of a mother-son business partnership in a newspaper advertisement. But Lewis argues that sons often worked as bookkeepers and clerks in their mothers' businesses, "suggesting that young men were often 'brought up' in business techniques" and that their mothers' businesses "served as a training ground for commercial careers . . . even if they did not move into their mothers' enterprises." Susan Ingalls Lewis, "Women in the Marketplace: Female Entrepreneurship, Business Patterns, and Working Families in Mid-Nineteenth-Century Albany, New York, 1830–1885" (Ph.D. diss, State University of New York, Binghamton, 2002), 228.

153. Mrs. A. Dannenberg, California v. 14, p. 318 and 319, RGDC.

154. Mrs. M. A. Soper, California v. 14, p. 61, RGDC.

155. When figured as a percentage of all married women in the reports, this figure is even more dramatic: 37 percent of all married businesswomen managed their businesses with the help of their spouses. RGDC.

156. Gamber makes this point about the degree to which husbands turned their wives' businesses to their own advantage. Gamber, *The Female Economy*, 46–52.

157. Mrs. E. E. Caswell, California v. 17, p. 11, RGDC. Of course, sometimes the arrangement could work the other way, too. For example, once Mrs. A. H. Makins married, her successful necktie manufactory became "virtually in [the] control" of her husband James, formerly a clerk in the City Tax Collectors Office. Within five years, in fact, James changed the name of the business to "Makins & Co.," erasing any public connection between his wife and the business. Mrs. A. H. Makins, California v. 14, p. 311, RGDC.

158. Mrs. E. E. Caswell, California v. 17, p. 11, RGDC; E. E. Caswell, business card, Ephemera File, Business-Clothing, Box F4, Folder 11: Business, Clothing, Hats, California, Huntington Library, San Marino, Calif.

159. Gamber, *The Female Economy*, 51.

160. A "partnership" was believed to exist even when a formal partnership agreement was not filed with the state. Participation in the profits of a business alone was thought to provide "strong presumptive evidence of a partnership in it," and California courts admitted books and receipts in lieu of a partnership agreement "if they afford[ed] any evidence" to prove that a partnership between two or more persons existed. F. P. Deering, *Deering's Annotated Codes and Statutes of California: Civil Code* (San Francisco: Bancroft-Whitney, 1886), 405–6.

161. Bankruptcy court records indicate that sometime between 1907 and 1909, husbands and wives in the San Francisco area began entering into formal partnership agreements. Though such cases are rare, at least one did occur in each sample year examined: 1909, 1912, 1915, and 1921. While this tiny sample hardly permits any penetrating conclusions here, it does provide enough evidence to suggest that in the first decade of the twentieth century, husband-wife business teams began formalizing partnerships that had previously been only implied by a couple's activities.

162. In an 1888 ruling in *Artman vs. Ferguson*, for example, the Michigan Supreme Court argued that the "mischief of allowing persons thus related to put themselves habitually in business antagonism" made permitting spousal partnerships unwise. In his opinion for the court Justice Long wrote: "The important and sacred relations between man and wife, which lie at the very foundation of civilized society, are not to be disturbed and destroyed by contentions which may arise from such a community of property and a joint power of disposal and a mutual liability for the contracts and obligations of each other." Floyd R. Mechem, ed., *Cases on the Law of Partnership*, 4th ed. (Chicago: Callaghan, 1924), 95.

163. Giuseppi Alexandro and Antoinetta Alexandro, case #6366, San Francisco, 1909, BCF. Note the Americanized spelling of the couple's last name. This is the spelling typically typed in the documents, while the couple signed their name "Alessandro."

164. Ibid.

165. Lawrence Estavan, "San Francisco Theater Research Monographs," San Francisco Works Progress Administration, 1939; cited in Maxine Seller, "Antoinetta Pisanelli Alessandro and the Italian Theater of San Francisco: Entertainment, Education and Americanization," in *Struggle and Success: An Anthology of the Italian Im-*

migrant Experience in California, ed. Paola A. Sensi-Isolani and Phylis Cancilla Martinelli (New York: Center for Migration Studies, 1993), 166.

166. Nenadic, "Social Shaping of Business Behavior," 631–32. The partnership referred to here is actually between a brother and sister, but the evidence on which it relies is quite remarkable. Nenadic actually reproduces the partnership agreement in her article.

167. Kwolek-Folland, *Incorporating Women*, 118–19.

168. Hasia R. Diner, *Erin's Daughters in America: Irish Immigrant Women in the Nineteenth Century* (Baltimore: Johns Hopkins University Press, 1983), 68, 67.

169. For more on the degree to which women's roles as household managers constituted economic engagement, see Kwolek-Folland, *Incorporating Women*.

170. "Memorandum to Mr. A. P. Giannini From The Women's Banking Department," BOAA.

171. One 1913 article published in *Ladies Home Journal* lambasted homemakers with the following reprimand: "If one-half the men conducted their commercial business as carelessly as the majority of women conduct their business of housekeeping, the country's bankruptcy courts would be running day and night." Mrs. Julian Heath, "How Housewives Waste Money," *Ladies Home Journal*, February 1913, 73; cited in Jennifer Scanlon, *Inarticulate Longings: The Ladies Home Journal, Gender, and the Promises of Consumer Culture* (New York: Routledge, 1995), 61.

172. Marchand, *Advertising the American Dream*, 168–69.

173. Lori D. Ginzburg, *Women and the Work of Benevolence: Morality, Politics, and Class in the 19th-Century United States* (New Haven: Yale University Press, 1990), 42, 41.

174. Kathleen W. Sander, *The Business of Charity: The Woman's Exchange Movement, 1832–1900* (Urbana: University of Illinois Press, 1998).

175. African American women are an important exception, since they were among the urban women who operated small businesses in San Francisco and since they also participated in middle-class charitable causes. See Chapter 1 for more on the experiences of black female business owners.

176. Diner, *Erin's Daughters*, 125. Some Irish women were involved in the operation of church-related organizations, but most of these were Catholic nuns.

177. For more on this see Willi Coleman, "African American Women and Community Development in California, 1848-1900," in *Seeking El Dorado: African Americans in California*, ed. Lawrence B. de Graaf, Kevin Mulroy, and Quintard Taylor (Seattle: University of Washington Press, 2001), 98-125.

178. See Gamber, *The Female Economy*.

CHAPTER 6

1. The longevity figures for San Francisco female proprietors were composed by following the careers of eighty-one businesswomen in both the R. G. Dun & Company credit reports, available only during the 1870s for San Francisco, and the 1878 *San Francisco Business Directory*. Used in tandem, these sources provide a reliable, if upwardly skewed (since the reports favored more-successful proprietors), portrait of women's business longevity. Because listings in city and business directories were inconsistent, used alone they would not provide an accurate view into the length of time women's businesses lasted. The majority of businesswomen in the reports (58 percent) were in the millinery, dressmaking, or clothing retail business. The remaining 42 percent ran fancy goods, dry goods, stationery, toy, furniture, liquor, artificial flower, hardware, regalia, and drug stores, as well as hair salons, groceries, confectioneries, and boardinghouses. California v. 14–20, RGDC.

2. The figure for Illinois businesswomen is from Lucy Eldersveld Murphy, "Her Own Sphere: Businesswomen and Separate Spheres in the Midwest, 1850–1880," *Illinois Historical Journal* 80 (Autumn 1987): 165. The figures for women in Boston are taken from Wendy Gamber, *The Female Economy: The Millinery and Dressmaking Trades, 1860–1930* (Urbana: University of Illinois Press, 1997), 36–37. Gamber's figures were composed by tracing the careers of proprietors in the 1860 census sample and are limited to businesswomen in the dressmaking and millinery trades. To underscore the upward bias of the credit reports, she states that milliners and dressmakers reviewed by Dun reporters stayed in business an average of nine years, as opposed to the six-year average she found for women business owners in the census. This difference suggests that if a sample similar to Gamber's were prepared from the census for San Francisco women the average number of years in business would likely be lower.

3. Women who closed their businesses and sold them to other female proprietors are covered extensively in Chapter 3 in the section on buying out or taking over an established business and so will not be discussed here. But like all business transactions at the end of a career, closing up shop required a certain amount of skill. Most women who chose to close their stores were headed someplace new, whether a new location or a new enterprise, and so wanted and needed to squeeze as much money out of the sale as possible. Whether selling the actual business or just the merchandise, businesswomen used ads, agents, and their negotiating skills to get the best deal.

4. Ruth Gillette Hutchinson, Arthur R. Hutchinson, and Mabel Newcomer, "A Study of Business Mortality: Length of Life of Business Enterprises in Poughkeepsie, New York, 1843–1936," *American Economic Review* 28 (September 1938), 514.

5. Mansel Blackford, *A History of Small Business in America*, 2nd ed. (Chapel Hill: University of North Carolina Press, 2003), 70.

6. Hutchinson, "A Study of Business Mortality," 501. Businesses in the crafts (including millinery) and in the service industry (including restaurants, saloons, and barbershops) fared about the same.

7. Ibid., 505. In *San Francisco City Directory, 1877/78* (San Francisco: Polk, 1877), 37 out of approximately 160 confectioners, or 23 percent, were women.

8. Paul H. Nystrom, *The Economics of Retailing: A Textbook for Colleges and Schools of Business Administration*, 2nd ed. (New York: Ronald Press, 1920), 307.

9. One study of female bankrupts at the beginning of the nineteenth century underscores that the San Francisco women who declared bankruptcy at the end of the 1800s and beginning of the 1900s simply followed in a long historical trend both of female commercial engagement and of women's use of American bankruptcy laws to manage their financial difficulties. Of the forty-eight women who filed for bankruptcy under the nation's 1841 law, forty-seven were voluntary bankrupts, indicating

women's willingness to avail themselves of all legal tools when faced with commercial crisis. See Karen Gross, Marie Stefanini, and Denise Campbell, "Ladies in Red: Learning from America's First Female Bankrupts," *American Journal of Legal History* 40 (January 1996), 1–40.

10. Because such a small number of women's cases were filed under the National Bankruptcy Act, bankruptcy court cases are not useful as a source for quantifying the proportion of businesswomen who failed. Credit reports, which are only available for the 1870s for San Francisco women, are therefore the only reliable way to establish the percentage of women whose businesses did not succeed. As a result, failure rates can only be created for the decade of the 1870s.

11. Peter R. Decker, *Fortunes and Failures: White-Collar Mobility in Nineteenth-Century San Francisco* (Cambridge: Harvard University Press, 1978), 308.

12. Finding based on sample of male small-business owners in industries comparable to those of female small-business owners in the R. G. Dun & Company credit reports, RGDC. For more information on this sample see the Note on Sources. Sarah Deutsch comes to similar conclusions in her examination of proprietors in Boston between 1890 and 1940. While on the one hand she argues that businesswomen failed at a rate twice that of businessmen, she concludes that the "closer similarities between total and female dry goods and variety stores could be partially explained by the lack of large-scale shops in either sector, so that *small* business women and *small* business men were relatively comparable in their success rates." See Sarah Deutsch, *Women and the City: Gender, Space, and Power in Boston, 1870–1940* (New York: Oxford University Press, 2000), 130 and 330 n. 76. This finding conforms with the conclusions of scholars such as Mansel Blackford, cited above, who argues that small-business proprietors generally failed at high rates.

13. Decker, *Fortunes and Failures*, 308.

14. Comparing the number of Poughkeepsie businesses from one year to the next with the Cleveland Trust Company index of industrial activity, Hutchinson and her colleagues found that "neither the 1907 nor the 1921 depression [were] reflected in the Poughkeepsie figures" for business mortality. Hutchinson, "A Study of Business Mortality," 510. This finding suggests that tying business mortality to economic downturns may not provide the most accurate picture of the causes of commercial failure.

15. Mrs. M. A. Soper, California v. 14, p. 61, RGDC.

16. Mrs. M. A. Soper, Kansas v. 15, p. 134, RGDC.

17. David Lavender, *California: A Bicentennial History* (New York: W. W. Norton, 1976), 119; Robert O'Brien, " '70s: Boom and Bust," *San Francisco Chronicle*, September 9, 1950, RCS.

18. Kevin Starr, *Americans and the California Dream, 1850–1915* (New York: Oxford University Press, 1973), 125.

19. O'Brien, " '70s: Boom and Bust."

20. Mrs. M. A. Soper, California v. 14, p. 61, RGDC. This language was not in any of the reports written about her Leavenworth business. See Mrs. Mary A. Soper, Kansas v. 14, p. 141, RGDC.

21. For articles on the depression throughout the rest of the country see "Coxey's

Army Aided," and "It Couldn't Prevent Poverty: A Widow Forced to Sell Much-Prized Lucky Cap," *San Francisco Chronicle*, April 2, 1894, 2–3; and "Labor and Capital-Strikers Anxious to Get Work," ibid., August 7, 1894, 2.

22. Soper's health must have begun to fail by 1894 because she was under the constant care of a doctor beginning in 1898. For more on the details of her life, see the end of this chapter. Mary A. Soper, "Duplicate Certificate of Death," August 21, 1911, California State Department of Health, in the author's possession. This document was possible to obtain only because Soper lived an unusually long life and died after 1906. All records prior to 1906 were destroyed in the earthquake and fire of that year.

23. *San Francisco Chronicle*, September 14, 1869.

24. Benjamin E. Lloyd, *Lights and Shades of San Francisco*, Chapter 74, "Kearney and Montgomery Streets: Fashionable Thoroughfares"; and Edward A. Morphy, "San Francisco's Thoroughfares: Montgomery Street," *San Francisco Chronicle*, June 1, 1919.

25. Lizzie Carter, case #1311, San Francisco, 1873, BCF.

26. Had Lizzie Carter made any decisions that hastened the failure of her business? Perhaps. By purchasing her drugs at Wakelee's, she may have been extravagant —one of the certain deadly sins for businesspeople, as the last chapter has demonstrated. The *Chronicle's* San Francisco Thoroughfares columnist, Edward A. Morphy wrote that "for many years the corner where Wakelee's drug store used to be, under the Occidental Hotel, was probably the most fashionable in the city. That is to say, if one stood there long enough he would see more leaders of local business, thought and fashion than at any other point in the city." Morphy, San Francisco's Thoroughfares, *San Francisco Chronicle*, June 1, 1919. Because of its location, Wakelee's was likely not the most affordable place to buy drugs.

27. Sallie Snow to her sister, November 21, 1868, SSP.

28. The 1868 epidemic was so serious that the *Oakland News* published an announcement that San Francisco was under quarantine and cautioned Oaklanders against paying "unnecessary visits to th[e] city during the prevalence of the small pox." Quoted in *Daily Alta California*, December 15, 1868.

29. *Daily Alta California*, September 6, 1868.

30. Angel Island was a quarantine station before it became an immigration station between 1910 and 1940, processing 175,000 mainly Chinese immigrants, some of them incarcerated in the island's primitive barracks for months at a time. See Him Mark Lai, Genny Lim, and Judy Yung, *Island: Poetry and History of Chinese Immigrants on Angel Island, 1910–1940* (Seattle: University of Washington Press, 1991).

31. Marilyn Chase, *The Barbary Plague: The Black Death in Victorian San Francisco* (New York: Random House, 2003), 12–13, 16, 54, 70, 194–95.

32. Ibid., 53.

33. "Cordon of City Police Is Drawn Around Chinatown," *San Francisco Examiner*, May 30, 1900, p. 3; cited in Chase, *The Barbary Plague*, 62.

34. Six pamphlets from the 'Anti-Jap Laundry League' are included in the Appendix of Lillian R. Matthews, "Women in Trade Unions in San Francisco," in *University of California Publications in Economics* 3, no. 1, ed. Adolph C. Miller (Berkeley: University of California Press, 1913).

35. Charles J. McClain, *In Search of Equality: The Chinese Struggle against Discrimination in Nineteenth-Century America* (Berkeley: University of California Press, 1994), 234–76.

36. Chase, *The Barbary Plague*, 173.

37. Ibid., 177.

38. Starr, *Americans and the California Dream*, 161.

39. Margaret De Witt to her mother, December 29, 1849, De Witt Family Papers, Bancroft Library, University of California, Berkeley, Calif.

40. Until 1866 San Franciscans relied on volunteer fire companies modeled after similar civic organizations in eastern cities such as New York, Boston, Philadelphia, and Baltimore. But in that year, the city replaced these volunteers with "a department of full time paid firemen." Decker, *Fortunes and Failures*, 109.

41. Mrs. A. H. Stoppelkamp, California v. 17, p. 104, RGDC.

42. "Rates of Insurance," Home Mutual Insurance Company, 1865, Huntington Library, San Marino, Calif.

43. See advertisement by Mrs. J. Wheelock for millinery goods she had for sale in the *Daily Alta California*, June 30, 1852.

44. "Fires Last Evening," ibid., September 12, 1871.

45. Clyde Griffen and Sally Griffen, "Small Business and Occupational Mobility In Mid-Nineteenth-Century Poughkeepsie," in *Small Business in American Life*, ed. Stuart W. Bruchey (New York: Columbia University Press, 1980), 128.

46. Duane A. Smith argues that "fireproof buildings placed at strategic points acted as a break among the surrounding wooden structures" in mining towns. Smith, *Rocky Mountain Mining Camps* (Bloomington: Indiana University Press, 1967), 95. Of course, as the 1906 fire illustrated, "fireproof" buildings were not, in fact, safe from incineration. Only scorched and hollow brick shells remained at the end of the three-day conflagration.

47. See, for example, Mrs. Margaret M. Nicholds advertisement in the *Daily Alta California*, November 3, 1855, for "first class private boarding . . . [in a] large fire proof brick house."

48. Baker's location in a brick building was also connected to her ability to procure insurance on her stock of millinery goods. Insurance companies assessed risk and assigned cost based on the likelihood that the stock being insured would be destroyed by fire. Thus in its 1865 pamphlet, the Home Mutual Insurance Company listed a "1st Class" rate of insurance for any brick or stone building with all openings protected by iron shutters. When such buildings were within twenty-five feet of a frame building, insurance cost nearly twice as much, while stores located in frame buildings were charged up to 5 percent more than those in brick ones. Moving into a brick building, therefore, made it easier and less expensive for Baker to procure a policy. "Rates of Insurance," Home Mutual Insurance Company, 1865, Huntington Library, San Marino, Calif.

49. Robert O'Brien, "Pageant of the Years—'60s: Grain, Grapes," *San Francisco Chronicle*, September 9, 1950, RCS.

50. Sallie Snow to her sister, November 21, 1868, SSP.

51. Ibid.

52. According to California historians Walton Bean and James Rawls, "early estimates of the loss of life put the figure at about 450." But, they continue, "more recent research has indicated that as many as 2,500 people may have been killed in the disaster and property valued at $1 billion was destroyed." Bean and Rawls, *California: An Interpretive History*, 5th ed. (New York: McGraw-Hill, 1988), 241. One admittedly unscholarly account of the earthquake ventures that the quake would have measured 8.25 on the Richter Scale. Barry Parr, *San Francisco* (Oakland, Calif.: Compass American Guides, 1996), 42.

53. Leigh added her comment on the earthquake and fire (in different ink and script) to her December 14, 1905, diary entry without listing a new date. Ella (Lees) Leigh, diary entry, December 14, 1905, Lees Family Papers, Bancroft Library, University of California, Berkeley, Calif.

54. Like other areas beyond the city center, the Western Addition—so called when the area was annexed in the 1870s for the city's expanding population—was used as a refuge for residents fleeing the four-day fire. Carrie Mangels, for example, wrote that in the midst of the confusion surrounding the earthquake and fire, "two men came around and told everybody to go to Oakland or the Western Addition, as they were going to dynamite as far as Polk Street." Carrie A. Mangels to her Uncle John, July 20, 1906, Carrie A. Mangels Papers, SFEFC. The famous row of nineteenth-century Victorian homes on Steiner Street, often called "the painted ladies" in tourist literature, is further evidence of the survival of pre-earthquake structures in the Western Addition. For a photograph of the neighborhood right after the disaster, see William Bronson, *The Earth Shook, the Sky Burned* (San Francisco: Chronicle Books, 1959), 89.

55. Bronson, *The Earth Shook*, 26–27, 36. One city resident reported that the majority of those camping out in tents were "of the poorer class and only paid from about $7 to $15 rent and as the main portion of the unburned district is composed of fine flats and residences with rents ranging from $25 to $50 and upwards, it will be sometime before they are housed." Carrie Mangels to unknown, no date, Carrie A. Mangels Papers, SFEFC.

56. Carrie A. Mangels to unknown, no date, Carrie A. Mangels Papers, SFEFC.

57. Bronson, *The Earth Shook*, 88.

58. Kevin Starr, "Thinking Catastrophically," in *San Francisco Chronicle*, March 31, 2006, 1906 Earthquake 100th Anniversary Commemorative: A Special Section Presented by the California Historical Society, April 2006. See also Philip L. Fradkin, "The Great Earthquake and Firestorms of 1906," in the same section.

59. Recent books on the disaster include Philip L. Fradkin, *The Great Earthquake and Firestorms of 1906: How San Francisco Nearly Destroyed Itself* (Berkeley: University of California Press, 2005); and Simon Winchester, *A Crack in the Edge of the World: America and the Great California Earthquake of 1906* (New York: HarperCollins, 2005). In his review of Fradkin's book Jeff Wiltse accuses the author of writing a "moralistic and judgemental account" in which "greedy, imperious, and racist" city leaders "subvert[ed] democracy, discriminating against the poor and racial minorities, and prioritizing economic redevelopment." *Reviews in American History* 33 (Winter 2005): 545–52.

60. *San Francisco City Directory, 1905* (San Francisco: Crocker-Langley, 1905); *San Francisco City Directory, 1907* (San Francisco: Crocker-Langley, 1907); *San Francisco City Directory, 1908* (San Francisco: Crocker-Langley, 1908). In each case, the classified business section of the directory was used to prepare these figures.

61. *San Francisco City Directory, 1905*; *San Francisco City Directory, 1907*; *San Francisco City Directory, 1908*. Because lodging houses were often listed in the directory as, for example, "The Abbey," with no proprietor, the figure listed here is for the number of female proprietors whose names were specifically listed. It almost certainly underestimates how many female lodging house owners there actually were.

62. These figures are estimates, composed by counting the number of columns under the heading "lodging" for each year and multiplying that number by ninety-two, the average number of names in each column. They estimate lodging house keepers only. *San Francisco City Directory, 1905*; *San Francisco City Directory, 1907*; *San Francisco City Directory, 1908*.

63. Bronson, *The Earth Shook*, 45. The page includes a photograph of the mayor's published proclamation, dated April 18, 1906.

64. Carrie A. Mangels to her Uncle John, July 20, 1906, Carrie A. Mangels Papers, SFEFC.

65. Bronson, *The Earth Shook*, 101, 103, especially photos. Crockery must have been in particular demand. In thanks to family members who sent a post-earthquake package, Mrs. Blight wrote, "The dishes came in mighty handy, it is very hard to get dishes here now as most of them all around are broken." Mrs. T. J. Blight to her Folks, May 11, 1906, Mrs. T. J. Blight Papers (MS 3463), SFEFC. Rummaging through the ruins also produced souvenirs that were popular with "tourists" who ferried over from the East Bay. Bronson, *The Earth Shook*, 166, photos.

66. Mother Symmes to Mabel and Harold Symmes, April 19, 1906, Edith Bonnell Papers (MS 3465), SFEFC.

67. Mrs. T. J. Blight to family, May 3, 1906, Mrs. T. J. Blight Papers (MS 3463), SFEFC.

68. "Reminiscences of Eddie Joseph, VP-Stores" (1959), Box B, IMC. Joseph claims that a shipment of French imports in the Custom House was spared in the fire and was sold by the Magnins in their makeshift location.

69. Edith Bonnell to Harold Symmes, no date, Edith Bonnell Papers, SFEFC. See also photo entitled "The Oyster Loaf and Chat Noir, 1617 Oak Street," picturing two hastily thrown-together shacks from which women sold food. California Historical Society, FN-33958.

70. Carrie Mangels to unknown, unknown date, Carrie A. Mangels Papers, SFEFC.

71. The Magnins reportedly benefited from a $50,000 loan from I. W. Hellman, president of Wells Fargo Bank, which he provided without security. John Magnin, Mary Ann Magnin's eldest son, who by then was in charge of the company's fortunes, brokered the deal. Such "gentlemen's agreements" were, of course, out of reach for typical women-owned businesses. "Chronology of Company History," IMC.

72. The distribution of relief funds was tracked and analyzed in Charles J. O'Connor et al., *San Francisco Relief Survey: The Organization and Methods of Relief*

Used After the Earthquake and Fire of April 18, 1906 (San Francisco: Russell Sage Foundation, 1913). For more on the use of these funds, see "Financing a New Business" in Chapter 3.

73. While earthquake insurance did not exist in 1906, many city residents held fire insurance policies and made claims for damages that resulted from the conflagration following the quake. Insurance companies were, of course, overburdened by the enormity of the loss and the resulting claims. Evidence of this can be found in Samuel Richards Weed, "My Early Experiences and Recollections of the Great Fires and the First Fire Department in San Francisco," Huntington Library, San Marino, Calif. But some insurance companies did pay customers' claims. William Bronson asserts that "only six companies made adjustments quickly and then paid off in full without delay and without asking cash discounts." Others used shady tactics to reduce the enormous sums they owed. Bronson, *The Earth Shook*, 111–14.

74. Maria J. Stacom, California v. 16, p. 341, RGDC; *San Francisco City Directory, 1877/78*; *San Francisco City Directory, 1889* (San Francisco: Crocker-Langley, 1889); *San Francisco City Directory, 1900* (San Francisco: Crocker-Langley, 1900); *San Francisco City Directory, 1905*; *San Francisco City Directory, 1908*.

75. Compared to Mary Soper, Stacom gets much less treatment in the credit reports. But what Dun evaluators did note about her is that when her business faced failure in 1876, rather than waiting for creditors to make a petition in bankruptcy against her, she called a meeting and asked them for an extension on her liabilities. Unsympathetic to her situation, the creditors moved forward with their petition against her, but her initiative highlights a rare and aggressive management style. Maria J. Stacom, California v. 16, p. 341, RGDC.

76. Decker, *Fortunes and Failures*, 92.

77. Ibid., 92.

78. Madame C. Goldberg, California v. 15, p. 5, RGDC.

79. Edward J. Balleisen, "Vulture Capitalism in Antebellum America: The 1841 Federal Bankruptcy Act and the Exploitation of Financial Distress," *Business History Review* 70 (Winter 1996): 473–516.

80. Mrs. C. M. Chapman, California v. 18, p. 123, RGDC.

81. Murphy & McCarthy, California v. 16, p. 324, RGDC.

82. *Daily Alta California*, September 2, 1870.

83. Contemporary San Franciscan Benjamin E. Lloyd, for example, wrote that "one, and sometimes two, of every four corners formed by the streets crossing each other, throughout the city, even in the remote suburbs, is generally occupied by a corner grocery." It was also common, Lloyd suggests, for these corner groceries to contain bar rooms, like Mrs. McCarthy's, which he says were "largely patronized as 'loafing places' by the mechanics, laborers and idlers, whose homes are in the neighborhood." Lloyd, *Lights and Shades*, 180–85.

84. Scott A. Sandage, *Born Losers: A History of Failure in America* (Cambridge: Harvard University Press, 2005), 5.

85. Susan Strasser, *Satisfaction Guaranteed: The Making of the American Mass Market* (Washington, D.C.: Smithsonian Institution Press, 1989), 65.

86. Deutsch, *Women and the City*, 127.

87. Hubert H. Bancrfot, *California Inter Pocula* (San Francisco, 1880), 341; cited in Decker, *Fortunes and Failures*, 91.

88. Gordon Morris Bakken, *Practicing Law in Frontier California* (Lincoln: University of Nebraska Press, 1991), 52. California made bankruptcy easy, Bakken writes, and in at least one way made debt collection more difficult for creditors. They only had two years from the "date of the accrual of an action for commencement of a lawsuit."(51) In plain language, once creditors placed an attachment on a debtor's assets, he or she only had two years to begin court proceedings for recovery of the money owed them. Even more importantly, California provided a fresh start for travelling debtors. State law prohibited a creditor from filing an attachment against a debtor unless the debt had been contracted in California. Thus businessmen and -women who contracted debts in New York could not be reached by their creditors once they relocated to California. As a result, Bakken writes, "California was known as a haven for debtors."(51)

89. Gamber, *The Female Economy*, 37.

90. Susan Ingalls Lewis finds the same rate of failure for Albany businesswomen in the R. G. Dun & Company credit reports: 46 out of 241, or about 20 percent, were listed as "out of business." Lewis, "Women in the Marketplace: Female Entrepreneurship, Business Patterns, and Working Families in Mid-Nineteenth-Century Albany, New York, 1830-1885 (Ph.D. diss, State University of New York, Binghamton, 2002), 226.

91. Lizzie Carter, California v. 20, p. 314, RGDC.

92. Mary A. Soper, "Duplicate Certificate of Death." While the certificate states that Soper was widowed, it lists no information about survivors. But the informant listed on her death certificate, Frank W. Dean, could provide no information about her family background, such as her mother's maiden name or father's place of birth. A family member would likely know such information.

93. Allan Goodman, family service manager, Cypress Lawn Memorial Park, letter to author, August 4, 1998.

94. Mary A. Soper, "Duplicate Certificate of Death."

CONCLUSION

1. G. K. Stephens and D. C. Feldman, "A Motivational Approach for Understanding Work Versus Personal Life Investments," *Research in Personnel and Human Resources Management* 15 (1997), 333-78; cited in Daniel C. Feldman and Mark C. Bolino, "Career Patterns of the Self-Employed: Career Motivations and Career Outcomes," *Journal of Small Business Management* 38 (July 2000): 2.

2. Marilyn M. Helms, "Women and Entrepreneurship: The Appealing Alternative," *Business Perspectives*, July 1997, 16.

3. Ibid.

4. Barbara De Lollis, "No 'Glass Ceiling' Over Women Entrepreneurs," *San Francisco Business Times*, September 18, 1992, 13.

5. Kathy Peiss, "'Vital Industry' and Women's Ventures: Conceptualizing Gender in Twentieth-Century Business History," *Business History Review* 72 (Summer 1998): 219.

6. "Nothing Ventured," *Business Week*, July 10, 2000, F28.

7. Susan Coleman, "Access to Capital and Terms of Credit: A Comparison of Men- and Women-Owned Small Businesses," *Journal of Small Business Management* 38 (July 2000): 37.

8. "Where Women Get Credit," *Inc.*, November 1999, 1.

9. The National Foundation for Women Business Owners, <http://www.nfwo .org/LocLink/BIZC/RESEARCH/LinkTo/5-11-1999/5-11-1999.htm> (October 15, 2000).

10. Wendy Gamber, "A Gendered Enterprise: Placing Nineteenth-Century Businesswomen in History," *Business History Review* 72 (Summer 1998): 188.

11. Candida G. Brush, "Research on Women Business Owners: Past Trends, a New Perspective, and Future Directions," *Entrepreneurship: Theory and Practice* 16 (Summer 1992): 5.

12. Research has shown, for example, that the top growth industries for women between 1987 and 1996 were construction, wholesale trade, transportation, communications, agribusiness, and manufacturing. Sharon Nelton, "Women's Firms Thrive," *Nation's Business*, August 1998, 38. Women's slow entry into such capital-intensive industries is certainly linked with the difficulty in accessing venture capital. Prior to 2000, women-owned firms only received 2–5 percent of the venture capital money distributed each year. In the first quarter of 2000, however, the figure rose to 12.7 percent, indicating a significant improvement in accessibility. Lyn Berry, "Women Search for Funds," *Denver Business Journal*, August 18, 2000, 1A; "Nothing Ventured," *Business Week*, July 10, 2000, F28.

SELECTED BIBLIOGRAPHY

—— ❖ ❉ ❖ ——

ARCHIVAL AND MANUSCRIPT SOURCES

Berkeley, Calif.
> Bancroft Library, University of California
>> Bourn and Ingalls Family Papers
>> De Witt Family Papers
>> Lees Family Papers
>> Mrs. Joseph Newmark Papers
>> Mary Ellen Pleasant Papers
>> Sallie Snow Papers

Cambridge, Mass.
> Baker Library, Harvard Business School
>> R. G. Dun and Company Collection

San Bruno, Calif.
> National Archives and Records Administration, Pacific Region
>> Bankruptcy Case Files, 1872–76, 1878, 1898–1900, 1903, 1906, 1909, 1912, 1915, 1918, 1921, Records of the U.S. District Court, Northern District of California, Northern Division, San Francisco, Records of U.S. District Courts (Record Group 21)

San Francisco, Calif.
> Bank of America Archives
>> Bank of Italy Collection
> California Historical Society
>> Benjamin Butler Papers

Jessie Anderson Cameron Papers
Hitchcock Family Papers
Lucy Jones Diary
Robert O'Brien, Riptides Column Scrapbook
Catherine Oliver, unsigned letter
Journal of Alfred and Chastina Rix
San Francisco Earthquake and Fire Collection
    Mrs. T. J. Blight Papers
    Edith Bonnell Papers
    Carrie A. Mangels Papers
Mary S. D. Smith Papers
Edward D. Weld Papers
San Francisco History Center, San Francisco Public Library
    I. Magnin Collection, SFH 2
    Trade Card Collection

San Marino, Calif.
    Huntington Library
        Bicknell Collection
        Business Women's Legislative Council of California Collection
        Home Mutual Insurance Company
        David Jacks Collection
        Lura Case Smith Papers
        Trade Cards, Ephemera Files
        Samuel Richards Weed, "My Early Experiences and Recollections of the Great Fires and First Fire Department in San Francisco"

GOVERNMENT DOCUMENTS

Hill, Joseph A. *Women in Gainful Occupations*. Census Monographs 9. Washington, D.C.: Government Printing Office, 1929.

U.S. Census Bureau. *Report on the Population of the United States at the Eighth Census*. Washington, D.C.: Government Printing Office, 1860.

———. *Ninth Census: The Statistics of the Population of the United States*. Washington, D.C.: Government Printing Office, 1872.

———. *Compendium of the Tenth Census*. Washington, D.C.: Government Printing Office, 1883.

———. *Report on the Population of the United States at the Eleventh Census*. Washington, D.C.: Government Printing Office, 1895.

———. *The Twelfth Census of the United States Taken in the Year 1900: Population*. Washington, D.C.: Government Printing Office, 1901.

———. *Thirteenth Census of the United States Taken in the Year 1910: Population, Occupation Statistics*. Washington, D.C.: Government Printing Office, 1914.

———. *Fourteenth Census of the United States Taken in the Year 1920: Population*. Washington, D.C.: Government Printing Office, 1921.

———. *Fifteenth Census of the United States, 1930: Population*. Washington, D.C.: Government Printing Office, 1933.

DIRECTORIES

San Francisco City Directory. San Francisco: Kimball, 1850, 1859/60. San Francisco: Gilman and Swanwick, 1872/73. San Francisco: Polk, 1877/78. San Francisco: Crocker-Langley: 1888, 1889, 1892, 1896, 1897, 1899, 1900, 1905, 1907, 1908, 1909, 1915, 1920.

NEWSPAPERS

Daily Alta California, 1851–90
San Francisco Bulletin, 1902–14
San Francisco Chronicle, 1850–1902

LEGAL STATUTES AND INTERPRETATIONS OF THE LAW

Blumberg, Grace Ganz. *Community Property in California*. Boston: Little, Brown, 1987.

Deering, F. P. *Deering's Annotated Codes and Statutes of California: Civil Code*. San Francisco: Bancroft-Whitney, 1886.

Index to the Laws of California, 1850–1920. Sacramento: California State Printing Office, 1921.

McMurray, Orrin K. *Community Property, Contributed to California Jurisprudence, 1930 Supplement*. Berkeley, Calif.: Bancroft-Whitney, 1930.

Mechem, Floyd R., ed. *Elements of the Law of Partnership*. 2nd ed. Chicago: Callaghan, 1920.

———. *Cases on the Law of Partnership*. 4th ed. Chicago: Callaghan, 1924.

Reppy, William A., Jr. *Community Property in California: Cases, Statutes, Problems*. Charlottesville, Va.: Michie Company Law Publishers, 1980.

Statutes of California and Digests of Measures . . . General Laws, Amendments to the Codes, Resolutions, and Constitutional Amendments passed by the California Legislature. 1979–80 Regular Session. Vol. 1. (St. Paul, Minn.: West Publishing, 1980).

The Statutes of California, passed at the Thirteenth Session of the Legislature, 1862. Sacramento, Calif.: Benj. P. Avery, State Printer, 1862.

Stocker, Archibald H. *Business Ownership Organization*. New York: Henry Holt, 1922.

PUBLISHED PRIMARY SOURCES

Ballou, Mary. *"I Hear Hogs in My Kitchen": A Woman's View of the Gold Rush*. New Haven: Yale University Press, 1962.

Bancroft, Hubert Howe. *History of California*. Vol. 24. 1890. Reprint, Santa Barbara, Calif.: Wallace Hebberd, 1970.

Boer, A. E. "Mortality Costs in Retail Trades." *Journal of Marketing* 2 (July 1937): 52–60.

Cleland, Robert Glass, ed. *Apron Full of Gold: The Letters of Mary Jane Megquier from San Francisco*. San Marino, Calif.: Huntington Library, 1949.

Eaves, Lucille. *A History of California Labor Legislation: With an Introductory Sketch of the San Francisco Labor Movement*. Berkeley: University of California Press, 1910.

Hutchinson, Ruth Gillette, Arthur R. Hutchinson, and Mabel Newcomer. "A Study of Business Mortality: Length of Life of Business Enterprises in Poughkeepsie, New York, 1843–1936." *American Economic Review* 28 (September 1938): 497–514.

Lloyd, Benjamin E. *Lights and Shades of San Francisco*. San Francisco: A. L. Bancroft, 1876.

MacGregor, William Laird. *Hotels and Hotel Life at San Francisco California in 1876*. San Francisco: San Francisco News Company, 1877.

Matthews, Lillian R. "Women in Trade Unions in San Francisco." In *University of California Publications in Economics* 3, no. 1, edited by Adolph C. Miller, Appendix. Berkeley: University of California Press, 1913.

McGarry, E. D. *Mortality in Retail Trade*. University of Buffalo Studies in Business 4 (1930).

Nystrom, Paul H. *The Economics of Retailing: A Textbook for Colleges and Schools of Business Administration*. 2nd ed. New York: Ronald Press, 1920.

O'Connor, Charles J., et al. *San Francisco Relief Survey: The Organization and Methods of Relief Used After the Earthquake and Fire of April 18, 1906*. San Francisco: Russell Sage Foundation, 1913.

Perry, Lorinda. *The Millinery Trade in Boston and Philadelphia: A Study of Women in Industry*. Binghamton, N.Y.: Vail-Ballou Company Press, 1916.

Soulé, Frank, John H. Gihon, and James Nisbet. *The Annals of San Francisco*. New York: D. Appleton, 1854.

Swett, John. *History of the Public School System of California*. San Francisco: A. L. Bancroft, 1876.

Victor, Frances Fuller. *The New Penelope, A Novella*. San Francisco: A. L. Bancroft, 1877.

Wright, Wilson, ed. *Luzena Stanley Wilson '49er: Memories Recalled Years Later for Her Daughter*. Oakland, Calif.: Eucalyptus Press, 1937.

Wyman, Walker D., ed. *California Emigrant Letters*. New York: Bookman Associates, 1952.

SECONDARY SOURCES

Averbach, Alvin. "San Francisco's South of Market District, 1850–1950: The Emergence of a Skid Row." *California Historical Quarterly* 52 (Fall 1973): 197–223.

Backhouse, Constance. "White Women's Labor Laws: Anti-Chinese Racism in Early Twentieth-Century Canada." *Law and History Review* 14, no. 2 (1996): 315–68.

Bakken, Gordon Morris. *The Development of Law on the Rocky Mountain Frontier: Civil Law and Society, 1850–1912*. Westport, Conn.: Greenwood Press, 1983.

———. *Practicing Law in Frontier California*. Lincoln: University of Nebraska Press, 1991.

Balleisen, Edward J. "Vulture Capitalism in Antebellum America: The 1841 Federal Bankruptcy Act and the Exploitation of Financial Distress." *Business History Review* 70 (Winter 1996): 473–516.

Banner, Lois W. *American Beauty*. New York: Alfred A. Knopf, 1983.

Barth, Gunther. *Instant Cities: Urbanization and the Rise of San Francisco and Denver*. New York: Oxford University Press, 1975.

Basch, Norma. *In the Eyes of the Law: Women, Marriage, and Property in Nineteenth-Century New York*. Ithaca, N.Y.: Cornell University Press, 1982.

Beasley, Delilah. *Negro Trail Blazers of California*. Los Angeles: James Stevenson, 1919.

Bederman, Gail. *Manliness and Civilization: A Cultural History of Gender and Race in the United States, 1880–1917*. Chicago: University of Chicago Press, 1995.

Benson, Susan Porter. *Counter Cultures: Saleswomen, Managers, and Customers in American Department Stores, 1890–1940*. Urbana: University of Illinois Press, 1986.

Berthoff, Roland. "Independence and Enterprise: Small Business in the American Dream." In *Small Business in American Life*, edited by Stuart W. Bruchey, 28–48. New York: Columbia University Press, 1980.

Bird, Caroline. *Enterprising Women*. New York: W. W. Norton, 1976.

Blackford, Mansel. "Small Business in America: A Historiographical Survey." *Business History Review* 65, no. 1 (Spring 1991): 1–26.

———. *A History of Small Business in America*. 2nd ed. Chapel Hill: University of North Carolina Press, 2003.

Blackmar, Elizabeth. *Manhattan for Rent, 1785–1850*. Ithaca, N.Y.: Cornell University Press, 1989.

Blewett, Mary H., *Men, Women, and Work: Class, Gender, and Protest in the New England Shoe Industry, 1780–1910*. Urbana: University of Illinois Press, 1988.

Blumin, Stuart M. *The Emergence of the Middle Class: Social Experience in the American City, 1760–1900*. New York: Cambridge University Press, 1989.

Boydston, Jeanne. *Home and Work: Housework, Wages, and the Ideology of Labor in the Early Republic*. New York: Oxford University Press, 1990.

Brechin, Gray. *Imperial San Francisco: Urban Power, Earthly Ruin*. Berkeley: University of California Press, 1999.

Bristol, Douglas, Jr. "From Outposts to Enclaves: A Social History of Black Barbers from 1750–1915." *Enterprise and Society: The International Journal of Business History* 5 (December 2004): 594–606.

Bronson, William. *The Earth Shook, the Sky Burned*. San Francisco: Chronicle Books, 1959.

Broussard, Albert S. *Black San Francisco: The Struggle for Racial Equality in the West, 1900–1954*. Lawrence: University Press of Kansas, 1993.

Bruchey, Stuart W., ed. *Small Business in American Life*. New York: Columbia University Press, 1980.

Burchell, Robert A. *The San Francisco Irish, 1848–1880*. Manchester, U.K.: Manchester University Press, 1979.

Castañeda. Antonia. "Women of Color and the Rewriting of Western History: The Discourse, Politics, and Decolonization of History." *Pacific Historical Review* 61 (November 1992): 501–33.

Chandler, Alfred. *The Visible Hand: The Managerial Revolution in American Business*. Cambridge: Harvard University Press, 1977.

———. *Scale and Scope: The Dynamics of Industrial Capitalism*. Cambridge: Harvard University Press, 1990.

Chase, Marilyn. *The Barbary Plague: The Black Death in Victorian San Francisco*. New York: Random House, 2003.

Chávez-García, Miroslava. *Negotiating Conquest: Gender and Power in California, 1770s to 1880s*. Tucson: University of Arizona Press, 2004.

Cherny, Robert W., and William Issel. *San Francisco, 1865–1932: Politics, Power, and Urban Development* (Berkeley: University of California Press, 1986).

———. *San Francisco: Presidio, Port and Pacific Metropolis*. Sparks, Nev.: Materials For Today's Learning, 1988.

Chused, Richard. "Married Women's Property Law: 1800–1850." *Georgetown Law Journal* 71 (June 1983): 1359–1425.

Cleary, Patricia. "'She Will Be in the Shop': Women's Sphere of Trade in Eighteenth-Century Philadelphia and New York." *Pennsylvania Magazine of History and Biography* 119 (July 1995): 181–202.

———. *Elizabeth Murray: A Woman's Pursuit of Independence in Eighteenth-Century America*. (Amherst: University of Massachusetts Press, 2000).

Cochran, Thomas. *200 Years of American Business*. New York: Basic Books, 1977.

Cocks, Catherine. *Doing the Town: The Rise of Urban Tourism in the United States, 1850–1915*. Berkeley: University of California Press, 2001.

Coleman, Willi. "African American Women and Community Development in California, 1848–1900." In *Seeking El Dorado: African Americans in California*, edited by Lawrence B. de Graaf, Kevin Mulroy, and Quintard Taylor, 98–125. Seattle: University of Washington Press, 2001.

Conlin, Joseph R. *Bacons, Beans, and Galantines: Food and Foodways on the Western Mining Frontier*. Reno: University of Nevada Press, 1986.

Cowan, Ruth Schwartz. *More Work for Mother: The Ironies of Household Technology from the Open Hearth to the Microwave*. New York: Basic Books, 1983.

Cross, Ralph Herbert. *The Early Inns of California, 1844–1869*. San Francisco: privately printed, 1954.

Cummings, Scott, ed. *Self-Help in Urban America: Patterns of Minority Business Enterprise*. Port Washington, N.Y.: Kennikat, 1980.

Dahlin, Michael, Carole Shammas, and Marylynn Salmon. *Inheritance in America: From Colonial Times to the Present*. New Brunswick, N.J.: Rutgers University Press, 1987.

Daily, Christine. "A Woman's Concern: Millinery in Central Iowa, 1870–1880." *Journal of the West* 21, no. 2 (1982): 26–32.

Daniels, Douglas Henry. *Pioneer Urbanites: A Social and Cultural History of Black San Francisco*. Philadelphia: Temple University Press, 1980.

Davidoff, Leonore, and Catherine Hall, eds. *Family Fortunes: Men and Women of the English Middle Class, 1780–1850*. New York: Routledge, 1987.

Davies, Margery W. *Woman's Place Is at the Typewriter: Office Work and Office Workers, 1870–1930*. Philadelphia: Temple University Press, 1982.

Davis, W. N., Jr. "Research Uses of County Court Records, 1850–1879 and Incidental Glimpses of California Life and Society, Part I." *California Historical Quarterly* 52 (Fall 1973): 160–241.

———. "Research Uses of County Court Records, 1850–1879 and Incidental Glimpses of California Life and Society, Part II." *California Historical Quarterly* 52 (Winter 1973): 338–65.

Decker, Peter R. *Fortunes and Failures: White-Collar Mobility in Nineteenth-Century San Francisco*. Cambridge: Harvard University Press, 1978.

Deutsch, Sarah. *Women and the City: Gender, Space, and Power in Boston, 1870–1940*. New York: Oxford University Press, 2000.

Deverall, William. *Railroad Crossing: Californians and the Railroad, 1850–1910*. Berkeley: University of California Press, 1994.

Dexter, Elisabeth A. *Colonial Women of Affairs: A Study of Women in Business and the Professions in America before 1776*. Boston: Houghton Mifflin, 1924.

Dicke, Thomas S. *Franchising in America: The Development of a Business Method, 1840–1980*. Chapel Hill: University of North Carolina Press, 1992.

Diner, Hasia R. *Erin's Daughters in America: Irish Immigrant Women in the Nineteenth Century*. Baltimore: Johns Hopkins University Press, 1983.

———. *Hungering for America: Italian, Irish, and Jewish Foodways in the Age of Migration*. Cambridge: Harvard University Press, 2001.

Dorsett, Lyle W. "Equality of Opportunity on the Urban Frontier: Access to Credit in Denver, Colorado Territory, 1858–1876." *Journal of the West* 18, no. 3 (1979): 75–81.

Drachman, Virginia G. *Enterprising Women: 250 Years of American Business*. Chapel Hill: University of North Carolina Press, 2002.

Friedman, Lawrence. "Law and Small Business in the United States: One Hundred Years of Struggle and Accommodation." In *Small Business in American Life*, edited by Stuart W. Bruchey, 305–18. New York: Columbia University Press, 1980.

Gamber, Wendy. "A Precarious Independence: Milliners and Dressmakers in Boston, 1860–1890." *Journal of Women's History* 4 (Spring 1992): 60–88.

———. *The Female Economy: The Millinery and Dressmaking Trades, 1860–1930*. Urbana: University of Illinois Press, 1997.

———. "A Gendered Enterprise: Placing Nineteenth-Century Businesswomen in History." *Business History Review* 72 (Summer 1998): 188–218.

———. "Tarnished Labor: The Home, the Market, and the Boardinghouse in Antebellum America." *Journal of the Early Republic* 22 (Summer 2002): 177–204.

Gardner, Martha Mabie. "Working on White Womanhood: White Working

Women in the San Francisco Anti-Chinese Movement, 1877–1890." *Journal of Social History* 33, no. 1 (1999): 73–95.

Gerber, David. "Cutting Out Shylock: Elite Anti-Semitism and the Quest for Moral Order in the Mid-Nineteenth-Century American Marketplace." *Journal of American History* 69 (December 1982): 615–37.

Gill, Tiffany. "Civic Beauty: Beauty Culturists and the Politics of African American Female Entrepreneurship, 1900–1965." *Enterprise and Society: The International Journal of Business History* 5 (December 2004): 583–93.

Ginzburg, Lori D. *Women and the Work of Benevolence: Morality, Politics, and Class in the 19th-Century United States*. New Haven: Yale University Press, 1990.

Glenn, Evelyn Nakano. "From Servitude to Service Work: Historical Continuities in the Racial Division of Paid Reproductive Labor." In *Unequal Sisters: A Multicultural Reader in U.S. Women's History*, 2nd ed., edited by Vicki L. Ruiz and Ellen Carol DuBois, 405–35. New York: Routledge, 1994.

Goldin, Claudia. "The Economic Status of Women in the Early Republic: Quantitative Evidence." *Journal of Interdisciplinary History* 16 (Winter 1986): 375–404.

———. *Understanding the Gender Gap: An Economic History of American Women*. New York: Oxford University Press, 1990.

Gonzalez, Deena J. "La Tules of Image and Reality: Euro-American Attitudes and Legend Formation on a Spanish-Mexican Frontier." In *Unequal Sisters: A Multicultural Reader in U.S. Women's History*, 2nd ed., edited by Vicki L. Ruiz and Ellen Carol DuBois, 57–69. New York: Routledge, 1994.

Griffen, Clyde, and Sally Griffen. *Natives and Newcomers: The Ordering of Opportunity in Mid-Nineteenth-Century Poughkeepsie*. Cambridge: Harvard University Press, 1978.

———. "Small Business and Occupational Mobility in Mid-Nineteenth-Century Poughkeepsie." In *Small Business in American Life*, edited by Stuart W. Bruchey, 122–41. New York: Columbia University Press, 1980.

Griswold, Robert L. *Family and Divorce in California, 1850–1890: Victorian Illusions and Everyday Realities*. Albany: State University of New York Press, 1982.

Gross, Karen, Marie Stefanini, and Denise Campbell, "Ladies in Red: Learning from America's First Female Bankrupts." *American Journal of Legal History* 40 (January 1996): 1–40.

Gumina, Deanna Paoli. *The Italians of San Francisco, 1850–1930*. New York: Center for Migration Studies, 1985.

Guy, Donna J. "The Economics of Widowhood in Arizona, 1880–1940." In *On Their Own: Widows and Widowhood in the American Southwest, 1848–1939*, edited by Arlene Scadron, 195–223. Urbana: University of Illinois Press, 1988.

Hendrickson, Robert. *The Grand Emporium: The Illustrated History of America's Great Department Stores*. New York: Stein and Day, 1979.

Herr, Elizabeth. "Women, Marital Status, and Work Opportunities in 1880 Colorado." *Journal of Economic History* 55 (June 1995): 339–66.

Hirata, Lucie Cheng. "Free, Indentured, Enslaved: Chinese Prostitutes in Nineteenth-Century America." *Signs* 5 (Autumn 1979): 3–29.

Hoff, Joan. *Law, Gender, and Injustice: A Legal History of U.S. Women*. New York: New York University Press, 1991.

Hoganson, Kristin L. *Fighting for American Manhood: How Gender Politics Provoked the Spanish-American and Philippine-American Wars*. New Haven: Yale University Press, 1998.

Hollis, Aidan. "Women and Microcredit in History: Gender in the Irish Loan Funds." Unpublished paper. <http:www.econ.ucalgary.ca/fac-files/ah/women andloanfunds.pdf>. May 2004.

Horowitz, Daniel. *The Morality of Spending: Attitudes toward Consumer Society in America, 1875–1940*. Baltimore: Johns Hopkins University Press, 1991.

Hudson, Lynn M. "A New Look, or 'I'm Not Mammy to Everybody': Mary Ellen Pleasant, a Black Entrepreneur." *Journal of the West* 32, no. 3 (1993): 35–40.

———. *The Making of "Mammy Pleasant": A Black Entrepreneur in Nineteenth-Century San Francisco*. Urbana: University of Illinois Press, 2003.

Hurtado, Albert L. *Intimate Frontiers: Sex, Gender, and Culture in Old California*. Albuquerque: University of New Mexico Press, 1999.

Ingham, John N. "Patterns of African-American Female Self-Employment and Entrepreneurship in Ten Southern Cities, 1880-1933." In *Black Business and Economic Power*, edited by Alusine Jalloh and Toyin Falola. Rochester, N.Y.: University of Rochester Press, 2002.

James, Marquis, and Bessie R. James. *Biography of a Bank: The Story of Bank of America, 1904–1953*. San Francisco: Bank of America Corporate Archive, 1954.

James, Ronald M., Richard D. Adkins, and Rachel J. Hartigan. "Competition and Coexistence in the Laundry: A View of the Comstock." *Western Historical Quarterly* 25, no. 2 (1994): 164–84.

Jameson, Elizabeth, and Susan Armitage, eds. *Writing the Range: Race, Class and Culture in the Women's West*. Norman: University of Oklahoma Press, 1997.

Jeffrey, Julie Roy. *Frontier Women: The Trans-Mississippi West, 1840–1880*. New York: Hill and Wang, 1979.

Jensen, Joan. "Cloth, Butter, Boarders: Women's Household Production for the Market." *Review of Radical Political Economics* 12 (Summer 1980): 14–24.

———. *Promise to the Land: Essays on Rural Women*. Albuquerque: University of New Mexico Press, 1991.

Jensen, Joan, and Darlis Miller. "The Gentle Tamers Revisited: New Approaches to the History of Women in the West." *Pacific Historical Review* 49 (May 1980): 173–213.

Jensen, Joan, and Gloria Lathrop. *California Women: A History*. San Francisco: Boyd and Fraser, 1987.

Johnson, Susan Lee. "'A Memory Sweet to Soldiers': The Significance of Gender in the History of the 'American West.'" *Western Historical Quarterly* 24 (November 1993): 495–517.

———. *Roaring Camp: The Social World of the California Gold Rush*. New York: W. W. Norton, 2000.

Jolly, Michelle E. "Inventing the City: Gender and the Politics of Everyday Life in

Gold Rush San Francisco, 1848–1869." Ph.D. diss., University of California, San Diego, 1998.

Jones, Jacqueline. *Labor of Love, Labor of Sorrow: Black Women, Work and the Family, from Slavery to the Present*. New York: Vintage Books, 1986.

Katzman, David M. *Seven Days a Week: Women and Domestic Service in Industrializing America*. New York: Oxford University Press, 1978.

Kessler-Harris, Alice. *Out to Work: A History of Wage-Earning Women in the United States*. New York: Oxford University Press, 1982.

———. *A Woman's Wage: Historical Meanings and Social Consequences*. Lexington: University Press of Kentucky, 1990.

———. *In Pursuit of Equity: Women, Men, and the Quest for Economic Citizenship in 20th-Century America*. New York: Oxford University Press, 2001.

Kowalewski, Michael. "Imagining the California Gold Rush: The Visual and Verbal Legacy." *California History* 71 (Spring 1992): 61–73.

Kwolek-Folland, Angel. *Engendering Business: Men and Women in the Corporate Office, 1870–1930*. Baltimore: Johns Hopkins University Press, 1994.

———. "Customers and Neighbors: Women in the Economy of Lawrence, Kansas, 1870–1885." *Business and Economic History* 27 (Fall 1998): 129–39.

———. *Incorporating Women: A History of Women and Business in the United States*. New York: Twayne Publishers, 1998.

Kurutz, K. D., and Gary F. Kurutz, *California Calls You: The Art of Promoting the Golden State, 1870–1940*. Sausalito, Calif.: Windgate Press, 2000.

Lai, Him Mark, Genny Lim, and Judy Yung. *Island: Poetry and History of Chinese Immigrants on Angel Island, 1910–1940*. Seattle: University of Washington Press, 1991.

Lamoreaux, Naomi. "Constructing Firms: Partnerships and Alternative Contractual Arrangements in Early Nineteenth-Century American Business." *Business and Economic History* 24 (Winter 1995): 43–71.

Larson, T. A. "Women's Role in the American West." *Montana: The Magazine of Western History* 24 (Summer 1974): 2–11.

Leach, William. *Land of Desire: Merchants, Power, and the Rise of a New American Culture*. New York: Pantheon Books, 1993.

Lebsock, Suzanne. *The Free Women of Petersburg: Status and Culture in a Southern Town, 1784–1860*. New York: W. W. Norton, 1984.

Lee, Erika. *At America's Gates: Chinese Immigration during the Exclusion Era, 1882–1943*. Chapel Hill: University of North Carolina Press, 2003.

Lemire, Beverly. "Petty Pawns and Informal Lending: Gender and the Transformation of Small-Scale Credit in England, circa 1600–1800." In *From Family Firms to Corporate Capitalism: Essays in Business and Industrial History in Honour of Peter Mathias*, edited by Kristine Bruland and Patrick O'Brien, 112–38. Oxford, U.K.: Clarendon Press, 1998.

Lerner, Gerda. "Placing Women in History: Definitions and Challenges," *Feminist Studies* 3 (Fall 1975): 5–14.

Levenstein, Margaret. "African American Entrepreneurship: The View from the 1910 Census." *Business and Economic History* 24 (Fall 1995): 106–22.

Levinson, Robert E. *The Jews in the California Gold Rush*. New York: Ktav Publishing House, 1978.

Levy, JoAnn. *They Saw the Elephant: Women in the California Gold Rush*. Hamden, Conn.: Archon Books, 1990.

Lewis, Susan Ingalls. "Beyond Horatia Alger: Breaking through Gendered Assumptions about Business 'Success' in Mid-Nineteenth-Century America." *Business and Economic History* 24 (Fall 1995): 97–105.

———. "Women in the Marketplace: Female Entrepreneurship, Business Patterns, and Working Families in Mid-Nineteenth-Century Albany, New York, 1830–1885." Ph.D. diss., State University of New York, Binghamton, 2002.

Light, Ivan H. *Ethnic Enterprise in America: Business and Welfare among Chinese, Japanese, and Blacks*. Berkeley: University of California Press, 1972.

Livesay, Harold. "Entrepreneurial Dominance in Businesses Large and Small, Past and Present." *Business History Review* 63 (Spring 1989): 1–21.

Locke, Mary Lou. "'Like a Machine or an Animal': Working Women of the Late Nineteenth-Century Urban Far West, in San Francisco, Portland, and Los Angeles." Ph.D. diss., University of California, San Diego, 1982.

Lotchin, Roger W. *San Francisco, 1846–1856: From Hamlet to City*. New York: Oxford University Press, 1974.

———. *Fortress California, 1910–1960: From Warfare to Welfare*. New York: Oxford University Press, 1992.

Malcolmson, Patricia. *English Laundresses: A Social History, 1850–1930*. Urbana: University of Illinois Press, 1986.

Marchand, Roland. *Advertising the American Dream*. Berkeley: University of California Press, 1985.

Marovich, Lisa A. "'Let Her Have Brains Too': Commercial Networks, Public Relations, and the Business of Invention." *Business and Economic History* 27 (Fall 1998): 140–61.

Matthei, Julie E. *An Economic History of Women in America: Women's Work, the Sexual Division of Labor, and the Development of Capitalism*. New York: Schocken Books, 1982.

McClain, Charles J. *In Search of Equality: The Chinese Struggle against Discrimination in Nineteenth-Century America*. Berkeley: University of California Press, 1994.

Modell, John, and Tamara K. Hareven, "Urbanization and the Malleable Household: An Examination of Boarding and Lodging in American Families." *Journal of Marriage and the Family* 35 (August 1973): 467–79.

Mohun, Arwen P. *Steam Laundries: Gender, Technology, and Work in the United States and Great Britain, 1880–1940*. Baltimore: Johns Hopkins University Press, 1999.

Murphy, Lucy Eldersveld. "Her Own Boss: Businesswomen and Separate Spheres in the Midwest, 1850–1880." *Illinois Historical Journal* 80 (Autumn 1987): 155–76.

———. "Business Ladies: Midwestern Women and Enterprise, 1850–1880." *Journal of Women's History* 3 (Spring 1991): 65–89.

Myres, Sandra L. *Westering Women and the Frontier Experience, 1800–1915*. Albuquerque: University of New Mexico Press, 1982.

Narell, Irena Penzik. "The Jewish 49er in the New Land of Milk and Honey." *The Californians* 4 (March–April 1986): 14–20.

Nelson, Paula M. "'Do Everything'—Women in Small Prairie Towns, 1870–1920." *Journal of the West* 36 (October 1997): 52–60.

Nenadic, Stana. "The Social Shaping of Business Behaviour in the Nineteenth-Century Women's Garment Trades." *Journal of Social History* 31 (Spring 1998): 625–45.

Neu, Irene D. "The Jewish Businesswoman in America" *American Jewish Historical Quarterly* 66, no. 1 (1976): 137–54.

Olegario, Rowena. *A Culture of Credit: Embedding Trust and Transparency in American Business*. Cambridge: Harvard University Press, 2007.

Ong, Paul. "An Ethnic Trade: The Chinese Laundries in Early California." *Journal of Ethnic Studies* 8 (Winter 1981): 95–113.

Peffer, George Anthony. *If They Don't Bring Their Women Here: Chinese Female Immigration before Exclusion*. Urbana: University of Illinois Press, 1999.

Peiss, Kathy. *Hope in a Jar: The Making of America's Beauty Culture*. New York: Henry Holt, 1998.

———. "'Vital Industry' and Women's Ventures: Conceptualizing Gender in Twentieth-Century Business History." *Business History Review* 72 (Summer 1998): 218–41.

Petrik, Paula. *No Step Backward: Women and Family on the Rocky Mountain Mining Frontier, Helena, Montana, 1865–1900*. Helena: Montana Historical Society Press, 1987.

Pollay, Richard W. "The Subsiding Sizzle: A Descriptive History of Print Advertising, 1900–1980." *Journal of Marketing* 49 (Summer 1985): 24–37.

Rappaport, Erika. *Shopping for Pleasure*. Princeton: Princeton University Press, 2000.

Rath, Jan., ed., *Immigrant Businesses: The Economic, Political, and Social Environment*. New York: St. Martin's, 2000.

Rawls, James, and Richard Orsi, eds. *A Golden State: Mining and Economic Development in Gold Rush California*. Berkeley: University of California Press, 1998.

Rohrbaugh, Malcolm J. *Days of Gold: The California Gold Rush and the American Nation*. Berkeley: University of California Press, 1997.

Rotundo, E. Anthony. *American Manhood: Transformation in Masculinity from the Revolution to the Modern Era*. New York: Basic Books, 1993.

Ryan, Mary P. *Women in Public: Between Banners and Ballots, 1825–1880*. Baltimore: Johns Hopkins University Press, 1990.

Sandage, Scott. *Born Losers: A History of Failure in America*. Cambridge: Harvard University Press, 2005.

Sander, Kathleen W. *The Business of Charity: The Woman's Exchange Movement, 1832–1900*. Urbana: University of Illinois Press, 1998.

Saxton, Alexander. *The Indispensable Enemy: Labor and the Anti-Chinese Movement in California*. Berkeley: University of California Press, 1971.

Scanlon, Jennifer. *Inarticulate Longings: The Ladies Home Journal, Gender, and the Promises of Consumer Culture*. New York: Routledge, 1995.

Schlissel, Lillian, Vicki Ruiz, and Janice Monk, eds. *Western Women: Their Land, Their Lives*. Albuquerque: University of New Mexico Press, 1988.

Schuele, Donna. "'None Could Deny the Eloquence of This Lady': Women, Law, and Government in California, 1850–1890." In *Taming the Elephant: Politics, Government, and Law in Pioneer California*, edited by John F. Burns and Richard J. Orsi, 169–98. Berkeley: University of California Press, 2003.

Schweninger, Loren. "Property Owning Free African-American Women in the South." *Journal of Women's History* 1 (Winter 1990): 13–44.

Scott, Joan. "Gender: A Useful Category of Historical Analysis." *American Historical Review* 91 (December 1986): 1053–75.

Scott, Mel. *The San Francisco Bay Area: A Metropolis in Perspective*. Berkeley: University of California Press, 1959.

Scranton, Philip. *Beauty and Business: Commerce, Gender, and Culture in Modern America*. New York: Routledge, 2001.

Seller, Maxine. "Antoinetta Pisanelli Alessandro and the Italian Theater of San Francisco: Entertainment, Education and Americanization." In *Struggle and Success: An Anthology of the Italian Immigrant Experience in California*, edited by Paola A. Sensi-Isolani and Phylis Cancilla Martinelli, 160–74. New York: Center for Migration Studies, 1993.

Shammas, Carole. "Re-Assessing the Married Women's Property Acts." *Journal of Women's History* 6 (Spring 1994): 9–30.

Siegel, Reva B. "Home as Work: The First Woman's Rights Claims Concerning Wives' Household Labor, 1850–1880." *Yale Law Journal* 103 (March 1994): 1073–1217.

Simpson, Lee M. A. *Selling the City: Gender, Class and the California Growth Machine, 1880–1940*. Palo Alto, Calif.: Stanford University Press, 2004.

Smith, Duane A. *Rocky Mountain Mining Camps*. Bloomington: Indiana University Press, 1967.

Soltow, James H. "Origins of Small Business and the Relationships between Large and Small Firms: Metal Fabricating and Machinery Making in New England, 1890–1957." In *Small Business in American Life*, edited by Stuart W. Bruchey, 192–211. New York: Columbia University Press, 1980.

Sorin, Gerald. *Tradition Transformed: The Jewish Experience in America*. Baltimore: Johns Hopkins University Press, 1997.

Sparks, Edith. "Capital Instincts: The Economics of Female Proprietorship in San Francisco, 1850–1920." Ph.D. diss., University of California, Los Angeles, 1999.

———. "Terms of Endearment: Informal Borrowing Networks among Northern California Businesswomen, 1870–1920," *Business and Economic History On-Line* 2 (Winter 2004): 1–12. <www.h-net.org/~business/bhcweb/publications/BEHonline/beh.html>

Stage, Sarah. *Female Complaints: Lydia Pinkham and the Business of Women's Medicine*. New York: W. W. Norton, 1979.

Stansell, Christine. *City of Women: Sex and Class in New York, 1789–1860*. Urbana: University of Illinois Press, 1987.

Starr, Kevin. *Americans and the California Dream, 1850–1915*. New York: Oxford University Press, 1973.

———. *Inventing the Dream: California through the Progressive Era*. New York: Oxford University Press, 1985.

———. *Material Dreams: Southern California through the 1920s*. New York: Oxford University Press, 1990.

Starr, Kevin, and Richard Orsi, eds. *Rooted in Barbarous Soil: People, Culture, and Community in Gold Rush California*. Berkeley: University of California Press, 2000.

Strasser, Susan. *Satisfaction Guaranteed: The Making of the American Mass Market*. Washington, D.C.: Smithsonian Institution Press, 1989.

Strom, Sharon. *Beyond the Typewriter: Gender, Class, and the Origins of Modern American Office Work, 1900–1930*. Urbana: University of Illinois Press, 1992.

Takaki, Ronald. *Strangers from a Different Shore: A History of Asian Americans*. Boston: Little, Brown, 1989.

Tenenbaum, Shelly. "Borrowers or Lenders Be: Jewish Immigrant Women's Credit Networks." In *American Jewish Women's History, A Reader*, edited by Pamela S. Nadell, 79–90. New York: New York University Press, 2003.

Tong, Benson. *Unsubmissive Women: Chinese Prostitutes in Nineteenth-Century San Francisco*. Norman: University of Oklahoma Press, 1994.

Trachtenberg, Alan. *The Incorporation of America: Culture and Society in the Gilded Age*. New York: Hill and Wang, 1982.

Turbin, Carole. *Working Women of Collar City: Gender, Class and Community in Troy, New York, 1864–1886*. Urbana: University of Illinois Press, 1992.

Walker, Juliet E. K. "Racism, Slavery, and Free Enterprise: Black Entrepreneurship in the United States before the Civil War." *Business History Review* 60 (Autumn 1986): 343–82.

———. *The History of Black Business in America: Capitalism, Race, Entrepreneurship*. New York: Macmillan Library Reference USA, 1998.

Wang, Joan. "Gender, Race and Civilization: The Competition between American Power Laundries and Chinese Steam Laundries, 1870s–1920s." *American Studies International* 40 (February 2002): 52–73.

Wiley, Peter Booth. *National Trust Guide to San Francisco: America's Guide for Architecture and History Travelers*. New York: Preservation Press, 2000.

Wong, K. Scott, and Sucheng Chan, eds. *Claiming America: Constructing Chinese American Identities during the Exclusion Era*. Philadelphia: Temple University Press, 1998.

Wooten, Charles W., and Barbara E. Kemmerer. "The Changing Genderization of Bookkeeping in the United States, 1870-1930." *Business History Review* 70 (Winter 1996): 541–86.

Wright, Doris Marion. "The Making of Cosmopolitan California: An Analysis of Immigration, 1848–1870, Part I." *California Historical Society Quarterly* 19 (December 1940): 330–45.

———. "The Making of Cosmopolitan California: An Analysis of Immigration, 1848–1870, Part II." *California Historical Society Quarterly* 20 (March 1941): 65–79.

Wright, Robert E. "Women and Finance in the Early National U.S." *Essays in History* 42 (2000), <http://etext.lib.virginia.edu/journals/EH/EH42/Wright42.html. May 2004.

Yeager, Mary, ed. *Women in Business*. 3 vols. Cheltenham, U.K.: Edward Elgar, 1997.

Yohn, Susan. "Crippled Capitalists: The Inscription of Economic Dependence and the Challenge of Female Entrepreneurship in Nineteenth-Century America." *Feminist Economics* 12 (April 2006): 85–109.

Yu, Renquiu. *To Save China, to Save Ourselves: The Chinese Hand Laundry Alliance of New York*. Philadelphia: Temple University Press, 1992.

Yung, Judy. *Unbound Feet: A Social History of Chinese Women in San Francisco*. Berkeley: University of California Press, 1995.

Zunz, Olivier. *Making America Corporate, 1870–1920*. Chicago: University of Chicago Press, 1990.

INDEX

Accommodations industry: and gender imbalance, 4, 11–12, 25, 39; female proprietors in, 8, 23; African American women in, 18, 51–52, 248 (nn. 133, 144); Irish women in, 18, 130, 223, 246 (n. 111); businesses in, 24; Chinese women in, 29, 52, 256 (n. 1); decline of female-owned businesses in, 30–31; and domestic tasks performed by women, 36–37, 85–86; statistics on, 37, 38, 41–42, 53, 196, 213–14, 215, 217, 242 (n. 56); and housing shortage, 37–39; capital intentions and market incentives in, 37–45; and temporary residents of San Francisco, 39, 41; and families' choice of boarding out, 39–40; in working-class environs, 40–41; and rebuilding of San Francisco after earthquake and fire, 43, 44; racial/ethnic background of female proprietors in, 53, 221–23; male proprietors in, 53, 225; buying out or taking over established businesses in, 105–6; modern improvements in, 138–41, 204; and tourism, 140–41; advertising for, 141; licensing fees in, 150, 151; purchasing decisions in, 152; debt collection in, 160–61, 279 (n. 62); employees in, 168–69; Chinese laborers in, 169; and earthquakes, 193–96; combined place of business and residence in, 279 (n. 61), 282 (n. 103). *See also* Boardinghouses; Hotels; Lodging houses; Restaurants

Accounting, 172, 283 (n. 131)

Advertising: for boardinghouses, 5–7, 72, 105, 231 (n. 8); trade cards for, 5–7, 135–38, 280 (n. 85); in early twentieth century, 116; in 1850s–60s, 125–27; for apparel industry, 125–27, 165; for millinery and dressmaking businesses, 126, 145–46, 165, 280 (n. 85); and tourism, 141; for hotels, 141, 166; direct-mail advertising, 145; advertising agencies, 145–46, 167; and prices of goods, 151; in newspapers and magazines, 165–66, 281 (n. 90); for beauty industry, 166; for retail industry, 166–67; return on investment in, 166–67, 281 (nn. 91, 93); research on, 276–77 (n. 129)

African American men: statistics on, 51, 54; in retail industry, 53–54, 248 (n. 148); in laundry industry, 54; as proprietors of businesses, 54, 224–25, 248 (n. 148); and credit, 89; racism against and segregation of, 89, 272 (n. 67); location of businesses of, 131; in gold rush California, 256 (n. 1)

African American women: in beauty industry, 18, 25, 145, 230 (n. 4), 237–38 (n. 8), 276 (n. 124); businesses run by, 18, 221–23, 248 (nn. 133, 144); in laundry industry, 18, 248 (n. 144); statistics on, 50, 51, 220–22, 248 (n. 144); in accommodations industry, 51–52, 248 (nn. 133, 144); wealth of, 59, 230 (n. 4); as domestic service workers, 65; and credit, 89; racism against and segregation of, 89, 272 (n. 67); as prostitutes, 119; location of businesses of, 131; and benevolent organizations, 181, 287 (n. 175); in apparel industry, 248 (n. 144); in retail industry, 248 (n. 144); as clerks, 252 (n. 48); in gold rush California, 256 (n. 1)

Agee, Posey, 172

Albany, N.Y., 17, 250 (n. 19), 295 (n. 90)

Alessandro, Antoinetta and Giuseppi, 178–79

Alimony laws, 70–71, 253 (n. 70)

Anderson, Diana O., 93–94

Anti-Coolie Co-Operative Laundry Association, 34, 48, 246 (n. 118)

Anti-Jap Laundry League, 34, 190

Apparel industry: female proprietors in, 8; characteristics of female proprietors in, 17; Hudson's clothing store, 22, 23, 237 (n. 1); businesses in, 24; male proprietors in, 30; decline of female-owned businesses in, 30, 33; and domestic tasks performed by women, 36; capital intentions and market incentives in, 37; racial/ethnic background of female proprietors in, 53, 221–23; and prostitutes, 61, 250 (n. 22); partnerships in, 99–100, 102; advertising for, 125–27, 165; location of businesses in, 128, 227; interior decor of businesses in, 132–33, 142–44; and display windows, 133–34, 142; and competition between department stores and small-scale proprietors, 141–46; inventory management in, 153; overbuying in, 157; debt collection in, 161–62; bank services for, 171–72; financial management in, 176; husbands' contributions to, 176; fire risks in, 192; in twenty-first century, 207; Irish women as proprietors in, 223; African American proprietors in, 235–36 (n. 46), 248 (n. 144); in Boston, 235–36 (n. 46), 239 (n. 28), 247 (n. 127), 259 (n. 24). *See also* Dressmaking business; Millinery business

Applefield, Eva, 103

Apprenticeships, 8, 46, 53, 172, 283 (n. 128)

Arden, Elizabeth, 145

Baker, Miss J. A., 192–93, 291 (n. 48)

Bakeries, 130, 192

Bakken, Gordon Morris, 295 (n. 88)

Baley, May, 169

Ballinger, Martha, 95–96, 262 (nn. 64–65)

Ballou, Mary, 121

Bancroft, Hubert Howe, 270 (nn. 41–42)

Banking industry, 24, 62, 94, 97–98, 170–72, 180, 232 (n. 18), 262 (n. 58), 263 (n. 73), 282 (nn. 115–16), 284 (n. 133). *See also* Loans

Bank of Italy, 24, 94, 97–98, 170–71, 172, 180, 262 (n. 58), 263 (n. 73), 282 (n. 116)

Bankruptcy: court records on, 5, 14, 50, 210–11; court proceedings for, 198–200; laws on, 279 (n. 60), 288–89 (n. 9), 289 (n. 10), 295 (n. 88)

Barbers, 225–26, 276 (n. 124)

Baschan, Bertha, 156–57

Baum, L. Frank, 142, 273 (n. 76)

Beach, Mrs. Eliza, 106

Bean, Walton, 267 (n. 134), 292 (n. 52)

Beauty industry: female proprietors in, 8; Jewish women in, 18; African American women in, 18, 25, 145, 230 (n. 4), 237–38 (n. 8), 276 (n. 124); businesses in, 24; expansion of opportunities for women in, 34–35; and beauty culture, 35; statistics on, 35, 215, 225–26; interior decor of businesses in, 144–45; location of beauty salons, 145; advertising for, 166; location of businesses in, 227

Berio, Miss, 24

Berry, Mrs., 24

Berthoff, Rowland, 231–32 (n. 12)

Beyersdorf, Louis, 90

Billiards, 123, 124, 127, 270 (n. 41)

Bird, Mr. and Mrs., 141

Birthrate, 75

Blackford, Mansel, 231–32 (n. 12), 233 (nn. 26, 29–30), 250 (n. 29), 259 (n. 30), 260 (n. 41), 273 (n. 80), 274 (n. 101), 289 (n. 12)

Blackmar, Elizabeth, 244 (n. 93)

Black women. *See* African American women

Blewett, Mary H., 240 (n. 33)

Blight, Mrs. T. J., 293 (n. 65)

Boardinghouses: advertising for, 5–7, 72, 105, 231 (n. 8); female proprietors of, 23, 24; and gender imbalance, 25, 39; Chinese women as proprietors of, 29, 52; and domestic tasks performed by women, 36, 269 (n. 21); purchase price for, 38, 39; statistics on, 38, 41–42, 51, 215, 217; location of, 40; single women as residents

of, 41; in antebellum period, 51, 235 (n. 44), 244 (n. 93), 258 (n. 9), 269 (n. 21); African American women as proprietors of, 51–52, 248 (n. 133); earnings from, 65, 70; fictional account of, 72; widowed women as proprietors of, 72, 254 (n. 82); partnership between apparel store and, 99–100; sale of, 107; employees of, 121, 138; physical labor required in, 121–22; Irish men as lodgers of, 130; Irish women as proprietors of, 130, 223, 246 (n. 111); furnishings of, 138; modern improvements in, 138–41, 204; purchasing decisions for, 152; expenditures on, 156; price of lodging in, 160; debt collection by, 160–61, 279 (n. 62); and earthquakes, 193, 196; racial/ethnic background of female proprietors of, 221–23; male proprietors of, 225–26; as combined place of business and residence, 279 (n. 61), 282 (n. 103). *See also* Accommodations industry

Booker, Mrs. H. E., 102

Bookkeeping. *See* Record keeping

Bookstores, 24, 233 (n. 29)

Borchard, Mrs., 174

Borden, Ivy, 32

Borgstrom, Minnie, 155–56

Borrowing money. *See* Loans

Bosley, Mrs., 105

Boston: statistics on female proprietors in, 33, 60; accommodations industry in, 37, 213–14; retail industry in, 61; female proprietors in colonial Boston, 71; interior decorating shop in, 144; milliners and dressmakers in, 161, 184, 201, 239 (n. 28), 247 (n. 127), 251 (n. 32), 264 (n. 79); debt collection by female proprietors in, 162–63; Women's Educational and Industrial Union in, 169; longevity of women's businesses in, 184; failure of businesses in, 201, 289 (n. 12); census

management, 66; male clerks, 66, 172–73, 177, 283 (n. 129), 284 (n. 133); gendered culture and feminization of, 66, 173, 252 (n. 53), 260 (n. 33), 283 (n. 131); education and training for, 66–67; independent contractors in, 67; statistics on, 67, 68, 74; exclusion of married women from, 68, 69; married and formerly married (widowed or divorced) women in, 68, 74; work week for, 69; African Americans in, 252 (n. 48)

Clothing stores. *See* Apparel industry

Cochran, Thomas, 259 (n. 27), 281 (n. 90), 283 (n. 124)

Colorado, 86–87, 255 (n. 102)

Confectionery businesses. *See* Candy and confectionery businesses

Conlin, Joseph, 270 (n. 36)

Cook, Miss, 24

Cook, Mrs. C., 29

Cosmetics. *See* Beauty industry

Cost accounting, 172

Cowan, Ruth Schwartz, 274 (n. 95)

Cowles, Mrs. Irene S., 111

Crawford, Mrs., 135–37

Credit, 48, 83–90, 97, 103, 154–59, 188, 205, 207–8, 257 (n. 6), 279 (nn. 49, 52), 283 (n. 119), 293 (n. 71). *See also* Loans

Credit cards, 207–8

Credit reports. *See* Dun (R. G.) & Company credit reports

Crocker, Charles, 7

Crocker, Ellen, 138

Croles, Mrs. G. W. M., 24, 107, 155

Curtain, Miner Andrew, 95

Customer relations: and trade cards, 5–7, 135–38; and appeal of female proprietors during gold rush, 57–59, 83, 115, 116–22, 146, 256 (n. 1); catering to customer pretensions after 1860s, 115–16, 122–27; and displays, 115–16, 131–38, 142, 273 (n. 76); and advertising, 116, 125–27; and location of businesses, 116, 127–31; and modern improvements, 116, 138–41, 204, 274 (n. 88); and plate-glass display windows, 133–34, 142; and brand-name products, 134–35; and interior decor of businesses, 142–45; and debt collection, 159–63. *See also* Advertising

Daniels, Douglas Henry, 276 (n. 124)

Dannenberg, Mrs. Amalie, 102, 109, 154, 174, 176, 265 (n. 117)

Davidoff, Leonore, 285 (n. 145)

Dazet, Mrs., 111–13

Debt. *See* Credit; Loans

Debt collection, 159–63, 279 (n. 62)

Decker, Peter, 198, 233 (n. 22), 236 (n. 52), 259 (n. 24), 271 (n. 57), 272 (n. 72)

De Gomez, Miss, 24

Department stores: competition between small businesses and, 13, 30, 67, 116, 132, 142, 166–67, 275 (n. 108); law on, 142; examples of, 142, 272 (n. 70); interior decor of, 142–43, 277 (n. 4); Magnin as female proprietor of, 148, 245 (n. 102), 272–73 (n. 73); reopening of, after earthquake, 197; hat and clothing departments of, 276 (n. 122); in London, 281 (n. 98)

Deutsch, Sarah, 260 (n. 40), 276 (n. 121), 284 (nn. 140, 143), 289 (n. 12)

Dewey, Mrs. S. A., 25

De Witt, Margaret, 191

Diner, Hasia R., 245–46 (n. 111)

Displays, 115–16, 131–38, 142, 273 (n. 76)

Divorced women. *See* Female proprietors; Widowed/divorced women

Doherty, Mrs. M. E., 132–33, 138, 150–51

Domestic and personal service workers: unmarried women as, 48, 64–65; race and ethnicity of, 48, 65; statistics on, 62, 65, 68, 241 (n. 42), 252 (n. 47); and gender imbalance, 64;

wages for, 64, 122, 251 (n. 40); in New York, 64, 251 (n. 40); married and formerly married (widowed or divorced) women as, 68, 71; in different cities, 241 (n. 42); Chinese men as, 251 (n. 39), 282 (n. 108)

Domesticity, commercial, 36–37, 58–60, 83, 85–86, 116–22, 173–74, 258 (n. 11)

Drachman, Virginia G., 234 (n. 33), 235 (n. 43)

Dressmaking business: and domestic tasks performed by women, 8, 36; apprenticeships in, 8, 53, 172, 283 (n. 128); female proprietors in, 24; decline in, 33; and prostitutes, 61; saving for, by female proprietors, 91; loans for, 95; partnership in, 101; location of, 105; credit for, 154, 279 (n. 52); and debt collection, 161; in Boston, 161, 184, 201, 239 (n. 28), 247 (n. 127), 264 (n. 79); advertising for, 165, 280 (n. 85); and lease agreements, 168; employees of, 168–69; bank services for, 171; financial management in, 174; and earthquake, 196; statistics on female proprietors in, 215, 247 (n. 127); African American women in, 236 (n. 46); in New Orleans, 236 (n. 46); as combined place of business and residence, 282 (n. 103); widows as proprietors in, 284 (n. 140). See also Apparel industry

Drugs and medicines, 29, 36, 79, 192, 258 (n. 11), 280 (n. 83), 290 (n. 26)

Dun (R. G.) & Company credit reports, 14, 49, 50, 78–79, 87–89, 104–5, 111, 151, 154–55, 163, 173, 176, 177, 209–10, 250 (n. 19), 256 (n. 104), 259 (n. 24)

Earthquakes, 4, 13, 14, 43, 94, 183, 184, 193–97, 205, 292 (nn. 52, 54–55)

Economy of San Francisco, 4, 13, 39,

40, 110, 125, 132, 185, 186–87, 206, 242 (n. 63), 267 (n. 134), 272 (n. 72)

Education of women, 66, 285 (n. 148). See also Training

Electric lights, 140

Elevators, 140

Emmons, Mrs., 154

Employment offices, 101

Emporium, 13, 30, 31, 132, 142, 272 (n. 70)

Ennis, Margaret, 111–13

Entrepreneurship: definition of, 231 (n. 9). See also Female proprietors; Male proprietors; Small businesses; and specific businesses

Esprit de Corp, 207

Ethnic and racial groups. See African American men; African American women; Chinese immigrants; Irish men; Irish women; Japanese immigrants; Jewish men; Jewish women; Mexican and Californio women; Race and ethnicity

Evans, Mrs. Jeanie, 107, 108

Evarts, Clara, 96, 262 (n. 64)

Ezell, Elizabeth, 143

Failure of small businesses: bankruptcy court records on, 5, 14, 50, 210–11; of female proprietors, 5, 103, 183–202, 227; statistics on, 62, 68, 185, 227, 230 (n. 1); and partnerships, 103; and natural disasters, 183, 184; commercial rebounds following, 183, 200–202; and longevity of women's businesses, 184–85; of male proprietors, 185, 200; and economic depressions, 185–87; risk management for prevention of, 186–87; and illnesses, 187–91, 205; and fires, 191–93, 195, 205; and earthquakes, 193–98, 205; and private settlement with creditors, 198; and bankruptcy proceedings, 198–200, 288–89 (n. 9)

Fairbanks, Madame, 271 (n. 46)

Family businesses. *See* "Mom-and-pop stores"

Federal Trade Commission, 172

Female proprietors: in twenty-first century, 1–3, 207–8; rewards and responsibilities of, 3, 230 (n. 2); significance of study of, 3–4, 17–19, 206–8; decline of, by 1920s, 4, 13–14, 20–23, 30–36, 54–55, 73–75, 81–82; research sources on, 5, 14, 50, 209–12; and failure of small businesses, 5, 103, 183–202, 205–6, 227; as financial managers, 7, 88, 148–82, 205; types of businesses operated by, 8, 24, 55; factors shaping business decisions of, 8–9, 19–20; demographics of, 9, 17–18, 45–54; domestic concerns of and child rearing by, 9–11, 69–71, 75, 76, 253 (n. 65); goals of, 10; and capital intentions and market incentives, 10, 36–45, 203–8; instinct and intuition of, 10, 37; compared to male proprietors, 10–11, 90–91, 93, 103–4, 172–73, 185; and gold rush, 12, 56, 57–62, 83, 85–87, 115, 116–22, 204, 256 (n. 1), 257 (n. 6); scholarship on, 16–19; race and nativity of, 17–18, 89–90, 220–23; as participants in urban marketplace, 18–19; overview of businesses of, 24–36; statistics on, 32, 50, 60, 64, 68–69, 74, 75, 207, 208, 213–23, 227; and commercial domesticity, 36–37, 58–60, 83, 85–86, 116–22, 173–74; and class status, 45–47, 244 (n. 97); and economic choice, 46–47, 73–75, 81–82; credit for, 48, 83–90, 154–59, 205, 207–8, 257 (n. 6), 279 (nn. 49, 52), 293 (n. 71); motivations of, for starting businesses, 56–82; as single (never-married) women, 63–68; in post-gold rush San Francisco, 63–73; as married and formerly married (widowed or divorced) women, 68–73, 76–81; in colonial period, 71; after 1920, 73–75; legal and personal cir-cumstances of married proprietors, 76–81, 92, 204, 254–55 (n. 95), 255 (nn. 97, 101, 102), 255–56 (n. 103), 257 (n. 6), 261 (nn. 155–57); start-up strategies by, 83–114, 205, 207–8; and raising capital through saving and borrowing money, 84, 90–98, 113, 207–8, 259 (n. 30), 261–62 (n. 57), 262 (nn. 58, 62, 65), 262–63 (n. 66), 275–76 (n. 120); and partnerships, 84, 98–104, 113, 178–79, 205, 264 (n. 93), 285 (n. 152), 286 (nn. 160–62), 287 (n. 166); buying out or taking over established businesses by, 84, 104–13, 205, 266–67 (n. 130), 267 (n. 135); and motherhood image, 86, 258 (n. 11); and customer relations, 115–47; location of businesses of, 116, 127–31, 227, 238 (n. 18); and household finances, 179–80, 205, 287 (n. 171); longevity of businesses of, 184–85; reentry into business world following failure of, 200–202; names of businesses of, 266 (n. 123); in late twentieth century, 296 (n. 12). *See also* Accommodations industry; African American women; Apparel industry; Beauty industry; Chinese immigrants; Irish women; Japanese immigrants; Laundry industry; Mexican and Californio women; Retail industry

Ferran, Mr. and Madame, 265 (n. 117)

Fiala, Mrs. S., 91–92, 260 (n. 42)

Fields, Deborah, 258 (n. 11)

Filipino-American War, 13, 42, 43

Financial management: female proprietors' lack of experience in, 10, 170–71, 173–74, 181–82, 205; and brand-name products, 134–35, 170; Magnin on, 148; areas of, 149; training in, 149; and male proprietors, 149, 172–73; tax and licensing fees for business owners, 150–51; purchasing decisions, 151–52; inventory management, 152–54; credit, 154–59, 188,

household finances, 179; in retail industry, 223; and religious organizations, 287 (n. 176). *See also* Female proprietors

Issel, William, 236 (n. 52)

Jacobs, Mrs. H., 89
Japanese immigrants, 34, 48, 49, 53–54, 65, 190
Jeffrey, Julie Roy, 28 (n. 11)
Jensen, Joan, 236 (n. 53), 257 (n. 6)
Jessica McClintock, Inc., 207
Jewish men, 89, 247 (n. 121)
Jewish women: in retail trade, 17–18, 89, 259 (n. 22); in beauty industry, 18; as entrepreneurs and Eastern European Jewish culture, 46; and credit networks, 48, 97, 259 (n. 22); stereotypes of, 89; and household finances, 179. *See also* Female proprietors
Job placement services, 101
Johnson, Mrs., 125–26
Johnson, Susan, 256–57 (n. 7)
Jordan, Mrs. C., 155
Jordan, Mrs. E. A., 35
Joseph, Eddie, 293 (n. 68)

Kearney, Dennis, 246 (n. 118)
Kessler-Harris, Alice, 231 (n. 11)
Kimball, Charles P., 38
Komfeld, Charles, 108, 265 (n. 110)
Kuck, Mrs. Meta, 109–10
Kwolek-Folland, Angel, 231 (n. 9), 232 (n. 18), 234 (n. 32), 235 (nn. 43, 45), 252 (n. 53), 258 (n. 11), 260 (n. 40), 266 (n. 122), 275 (n. 108), 277 (n. 6), 284 (n. 140), 285 (n. 148)

Land Act (1851), 51
Largent, Ida, 168
Lathrop, Gloria, 236 (n. 53)
Laundry industry: Chinese immigrants in, 4, 12, 34, 48, 49, 54, 118, 131, 190, 206, 240–41 (n. 39), 247 (n. 126), 272 (n. 68), 282 (n. 108);

female proprietors in, 8; Irish immigrants in, 18, 48, 49–50, 223; African Americans in, 18, 54, 248 (n. 144); businesses in, 24; decline of female-owned businesses in, 33–34; Japanese immigrants in, 34, 48, 49, 54, 190; racist response to Chinese and Japanese immigrants in, 34, 48, 131, 190, 206, 240–41 (n. 39), 246 (n. 118), 247 (n. 126); male proprietors in, 34, 48–50, 54, 225–26; and manglers, 34, 240 (n. 34); and domestic tasks performed by women, 36; statistics on, 52–53, 215, 240 (n. 37), 241 (n. 42), 242 (n. 56); racial/ethnic background of female proprietors in, 52–53, 221–23, 247 (n. 128); location of businesses in, 129–30, 240 (n. 37); and smallpox epidemic, 188–89; and bubonic plague, 190–91; fire risks in, 192; competition between whites and Chinese immigrants in, 247 (n. 126); sale of laundry business, 265 (n. 117)

Lawlor, Miss, 101
Lawrence, J., Jr., 103
Laws: on divorce, 69, 76; on alimony, 70–71, 253 (n. 70); on married women's rights, 76–81, 92, 204, 254–55 (n. 95), 255 (nn. 97, 101–2), 255–56 (n. 103), 260 (n. 35), 260–61 (n. 45), 261 (nn. 47–49); on protection of married women's wages, 77, 260 (n. 36), 260–61 (n. 45); on married women's businesses, 79–81, 92, 204, 255 (nn. 97, 101–2), 255–56 (n. 103), 257 (n. 6), 261 (nn. 48–49); on partnerships, 101–2; anti-Chinese laws, 131; on department stores, 142; on payment by customers, 160; Married Women's Property Acts, 254–55 (n. 95), 261 (n. 47); on bankruptcy, 279 (n. 60), 288–89 (n. 9), 289 (n. 10), 295 (n. 88)

Leach, William, 273 (n. 76)
Lease agreements, 168

Lee, Erika, 232 (n. 20), 238 (n. 15), 240 (n. 38)

Leigh, Ella, 195

Leroy, Mme., 154

Lester, Mrs., 135–37

Leuenberger, Caroline Louise, 159, 279 (n. 54)

Levenstein, Margaret, 231 (n. 9)

Levy, JoAnn, 236 (n. 53)

Lewis, Susan Ingalls, 232 (n. 13), 234 (n. 33), 235 (n. 44), 244 (n. 97), 260 (n. 40), 285 (n. 152), 295 (n. 90)

Licensing and tax fees, 150–51, 277 (n. 12)

Lichtenstein, Mrs. L. H., 73, 91

Life insurance. *See* Insurance industry

Limerick, Patricia Nelson, 250 (n. 27)

Liquor license, 150, 151

Livesay, Harold, 231 (n. 9)

Lloyd, Benjamin E., 39, 40, 128, 133, 294 (n. 83)

Loans, 84, 93–98, 113, 207, 262 (nn. 57–58, 62, 65), 262–63 (n. 66), 275–76 (n. 120), 283 (n. 119), 293 (n. 71). *See also* Credit

Location of businesses, 116, 127–31, 227, 238 (n. 18)

Locke, Mary Lou, 253 (n. 65)

Lodging houses: female proprietors of, 23, 24; and gender imbalance, 25, 39; location of, 30–31, 41; and domestic tasks performed by women, 36; and families' choice of boarding out, 39–40; motivation for starting, 78; sale of, 111; furnishings of, 138, 139; modern improvements in, 138–41; and lease agreements, 168; employees in, 169; and earthquake, 196; statistics on female proprietors in, 215, 217; as combined place of business and residence, 279 (n. 61). *See also* Accommodations industry

Long, Sue, 28

Los Angeles, Calif.: population of, 232 (n. 19); domestic and personal service in, 241 (n. 42); male-to-female ratio in, 243 (n. 68); Mexican and Californio women in, 247–48 (n. 132); child-rearing responsibilities of working women in, 253 (n. 65)

Lotchin, Roger W., 270 (n. 36)

Lucas, Robert, 76

Lukens, Rebecca, 285 (n. 148)

Lumbering, 38

Lynch, Mrs. Elizabeth, 30

Lyons, Julia and James, 70, 168

MacGregor, William Laird, 40

Magnin, Grover, 148

Magnin, Joseph, 293 (n. 71)

Magnin, Mary Ann, 148, 197, 245 (n. 102), 272–73 (n. 73), 277 (n. 4), 293 (n. 71)

Maita, Frances, 151

Makins, Mrs. A. H., 286 (n. 157)

Malcolmson, Patricia, 240 (n. 37)

Male clerks, 66, 90–91, 172–73, 177, 283 (n. 129), 284 (n. 133)

Male proprietors: domestic concerns of, 9–10; and "mom-and-pop stores," 10, 11, 175, 232 (n. 16), 284 (n. 143); compared to female proprietors, 10–11, 90–91, 93, 103–4, 172–73, 185; in apparel industry, 30; in laundry industry, 34, 49–50, 225–26; in retail industry, 35, 53–54, 218–19, 225–26, 248 (n. 148); race and nativity of, 48–49, 53–54, 224–26, 247 (n. 121), 248 (n. 148), 248–49 (n. 149); in accommodations industry, 53, 225–26; credit reports of, 87–88, 173; business experience of, 88; credit for, 88, 103; savings as start-up strategy of, 90–91, 259 (n. 30); loans for, 93, 262 (n. 62), 262–63 (n. 66); and partnerships, 103–4, 178–79, 264 (n. 93), 285 (n. 152), 286 (nn. 161–62), 287 (n. 166); location of businesses of, 129, 238 (n. 18); financial management skills of, 149, 172–73; failure of businesses of, 185, 200; in barber/hair industry, 225–26; as tailors, 248 (n. 148). *See also* African American men; Chinese immigrants; Irish men; Japanese immigrants

Malone, Annie Turnbo, 145

Mangels, Carrie, 292 (n. 54)

Marchand, Roland, 276–77 (n. 129), 281 (n. 93)

Marchard, Mrs. C., 35

Maritime trade, 39, 41, 60–61

Marketing. *See* Advertising

Married women. *See* Female proprietors

Married Women's Business Act, 92

Married Women's Property Acts, 254–55 (n. 95), 261 (n. 47)

Martineaut, Mrs. Josephine, 108, 154, 265 (n. 110)

McAuliff, Mrs. F., 25

McCarthy, Mrs., 199–200, 294 (n. 83)

McClain, Charles J., 241 (n. 39)

McGearny, Miss Eliza, 63–64

McLeod, Mrs., 107

Medicines. *See* Drugs and medicines

Megquier, Mary Jane, 58, 62, 121–22

Mercer, Mr. and Mrs. Charles H., 79, 154, 163, 176

Mexican and Californio women, 51, 118, 119, 247–48 (n. 132), 256–57 (n. 7)

Michelsen, M., 188–89

Military bases, 13, 42–43

Miller, William, 119

Miller, Mrs. Stites, 5–7

Milligan, Ellen, 265 (n. 117)

Millinery business: and domestic tasks performed by women, 8, 36; apprenticeships in, 8, 46, 53, 63, 172, 283 (n. 128); female proprietors in, 24; examples of, 24–25, 30, 63, 108–9, 132–33, 163, 198, 274 (n. 84); decline in, 33; and prostitutes, 61; saving for, by female proprietors, 91; sale of, 106, 107, 109, 265 (nn. 110, 114); purchase of, by single women, 108–

9; advertising for, 126, 145–46, 280 (n. 85); location of, 128, 227; trade cards for, 135–37, 280 (n. 85); interior decor and furnishings of, 143–44, 156; financial management in, 150–51, 174, 176, 177, 181; credit for, 154, 155–56, 279 (n. 52); expenditures for, 155–56; and overbuying, 157; and debt collection, 161, 162; in Boston, 161, 184, 201, 239 (n. 28), 247 (n. 127), 251 (n. 32), 264 (n. 79); record keeping for, 163; husbands' contributions to, 176, 177; failure of, due to illness, 188; fire risks in, 192–93; and earthquake, 196, 198; bankruptcy of, 199, 201; statistics on female proprietors in, 215, 247 (n. 127); African American women in, 236 (n. 46); in New Orleans, 236 (n. 46); in Philadelphia, 251 (n. 32); purchase price for, 265 (nn. 110, 114); financial difficulties of, 270–71 (n. 46); widows as proprietors in, 284 (n. 140). *See also* Apparel industry

"The Misadventures of Charley," 45, 46

Mish, Mrs. Sarah, 135, 136, 274 (n. 84)

Modernization: in retail industry, 138, 157–58, 274 (n. 88); in accommodations industry, 138–41, 204; in household appliances, 139

"Mom-and-pop stores," 10, 11, 175, 232 (n. 16), 284 (n. 143)

Mondelet, Marie, 123–24, 125, 127, 270 (n. 39)

Money management. *See* Financial management

Moody, Clara, 152, 180, 278 (n. 19)

Morley, Doris, 103

Morphy, Edward A., 290 (n. 26)

Morrell, Mrs., 32

Morris, Mrs. E., 126–27

Morris, Mrs. O. E., 31–32

Motherhood image, 86, 258 (n. 11). *See also* Domesticity, commercial

Murphy, Lucy Eldersveld, 234 (n. 35)
Murphy, Mrs. Michael C., 71–72
Music store, 152
Myres, Sandra L., 237 (n. 42)

Nathorst, Annie, 168
National Foundation for Women
  Business Owners, 208
Natural disasters. *See* Earthquakes;
  Fires
Nenadic, Stana, 287 (n. 166)
Nevada City, Calif., 38, 85, 135–37, 257
  (n. 3)
Newman, Bessie, 103
Newmark, Mrs. Joseph, 76–78
New Orleans, La.: statistics on female
  proprietors in, 33, 239 (nn. 25–26);
  accommodations industry in, 213–
  14; census records on, 232–33 (n. 21);
  African American proprietors in,
  236 (n. 46); laundry industry in, 240
  (n. 37)
The New Penelope (Victor), 72–73
New York, N.Y.: statistics on female
  proprietors in, 33; accommodations
  industry in, 37, 213–14; maritime
  trade in, 60; domestic servants in,
  64, 122, 251 (n. 40); Harlem, 131;
  banks in, 171, 172; wholesalers in, 174;
  census records on, 232–33 (n. 21);
  laundry industry in, 240 (n. 37);
  Earnings Act (1860) in, 255 (n. 97);
  volunteer fire companies in, 291
  (n. 40)
Nicholds, Mrs. Margaret M., 291
  (n. 47)
Noyes, Mrs. Nancy C., 93, 95, 138
Nucleus House, 25, 29
Nursing, 62, 71
Nystrom, Paul, 173

Oakland, Calif., 241 (n. 42), 243 (n. 68)
O'Brien, Robert, 167
Office workers. *See* Clerical occupa-
  tions

Olegario, Rowena, 259 (n. 24)
Oshkosh, Wis., 185
Oysters, 124, 270 (n. 42)

Palmer, Mrs. J. B., 279 (n. 62)
Panama Pacific Exposition (1915),
  140–41
Parker, Ellen, 279 (n. 62)
Partnerships, 84, 98–104, 113, 178–79,
  205, 264 (n. 93), 285 (n. 152), 286
  (nn. 160–62), 287 (n. 166)
Patent medicines. *See* Drugs and medi-
  cines
Peddlers, 156–57
Peffer, Anthony, 238 (n. 15)
Peiss, Kathy, 230 (n. 4)
People v. Irene S. Cowles, 111
Perkins, George C., 151
Perry, Lorinda, 251 (n. 32)
Phelan, James, 189
Philadelphia, Pa., 251 (n. 32), 291 (n. 40)
Phillips, Madame, 145, 276 (n. 124)
Pierson, Mrs. C., 126
Pinkham, Lydia, 258 (n. 11), 280 (n. 83)
Pioche, Francis L. A., 270 (n. 39)
Plague, 189–91, 205, 290 (n. 30)
Plate-glass display windows, 133–34,
  142
Pleasant, Mary Ellen, 51–52, 59, 62
Plumbing, 139, 140
Pollay, Richard W., 271 (n. 52)
Pommer, Eva, 159
Portland, Oreg., 241 (n. 42), 253 (n. 65)
Poughkeepsie, N.Y., 61, 185, 289 (n. 14)
Powell, Mrs., 24
Proprietors. *See* Female proprietors;
  Male proprietors; *and specific busi-
  nesses*
Prostitution: and gender imbalance,
  58; Chinese women as prostitutes,
  61, 119, 238 (n. 15), 269 (n. 17); and
  apparel industry, 61, 250 (n. 22); and
  race, 119, 256 (n. 1); research studies
  on, 249 (n. 17); in Albany, N.Y., 250
  (n. 19)

Pulfer, Johanna, 93
Purchasing decisions, 151–52

Quigley, Mrs., 174

Race and ethnicity: types of businesses for foreign-born women, 17–18, 52–53, 221–23; of female proprietors, 17–18, 89–90, 220–23; of male proprietors, 48–49, 53–54, 224–26, 247 (n. 121), 248 (n. 148), 248–49 (n. 149); statistics on, 50, 51, 220–26, 248–49 (n. 149); of foreign-born women, 50, 220–23; and credit, 89–90; stereotypes based on, 89–90; and prostitution, 119, 256 (n. 1); and location of businesses, 131; of foreign-born men, 224–26, 245 (n. 108), 248 (n. 148), 248–49 (n. 149); in gold rush California, 256 (n. 1). *See also* African American men; African American women; Chinese immigrants; Irish men; Irish women; Japanese immigrants; Jewish men; Jewish women; Mexican and Californio women
Railroads, 7, 12, 13, 40, 128, 172, 274–75 (n. 102)
Rappaport, Erika, 281 (n. 98)
Rawls, James J., 267 (n. 134), 292 (n. 52)
Ready, Miss, 24
Real estate prices, 38–39, 123, 270 (n. 36)
Record keeping, 163–64, 172, 205, 283 (n. 131)
Reed, Miss E. L., 108–9
Reed, Miss F. W., 107, 108–9
Religious and charitable organizations, 180–81, 205, 287 (nn. 175–76)
Restaurants: and gender imbalance, 11–12, 25; female proprietors of, 23, 24; examples of, 28, 29, 105–6, 123–24, 152; and domestic tasks performed by women, 36–37, 85–86; and families' choice of boarding out,

39–40; location of, 41, 127, 129–30; statistics on, 42, 217; cosmopolitan restaurants, 123–25, 270 (n. 39); in department stores, 142; licensing fees for, 150; purchasing decisions for, 152; modern improvements in, 158; word-of-mouth advertising for, 165; financial management in, 176; and bubonic plague, 191; fire risks in, 192; racial/ethnic background of female proprietors of, 221–23; Irish women as proprietors of, 223; male proprietors of, 225–26; Chinese proprietors of, 282 (n. 108). *See also* Accommodations industry
Retail industry: female proprietors in, 8; characteristics of female proprietors in, 17–18; Jewish women in, 17–18, 89, 259 (n. 22); businesses in, 24, 36, 218–19; male proprietors in, 35, 53–54, 218–19, 248 (n. 148); statistics on, 35–36, 131–32, 218–19; capital intentions and market incentives in, 37; in Boston, 61; and niche production, 67; widowed women in, 71–72; credit for female proprietors in, 88–89, 154, 159; start-up strategies for, 91–92; partnerships in, 99–100, 102; sale of retail businesses, 106–7, 108, 109–13, 265 (nn. 110, 114); location of businesses in, 128–30; and display windows, 133–34, 142; and brand-name products, 134–35, 170; modern improvements in, 138, 157–58, 274 (n. 88); and competition between department stores and small-scale proprietors, 141–46; interior decor of businesses in, 142–44; debt collection in, 161–62; advertising for, 166–67; employees in, 168–69; accounting system for, 172; business closings in, 185; and earthquake, 196; racial/ethnic background of female proprietors in, 221–23; Irish women as proprietors in, 223; African

system for, 172; financial success of, 230 (n. 1); definition of, 233 (n. 30). *See also* Accommodations industry; Apparel industry; Beauty industry; Female proprietors; Laundry industry; Male proprietors; Retail industry; *and specific businesses*

Smallpox, 188–89, 290 (n. 28)

Smith, Duane A., 291 (n. 46)

Smith, Mrs., 59–60

Snow, Sallie, 188, 193

Social class of female proprietors, 45–47, 244 (n. 97)

Soper, Mrs. Mary A., 176, 186–87, 202, 290 (n. 22), 295 (n. 92)

Sorin, Gerald, 259 (n. 22)

Spanish-American War, 13, 42

Spanish surnames, 50. *See also* Mexican and Californio women

Stacom, Maria J., 197–98, 294 (n. 75)

Stage, Sarah, 258 (n. 11)

Stanford, Leland, 7

Stanyan, Mrs. Marie, 32

Starr, Kevin, 270 (n. 43)

Start-up strategies: credit, 83, 85–90, 97, 205, 207–8, 257 (n. 6); raising capital through saving and borrowing money, 84, 90–98, 113, 207–8, 259 (n. 30), 262 (nn. 57–58, 62, 65), 262–63 (n. 66), 275–76 (n. 120); loans, 84, 93–98, 113, 207, 262 (nn. 57–58, 62, 65), 262–63 (n. 66), 275–76 (n. 120); partnerships, 84, 98–104, 113, 205, 264 (n. 93); buying out or taking over established businesses, 84, 104–13, 205, 266–67 (n. 130), 267 (n. 135); savings, 90–93, 259 (n. 30); in twenty-first century, 207–8; venture capital for, 296 (n. 12)

Steel, Valerie, 239 (n. 27)

Stein, Margaret, 169

Stern, David, 25, 238 (n. 12)

Stevens, Lilly, 157, 169, 171

Stevenson, Robert Louis, 167

Stewart, Martha, 258 (n. 11)

Stock market investment, 167–68

Stone, Mrs., 174

Stoppelkamp, Mrs. A. H., 28–29, 191

Strasser, Susan, 274 (n. 101), 284 (n. 143)

Strauss, Levi, 35

Strom, Sharon, 252 (n. 48)

Supreme Court cases, 241 (n. 39)

Tailors, 248 (n. 148)

Tarbox, Helen, 151, 157, 279 (n. 49)

Tax and licensing fees, 150–51, 277 (n. 12)

Teaching and school administration, 48, 62, 65, 68, 74, 252 (nn. 46–47)

Telephones, 138

Theaters, 31, 178–79

Thomas, Mrs. Jane, 91, 107, 108, 155, 265 (n. 110)

Thompson, Miss May, 102, 154

Tighe, Lucille, 44

Tighe, Mrs. Mary Frances, 43–44

Tobacco store, 28

Touchard, Mrs., 99–100

Tourism, 140–41, 190, 274–75 (n. 102), 275 (n. 105)

Trachtenberg, Alan, 233 (n. 25)

Trade cards, 5–7, 135–38, 280 (n. 85)

Training: for clerical occupations, 66–67; in financial management, 149. *See also* Education of women

Twain, Mark, 42, 122, 243 (n. 82)

United Iron Works, 42

Unmarried women. *See* Single (never-married) women

Uznay, Frances, 155

Van Winkle, Miss E., 91, 174

Venture capital, 296 (n. 12)

Victor, Frances Fuller, 72–73

Vioget, Mrs., 96, 262 (n. 65)

Wages: of domestic servants, 64, 122, 251 (n. 40); of teachers, 65,

252 (n. 46); protection of married women's wages, 77, 260 (n. 36), 260–61 (n. 45); sex differences in, 91; of cooks, 122; owed to employees by female proprietors, 168–69; of garment workers, 266 (n. 119)

Walker, Juliet E. K., 236 (n. 46), 237–38 (n. 8), 248 (n. 137)

Walker, Madame C. J., 145, 230 (n. 4)

Ward, Mrs., 79

Warner, Ida, 158

Warren, Ida, 140, 276 (n. 126)

Washerwomen, 24, 33–34, 41, 240 (n. 37). *See also* Laundry industry

Washington, Mrs., 24

Watson, Ethel, 103, 152

Wells, Olive, 139, 279 (nn. 49, 62)

Wheelan, Mrs. F., 109

White, Miss C. T., 25

Widowed/divorced women: employment of, 68, 74; as proprietors, 68–73, 254 (n. 82); legal status of, 69; statistics on, 69, 73, 174, 284 (n. 141); and child rearing, 69–71, 253 (n. 65); and alimony laws, 70–71, 253 (n. 70); charges of dereliction of duty against wives in divorce cases, 76; start-up strategies of, 91, 108; business rehabilitation funds for, 94; credit for divorced women, 155; financial management skills of, 174–76; in millinery and dressmaking trades, 284 (n. 140). *See also* Female proprietors

Wilson, Luzena Stanley, 38, 57–58, 62, 85–87, 116–19, 122, 124, 127

Wiltse, Jeff, 292 (n. 59)

Wimmer, Mrs. Peter, 60

Wolff, Mrs. Henry, 253 (n. 70)

Women in business. *See* African American women; Chinese immigrants; Female proprietors; Irish women; Japanese immigrants; Jewish women; Mexican and Californio women

Women's education. *See* Education of women

Woods, Miss, 105

Woods, Miss C. L., 109, 265 (n. 110)

Worth, Mrs. E. R., 25, 238 (n. 12)

Wyman, Mr., 107

Wyman, N. J., 90

Yeager, Mary, 233 (n. 26), 234 (n. 32)

Yick Wo v. Hopkins, 241 (n. 39)

Yung, Judy, 238 (n. 15), 282 (n. 108)